The Art of Louis Comfort Tiffany

The Art of Louis Comfort Tiffany

An exhibition organized by
The Fine Arts Museums of San Francisco
from the collection of the
Charles Hosmer Morse Foundation

by Donald L. Stover
Ednah Root Curator of American Art, 1980–81

M. H. de Young Memorial Museum

25 April through 8 August 1981

This catalogue was published on the occasion of the exhibition *The Art of Louis Comfort Tiffany*, organized by The Fine Arts Museums of San Francisco from the collection of the Charles Hosmer Morse Foundation. Both catalogue and exhibition were supported by The Museum Society and funded by a grant from Shaklee Corporation.

The Art of Louis Comfort Tiffany is a title that was first used by The Toledo Museum of Art for their exhibition of sixty objects from the collection assembled by Hugh and Jeannette McKean, November 12–December 17, 1978.

Photographs reproduced from *The Lost Treasures of Louis Comfort Tiffany*. Copyright © 1980 by Hugh F. McKean. Reproduced by permission of Doubleday & Company, Inc.: cover and color plates on pp. 18, 19, 22, 87, 94.

Frontispiece:
Louis Comfort Tiffany, by Joaquin Sorolla y Bastida (1863–1923), 1911. Oil on canvas, 59¼ x 88¾ in (150.5 x 225.5 cm). Courtesy of the Hispanic Society of America.

Cover: *Wisteria Transom* (detail), stained glass, ca. 1910. Cat. no. 60

Contents

Foreword   7

Acknowledgments   9

Introduction

     Louis Comfort Tiffany   13

Catalogue

     Paintings   29

     Photography   39

     Windows   45

     Lamps   57

     Glass   67

     Ceramics   81

     Metals, Enamels, and Jewelry   89

     World's Columbian Exposition Chapel   103

     Laurelton Hall   109

     Awards and Decorations   116

     Tiffany's Contemporaries   117

Selected Bibliography   123

Foreword

Although exhibitions and publications have examined various aspects of the work of Louis Comfort Tiffany, no exhibition to date has examined the beauty and importance of his diverse creativity within the context of his total production. In presenting this exhibition, The Fine Arts Museums of San Francisco have drawn upon the remarkable collection assembled by Mr. and Mrs. Hugh F. McKean, now entrusted to the Morse Gallery of Art, Winter Park, Florida. Operated by the Charles Hosmer Morse Foundation, the Morse Gallery was founded in 1942 by Mrs. McKean in honor of her grandfather.

Louis Comfort Tiffany had in the last quarter of the nineteenth century distinguished himself as a painter and insured for himself a unique place in the development of American Art. As an artist, patron, and entrepreneur, he was a peer of the arts and social aristocracy of the period. By the end of the century his innovative work with stained glass and interior design had made his name well known throughout America, and his artistic influence was internationally accepted and acclaimed. But his fame was quickly eclipsed by the rapid changes in style and taste that marked the first decades of the twentieth century. Only in recent years has the perspective afforded by the passage of time allowed for scholarly reevaluation of his importance. Studies into the American manifestations of the Arts and Crafts Movement, Art Nouveau, and the foundations of modern art have confirmed the importance of his work and his influence within each of these areas.

Toward the end of his life, Tiffany established the Louis Comfort Tiffany Foundation and under its auspices invited promising young artists to work as Tiffany fellows in residence at his Long Island estate. Hugh McKean was selected as a Tiffany fellow following his graduation from Rollins College and was invited to spend two months at Laurelton Hall. It was during this brief period spent as the personal guest of Louis Comfort Tiffany that Mr. McKean was to meet the artist and to perceive something of the unique concepts of art and beauty from which Laurelton Hall had been created, and for the preservation of which Tiffany had established and endowed his foundation. In the years that followed Tiffany's death in 1933, the foundation came to view Laurelton Hall not so much as the embodiment of a vision, but as a financial liability. In 1946, the house and its estate were sold, the vast collections were dispersed at public auction, and it appeared that Tiffany's vision was lost forever.

Hugh McKean, with his wife Jeannette, had begun to acquire significant examples of the art of Louis Comfort Tiffany, and following the fire that destroyed Laurelton Hall in 1957, they visited the ruins. As a consequence of their efforts to salvage what had survived, they found themselves in possession of windows, wall coverings, and architectural elements. The garden loggia with its poppy-capped columns now installed in the American Wing at the Metropolitan Museum of Art, New York, was a gift from the McKeans. They also acquired the Columbian Exposition Chapel, which for the third time in its history was to be without a building to house it. Through the years the McKeans have continued to add to the collection, and now more than 4,000 objects comprise the most comprehensive assemblage of the art produced by and for Louis Comfort Tiffany. The collection also includes major examples of the work of other artists who were Tiffany's antecedents, contemporaries, and followers.

Although the Morse Foundation has previously made objects available for loaned exhibitions, the scale of the endeavor that we suggested posed obvious logistical problems. Tiffany himself once remarked that "the main body of my work deals with very brittle matter, namely glass." The prospect of transporting across the continent such fragile objects as blown glass vases and windows of considerable size and weight was cause for understandable concern. Under the direction of Hugh McKean, the staff of the Morse Gallery, after a great deal of experimentation and testing, developed a system of packing, crating, and handling and shipping the objects. Although the exhibition was now feasible, the cost estimated for packing, transportation, and the installation in San Francisco appeared unmanageable.

The problem was resolved when Shaklee Corporation expressed its interest in assisting the project. J. Gary Shansby, President and Chief Executive Officer of Shaklee Corporation, liked the idea from the start. "Tiffany was American, innovative, and a leader in his field. We are delighted to be able to help in bringing this exhibition to the San Francisco Bay Area." It is Shaklee's grant, combined with the support of The Museum Society, that has made this exhibition a reality.

The Art of Louis Comfort Tiffany is a major decorative art exhibition to be presented exclusively in San Francisco, and it was created by the American Art Department of The Fine Arts Museums of San Francisco. The department has flourished remarkably in recent years. The gift of the collection of Mr. and Mrs. John D. Rockefeller 3rd redefined what was already an American paintings and sculpture collection of considerable scope and justified the development of a center for the study of American art. Two Bothin Helping Fund grants have resulted in the creation, within the reference library at the de Young Museum, of an American Art Library Collection. It complements the collection of primary sources and documents available on microfilm in the adjacent West Coast

Area Center of the Smithsonian Institution's Archives of American Art.

Recognizing the potential of the collection and the resources available, Ednah Root, a friend of the Museums and herself a practicing artist, established the Ednah Root Curatorial Chair for American Art and proposed that its occupant pursue research, lecture, organize exhibitions, and prepare publications. The Tiffany exhibition is the most ambitious project to be realized thus far under the Ednah Root Chair.

The exhibition has been organized by Donald L. Stover who, as Associate Curator for American Decorative Arts, had directed its development since 1977. His appointment to the Ednah Root Chair for the 1980–81 term has provided him with the opportunity to bring this project to its completion. I am grateful that he accepted the challenge with enthusiasm, juggled normal activities, and discharged his assignment with precision and style.

I am sure that the many visitors who enjoy this exhibition join me in expressing their appreciation to Hugh and Jeannette McKean for having assembled and preserved this important collection and thereby insured the stature of Louis Comfort Tiffany as a unique American artist; to the McKeans and the trustees of the Charles Hosmer Morse Foundation for having made the collection available to us; to J. Gary Shansby and Shaklee Corporation for their financial support; to Ednah Root for her vision and generous patronage of specific activities of the exhibition; to The Museum Society for its assistance; and to the staffs of the Charles Hosmer Morse Foundation, the Morse Gallery of Art, and The Fine Arts Museums of San Francisco for their patient, tireless, and professional efforts in assembling, preparing, and realizing this catalogue and exhibition.

Ian McKibbin White
Director of Museums

Acknowledgments

In the presentation of this exhibition and its publications I am indebted to many people for their support in bringing the project to completion. The Board of Trustees of The Fine Arts Museums of San Francisco and its president, Walter S. Newman, and the Board of Directors of The Museum Society and its chairman, Mrs. G. Gordon Bellis, endorsed this exhibition as a concept and remained committed to it throughout its realization. The encouragement and advice of Ian McKibbin White, Director of Museums, has been invaluable. To all of these people, I would like to express my gratitude. I have also appreciated the considerable expertise, assistance, and cooperation of Stephen Dykes, Deputy Director for Administration, and his assistant, Barbara Whitney; Helen Moss, Deputy Director for Development, and Julie Mackaman, Grants Officer; Thomas Seligman, Deputy Director for Education and Exhibitions; Gus Teller, Deputy Director for Operations; and Judith Teichman, Deputy City Attorney.

For their hard work, dedication and patience, not only in behalf of this exhibition, but also in maintaining the normal operation of my office, I am indebted to Kate Northcott, Project Coordinator for this exhibition; Deborah Fenton, Graduate Intern, University of Michigan; Lee Hunt Miller, Curatorial Assistant for American Decorative Arts; and Gloria M. Ravitch, Curatorial Assistant, Department of Sculpture and Decorative Arts.

The installation of this exhibition has been complicated and demanding work. I gratefully acknowledge the talents and special skills of Robert Davis, Exhibition Designer; Ron Rick, Senior Graphic Designer; Kate Weese, Graphic Designer; William White, Technical Coordinator; Michael Sandgren, Packer; Thérèse Chen and Paula March Romanovsky, Registrars; James Bernstein, Elizabeth Cornu, and Robert Futernick, Conservators; Niccolo Caldararo, Darryl Greig, and Karen Werner, Technicians, and the crew responsible for constructing and mounting the installation.

For their assistance in the production of the publications that have accompanied this exhibition, I would like to thank Ann Heath Karlstrom, Publications Manager; Mary Foard, who edited the catalogue; Pamela Forbes, Editor and Production Manager of *Triptych*; Renée Beller Dreyfus, Associate Curator for Education and Interpretation; and Kenneth Keen, who typed the manuscript of the catalogue. I am also grateful to Ed Watchempino, Art Director of Shaklee Corporation, for his work in the design and production of materials used for publicizing the exhibition.

The Fine Arts Museums of San Francisco are fortunate to have an exceptional staff, and among those whose professional expertise and cooperation have made the organization of this exhibition such a pleasure are Gail Docktor, Chief Public Information Officer; Charles Long, Public Information Officer; Lucy Martell, Curator of Public Programs, and her assistants, Jim Baldocchi and Jean Chaitin; Jane Nelson, Head Librarian; Charlotte Elkins, Librarian, the Bothin American Art Library Collection; Lois Gordon, Museum Teaching Assistant; Nativity D'Souza, General Manager, The Museum Society; and Alice Fischer, Executive Secretary, The Museum Society. To these individuals and the members of the dedicated staffs of The Museum Society and The Fine Arts Museums—my colleagues—I express my sincere gratitude.

Mrs. Robert E. Hunter of The Museum Society's Board of Directors provided an enormous service in her role as coordinator of special events, and Wally Goodman's advice regarding logistics management for visitors to the exhibition was a welcome and valuable contribution. In addition, I wish to thank Mrs. Carmine Guerro, Chairman of the Docent Council; Kay Millar, Chairman of Docent Training for the exhibition; all of the members of our Docent Council; Kathy Baldwin, Volunteer Coordinator; and all of the members of the Volunteer Council. These men and women who give unselfishly of their time and talent comprise one of the major resources of these museums.

Hugh and Jeannette McKean and the remarkable collection they assembled have made this exhibition possible; to them I express my deepest gratitude not only for their interest and support, but also for their many kindnesses and hospitality extended throughout the past four years. David Donaldson, Curator of the Morse Gallery of Art, has provided invaluable assistance not only in sharing his knowledge of the collection but also in preparing and installing the objects in the exhibition. Gus Legard packed and crated the objects for their safe shipment and accompanied David Donaldson to San Francisco to assist in supervising their installation. To these gentlemen and the staff of the Morse Gallery and to the Charles Hosmer Morse Foundation and its board, I extend my appreciation.

The Museums are very fortunate to have the support of Ednah Root, patron of the chair that I have the pleasure to hold for this year. Her generosity has been an important element in the activities surrounding the presentation of the exhibition, and I offer her my sincerest thanks.

Donald L. Stover
Ednah Root Curator of American Art

Introduction

Magnolia Window (cat. no. 39)

Louis Comfort Tiffany

Louis Comfort Tiffany was born in New York City on February 18, 1848, the eldest son of Charles L. and Harriet Young Tiffany. Charles Lewis Tiffany was the son of a successful Connecticut millowner and merchant and a sixth generation American who could trace his heritage to the Massachusetts Bay Colony. Harriet Young Tiffany was the daughter of Ebeneezer Young, a former member of the United States House of Representatives from Connecticut and the sister of John B. Young. John Young and Charles Tiffany had left Connecticut in 1837 and had established in New York City the firm of Tiffany and Young, merchants in fancy goods and stationery. As this venture prospered J. L. Ellis was admitted to the partnership, and the firm of Tiffany, Young and Ellis began to establish a reputation as purveyors of an impressive line of luxury goods which included, in addition to stationery, "porcelain, glass, bronzes, toilet articles, gloves, fancy French furniture, Chinese goods, papier mâché, cutlery, games, and French Jewelry."[1] In the year of Louis Tiffany's birth, the firm made a fortuitous decision to direct their enterprise and resources to the retail of precious stones and the production of silverware.[2] This decision and the subsequent retirement of John Young and J. L. Ellis resulted in the creation of the soon to be internationally prestigious firm of Tiffany and Company.[3]

The success of his father's business insured young Louis Tiffany of a comfortable if strict childhood. Never inclined toward scholarship, he has been characterized as a "... talented, creative child ... mercurial in his interests ... fond of animals ... a leader among his peers and always in trouble with his elders."[4] His formal education consisted of his attendance at the Flushing Academy on Long Island and the Eagleswood Military Academy in New Jersey.[5] Upon completion of his studies, seventeen-year-old Louis boarded the *Scotia* in November of 1865 and sailed for Europe. A chronicle of this trip survives in the form of a small sketchbook containing fifty studies in various media of places that he visited (see no. 2). Little else is known about this voyage; however, it was influential in convincing Louis Comfort Tiffany to pursue a career as an artist. Upon his return to the United States in March of 1866 he announced his intention to study art rather than to attend college. In the fall of that year he entered the Antique classes at the National Academy of Design for what was to be his only formal "study." As he later recalled, "at the age when a youth in his circumstances is pretty sure to be at the University he was haunting the studios of George Inness, N.A. and Samuel Colman, N.A."[6] At the age of nineteen he exhibited a watercolor at the National Academy of Design and returned to Europe where he studied in the Paris atelier of Leon Charles Adrien Bailly.

Page from Tiffany's sketch book, **My First Visit to Europe** (cat. no. 2)

Upon his return to the United States in 1868, Louis Comfort Tiffany, now twenty-one, asserted his independence and took up residence with other aspiring young artists at the Y.M.C.A. across the street from the National Academy of Design.[7] This move signaled no apparent break with his family; his relationship with them remained cordial and it can be assumed that his father continued to provide him with financial support. He returned to Europe in 1870 and proceeded to North Africa where he visited Morocco, Algeria, Tunisia, and Egypt.[8] His travel in North Africa profoundly influenced both the eye and art of the young artist and he later observed "When first I had a chance to travel in the East and to paint where the people and the buildings also are clad in beautiful hues, the pre-eminence of color in the world was brought forcibly to my attention. I returned to New York wondering why we made so little use of our eyes, why we refrained so obstinately from taking advantage of color in our architecture and our clothing when Nature indicates its mastership."[9]

The decade of the 1870s was a productive period for Tiffany and was to be marked by his increasing stature as a painter and a diversification of his interest into other

Tiffany's ink sketch for the Tiffany home at the corner of 72nd Street and Madison Avenue. 4½ x 7½ in (11.4 x 19 cm) Photograph: Schopplein Studio.

fields of creative expression. Subject matter from his African travels began to appear along with his landscape pictures in watercolor and oil, and his work began to attract attention and generate discussion among the critics. At the age of twenty-two he became the youngest member elected to membership in the Century Club, and in 1871 he was made an associate of the National Academy of Design. In addition to exhibits at the Academy, Tiffany was exhibiting his work with the Brooklyn Art Association and the American Watercolor Society.[10]

In 1871 Louis Comfort Tiffany met Mary Woodbridge Goddard whom he later married on May 15, 1872. During the period of their courtship he became a frequent visitor in the Connecticut home of Donald G. Mitchell, an essayist who was as interested and influential in the decorative arts as he was in literature.[11] He and Edward C. Moore, general manager and chief designer for the silverware operations of Tiffany & Company, encouraged Tiffany to consider both the need in America for greater artistic effort in the decorative arts and the possibilities for creative expression beyond the brush and canvas. Additionally, Moore was in the process of assembling one of the most important collections of oriental and Near Eastern art in the United States and was undoubtedly influential in stimulating Tiffany's interest in collecting.[12] As collectors both Tiffany and Moore shared an interest in oriental art and the ancient glass of Egypt, Rome, and Syria. Tiffany's pursuit of the former resulted in his introduction to Samuel Bing, a Parisian dealer and art critic; and his fascination with the latter resulted in his experimentation with iridescent glass. Both were to be extremely important in shaping the ultimate career of Louis Comfort Tiffany.

Tiffany's first child, named Mary Woodbridge, after his wife, was born April 3, 1873. The following year while the Tiffany family was traveling in France, his first son was born. Named Charles Louis, the child survived for only a few weeks, and Louis's wife, always a frail woman,

was never to regain her health. Tiffany and his family returned to the United States in the spring of 1875; he continued to paint and exhibit his works and resumed his experiments with glass.

In 1876 he exhibited three of his oils and six watercolors at the American Centennial Exposition in Philadelphia.[13] This exposition exerted an enormous influence not only upon its exhibitors and visitors but upon the arts and the art consciousness of the entire nation. Although America's achievements in industry, commerce, and agriculture were roundly praised, American design, particularly design for the domestic environment, was singled out for its dependence upon European precedent and its lack of originality. Tiffany's friend and mentor, Donald G. Mitchell, was Chairman of Judges for Decorative Arts, and Louis must have been familiar with the enormous volume of criticism, discussion, and debate on the subject engendered by the Exposition. The discussions regarding the potential of stained glass must have interested him particularly, for although Louis's interest in the decorative arts was increasing, his five years of experimentation with glass had already resulted in the creation of his first ornamental window for the Church of the Sacred Heart in New York. Given his interest in the Near East, Tiffany must have noted the architectural contributions of Frank Furness at the Exposition and visited the dazzling new building he had designed for the Pennsylvania Academy for the Fine Arts. In the decoration for the latter, Furness had made lavish and original use of color, texture, and lustrous polychromed glass tiles.[14] Tiffany must also have been aware of John La Farge's involvement with the interior decoration and windows for H. H. Richardson's Trinity Church which was under construction in Boston.[15] La Farge, a member of the National Academy of Design, shared as a fellow artist not only Tiffany's interest in the potential of stained glass but also his concern for what was perceived as the conservative and provincial attitude of the Academy toward the work of many younger American artists. In 1877 Tiffany and La Farge joined George Inness, Augustus Saint-Gaudens, George de Forest Brush, Thomas Eakins, Homer Martin, Albert Ryder, John Singer Sargent, and James McNeill Whistler in forming the Society of American Artists.[16] The Society, of which Tiffany was elected treasurer, proposed not so much to supplant the National Academy as to provide a vehicle for the exhibition of new trends in American art. Although active with the Society, Tiffany continued to participate in exhibitions at the National Academy. He was frequently criticised for his non-academic and frequently non-romantic subject matter, but his increasing maturity as an artist gained him a reputation as one of America's important young artists and his pictures commanded relatively high prices.

With his success as a painter came an increasing diversification of artistic interests. To painting and his continuing work and experimentation with glass, Tiffany added photography and interior design. By the time of

13 **My Family at Somesville,** oil on canvas, 1888.

the birth of his second son, named Charles Lewis in honor of his father, on January 7, 1878, Tiffany was preparing to move his growing family into new quarters on the top floor of the Bella apartment building at 48 East 26th Street in New York. The decoration of this apartment provided him with the opportunity to explore and exploit concepts of the applied arts that he had been developing for some years. The finished product was to bear the personal imprint of Louis Comfort Tiffany and signaled the maturation of his interest in the decorative arts. Occupied in 1879, the apartment incorporated furniture of various styles that included examples of English and American design of the late eighteenth and early nineteenth centuries, oriental rugs, his growing collection of oriental and Near Eastern art, ornamental windows, glass mosaics, and tiles in an environment carefully worked out to the smallest detail. The overall effect was hailed by Donald Mitchell as having "welded the decorative art of the West and the East into one harmonious whole."[17] Here on August 24th of that year his daughter Hilda Goddard was born.

Louis Comfort Tiffany and Associated Artists

Having experienced the possibilities of decorative design, Tiffany embarked on a new venture. In 1878 he formed his first company, Louis C. Tiffany and Company, which was created to operate a glasshouse which he established to bring together his various work and experimentation with glass.[18] The following year, in conjunction with Candace Wheeler, Samuel Colman, and Lockwood de Forest, he proposed entering the field of professional interior design under the name of Louis Comfort Tiffany and Associated Artists. The publicity that had been attracted by Tiffany's apartment at the Bella and certainly the social entrée provided by the Tiffany name assured them the important commissions that were to establish their reputation. Although each of the Associated Artists had specific responsibilities, Tiffany was the dominant artistic force, and the same originality that had distinguished his painting was to be found in his decoration. Tiffany found ample opportunity for the introduction of his glass into the decoration designed by the Associated Artists. In addition to glass tiles he introduced transparent glass mosaics for windows, screens, and transoms. In the few years of their existence the Associated Artists were to decorate some of the most important houses and public buildings of the period and could count among their clients New York's Union League, Samuel Clemens, Ogden Goelet, Hamilton Fish, and Cornelius Vanderbilt II. In 1881 they were awarded the prestigious contract to redecorate the State Rooms at the White House for President Chester Arthur.

Although the activities of the Associated Artists occupied much of his time, Tiffany continued to paint and experiment with glass. Two successive fires had destroyed his new glasshouse, and although he had been forced to move his experiments to the Heidt glasshouse in Brooklyn he applied for and was awarded three patents for glass and glass technology. Despite the obvious success of the Associated Artists, each of the artists was becoming increasingly anxious to proceed with their individual interests, and their association was amicably dissolved in 1883. Candace Wheeler later observed that the time had come for her to devote herself "to art in a way which would more particularly help women," and she noted that "Mr. Tiffany was rather glad to get rid of all of us, for his wonderful experiments with glass iridescence meant far more to him at the time than association with other interests."[19]

All of Tiffany's time had not been occupied by either the Associated Artists or his work with glass. In 1881 he was elected to full membership in the National Academy of Design, and during this period he became involved in additional artistic ventures including fabric, wallpaper, and book design. More significantly, he was contracting for decorative elements for a new house that he was planning to build.[20] This house, designed by Tiffany (with technical and working drawings supplied by Stanford White) for his father, was to occupy the corner of Madison Avenue at 72nd Street and proposed to shelter the entire Tiffany family under one roof.

On January 22, 1884 Mary Woodbridge Goddard, Tiffany's wife of almost twelve years, died. Following her death Tiffany distracted himself with a brief if unprofitable venture into theater design. The Associated Artists' first commission had been the curtain for the Madison Square Theater, and during its production Tiffany had become acquainted with Steele MacKaye. In 1884 MacKaye proposed opening a new theater to be called the Lyceum, and in exchange for a percentage of the profits from its operation Tiffany agreed to decorate the interior. The Lyceum was the first theater to be lighted entirely by electricity, and Tiffany was given the opportunity to work directly with Thomas A. Edison in the installation of the lighting.[21] Although the new theater proved a financial disaster, Tiffany's decoration was well received and the New York *Morning Journal* observed, "It belongs to no school unless the ultra-aesthetic—the school of Wilde outdone by MacKaye ... everything was a departure from the hackneyed form of theatrical decoration. The electric light from clustered globes pendant from the ceiling is soft and pleasantly diffused. Similar lights smoulder under green sconces along the face of the gallery, like fire in monster emeralds ... but these things are not obtrusive. A master hand has blent them into a general effect, avoiding all aggressive detail."[22]

Following the Lyceum debacle, in 1885 Tiffany turned his attention back to his work with glass and the decoration of the Tiffany mansion then nearing completion. For reasons not fully understood Charles L. Tiffany never moved into the house; however, Louis and his family occupied the upper floors and created within the vast gabled garret a studio that became the wonder of the city. In the decoration of the apartment Tiffany gave free reign to his considerable and diverse creative talent, incorporating a masterful manipulation of space, light, and shadow. Contemporary descriptions are numerous, and all are unanimous in noting the ethereal quality of the studio where light from either the windows of pale tinted glass or the fires burning in the great four-sided, free-standing fireplace played over a fantasy of oriental carpets, potted palms, wicker furniture, early American chairs, and fur-covered divans beneath glittering globes of blown glass and lamps suspended from decorative chains which like the great sculpted mass of the chimney disappeared into the lofty darkness above. Tiffany was to occupy this residence until his death, and he continued to decorate it with some of his finest windows and use its diverse interior vistas as subjects or backgrounds for numerous paintings. With the completion of the house and studio Tiffany reorganized his business activities and on December 1, 1885 incorporated the Tiffany Glass Company.

Tiffany Glass Company

After having been a widower for nearly three years, Louis Comfort Tiffany married Louise Wakeman Knox on November 9, 1886. On September 24 of the following year, Louise gave birth to twins, Louis Comfort and Julia de Forest. At the time of their birth Tiffany was designing the interiors for the Ponce de Leon Hotel which Bernard Maybeck had designed for Henry M. Flagler in St. Augustine, Florida. The success of the Tiffany Glass Company and the increasing scale of their operation, both for the creation of stained glass windows and interior design on the scale of the Ponce de Leon Hotel, had required the hiring of additional designers and artists. Like his father, Tiffany possessed considerable organizational talent; he also had a unique ability to identify compatible artistic talents and to direct them in ways that compromised neither his insistence upon total artistic control nor the creative expression of his associates. This organization of his shops freed Tiffany from much of the routine activity of his business and allowed him to explore his own creative instincts and to pursue his personal interests. He enjoyed outings with his family, and his children and his new wife provided him with familial subject matter for both his brush and his camera. The period of the late 1880s produced some of his finest work in both media. This period of relative calm and happiness was attended by the birth of yet another child, Annie Olivia, on December 29, 1888.

The following year Tiffany was again traveling in Europe, and while in Paris he visited the Universal Exposition where he had a painting on exhibit. He was, no doubt, surprised to find that stained glass windows made from the new "American glass" were attracting much attention and praise. These windows, constructed of glass not unlike that which he had developed and used for his windows, were exhibited by Healy and Millet of Chicago, M. Galland (a Frenchman recently returned from America), and John La Farge.[23] Although Tiffany and La

Louis Comfort Tiffany (1848–1933)

Farge had experimented and worked at the same time at the Heidt glasshouse and each had been awarded separate patents for their respective efforts, Tiffany had been preempted in terms of international recognition. This was not to occur again.

On his return to the United States, Tiffany involved himself in two major new projects. The H. O. Havemeyers, personal friends of the Tiffany family, lovers of art and music, and important collectors of fine art, had asked him to decorate their mansion at 848 Fifth Avenue. Tiffany, who was assisted by Samuel Colman, could not have found this commission more to his liking nor the Havemeyers more compatible patrons. The resulting interiors delighted his clients and were roundly praised by most who saw them. Samuel Bing observed that ". . . the ingenious eclecticism responsible for these interiors has so skillfully combined disparate elements, integrating them so artfully, that we are left with an impression of perfect harmony."[24] If the Havemeyers and the critics supportive of innovative and original design were pleased by Tiffany's decorating concepts, there were others who preferred the acceptability and security of historical style. Without divulging the client, Samuel Bing also reported that "a name synonymous throughout the world with enormous wealth had commissioned

129 "Jack-in-the-Pulpit" Vase, Favrile glass, ca. 1912.

91 Spider Web Table Lamp, ca. 1900.

Tiffany to design the decor and furnishings of a formal sitting room to be based upon the artist's ideas. The expense came to over one hundred thousand dollars. But after the housewarming, when it had become apparent that the break with consecrated rules had horrified the visitors, the whole installation was promptly demolished and replaced by a decor pure Louis XVI."[25]

The other major project of this period was Tiffany's decoration of The Briars, his own new country estate near Oyster Bay on Long Island. The large shingled and shuttered house with its Tuscan-columned terraces and arbors was situated in the midst of landscaped gardens and grounds that were punctuated by a high, ogival-roofed clock tower. The antithesis of the massive, sheltering mansion at Madison and 72nd streets, The Briars opened itself to its surroundings. The interiors were light, airy, and restrained, and instead of volumetric space with its interplay of light and shadow, the spaces were clearly delineated and marked by a surprisingly modern, minimal quality. Tiffany's children were fond of The Briars, and the family passed many pleasant summers there.

The Tiffany Glass and Decorating Company
In 1892 Tiffany reorganized his glass company as the Tiffany Glass and Decorating Company and began the work for a major exhibition at the Columbian World's Exposition. Although he was to exhibit eight paintings at Chicago, the opportunity to exhibit his glass and decoration, missed in Paris in 1889, was not to escape him in 1893. In a pamphlet on his exhibition, issued by the Tiffany Glass and Decorating Company, Tiffany informed the public that "we have endeavored, in our exhibit, to bring before the eyes of the visitors to the World's Fair various objects from different departments in order to illustrate the scope of our business. . . . It will be seen . . . that there is hardly a material known to the decorator but what we employ in our work, and that, in fact, we cover the whole field of decoration—frescoes and mural paintings, colored glass windows, marble and glass mosaics, wood-carving and inlaying, metal work, embroideries, upholsteries, and hangings."[26] The exhibit itself consisted of three major sections described as the Dark Room, the Light Room, and the Chapel. In the two decorated and furnished rooms, separated only by a "portiere made of green tapestry shot with threads of gold and richly embroidered in various tones of golden colored silks," the disparate decorative concepts that had found expression in his studio at the 72nd Street house and in The Briars were juxtaposed.[27] Ironically, one of the two windows installed in the Light Room was after a painting entitled *Feeding the Flamingoes* in which Tiffany depicted a corner of his studio. The exhibition of the Tiffany Glass and Decorating Company was pure Louis Comfort Tiffany and, like Louis Sullivan's facade for the Transportation Building, represented but one side of the polemic that marked America's self-conscious search for artistic identity in the last quarter of the nineteenth cen-

tury. For those who sought that identity in the emulation of classical and renaissance precedents, the Exposition was a monument to American achievement in the arts. For others who, since the Centennial, had been hoping for the emergence of a truly American art, there was little consolation.

In describing his exhibit, Tiffany affirmed his position within this debate and stated that the aim of his company was "not so much to imitate the work of the past, as the introduction of new and original ideas, at the same time making it equal in merit with the best that has been done."[28] In this regard his efforts did not go unnoticed. A professor from the Imperial Museum at Berlin reported to his government that he "found little work exhibited at Chicago that did not bear traces of the study of European art methods, but amongst the truly original work exhibited was the stained glass and jeweled filigree work of the Tiffany Glass and Decorating Company."[29] This unidentified professor purchased examples of Tiffany's work and not only proposed to exhibit it at Berlin but also proposed a treatise on it as "judged by European standards."[30] By any standard, the Tiffany exhibit, one of the most popular at the fair, was a success and he was awarded no less than fifty-four medals for his effort. Additionally, his importance as an artist in stained glass had been acknowledged. La Farge had been acclaimed in Paris for his use of the new "American glass," but after Chicago this material was to be as frequently referred to as "Tiffany glass."[31] The rivalry between the two artists erupted into a public debate, and when Tiffany published a rare article entitled "American Art Supreme in Colored Glass" which appeared in *The Forum*, July 1893, La Farge immediately responded with a pamphlet entitled "The American Art of Glass: To Be Read in Connection with Mr. Louis C. Tiffany's Paper in the July Number of *The Forum*." This debate prompted considerable discussion within the trade for the remainder of the decade.

In 1893 Tiffany established a new glasshouse at Corona, Long Island. This facility, which was subsequently to be known as the Tiffany Furnaces, has traditionally been assumed to have been the first glasshouse operated by Tiffany since the unsuccessful attempt in 1878–1879. Although he is known to have moved his experimentation with glass to Heidt's glasshouse in the early 1880s, the consistent quality of the glass used by Tiffany and the volume of his production prior to 1893, including the exhibition at Chicago, suggests a production facility under his control. Such a facility may in fact have been operated by the Tiffany Glass Company. At the time of its incorporation, December 1, 1885, it was stated that the company was to "provide the manufacture of glass and other materials and the use and adaptation of the same to decorative and other artistic work of all kinds."[32] Apparently the company did manufacture glass, and seven years after its incorporation it listed among its assets "its plant and stock in trade used in connection with the manufacture of glass. . . ."[33] The location of this plant is not at this time known, but the company's reorganization in 1892 under the laws of the state of New Jersey perhaps offers a clue. Early company documents are captioned "Tiffany Glass and Decorating Company of Jersey City, New Jersey, and New York, N.Y." It is during this period that the name "Favrile" became the registered trade name for glass produced by Tiffany, and in its patent application for the trademark the company stated that the name had been adopted for use on "decorative glass or vitrified bodies manufactured by said corporation and used in making colored or stained glass windows, mosaics, glassware, or used in conjunction with other substances in manufacture or the arts. . . ." Additionally, it stated that "this trademark has been continuously used by said corporation since its incorporation. . . ."[34] The name Favrile derives from the Old English word "fabrile" meaning "handmade," and it has been traditionally accepted that the name was suggested by A. J. Nash whom Tiffany had brought from Stourbridge, England to build a glass factory.[35] It has also been accepted that the factory referred to by Tiffany was the facility at Corona. However, the evidence cited above implies an earlier association of Tiffany and Nash and the existence of a glasshouse that predates Corona.

By 1894 the Tiffany furnaces at Corona were producing a wide variety of products ranging from "wrought or blown" forms described as "foliated, convoluted, cylindrical, globular or cubicle, of one color or many, laminated, floriated or foliatious" to flat glass described as "Tiffany Favrile Fabric Glass, Tiffany Favrile Sunset Glass, Tiffany Favrile Horizon Glass, Tiffany Favrile Twig Glass, Tiffany Favrilé Lace Glass, &c."[36] Also at this time, Tiffany had been elected to membership in the French Société Nationale des Beaux-Arts, and he had been named a director of his father's company.[37]

The following year Tiffany's association with Samuel Bing, the influential Parisian art dealer, critic, and promoter, became increasingly important. In publishing a major treatise entitled *La Culture Artistique en Amérique*, Bing commended Tiffany for his artistic achievements, and in discussing the emergence in America of an art industry he noted "vast workshops that integrate numerous branches of art (such as that of Louis Tiffany)" and "the harmonic fusion of the objects produced."[38] Bing, who was planning a new gallery, commissioned Tiffany to produce a series of stained glass windows from designs by Paul Ranson (who designed two), Eugène Grasset, Felix Vallotton, Pierre Bonnard, Edouard Vuillard, Paul Sérusier, Ker-Xavier Roussel, Henri-Gabriel Ibels, and Henri de Toulouse-Lautrec.[39] The completed windows were exhibited in the annual Salon du Champ-de-Mars and at Bing's new gallery which opened December 26, 1895. Named Le Salon de L'Art Nouveau, the gallery was to exhibit the work of such notable artists as René Lalique, Auguste Rodin, Aubrey Beardsley, and Charles Rennie Mackintosh.[40] Samuel Bing also became the exclusive agent for the sale of Tiffany's art and his principal promoter in Europe.

Eggplants Transom (cat. no. 37)

Tiffany Studios

In the last years of the nineteenth century Tiffany continued to expand his operations and to direct his attention to new media for artistic expression. At the Corona furnaces, experimentation with pottery and enamels was under way, and a foundry and metal shop were added. The ecclesiastical department was now supplying tombstones and funerary monuments in addition to windows and church furnishings, and the decorating department had acquired a firm for the production of furniture. This expanded and diversified operation came to be known collectively as the Tiffany Studios.[41] In 1899 Samuel Bing promoted an exhibition at the Grafton Galleries in London to display the expanded production of the Studios, and the catalogue of this exhibition provides a survey of the range of Tiffany's work at this time.[42] In addition to an assortment of "Vases, bowls and flower-forms, plaques, pendants for electric light, lamp and candle-shades, wine glasses, &c," he exhibited thirteen windows including two entered as "12. Egg-plant" and "13. Head of Joseph of Arimathea, from 'The Entombment'—a window of Louis C. Tiffany exhibited at the World's Fair in Chicago, now in the Cathedral of St. John the Divine, New York City" (see nos. 37 and 43), five major mosaics, and forty-two examples of lamps and metal work including the entries "1. Portable electric reading lamp in green glass and green bronze" (possibly like no. 73), "6. Portable electric reading lamp in green metal and leaded glass, Nautilus shell" (see no. 72), "7. Portable oil lamp in green bronze and glass with leaded shade, dragon-fly design" (see shades, nos. 87 and 88), and "30. Candelabra (one light) in metal with glass blown inside" (see no. 186).[43] In discussing this exhibition in *The Studio*,

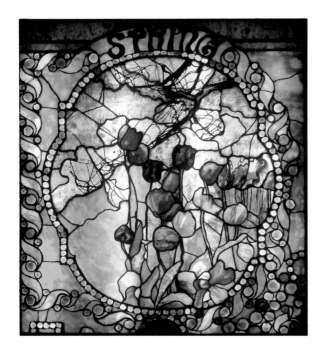

51–54 **The Four Seasons**, stained glass, ca. 1900.

Horace Townsend observed, "Among the many art exhibitions which have been put before Londoners this season the historian of the future . . . will probably find that among those which chiefly claim his attention, not alone for their intrinsic interest but for their influence upon contemporary art, that which Mr. S. Bing, of Paris, has gathered together at the Grafton Galleries will hold a distinguished place. . . . We have heard much in past years of what may almost be called this new art of Mr. Tiffany's . . ., which has so attracted the attention of European connoisseurs that in many of the museums in Europe . . . small collections have been gathered together as object lessons for the local craftsmen."[44]

At the dawn of the twentieth century few Americans and certainly no American artist enjoyed so universal a reputation as Louis Comfort Tiffany. His father had made the Tiffany name synonymous with wealth and luxury, and Louis had made it synonymous with excellence of craftsmanship, originality of design and good taste. His achievements as a painter had been recognized, and art historically his name was being included along with William Merritt Chase, Samuel Colman, Thomas Eakins, George Inness, John Singer Sargent, and James Abbott McNeill Whistler in a "marvelous list of names, embracing nearly all those who, by their lofty standard, have helped to raise the standard of modern American art."[45] Examples of his work in glass had found their way (either by gift, purchase, or placement by Tiffany himself) into the permanent collections of virtually every major museum in the United States. Internationally, Tiffany glass had been acquired by such prestigious museums as the Victoria and Albert Museum in London, the Musée des Arts Décoratifs in Paris, the Brussels Museum, the Kestner Museum in Hanover, the Kunstgewerbe Museum in Berlin, as well as other museums as distant as Tokyo. At the great Exposition Universelle in Paris, Tiffany exhibited, among other things, his dragonfly lamps and a pair of monumental windows, including The Four Seasons (see nos. 51–55). It was noted that "his work is all the more preeminent at the Exposition of 1900, especially his Favrile vases, because it is now surrounded by imitations and parodies from all over Europe and gains by inevitable comparisons."[46] His exhibit in Paris was awarded a Grand Prix and five gold medals, and he was made a Chevalier de la Légion d'Honneur. He was awarded gold medals at each of the expositions held in 1901 in Buffalo, Dresden, and St. Petersburg. At Paris in 1900 Louis Comfort Tiffany found himself at the apogee of his career; however, by 1902 in Turin his work, which had become recognized and widely imitated, was viewed as less sensational. Tiffany, now fifty-four years old, received the Grand Prix, but, some of the work of other artists represented in the exhibition was marked by a significant shift in emphasis. It has been observed that "one could see at Turin designs which were no longer derived from a desire for 'artistic' form but from an interest in construction and pure form."[47] In that same

year President Theodore Roosevelt commissioned the firm of McKim, Mead and White to refurbish the White House. The work installed by Tiffany in 1882 was torn out, and the rooms were "restored" to their "original" classicism.

The Laurelton Hall Years
On February 18, 1902, Charles Louis Tiffany died. Louis Comfort Tiffany inherited his share of his father's fortune and was named Vice-President and Art Director of Tiffany and Company. He formally reorganized his personal business enterprises under the name of Tiffany Studios and the showrooms were moved to Madison Avenue at 45th Street. He purchased property near Cold Spring Harbor and began planning a new country home. This house, to be built on the site of an old resort hotel, was to retain its original name, Laurelton Hall, and would occupy much of Tiffany's time for the next few years. In June of 1903, in recognition of his achievements and his designs for the celebration of its bicentennial, Yale University awarded Tiffany an Honorary Master of Arts Degree.

In the summer of 1904 Louise Knox Tiffany died, and Louis, again a widower, supervised completion and decoration of Laurelton Hall. He continued to pursue his ideals and his art in spite of the changing climate of taste and criticism and continued to exhibit, receiving gold medals at St. Louis in 1904, Jamestown in 1907, and the Grand Prize at Seattle in 1909. He experimented with and began the production of a line of artistic jewelry that was marketed through Tiffany & Company and described in their Blue Book as "Designed and made under the personal supervision of Mr. Louis C. Tiffany. No pieces duplicated. Among the features of this work are the remarkable color effects obtained in the combinations of gold and enamel with precious and semi-precious stones."[48] Tiffany Favrile pottery was introduced commercially in 1905 and was in production by 1906. The ecclesiastical department continued to prosper and the decorating department continued to receive some important commissions, including the Frank C. Havens house in Oakland, California, decorated by Tiffany in collaboration with Lockwood de Forest in 1908.[49] In 1909 he received the commission to produce a mosaic mural for the fire curtain in the Palacio de Bellas Artes in Mexico City. Completed in 1911, the mural, which was composed of two hundred three-foot-square panels and measured thirty-six feet in height, depicted the neighboring volcanoes, Popocatépetl and Iztaccíhuatl. Tiffany was also involved in the design of the mechanics required to raise the twenty-seven-ton curtain.[50]

In 1913 Tiffany staged the first of several lavish fetes which were consciously intended to be "artistic events" or what today might have been called "art happenings." It is ironic that his Egyptian Fete gathered together the elite of New York's art and social establishment a few short weeks before the now famous Armory Show was to unveil the new art of the twentieth century. Tiffany, whose career had been marked by his rejection of the past, the academic and the traditional, and by his brilliant pursuit of innovation and originality, placed himself squarely in opposition to the new "modern" movement and noted that "the 'modernists,' as they are called for want of a better term, wander after curiosities of technique, vaguely hoping they may light on some invention which will make them famous. They do not belong to art; they are untrained inventors of the processes of the arts."[51] Tiffany, a visionary who had been ahead of his time in the nineteenth century, soon came to be viewed as an eccentric relic of an all too recent past.

In 1914 he produced a ghost-written autobiography in which he reflected upon his life, his work, and his concepts of art and beauty. Actually written by Charles DeKay from Tiffany's recollections in a series of interviews, 502 hand-bound copies in covers of Tiffany's design were privately printed at his own expense by Doubleday, Page, & Company. The volumes were numbered, inscribed, and presented by Tiffany to those he felt would appreciate his message. Volume number one was inscribed *to Mr. and Mrs. Charles L. Tiffany, My dear son and daughter, Merry Xmas 1914* (see no. 1). The following year he exhibited at the Panama-Pacific International Exposition in San Francisco where he was awarded both a gold and silver medal (see nos. 236 and 237). Tiffany had originally planned to exhibit The Bathers, a large and important figural window in which he claimed to have at last eliminated all surface painting. He stated that even the flesh tones of the figures "are built up of what I call 'genuine' glass, genuine because there are no tricks of the glassmaker needed to express the flesh."[52] Regrettably, a dispute with the fair officials regarding the artificial lighting of the window prompted Tiffany not to exhibit it.[53] Another project then underway, however, was to result in the creation of an American masterwork. On the occasion of the completion of his magnificent mosaic translation of Maxfield Parrish's design for The Dream Garden installed in the Curtis Publishing Company Building in Philadelphia, Tiffany noted, "I trust it may stand in the years to come for a development in glass-making and its application to art which will give to students a feeling that in this year of nineteen hundred and fifteen something worthy has been produced for the benefit of mankind...."[54] Tiffany's unequivocal pursuit of aesthetic excellence, technological innovation, and strict adherence to the integrity of his materials show no signs of diminution in the execution of this important commission.

For the remainder of his life Tiffany was to devote his time and his fortune to efforts intended to ensure that his vision for the arts in America would not be forgotten. In 1918 he established and endowed the Louis Comfort Tiffany Foundation and entrusted to it the care and maintenance of Laurelton Hall and his personal collections contained therein. The following year the Tiffany Studios were again reorganized and although he retained the title of president and art director, he effectively retired from active participation in their operation. The years of his retirement were spent in traveling, painting, enjoying his grandchildren, and in observing the work of the artists who as Tiffany Fellows came to Laurelton Hall under the sponsorship of his foundation. In 1928 Louis Comfort Tiffany disassociated himself from the Tiffany Studios, and the Tiffany Furnaces were sold to Douglas Nash, son of Arthur J. Nash, Tiffany's former associate. In 1931 he was recognized by the National Academy of Design on the occasion of his fiftieth anniversary as an academician. In that same year Douglas Nash closed the furnaces at Corona for good, and the following year the Tiffany Studios were declared bankrupt.

On January 17, 1933, Louis Comfort Tiffany died in the house he had built at 72nd Street and Madison Avenue. His obituary in *Art News* noted that "Mr. Tiffany was generally regarded as one of the earliest exponents of the modern art movement in the United States, and at one time his painting, glass, and architectural designs aroused considerable controversy."[55]

1. Charles H. Carpenter, Jr. with Mary Grace Carpenter, *Tiffany Silver* (New York, 1978), p. 8. This work is an authoritative study of the history of the company founded by Charles L. Tiffany.

2. Ibid.

3. Ibid., pp. 13–14.

4. Robert Koch, *Louis C. Tiffany, Rebel in Glass* (New York, 1964), p. 6. This is the principal biography of Louis Comfort Tiffany. Koch has authored numerous books, articles, and papers on Tiffany and his work.

5. Hugh F. McKean, *The "Lost" Treasures of Louis Comfort Tiffany* (Garden City, N.Y., 1980), p. 2. With his wife, Jeanette, the author of this important work assembled the collection now in the Morse Gallery of Art, Winter Park, Florida, from which this exhibition has been drawn. McKean, director of the Morse Gallery and president of the Charles Hosmer Morse Foundation, is a former Tiffany Foundation Fellow.

6. Charles DeKay, *The Art Work of Louis C. Tiffany* (New York, 1914), p. 8.

Gary A. Reynolds, *Louis Comfort Tiffany: The Paintings*, exhibition catalogue, The Grey Art Gallery and Study Center, New York University, March 20–May 12, 1979, p. 9, states that George Inness had moved his studio from Massachusetts to Eaglewood, N.J., in 1864.

7. Koch, p. 7.

8. Considerable difference of opinion exists in the literature concerning the date of this trip. Although Koch notes that Tiffany and Colman traveled together in the spring of 1869 (p. 7), this appears unlikely. Reynolds rather convincingly dates Tiffany's trip in the summer of 1870 (p. 15), and Wayne Craven, in his article "Samuel Colman (1832–1920): Rediscovered Painter of Far-Away Places," *American Art Journal* 8 (May 1976), pp. 16–37, places Colman in Spain and North Africa in 1861–62 and not again until 1871–1875.

9. Louis C. Tiffany, "Color and Its Kinship to Sound," address before the Rembrandt Club of Brooklyn, 1917, reprinted by Robert Koch, *Louis C. Tiffany's Art Glass* (New York, 1977) pp. 35–39.

10. Reynolds provides a detailed account of Tiffany's participation in exhibitions of this period.

11. Koch, *Rebel in Glass*, p. 8.

12. Carpenter, pp. 27–28.

13. Koch, *Rebel in Glass*, p. 6.

14. For further discussion of Furness's work at the exposition and at the Pennsylvania Academy, see James F. O'Gorman, *The Architecture of Frank Furness* (Philadelphia, 1973).

15. For further discussion of LaFarge's work on Trinity Church, see Helene Barbara Weinberg, "The Early Stained Glass Work of John LaFarge (1835–1910)," *Stained Glass* 67 (Summer 1972), pp. 7–10.

16. Reynolds, p. 43; McKean, p. 3.

17. Koch, *Rebel in Glass*, p. 17.

18. A short-lived venture, the glasshouse employed Andrea Boldini, a Venetian glassmaker, as foreman.

19. Candace Wheeler, Document #1, Mark Twain Memorial Collection, cited by Wilson H. Faude, "Associated Artists and the American Renaissance in the Decorative Arts," *Winterthur Portfolio* 10 (1975), pp. 127–128.

20. Anne Suydam Lewis, *Lockwood de Forest: Painter, Importer, Decorator*, exhibition catalogue, Heckscher Museum, 1976, p. 17. Although Lewis assumed this new house to be the Bella apartment, the letter cited is dated November, 1882; given de Forest's subsequent observation that two years were required to complete the 1890 commission for a room for the Columbian Exposition, it is reasonable to assume that the new house being discussed was the house at 72nd and Madison occupied in 1885.

21. Koch, *Rebel in Glass*, p. 61.

22. Ibid.

23. Herwin Schaefer, "Tiffany's Fame in Europe," *Art Bulletin* (December 1962), p. 311.

24. Samuel Bing, *La Culture Artistique en Amérique* (Paris, 1895), translated by Benita Eisler and published by The MIT Press in *Artistic America, Tiffany Glass, and Art Nouveau* (Cambridge, 1970), p. 130. Although the Havemeyer House is not cited in Bing's narrative, this passage is footnoted with a description of the "Rembrandt Room of H. O. Havemeyer in New York."

25. Ibid., p. 148.

26. Tiffany Glass and Decorating Company, *A Synopsis of the Exhibit of the Tiffany Glass and Decorating Company in the American Section of the Manufactures and Liberal Arts Building at the World's Fair, Jackson Park, Chicago, Illinois, 1893, with an Appendix on Memorial Windows* (New York, 1893), p. 3.

27. Ibid., p. 7.

28. Ibid., p. 4.

29. "Tiffany Glass and Decorating Company's Exhibit at the Columbian Exposition," *The Decorator and Furnisher,* 23 (October 1893), p. 9.

30. Ibid.

31. Schaefer, p. 311.

32. Koch, *Rebel in Glass*, p. 69.

33. Ibid., p. 70.

34. Document, United States Patent Office, filed September 26, 1894, reproduced by Koch, *Rebel in Glass*, p. 118.

35. DeKay, p. 25.

36. Document, United States Patent Office, reproduced by Koch, *Rebel in Glass*, p. 118.

37. McKean, p. 6; Reynolds, p. 54.

38. Bing, p. 152.

39. Schaefer, p. 315.

40. McKean, p. 5.

41. Although the name "Tiffany Studios" appeared as early as 1896, the company was not formally organized under that name until 1902.

42. The text of this catalogue is reprinted by Robert Koch, *Louis C. Tiffany's Glass-Bronzes-Lamps* (New York, 1971), pp. 85–88.

43. Ibid.

44. Schaefer, p. 316.

45. McKean, p. 26.

46. Schaefer, p. 317.

47. Ibid., p. 331.

48. *Tiffany & Company Blue Book* (New York, 1910), p. 658.

49. Lewis, n. 30, p. 31.

50. McKean, p. 145.

51. Louis C. Tiffany, "What is the Quest of Beauty?" *The International Studio* 58 (April 1916), p. lxiii.

52. Ibid.

53. The window was installed in the living room at Laurelton Hall where it remained until its destruction in the fire in 1957.

54. Louis C. Tiffany, quoted by McKean, p. 147.

55. "Louis C. Tiffany," obituary, *The Art News* 31 (January 21, 1933), p. 8.

Catalogue

Dimensions are given in both inches and centimeters, height preceding width preceding depth or diameter. Where exceptions to this order and form occur, the dimension given is identified by the appropriate initial.

10

Paintings

Louis Comfort Tiffany's decision to pursue a career as an artist rather than to attend college has been viewed by some as a rebellious act with potentially serious economic consequences. There is no evidence to suggest that this was actually the case. The success of artists such as Frederick Church and some of his contemporaries, undoubtedly known to the Tiffany family, had greatly enhanced the stature of art as an acceptable profession. Also, the possible influence and encouragement of Charles L. Tiffany has been underestimated, considering his support and encouragement of the fine arts and his personal involvement in the arts as a Fellow of the National Academy of Design, a founder of the New York Society of Fine Arts, and a trustee of the Metropolitan Museum of Art.[1] If the elder Tiffany did not encourage his son's decision, it is apparent that he provided the financial support for him to study, travel, and pursue his career.

Tiffany's study, first with George Inness and then in Paris with Leon Charles Adrien Bailly, was casual at best. Of the former he recalled only that Inness had "set high ideals before the student" and that he "...did not give instruction in painting; his way was to criticize or appreciate the work."[2] Of Bailly he recalled that he "took particular pains with the young American."[3]

There is little evidence in Tiffany's work to suggest that Bailly had significant influence and, given his inability to fully master figure drawing, it seems that the Paris method of intensive instruction in drawing from life and plaster casts had even less. Elements of Inness's technique and what has been described as the "jewel-like surfaces" of his pictures do, however, appear as major elements in Tiffany's mature painting style.[4] A more profound influence was to be exerted by Tiffany's friend and future colleague, Samuel Colman. A landscape painter, Colman worked in the tradition of the Hudson River School, though his work was marked by a less picturesque quality, a greater fidelity in the depiction of nature, and a refined sense of color. Although Tiffany referred to himself as a student of Colman, it remains unclear whether his "study" involved any formal instruction. A similarity in the pictures of Dobbs Ferry by Tiffany and Colman (see nos. 3 and 3a) can be seen not only in the near duplication of subject matter but also in their approach to the handling of composition, color, and atmospheric quality. This relationship was observed as early as 1879 when it was noted that "Mr. Louis C. Tiffany is another of our artists who has chosen and very happily rendered a class of subjects similar to those painted by Mr. Colman, and has shown the same love and appreciation for color. Like him, too, he has wrought with equal effects in oil and water-colors."[5] Both Tiffany and Colman traveled extensively, and the sites they visited, particularly in North Africa, provided each of them with subject matter for many of their paintings. Working from sketches and photographs, Tiffany completed his pictures in his studio.

Tiffany himself would have agreed with the critic cited above who made reference to his appreciation for color. He frequently referred to himself as a colorist, and in the small, quickly rendered sketches executed in oil and watercolor Tiffany's perception of subject in terms of color is most salient (see nos. 11 and 12). In discussing this perception, Tiffany observed that "only a few have combined with an inborn color-sense the chance to study and develop this original gift... this primal natural instinct...."[6] Color to Tiffany was the vehicle through which the natural world was perceived and the medium through which the beauty of nature could be depicted. This relationship was inseparable in his mind and would characterize the unique quality that he would bring not only to his paintings but to all of his art.[7] In acknowledging the rightness and beauty inherent in nature, Tiffany, aware of but not educated into the inhibition of the classical ideal imposed by the academies, was freer in his perception of beauty in the natural world that recommended itself as appropriate for subject matter. As a consequence, he perceived beauty, not pictures, in the natural world of his studio, travels, and experience and painted pictures in which he strove to fix that beauty in oil and watercolor.

Cosmopolitan and active in both art organizations and exhibitions, Tiffany assimilated the influence of other contemporary artists; but his unique perception, which could find beauty in the slums of New York or in a sow nursing her young, marked his paintings with a special quality. This quality was to delight some critics and confound others. Writing in *Century* in 1881, William C. Brownell observed, "Some of the most attractive of his works that we remember were of the naturally unromantic, not to say hideous, 'localities' to be found in this city.... This seemed for a time, indeed, so clearly Mr. Tiffany's true line that it is hardly probable that he has seriously compromised the qualities to which he owed his success... but what is worth noticing is that... he brings to bear all the invention and taste with which he is endowed, and that at the beginning of his career as a painter he was content to lean upon whatever intrinsic interest might belong to such material as deserts and dromedaries."[8]

Although Tiffany maintained artistic credibility with the traditional and conservative National Academy of Design while at the same time identifying with the progressive ideas that resulted in the formation of the Society of American Artists, he saw himself as a man apart. His apparent presumption in describing himself this way reflects an awareness of fact, rather than arrogance, that has been borne out by art historical study. Although Tiffany's work has been discussed in connection with that of the Hudson River School, the Luminists,[9] or the Ashcan School, it remains fundamentally apart from any school or movement. His straightforward rendering of either exotic sites or mundane activities contrasts with the picturesque exploitation of the exotic or the social comment that characterizes the work of many of his contemporaries. The special quality of Tiffany's paintings was well received by a discriminating public and circle of collectors, but, in spite of his success, his interest in other areas of creative expression was to occupy an increasing amount of his time. Although he was to continue to paint for the rest of his life, he produced his finest works in the decades of the 1870s and 1880s, and in the exhibitions that followed the World's Columbian Exposition in 1893 it was to be his glass and accomplishments in the decorative arts that would attract attention, stimulate controversy, and insure his fame.

1. Gertrude Speenburg, *The Arts of the Tiffanys* (Chicago, 1956), p. 27.

2. Charles DeKay, *The Art Work of Louis C. Tiffany* (New York, 1914), p. 8.

3. Ibid.

4. Gary Reynolds, *Louis Comfort Tiffany: The Paintings,* exhibition catalogue, The Grey Art Gallery and Study Center, New York University, March 20–May 12, 1979, p. 9. This catalogue provides the most comprehensive examination to date of Tiffany's little-known career as a painter. It also gives information regarding contemporary exhibitions and criticism, as well as discussion of his influences, style, and techniques.

5. S. G. W. Benjamin, *Our American Artists* (New York, 1879; reprinted ed., 1977); cited by Reynolds, p. 14.

6. Louis Comfort Tiffany, "Color and Its Kinship to Sound," address before the Rembrandt Club of Brooklyn, 1917, reprinted by Robert Koch, *Louis C. Tiffany's Art Glass* (New York, 1977), p. 38.

7. Ibid., pp. 36–37.

8. William C. Brownell, "The Younger of American Painters," *Century* 72 (July 1881), p. 328; cited by Reynolds, p. 40.

9. See Reynolds.

1 The Art Work of Louis Comfort Tiffany, 1914
Book; cover design by Louis Comfort Tiffany
Fly leaf inscribed: *No. 1 to Mr. and Mrs. Charles L. Tiffany, My dear son and daughter, Merry Xmas 1914*
CHMF ARCHIVE
Though frequently referred to as Tiffany's autobiography, the book was written anonymously by Charles de Kay and was based on personal interviews and Tiffany's recollections. An edition of 502 copies was printed at Tiffany's expense by Doubleday, Page, and Co.

2 My First Visit to Europe, dated *Nov. 1865– March 1866*
Sketch book; 5 3/16 x 4 1/2 in (13.2 x 11.4 cm)
Signed: *L.T.* (each sketch)
CHMF 74-6
This little sketch book contains fifty studies by Louis Comfort Tiffany and chronicles his voyage on board the *Scotia* and his visits to England, Ireland, France, and Italy.

3 On the Hudson River at Dobbs Ferry, ca. 1880
Oil on canvas; 12 1/2 x 27 1/2 in (31.8 x 69.8 cm)
Signed: *Louis C. Tiffany*
CHMF 78-13
The influence of the Hudson River School is evident in this picture, but Tiffany, like others of the second generation of that school, has incorporated his interest in the atmospheric quality of light. Although pictures of this type have been cited as evidence of his link to the Luminist painters, his unconcerned brushwork exhibits a greater freedom than that usually seen in their work. The freely painted areas of low-key color at the left are not unlike that seen in the mature work of Tiffany's other teacher, George Inness.

3a Dobbs Ferry, by Samuel Colman, ca. 1880
Oil on canvas; 16 3/8 x 40 in (41.4 x 101.6 cm)
Unsigned
CHMF P-11-81
This painting by Samuel Colman (1832–1920), like Tiffany's of the same subject (see no. 3), probably was painted from sketches made on a joint trip to Dobbs Ferry. Both in style and subject matter the picture demonstrates Colman's kinship with the Hudson River School of landscape painters.

3

3a

4 Figure Study of an Arab, ca. 1875
Watercolor on paper; 14 x 7½ in (35.6 x 19 cm)
Unsigned
CHMF 55-28
One of a group of similar studies made by Louis Comfort
Tiffany on one of his visits to North Africa in the 1870s.
Here, as in other studies from this series (nos. 5, 6, and 7),
Tiffany is not so much concerned with the figure as with
the light, shadow, and the drapery of the costume.

5 Figure Study of an Arab, ca. 1875
Oil on canvas; 9¼ x 7½ in (23.5 x 19.05 cm)
Unsigned; pencil inscription on mat: *Painted by*
Louis C. Tiffany
CHMF 55-27

6 Figure Study of an Arab, ca. 1875
Oil on canvas; 10 x 7½ in (25.4 x 19.05 cm)
Unsigned; pencil inscription on mat: *Painted by*
Louis C. Tiffany
CHMF 55-26

7 Figure Study of an Arab Musician, ca. 1875
Watercolor on paper; 9½ x 7½ in (24.1 x 19 cm)
Unsigned
CHMF 55-25

8 Fruit Vendors under the Sea Wall at Nassau, 1872
Oil on canvas; 8⁷⁄₁₆ x 10¹⁄₁₆ in (21.5 x 25.6 cm)
Signed lower left: *L. Tiffany*
CHMF 69-15
This painting is a smaller version of the large painting
that Tiffany exhibited at the National Academy of Design in 1870. Like the other genre pictures from Cairo
and Tangiers that he exhibited in the 1870s, this painting
demonstrates Tiffany's nonjudgmental fascination with
the mundane activities of life. This fascination can also be
seen in many of Tiffany's photographs.

9 European Merchant's House, ca. 1877
Watercolor on paper; 11½ x 18½ in (29.2 x 47 cm)
Signed lower right: *Louis C. Tiffany*
CHMF 75-7
As a painter, Tiffany was perhaps most successful with
watercolors. In works such as this, he was able to achieve
in a finished picture something of the freshness and spon-
taneity seen in his preliminary oil sketches.

7

8

10 Old Mill at Frieburg, 1877
Watercolor on paper; 13 1/2 x 19 1/2 in (34.3 x 49.5 cm)
Signed lower right: *Louis C. Tiffany*
CHMF 75-6
This painting, like much of Tiffany's work, reflects a
precise perception of subject matter. Cropped as tightly
as a photograph, the picture derives its beauty not from
the picturesque profile of its architecture but rather from
the sensitive handling of color, texture, and the interplay
of light and shadow on but a portion of the mill.
A larger version of this painting hung in the living room
at Laurelton Hall.

11 Study of Women at Market, undated
Oil on panel; 6 3/4 x 5 1/2 in (17 x 14 cm)
Unsigned
CHMF 55-21
Tiffany apparently liked to sketch in oil on small pieces of
wood. This, like other such sketches, was probably a
study for a larger work and, like many of his paintings
and photographs, depicts the everyday activities of common folk. Although Tiffany was frequently criticized for
the inappropriateness of this subject matter, it represented some of his finest work.

12 My Family at Somesville, ca. 1888
Oil sketch on wood; 5 1/4 x 8 1/8 in (13.3 x 20.4 cm)
Unsigned
CHMF 55-23
Sketched while on an outing with his family into the
fields near Somesville, Maine, this panel was a study for
Tiffany's larger painting of the same title (no. 13).

13 My Family at Somesville, 1888
Oil on canvas; 24 x 36 in (26.5 x 91.4 cm)
Unsigned
CHMF 73-1
Based on a small oil sketch (no. 12), this painting depicts
Tiffany's children, Charles Lewis, Mary Woodbridge,
and the twins—Louis Comfort and Julia de Forest—with
his wife Louise and a nurse. Obviously comfortable with
this familial subject, Tiffany handled the figures with an
ease not found in his painting *Spring* (no. 15). The treatment of the surrounding Maine countryside exhibits the
luminous atmospheric quality that characterizes many of
his best landscapes. Although unsigned, this picture and
its study were displayed at Laurelton Hall.

12

14 **Night in a Tropical Garden,** ca. 1890
Oil on canvas; 22⅞ x 27⅞ in (58 x 70.7 cm)
Signed lower right: *Louis C. Tiffany*
CHMF 78-12
Despite its title, this painting depicts a portion of the tiers
of balconies in Tiffany's studio in the Madison Avenue
house he designed for his family in 1885. It relates both in
detail and in its use of scintillating light in a darkened
atmosphere to other paintings of the studio and appears
in contemporary photographs of it. There are other paintings of the studio that were given titles not reflecting the
actual subject matter. Notable among these is the painting *Feeding the Flamingos*, which was later executed in
glass. Although it depicts an adjacent corner of his studio, it was described by Tiffany in 1893 as depicting the
court of a Roman house.

15 **Spring,** ca. 1898
Oil on canvas; 58½ x 94½ in (148.6 x 240 cm)
Signed lower left: *Louis C. Tiffany*
CHMF 70-1
Figural allegory is rare in Tiffany's painting, and this
work reveals the dominance of his love of nature over the
classical ideal that permeated much of the establishment
art of the American Renaissance. As a member of the
establishment, he was aware of this ideal and of the work
of such artists as Thomas Dewing and Will Low. Tiffany,
however, having avoided academic training and discipline, never mastered figural drawing. In this attempt, his
figures possess neither the repose or spontaneity of natu-
ralism nor the idealized monumentality of allegory. They
become, rather, a tabloid suspended in and overpowered
by the landscape. Symbolic expression for Tiffany was to
be found in nature, and in works such as the Four Seasons
he is most eloquent (nos. 51-54).

14

15

16

16 Sow with Piglets, ca. 1900
Watercolor on paper; 19 x 24¾ in (48.3 x 62.9 cm)
Signed lower right: *Louis C. Tiffany*
CHMF 64-30
In its original Tiffany Studios frame, this watercolor
reflects both Tiffany's eye for non-idealized nature and
his freedom from the classical restraint of academic subject matter. The warm colors of autumn and the abundance of its harvest appear frequently in Tiffany's paintings and stained glass (see nos. 37, 53, 56, 59).

17 Palm Trees at Karnac, dated 1908
Watercolor on paper; 26¾ x 19¾ in (67.9 x 50.2 cm)
Inscribed lower left: *Karnac Feb 08*; signed lower right:
LCT
CHMF 77-17
In 1908, Tiffany chartered a yacht for a trip up the Nile
River. This watercolor study of palm trees was painted
on that trip.

18 Yellowstone Canyon, dated 1917
Watercolor on paper; 17⅜ x 11¾ in (44.2 x 29.8 cm)
Signed lower left: *Louis C. Tiffany*
CHMF 77-35
Tiffany, who had begun his career as a landscape painter,
painted numerous watercolors of places he visited in his
frequent travels. At the age of sixty-nine he painted this
picture of a site visited by many of the landscape painters
of the nineteenth century.

22

Photography

Less well known than his painting, Louis Comfort Tiffany's experiments with and use of photography represent a significant aspect of his artistic diversity and provide a rare and often personal insight into his approach to creative expression. The circumstances of his introduction to photography are not recorded, but Hugh McKean has suggested the inevitability of his interest in the field: "The camera was new and challenging when Tiffany was young, and new things fascinated him. . . ."[1]

His earliest associations with photography appear to have been with its use as a tool for his painting (see no. 19). Like many of his contemporaries, Tiffany saw the worth of such a tool, though it should be noted that this did not preclude his production of sketches and studies from life. Although he would continue to produce or acquire photographs for this purpose and expand its utility to include the documentation of his own work and that of the Tiffany Studios, his inquiring mind led him to explore other potentials of the camera.

As early as 1877 he was experimenting with motion photography, and in 1906 it was reported that he "shared with Eadweard Muybridge the honor of being one of the first to take instantaneous photographs of birds and animals in motion" (see no. 20).[2] Little is known about these early experiments, but there survive among his work various series of photographic studies which chronicle both human and animal motion within a progressing activity. In these series the subtle aspects of task performance are candidly captured, suspending in time the spontaneity of physiological action and response. These studies also reveal the nonjudgmental perception of beauty in the naturally unromantic that marks so much of his work in painting and in stained glass. Although some of these images were to be used as studies for paintings, others were selected and processed into finished photographic prints.

Other prints reveal that Tiffany had become cognizant of the artistic validity of the photograph in its own right. In these works compositional elements are as carefully manipulated as the elements of a still life painting. In an article on Laurelton Hall, published in 1907 and illustrated with photographs by Louis Comfort Tiffany, the artist, in discussing a sketch in progress, described his compositional approach in terms equally appropriate to photographic imagery: "See, the trees must be grouped together a little—so—to let a little more of the lake come into view. We need that reflected light and movement, and as you see, I have indicated enough of the body of the house to complete the composition. The picture should stop there—just beyond the tower."[3] On the opposing page a photograph entitled *First View of the House from the Road* illustrates a portion of Laurelton Hall and its tower as seen through the trees with the shimmering reflected light of the harbor beyond.

The survival of some prints and studies later discovered to be by photographers other than Tiffany, but mounted on mats which bear the Louis C. Tiffany stamp, raised the question as to whether Tiffany ever actually handled a camera. Subsequent research concludes, however, that the stamp indicates inclusion in a Tiffany collection rather than an identification of the artist. Another confirmation of Tiffany's work as a photographer is the mention of his photographic studio in articles contemporary with the construction of the house at Madison and 72nd streets.

Comparative analysis of photographs in the collection of the Charles Hosmer Morse Foundation and others that descended in the Tiffany family reinforce an attribution to Tiffany and provide a partial explanation for the confusion. A large number of photographs survive that were made in the course of a canal boat trip made by the Tiffany family, friends (including Lockwood de Forest), and servants. At least two cameras were taken on this outing and appear in the photographs. More often than not, Tiffany himself does not appear in the photographs, but in one print he is seen holding a camera in front of an old man and a goat surrounded by children. Prints of this old man also appear in the album. It can therefore be assumed that some of the pictures in the album are by Tiffany and some are by another member of his party. That both should be included in this chronicle of a family outing is not surprising, nor is the inclusion of the work of other artists in Tiffany's collection of photographs.

Much additional research remains to be done in this area and, as with some of the windows, a firm attribution may not be possible. But sufficient material and documentation does exist at this time to support Tiffany's position as an important early proponent and practitioner of photography as an art form.

1. Hugh F. McKean, *The "Lost" Treasures of Louis Comfort Tiffany* (Garden City, N.Y., 1980), p. 251.
2. Gary A. Reynolds, *Louis Comfort Tiffany: The Paintings*, exhibition catalogue, The Grey Art Gallery and Study Center, New York University, March 20–May 12, 1979, p. 43. Also see quote cited by McKean, p. 251.
3. Samuel Howe, "The Dwelling Place as an Expression of Individuality," *Appletons Magazine* (February 1907), p. 55.

19

19   Market Day outside the Walls of Tangier, ca. 1871
4 x 9¾ in (10.2 x 24.8 cm)
Unsigned; inscribed: *Tangiers / May 5 / Market place* (on
the back)
CHMF 65-30-473
Although it cannot be said with certainty that Tiffany
took this photograph, it is certain that he used it as a
study for the important oil painting *Market Day outside
the Walls of Tangier, Morocco.* The painting, dated 1873,
was exhibited at the National Academy of Design in
that year.

20   Sea Bird in Flight, dated 1884
3⅞ x 5½ in (9.7 x 14 cm)
Stamped on mat: *Louis C. Tiffany*
CHMF ARCHIVE
The graceful motion of this elegant sea bird has been
suspended by the camera. Tiffany was experimenting
with instantaneous motion photography as early as 1877.

21   Sailboats on the Beach, ca. 1888
6 x 8¼ in (15.2 x 21 cm)
Stamped on mat: *Louis C. Tiffany*
CHMF ARCHIVE
A print from a series of photographs of boats on the
beach at Sea Bright, New Jersey.

20

21

22 Coastal Scene with Boy and Boats, ca. 1888
6 x 8¼ in (15.2 x 21 cm)
Stamped on mat: *Louis C. Tiffany*
CHMF ARCHIVE
A print from one of several series of photographs taken at Sea Bright, New Jersey. The placement of the oars and rake may have been composed for the photograph.

23 Four Studies of Figures, Boats, and Carts, ca. 1888
2¾ x 4 in (7 x 10.2 cm)
Stamped on mat: *Louis C. Tiffany*; pencil notations on mat refer to an index system for negatives
CHMF ARCHIVE
Four studies from one of several series of photographs taken at Sea Bright, New Jersey. These studies are from a series of candid photographs that chronicle the activities of "fisher folk" and the movement of the catch from the boats to the fishmonger.

24 Coastal Scene with Men, Boats, and Carts, ca. 1888
6 x 8⅛ in (15.2 x 46.1 cm)
Stamped on mat: *Louis C. Tiffany*
CHMF ARCHIVE
A print from the "fisher folk" series, Sea Bright, New Jersey.

25 Shanties at Sea Bright, New Jersey, ca. 1888
8⅛ x 8¼ in (20.7 x 21 cm)
Stamped on mat: *Louis C. Tiffany*
CHMF ARCHIVE
A print possibly from the "fisher folk" series. The quaint structures illustrated here appear in the background of other photographs of this series. The buildings may have been used for smoking or storing fish.

26

26   **Six Studies at Sea Bright, New Jersey,** ca. 1888
Each image: 2¾ x 4 in (7 x 10.1 cm)
Unsigned; the portion of the mat with the stamp is
missing
CHMF ARCHIVE
This mat includes studies from the "tin peddler" series.
The study at the upper left was the source for a major
watercolor by Tiffany. Entitled *Tin Peddler at Sea Bright,
New Jersey*, it was exhibited at the American Watercolor
Society in 1889.

27   **Eight Studies from a Trip on a Canal Boat,** ca. 1886
Each image: 3 x 4 in (7.6 x 10.2 cm)
Stamped on mat: *Louis C. Tiffany*; pencil notations be-
low two images: *85 Neg* and *80 Neg*
CHMF ARCHIVE
Sixty-eight finished prints from this canal trip were
mounted and bound into an album that descended in the
Tiffany family.

28   **Pet Dog,** undated
4½ x 6½ in (11.4 x 16.5 cm)
Stamped on mat: *Louis C. Tiffany*
CHMF ARCHIVE
Candid photograph of a pet dog, possibly taken at The
Briars.

29   **Nine Studies of Trees in a Rural Landscape,** undated
Each image: 3 x 4 in (7.6 x 10.2 cm)
Stamped on mat (twice): *Louis C. Tiffany*; pencil nota-
tions on mat refer to an index system for negatives
CHMF ARCHIVE
The study annotated 76 may have been used as a source
for the cluster of gnarled trees that dominate the fore-
ground of the large landscape window made by Tiffany
for the Russell Sage Memorial Chapel, Far Rockaway,
Long Island.

30   **Landscape Study with Trees,** undated
8¼ x 6⅛ in (21 x 15.7 cm)
Stamped on mat: *Louis C. Tiffany*
CHMF ARCHIVE

31   **Landscape Study with Waterfalls,** undated
Each image: 4¾ x 3¾ in (12 x 9.5 cm)
Stamped on mat: *Louis C. Tiffany*
CHMF ARCHIVE

32   **Study of Snowball Blossoms,** undated
15¼ x 18½ in (38.7 x 47 cm)
Stamped on mat (three times): *Louis C. Tiffany*
CHMF ARCHIVE
The snowball bush (a cultivated shrub of the genus
Viburnum) with its aptly named blossoms was used by
Tiffany for both lampshades and windows (no. 58).

33 Study of Lilac Blossoms, undated
13¾ x 17¼ in (35 x 43.8 cm)
Stamped on mat (three times): *Louis C. Tiffany*
CHMF ARCHIVE

34 Study of a Poinsettia Blossom, undated
7 x 9½ in (17.8 x 24.1 cm)
Inscribed: *11321F* (on the negative)
CHMF ARCHIVE
One of a series of floral studies that survived with the
Tiffany photographs.

35 Study of Mounted Specimens of Queen Anne's Lace,
undated
7½ x 9¼ in (19 x 23.5 cm)
Unsigned
CHMF ARCHIVE
Queen Anne's lace, also known as wild carrot, was frequently used as a floral motif by Tiffany, finding expression in such diverse objects as the enameled and jeweled
brooch exhibited in St. Louis in 1904 and the bronze base
of a candlestick (no. 186).

**36 Study for a Floral Lamp Shade with Daffodils and
Foliage,** ca. 1905
7½ x 7¼ in (19 x 18.4 cm)
Unsigned
CHMF ARCHIVE
This remarkable photograph documents the direct use of
nature as source material for design. Tiffany Studios did
produce such a shade and in 1906 catalogued under
leaded shades, no. 1497, a 20-in. "Daffodil Cone."

35

36

32

43

62

Windows

Tiffany's interest in and fascination with glass, and windows in particular, can be traced to his visit to Europe in 1870; he later recalled, "Naturally I was attracted to the old glass in windows of the twelfth and thirteenth centuries which have always seemed to me the finest ever!"[1] Returning to America, he was confronted with the problem of "what was to be done for the windows" of his own studio and home, since "all windows were poor in quality and color."[2] By 1872 he had begun to experiment with making glass in his studio; he subsequently moved those experiments to Thill's glasshouse in Brooklyn. Encountering what he referred to as "the prejudice and mental habits of glass makers," he established his own glasshouse and began to study the chemistry and technology of glassmaking.[3] When fires destroyed his first two glasshouses, he continued his work at Heidt's glasshouse.

By 1881 the success of his experiments was described in an article in *Scribner's*. Discussing the "new styles of opalescent glass," and "new methods of mixing colors in the glass house," it described the production processes as follows:

The hot glass, while at a red heat, is rolled with corrugated rollers, punched and pressed by various roughened tools, or is squeezed and pressed up into corrugations by lateral pressure, or is stamped by dies. The "bull's-eyes" produced in making sheet glass, by whirling it round on a rod while still soft, are also cut into various shapes or, while still soft, are gently pressed into new shapes.... Next to this comes a revival and modification of the old Venetian method of imbedding bits of colored glass in sheets of clear glass. This is done by scattering filaments and irregular bits of colored glass on the table on which plate glass is made, and then pouring the hot glass (either white or colored) over the table and rolling it down in the usual manner to press the colored threads or pieces into the sheet.... Lastly comes one of the most original features of all, and this is the use of solid masses and lumps of glass pressed while hot into moulds, giving a great number of facets like a cut stone, or by taking blocks of glass and roughly chipping them into numerous small faces. These, when set in the window, have all the effects of the most brilliant gems, changing their shade of color with every changing angle of vision."[4]

All of the glass described above appears in and is characteristic of Tiffany windows; the molded, chipped and faceted pieces occur more frequently in those produced prior to 1900.

Though Tiffany's success in the pursuit of unique types of glass or innovative processes of glass production was remarkable, it seems insufficient explanation for his years of near obsessive experimentation with the medium. It should be remembered, however, that it was the son of Charles L. Tiffany who had been attracted to the beauty of "the skies and stars—the gems" that he had seen translated into the stained glass of the thirteenth century.[5] In that attraction can be seen the genesis of his artistic perception of glass as a vehicle for artistic expression. As a child he had been fascinated by the color and brilliance of the gems that formed the stock and trade of his father's firm. Intrinsically possessing both value and beauty, these stones required nothing more than to be cut, polished, and mounted in such fashion as to maximize those qualities. Tiffany's response to these gems was to be but part of his awakening as an artist. As he later observed, "When the savage searches for the gems from the earth or the pearls from the sea to decorate his person, or when he decorates the utensils of war or peace in designs and colours, he becomes an artist in embryo, for he has turned his face to the quest of beauty."[6] For Tiffany it was not enough simply to perceive beauty; growth as an artist required that the efforts of his mind and hands be directed to that quest, so that his art might "interpret the beauty of ideas and visible things, making them concrete and lasting."[7] From his experiments with glass, Tiffany, like the glassmakers of the thirteenth century, began to translate the beauty of nature into "the speech of stained glass."[8] Beauty, therefore, became fixed in a visible thing and that thing was the glass itself.

Writing in 1893, Tiffany reflected that "those of us in America who began to experiment in glass were untrammelled by tradition and were moved solely by a desire to produce a thing of beauty...."[9] The beautiful object thus produced, like a jewel, required nothing more for its presentation than to be mounted into a setting that would enhance its intrinsic qualities. Therefore, in the creation of a window like no. 40, Tiffany has used a window to exhibit and enhance the beauty he had fixed into two great cabochons of glass. It has been proposed that some of these early windows established him as a master of abstraction, anticipating American abstract-expressionist painting. If this is true, Tiffany's abstraction conforms with the philosophical justification for such art found in Plato: "I do not now intend by beauty of shapes what most people would expect, such as that of living creatures or pictures, but ... straight lines and curves and the surfaces or solid forms.... These things are not beautiful relatively, like other things, but always and naturally and absolutely."[10]

Having created a material imbued with both color and beauty, Tiffany the painter responded to stained glass and the brilliant potential for translucent color that he had long sought to achieve on canvas and paper. However, Tiffany the glassmaker abhorred the custom of painting on stained glass that had prevailed since the thirteenth century, and, although he admired the mosaic purity of the ancient windows, he realized that the primitive simplicity so appropriate to an old cathedral would not suffice for his own time. His efforts to expand the potential of his new medium were described by S. Bing in 1898: *For years Tiffany gave himself up to these engrossing researches, and gradually succeeded in making a glass which answered the requirements to a wonderful degree. By the blending of colour he causes the sheet of glass to convey the effect of a cloudy sky, or of rippling water, or again the delicate shades of flowers and foliage. For drapery, in all its truth of suppleness and outline, he operates in a most ingenious manner upon the material while it is cooling, putting into it an infinite variety of folds and wrinkles. Even then he has not done perfecting, but can communicate to the glass quite a special plastic surface. New tones are to be found on his palette, and he has quite new processes, as for instance the superposition of several plates of different colours, by which the aspect of the work is changed in the most unexpected ways.*[11] The success of these efforts provided Tiffany with a "palette" consisting of "five thousand colors and hues" represented in "as many as 200 tons of glass in the form of ovals about three feet long . . . stored in the bins of the Tiffany Studios."[12]

The two studies for the Entombment window provide a rare opportunity to share in the translation of a concept, formed in the mind of the artist, into a masterpiece "painted" with glass. As an artist, Tiffany considered himself a colorist and defended the supremacy of color over form and line.[13] In his oil sketch for this window, Tiffany fixes his concept in color laid down with bold strokes of the brush. Form appears only in its modeling in light, and there is scarce evidence of line. In the subsequent glass study, line appears in the form of the lead cames which support the composition, which has been translated into a sketch on a mosaic of translucent color. In the completed window, this mosaic is constructed of glass carefully selected to provide or imply the requisite detail, while faces, hands, and flesh tones have been achieved with enamel. The result is a masterpiece of the art of Louis Comfort Tiffany. At once both a painting and a window, it reveals the artist's strict adherence to his principles as a painter and his mastery of glass as a medium for painterly expression.

Although he was not to limit himself to the production of windows from his own designs, he exercised the same mastery of his craft in the execution of designs by other artists (see nos. 48 and 49). For the work produced in his studios, he imposed the same standards of excellence on his artists and designers that he imposed on himself; and all sketches, proposals, and finished windows required his personal approval.

1. Louis C. Tiffany, "Color and Its Kinship to Sound," address before the Rembrandt Club of Brooklyn, 1917, reprinted by Robert Koch, *Louis C. Tiffany's Art Glass* (New York, 1977), pp. 35–39.
2. Ibid.
3. Ibid.
4. "American Progress in the Manufacture of Stained Glass," *Scribner's Monthly* (January 1881), pp. 485–486.
5. Louis C. Tiffany, "The Quest of Beauty," reprinted by Koch, *Tiffany's Art Glass*, p. 35.
6. Ibid.
7. Ibid.
8. Ibid.
9. Louis C. Tiffany, "American Art Supreme in Colored Glass," *The Forum* 15 (July 1893), p. 623.
10. Peter Murray and Linda Murray, *A Dictionary of Art and Artists* (Baltimore, 1949), p. 13.
11. Samuel Bing, from *Kunst und Kunsthandwerk*, Vol. I (1898); translation published by the MIT Press in *Artistic America, Tiffany Glass, and Art Nouveau* (Cambridge, 1970), pp. 201–202.
12. Hugh F. McKean, *The "Lost" Treasures of Louis Comfort Tiffany* (Garden City, N.Y., 1980), p. 237.
13. Tiffany, "Color and Its Kinship to Sound," p. 37.

37 Eggplants Transom, 1879

31 x 41 in (78.7 x 104.1 cm)
Unsigned; possibly the transom designed and executed by Louis Comfort Tiffany for the dining room of the Kemp residence, decorated by Tiffany in 1879
CHMF 71-3

This mosaic transom depicts richly figured purple eggplants with amber and green foliage entwined in a yellow trellis on a ground of clear glass. In true mosaic tradition, detail is inherent in the pot metal which has been carefully selected for shape, gradation of color, and its orientation in the composition. A companion transom depicts squash plants. These transoms continued a frieze painted upon a gold ground that surrounded the dining room and depicted gourds, pumpkins, and other autumnal fruit. The decoration of this room was published and the transom illustrated as early as 1881.

Tiffany is known to have made at least one other set of similar transoms, possibly for his own dining room at the Bella apartment where the overmantle was painted with pumpkins and corn. One of the sets of transoms was exhibited by Tiffany at the Grafton Galleries in London in 1899. This panel was later installed in the living room at Laurelton Hall.

38 Jeweled Gothic Window, 1880–1890
30 x 56 in (76.2 x 142.2 cm)
Unsigned; Tiffany Glass and Decorating Company, installed in the painting gallery at Laurelton Hall
CHMF 61-1
Richly colored spheres and cullets of green, blue, and yellow glass are set like jewels into a heavy matrix of lead. Possibly two spandrels from a large circular window, this window was reworked to its present form when it was installed at Laurelton Hall.

39 Magnolia Window, ca. 1885
52⅞ x 55¾ in (134.6 x 141.6 cm)
Unsigned; designed by Louis Comfort Tiffany for the residence he designed and built for the Tiffany family at Madison Avenue and 72nd Street, New York City
CHMF 58-13
These three panels from a bay window depict *Magnolia soulangiana* against a ground of clear glass; the blossoms, formed of deeply folded drapery glass, are set in lead cames that have been naturalistically sculpted as branches.

  These panels were later installed as a screen in the windows of a hallway between the court and the dining room at Laurelton Hall.

40 Abstract Window, 1892-1900
31⅛ x 43¼ in (78.9 x 109.8 cm)
Unsigned; Tiffany Glass and Decorating Company, displayed for many years in the showrooms of the Tiffany Studios
CHMF 74-22
Two large cabochons of glass, one the center of a medallion of interlaced "C" and "S" scrolls, are set into a ground of greenish-yellow textured glass in an architectonic surround framed with translucent white opalescent glass tiles.

41 The Medallion Window, ca. 1892
146 x 47⅜ in (370.8 x 120.4 cm)
Unsigned; made for exhibition, later installed at Laurelton Hall
CHMF U-73
This Gothic lancet window was executed to display the application of Tiffany's Favrile glass to a design in the manner of the thirteenth century.

41

42　Field of Lilies, 1892
122½ x 103¼ in (311.1 x 262.3 cm)
Unsigned; Tiffany Glass and Decorating Company,
designed by Louis Comfort Tiffany for the chapel he
exhibited at the World's Columbian Exposition,
Chicago, 1893
CHMF U-71
This mosaic window depicts a classically detailed, col-
umned loggia overlooking a distant landscape beyond a
field of lilies. When originally installed in the baptistry of
the chapel, the central panel included the figure of an
angel. The reason for removing the angel is not known;
however, the use of the copper foil technique in the
present panel suggests that the change was made after
1900. The window appears today as it was in 1916 when
installed in the chapel at Laurelton Hall.

43　The Entombment, 1892
99⅛ x 69½ in (252 x 176.5 cm)
Unsigned; Tiffany Glass and Decorating Company, after
a design by Louis Comfort Tiffany for the chapel he
exhibited at the World's Columbian Exposition,
Chicago, 1893
CHMF 58-12
Among the most painterly of Tiffany's windows, the
Entombment window was described by Tiffany as being
"built upon what is called the mosaic system. No paints
or enamels have been used . . . except in the flesh of the
various figures." The head of Joseph of Aramathea is a
portrait of Louis' father, Charles L. Tiffany. The same
subject and composition was used again in 1930 in the
Tree of Life window, the last known to have been made by
Tiffany.

44　Sketch for the Entombment, 1892
Oil on panel; 8 x 5¾ in (20.3 x 14.6 cm)
Unsigned
CHMF 55-20
This oil sketch appears to be the first study for the window. Photographs printed from the original Tiffany Studios glass negatives illustrate additional, larger studies,
including detailed studies for the figures and a full-scale
cartoon.

45　Study for the Entombment, 1892
Leaded glass; 28⅜ x 20³⁄₁₆ in (72.1 x 51.3 cm)
Unsigned
CHMF 76-7
This panel was created as a study to translate the sketch
for the window (see no. 44) into transparent color.

46　Christ, Ruler of the Universe, 1892
DIAM. 105 in (266.7 cm)
Unsigned; Tiffany Glass and Decorating Company, from
a design by Louis Comfort Tiffany for his chapel at the
World's Columbian Exposition, Chicago, 1893
CHMF 62-37
This mosaic window, in the form of a circumscribed
Greek cross centered with a medallion, depicts Christ
enthroned with orb and scepter. Four medallions within
the cross portray scenes from the life of Christ. The
spandrels display a crown of thorns surrounded by small
blossoms.

47　Jesus Blessing Saint John, 1892
DIAM. 106¼ in (269.9 cm)
Unsigned; Tiffany Glass and Decorating Company, from
a design by Louis Comfort Tiffany for his chapel at the
World's Columbian Exposition, Chicago, 1893
CHMF 74-19
This mosaic window, also in the form of a circumscribed
Greek cross centered with a medallion, depicts Jesus
bestowing his blessing on Saint John. Medallions in the
spandrels display the apocalyptic symbols of the four
evangelists—which are repeated in the mosaics of the
altar frontal for the chapel.

　The window appears to have been conceived of as a
great jeweled brooch, the glass having been selected,
shaped, and "set" to display its jewel-like quality.

40

49

48   Young Woman at a Fountain, 1894

55 5⁄8 x 34 3⁄4 in (141.5 x 88.3 cm)

Unsigned; Tiffany Glass and Decorating Company, after a painting, *Aurora*, by Will Low (collection of The Metropolitan Museum of Art, New York)

CHMF 66-4

In this figural window, "painting" (in enamels fired onto glass) has been limited to the flesh tones. The remainder of the window is a true glass mosaic, the detail of drapery, foliage, shadows, and textures being in the pot metal. Effects such as the fall of water are achieved by overlaying pieces of glass in a technique known as plating.

49   Girl Picking Gourds, 1897

52 1⁄2 x 45 3⁄8 in (133.4 x 115.3 cm)

Unsigned; Tiffany Glass and Decorating Company, from a design by the English painter, Sir Frank Brangwyn.

CHMF U-70

Exhibited in 1899 at the Grafton Galleries in London, this window represents Tiffany's continuing effort to eliminate enameling in a mosaic window. The detail of the face and hands has been worked directly into a piece of glass which has been plated with a piece of flesh-colored pot metal. This window demonstrates Tiffany's use of designs by other artists as subjects for his windows, the most famous of these being the series of ten windows commissioned by Samuel Bing from designs by Bonnard, Grasset, Ibels, Ransom, Roussel, Sérusier, Toulouse-Lautrec, Vallotton, and Vuillard. These were exhibited in Paris in 1895.

50   Three-Dimensional Window, 1890–1900

48 x 48 in (121.9 x 121.9 cm)

Unsigned; Tiffany Glass and Decorating Company, formerly installed in the art gallery at Laurelton Hall.

CHMF 61-2

Three-dimensional, the surface of this window is projected forward by the out-rounded border of peacock feather "eyes." The three-lobed arch features medallions of chipped and faceted "jewels" of clear glass. Though the original context for this window is not known, it may have been made as a fire screen. It was installed as a window at Laurelton Hall.

51   Spring, a panel from the Four Seasons, ca. 1900

40 x 39 1⁄4 in (101.6 x 99.7 cm)

Unsigned; Tiffany Glass and Decorating Company, from the window designed by Louis Comfort Tiffany for exhibition at the Exposition Universelle, Paris, 1900

CHMF 57-18

The word SPRING is worked into the composition of this panel which depicts multi-colored tulips and the leafless branches of trees. This window is a panel from the large Four Seasons window which was installed at the entrance

45

49

to the exhibition of the United States at the Paris exposition of 1900. The large composition included in its border the monogram of Louis Comfort Tiffany and the word *Favrile* and was centered with the inscription ABUNDANCE/AND PEACE/AND PROS/ PERITY ANNO/ DOMINI/ MDCCCC. The panels were separated and mounted in their present borders when they were installed at Laurelton Hall. En suite with nos. 52-54.

52   Summer, a panel from the Four Seasons, ca. 1900
39⅛ x 35¼ in (99.5 x 89.5 cm)
Unsigned; Tiffany Glass and Decorating Company, from the window designed by Louis Comfort Tiffany for exhibition at the Exposition Universelle, Paris, 1900
CHMF 57-17
The word SUMMER is worked into the composition of this panel which depicts bright red poppies and pendant foliage against a distant landscape. En suite with nos. 51, 53 and 54.

53   Autumn, a panel from the Four Seasons, ca. 1900
39⅞ x 36⅜ in (101.1 x 92.5 cm)
Unsigned; Tiffany Glass and Decorating Company, from the window designed by Louis Comfort Tiffany for exhibition at the Exposition Universelle, Paris, 1900
CHMF 57-19
The word AUTUMN is worked into the composition of this panel which depicts the abundance of the season and includes grapes, ears of corn, and boughs laden with apples. En suite with nos. 51, 52, and 54.

   A figural window also entitled Autumn was exhibited at Chicago in 1893 and may have been one of the Four Seasons exhibited in Paris and London in 1892.

54   Winter, a panel from the Four Seasons, ca. 1900
39⅝ x 33 in (100.3 x 83.8 cm)
Unsigned; Tiffany Glass and Decorating Company, from the window designed by Louis Comfort Tiffany for exhibition at the Exposition Universelle, Paris, 1900
CHMF 62-33
The word WINTER is worked into the composition of this panel which depicts pine boughs with snow. The pine needles are filaments of dark glass that were fused into the colored glass while it was still molten. En suite with nos. 51-53.

48

47

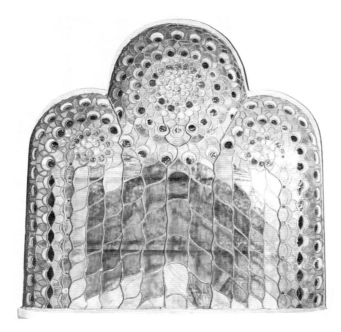

50

55 Eagle, a panel from the Four Seasons, ca. 1900

17⁷⁄₁₆ x 80⁵⁄₈ in (44.5 x 204.7 cm)
Signed: Louis Comfort Tiffany monogram
CHMF 57-20

Forming the top of the original border for the Four Seasons window, this panel depicts the American eagle, its wings outstretched above medallions into which are worked the monogram of Louis Comfort Tiffany and the word *Favrile*. The panel was separated and reworked to its present form when it was installed as a second-floor transom in the Poppy Loggia at Laurelton Hall. En suite with nos. 51-54.

56 Pumpkins and Beets, 1900-1905

44¼ x 56⅛ in (112.4 x 142.6 cm)
Unsigned; Tiffany Studios, after a design by Louis Comfort Tiffany
CHMF U-74

This mosaic window depicts pumpkins and beets amid rich green and purple foliage and trailing tendrils on an amber ground. The abundance of autumn was a favorite theme for Tiffany. In addition to the Kemp transoms, the Heckscher door panels, and the Autumn panel from the Four Seasons, he used it in an overmantle painting in the Bella apartment and as the background for his painting *Sow with Piglets*. The ribs of the large pumpkin are formed by lead cames which separate narrow pieces of amber glass which have been plated over with a single piece of amber-colored glass shaded to red. The tendrils of the pumpkin vine are trailings of dark glass fused into the amber glass while both were still molten.

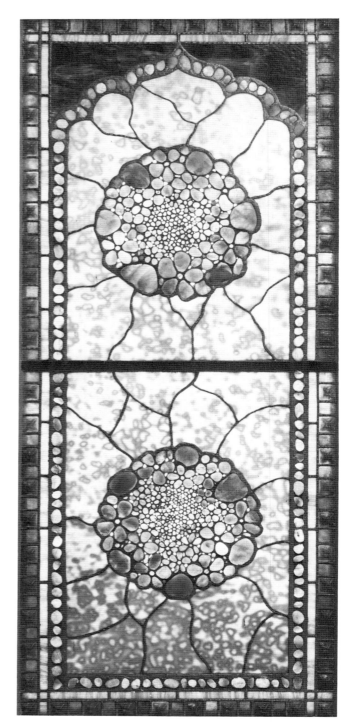

57

57   Pebble Window, after 1902
59⅝ x 25¾ in (151.4 x 65.4 cm)
Unsigned; Tiffany Studios, for the residence of Joseph Briggs, Jersey City, New Jersey
CHMF 58-16
This mosaic window has two medallions of stylized florettes of natural, translucent quartz pebbles and small chipped cullets of clear glass on a ground of mottled amber. The top is shaped as a cusped arch against a marbleized blue, and the whole is framed with bands of amber and red.

Joseph Briggs had been Tiffany's foreman and later managed Tiffany Studios until their liquidation.

58   Snowball Transom, after 1904
26 x 32 in (66 x 81.3 cm)
Unsigned; Tiffany Studios, from a design by Louis Comfort Tiffany, formerly installed in the living room at Laurelton Hall.
CHMF 58-15
This mosaic transom depicts a pendant bough of snow-ball bush, with mottled white blossoms and green foliage, against wisteria blossoms on a ground of blue marbled with greens and yellows. According to family tradition, this window was a particular favorite of Tiffany's.

59   Heckscher Door Panels, ca. 1905
122 x 135 in (309.9 x 342.9 cm)
Unsigned; Tiffany Studios, for the Heckscher residence, New York City
CHMF 58-11
Actually four door panels with their transoms, the "window" depicts a trellis on which entwine grape, squash, pumpkin, and tomato vines against a ground of clear glass. Similar both in concept and subject matter to the Eggplants transom, this window exhibits Tiffany's mastery of the transparent mosaic and its application as a screen, integrating interior and exterior spaces while providing protection from the elements. Its construction includes both lead cames and soldered copper foil.

60   Wisteria Transom, ca. 1910
36¾ x 47⅝ in (93.3 x 120.9 cm)
Unsigned; designed by Louis Comfort Tiffany for the dining room at Laurelton Hall
CHMF 59-9b
This transom is one of the series of transoms installed above the clear glass doors that lead from the dining room to the Daffodil Terrace at Laurelton Hall. The transoms have an upper border of dark mottled blue tiles and depict a trellis entwined with wisteria vines and pendant clusters of blossoms on a ground that varies from marbled blues to clear. They were designed to duplicate, year round, the springtime blossoms of a wisteria vine that grew outside of the windows. En suite with nos. 61 and 62.

61   Wisteria Transom, ca. 1910
36⅞ x 47⅝ in (93.5 x 120.9 cm)
Unsigned; designed by Louis Comfort Tiffany for the dining room at Laurelton Hall
CHMF 59-9c
En suite with nos. 60 and 62.

62   Wisteria Transom, ca. 1910
36⅞ x 95⅝ in (93.5 x 242.8 cm)
Unsigned; designed by Louis Comfort Tiffany for the dining room at Laurelton Hall
CHMF 59-10
En suite with nos. 60 and 61.

63   Jeweled Transom, 1900–1916
8¾ x 87 in (22.2 x 221 cm)
Unsigned; originally part of the Adoration window
CHMF 62-37-2
Composed of jewel-like cullets of glass, this transom originally formed the lower border of the Adoration window. This window, based on a painting that Tiffany exhibited as early as 1888, was installed above the door in the chapel as it was reconstructed at Laurelton Hall. The transom was separated from the larger window when it and several of the other windows and the altar were removed from the chapel.

59

60

64   Presentation Study for a Window, after 1902
12 x 9½ in (30.5 x 24.1 cm)
Mat signed lower right: *Louis C. Tiffany* (under
Approved by); mat inscribed with title block: *Ecclesiastical Department/Tiffany Studios/New York City N.Y.*;
other inscriptions on mat: *Sketch no. 3466*; *Suggestion
of/Ornamental Window/for/Mrs. Thomas F. Murtha/
New York N.Y./In Mausoleum/Woodlawn Cemetery*
CHMF 62-22

65   Preliminary Study for a Landscape Window,
ca. 1902
16⅜ x 10⅜ in (41.5 x 26.3 cm)
Signed lower right: *Louis C. Tiffany* (under *Approved
by*); mat inscribed: *No. 3880*; *Suggestion No 2 for/Land-
scape Window Rosehill Mausoleum*
CHMF 62-24

66   Miniature Wreath Window, 1900-1910
7¼ x 4½ in (18.4 x 11.4 cm)
Inscribed: *Tiffany Favrile Glass*
CHMF 68-4
This miniature window was a study for a larger window
installed in a residence in Dubuque, Iowa. In its simple,
geometric ground it related to windows Tiffany provided
for the Veteran's Room at New York's Seventh Regiment
Armory (1880) and the Union League Club (1880).

67   Julia Henop Memorial Window, before 1902
87¾ x 49¼ in (222.9 x 125 cm)
Inscribed: *Tiffany Glass and Decorating Company*; *In
Loving Memory of/Julia Henop/Died March 10, 1887*
CHMF 74-11
This window is one of eleven Tiffany windows installed
in 1908 in the chapel at the residence of the Association
for the Relief of Respectable, Aged, and Indigent
Females, 891 Amsterdam Avenue, New York City. The
inscription of the Tiffany Glass and Decorating Company indicates that the window predates the construction
of the chapel and that it was moved to the chapel from
some other location in the residence.

68   Hicks Memorial Window, 1892
87¾ x 49¼ in (222.9 x 125 cm)
Inscribed: *In memoriam Almy Townsend Hicks, born
March 4, 1795 and died December 18, 1862, Charlotte
Brevoore Hicks, born October 13, 1798 and died Decem-
ber 31, 1882*
CHMF 74-12
This window was installed as a pendant to the Henop
Memorial in the chapel of the Association residence;
both windows have identical borders.

69   Door to a Wine Cabinet, 1885
Wood, metal, and glass; 30⅝ x 25½ in (77.7 x 64.1 cm)
Unsigned; probably from the house Louis Comfort Tiffany designed and decorated for the Tiffany family at
72nd Street and Madison Avenue.
CHMF 64-34
This door reflects Tiffany's attention to detail, creative
use of glass, and interest in Near Eastern woodwork. The
concept of this small door was repeated in the design for a
mausoleum door executed in 1895.

67

68

61

70 **Fragments of Leaded Glass Windows from the Ruins of Laurelton Hall**

CHMF 78-147

Numerous windows were destroyed in the fire that raged through Laurelton Hall on March 6, 1957. Among these was the large window, The Bathers, which was intended for exhibition at the Panama-Pacific International Exposition, San Francisco, 1915.

71 **Fragments of Leaded Glass Windows from the Ruins of Laurelton Hall**

CHMF 78-131

Lamps

In his work as a painter, in his experiments with glass, in the design and decoration of houses, and in the creation of windows, Louis Comfort Tiffany explored and exploited the properties of light. To Tiffany, it was impossible to separate light and color. In discussing this phenomenon he stated, "light is composed of vibrations of different wave lengths, each vibration giving a different color; when all vibrate together, the result is white light. Were it not for these vibrations, what form, what lines could be seen? We could then only feel form, detect shape by the tactile sense."[1] Tiffany's exploration of the possibilities of artificial illumination for the exhibition of his glass came as a natural progression of his interest and beliefs. In addition, the opportunity to adapt the material to the more plastic forms associated with lighting presented a new challenge.

Tiffany used gas lighting in the decoration of his apartment at the Bella and, while with the Associated Artists, installed wrought iron gasoliers in the Seventh Regiment Armory. In 1882, he explored the reflective properties of his glass in artificial light when, as part of the redecoration of the White House, he installed "four circular sconces," each described as having "seven gas-jets . . . provided with a background, or rosette, three feet in diameter, composed of fantastic shapes of colored glass interspersed with little mirrors to produce a scintillating effect of great variety and brilliancy, which is enhanced by the pendant drops of iridescent glass affixed to the arms that hold the jets."[2]

Soon after Thomas Alva Edison invented the incandescent electric lamp in 1879, Tiffany was experimenting with the potential of electricity for artificial illumination. In 1885 he collaborated with Edison on the lighting of the Lyceum Theatre and later explored the design potential of this technological triumph in the decoration of the Havemeyer House. Now freed from tradition, the problem of fuel supply, and the restraints imposed by combustion, he designed fixtures that provided illumination in decorative forms never before possible. Samuel Bing, who had visited the Havemeyer House, observed that "American genius, faced with this barely conquered force, discerned not only the scope of its future role but had a clear vision of the particular forms into which it should be incorporated."[3]

At the Columbian Exposition he supplied a chandelier for the Women's Building and a massive electrolier for his own exhibit. The latter was awarded a gold medal for the artful integration of the technology of electricity into the design of this fixture. In his exposition chapel Tiffany also displayed a spectacular mosaic baptismal font (see no. 214), the domed cover of which consisted of leaded glass silvered on the inside. Although not translucent,

this dome portended the structure and concept of the leaded shades that were to become synonymous with Tiffany's name. These early fixtures, created to fill special orders or for exhibition, were undoubtedly designed by and produced under the supervision of Tiffany.

Shortly after the Columbian Exposition, Tiffany began marketing lamps; and in 1898 the Tiffany Glass and Decorating Company issued a booklet on its "Tiffany Favrile Glass-lamps," which, in addition to globes and shades, featured blown glass oil lamps.[4] Although most of the glass illustrated relates to other blown glass produced by Tiffany at this time, one shade appears to be of leaded glass. On February 1, 1899, Tiffany applied for a design patent for an electric lamp with a nautilus shell shade. The same year, this lamp and an identical lamp, shaded with a nautilus shell constructed of leaded glass, were exhibited at the Grafton Gallery in London. In addition to the nautilus lamps, Tiffany exhibited twenty-six other lamps including one "with leaded shade, dragon-fly design." The production of these lamps and the other metal work exhibited in London coincided with the establishment of the metal furnaces at the Corona glasshouse in 1898.[5]

By 1906 the Tiffany Studios had catalogued 106 entries for oil lamps, 183 electric lamps, 127 leaded shades, and 18 hanging shades.[6] Although some bases and shades were designed as complete compositions, others were interchangeable. In addition to bronze, some bases incorporated glass and glass mosaics. Ceramic bases originally supplied by art potteries, notably Grueby, were later supplied by Tiffany himself.[7]

Although Tiffany was to leave the designing of most shades and bases to others, each design proposed required his personal approval.[8] Consequently, his lamps exhibit the same high standards of design and quality of workmanship that marked every object marketed under Tiffany's name. The duplication of lamp designs, however, contributed to accusations of commercialism and speculation concerning Tiffany's artistic integrity regarding their production. The fact remains that, although the patterns were standardized, the beauty of each lamp is derived from the selection and juxtaposition of the individual pieces of stained glass used in its construction. As has been noted previously, color was always Tiffany's most important consideration. In discussing the art of "the men of the East who supplied barbarians with rugs and figured textiles," he observed, "Their designs were spots or tracts of color, and during the course of time they learned through reasoning and instinct that a fine design can be spoilt if the wrong combinations and juxtaposition of colors are chosen. We have to discover as they did what marvelous power one color has over another, and what the relative size of each different tract of color means to the result—what the mass of each different color means for the effect of the design as a whole!"[9] Therefore, we should assume that, to Tiffany, each of his lamps was as unique as the eye of the artisan who approached the glass bins at Corona and, either through reasoning or instinct, introduced the beauty of color into the design of each lamp (see nos. 87 and 88).

1. Louis C. Tiffany, "Color and its Kinship to Sound," address before the Rembrandt Club of Brooklyn, 1917, reprinted by Robert Koch, *Louis C. Tiffany's Art Glass* (New York, 1977), p. 38.

2. Robert Koch, *Louis C. Tiffany, Rebel in Glass* (New York, 1964), p. 6.

3. Samuel Bing, *La Culture Artistique en Amérique* (Paris, 1895), translated by Benita Eisler and published by The MIT Press in *Artistic America, Tiffany Glass, and Art Nouveau* (Cambridge, 1970), p. 177.

4. Koch, *Louis C. Tiffany's Glass-Bronzes-Lamps* (New York, 1971), pp. 120-121.

5. Hugh F. McKean, *The "Lost" Treasures of Louis Comfort Tiffany* (Garden City, N.Y., 1980), p. 237.

6. Koch, *Glass-Bronzes-Lamps*, pp. 163–186.

7. Gertrude Speenbugh, *The Arts of the Tiffanys* (Chicago, 1956), p. 68.

8. Robert Koch discusses the various lamps and their designers in *Rebel in Glass*, p. 134. In *Glass-Bronzes-Lamps*, he reproduced Tiffany Studios watercolor designs for a lamp and hanging shade. Each bears Tiffany's signed approval.

9. Tiffany, "Color and its Kinship to Sound," p. 38.

72 Nautilus Lamp, 1899-1902

H. 13 ½ (34.3 cm)
Inscribed: *Tiffany Studios/New York*, with the Tiffany Glass and Decorating Company monogram and the number 21345
CHMF 69-2

Considered one of the earliest production lamps made by Tiffany, the Nautilus lamp was granted a patent on May 2, 1899. The lamp was available with either a natural nautilus shell or a coppered glass shell. By 1906 there were eight models available, including one with a bronze mermaid sculpted by Louis A. Gudebrod. It is interesting to note that the leaded shade was more expensive than the natural shell shade. A Nautilus lamp was included at the exhibition staged by S. Bing at the Grafton Galleries in London in 1899.

73 Scarab Lamp, 1900-1902

H. 8 ½ (21.6 cm)
Base inscribed: 269/*Tiffany Studios/New York*, with the Tiffany Glass and Decorating Company monogram
CHMF 70-12

The blue-green iridescent Favrile glass scarab used as a shade for this lamp is an example of the many uses Tiffany found for these interesting molded scarabs. Produced in a variety of sizes, they were frequently treated as gemstones and set in 18-karat gold to be marketed as stickpins, studs, cuff links, etc. The large scarab here is treated in similar fashion, set not unlike the stone of a ring, and when lighted, recalls the description of the electric sconces Tiffany supplied for the Lyceum Theatre in 1885 which were noted to be "like fire in monster emeralds."

74 Turtleback Lantern, 1900-1905

H. 6 ¼ in (15.9 cm)
Unmarked
CHMF 58-19

This square bronze lantern is open at the top and set with bluish-purple iridescent glass turtleback tiles.

75 Turtleback Hanging Shade, 1902-1904

H. 13 in (33 cm); DIAM. 17 ½ in (44.5 cm)
Unmarked; from the living room at Laurelton Hall
CHMF 64-9

This bronze dome is set with iridescent green turtlebacks. One of a set of three, it and the others hung beneath and were movable along an iron yoke suspended by and mounted with Japanese sword guards (tsuba) from Tiffany's collection. The globes (no. 76), suspended at the ends of the yoke, were also part of this chandelier. Tiffany used a similar concept for a chandelier installed in the Veteran's Room at the Seventh Regiment Armory decorated by the Associated Artists in 1880.

72

73

76, 75

76 Pair of Hanging Lamps, 1902-1904
H. 14 in (35.6 cm); DIAM. 13 ½ in (34.3 cm)
Unmarked; from the living room at Laurelton Hall
CHMF 56-44 a and b
These open bronze globes are set with iridescent green turtlebacks, blue and green leaded glass panels, and have hinged discs of orange iridescent glass at the bottom. En suite with no. 75.

77 "Moorish" Chandelier, after 1904
Bronze and Favrile glass; H. 24¼ in (62.2 cm); DIAM. 14 in (35.6 cm)
Unmarked; from the residence of Joseph Briggs
CHMF 59-2
A hollow bronze core in an attenuated acorn shape forms the standard, from which develop twelve conforming fins of pierced bronze and six pendant arms which terminate in blown Favrile shades.

78 Study for a Wall Light, 1892-1902
Watercolor; 13½ x 10¼ in (34.3 x 26 cm)
Inscribed: *5658 for R.P. Martin of Akron, Ohio*
CHMF PR-5-72

79 Study for a Newel Lamp, 1892-1902
Watercolor; 13½ x 10¼ in (34.3 x 26 cm)
Inscribed: *#4885 for W.E. Bemis Larchmont, New York*, and with the Tiffany Glass and Decorating Company stamp
CHMF PR-6-72

80 Mushroom Table Lamp, after 1902
H. 18 in (45.7 cm); DIAM. 16 in (40.6 cm)
Base inscribed: *Tiffany Studios/New York/337*
Shade inscribed: *Tiffany Studios/New York/1424*
CHMF 66-29
The shade of this lamp, in the shape of a mushroom cap, is composed of coppered Favrile glass between six articulated ribs of bronze. It rests upon an inverted mushroom with a naturalistically modeled stem and a base representing the gills found on the underside of the pileus of the mushroom. Despite the entomological discrepancy, these lamps have come to be referred to as Spider lamps (the spider, an arachnid, has eight legs). An identical lamp is illustrated in the Tiffany Studios album, and the pattern numbers noted for the base and the shade are identical with those on this lamp. Electric, fitted with three bulbs, the lamp was catalogued by the Tiffany Studios as an electric lamp, no. 337, "Mushroom, standard, small." The entry for number 1424 was omitted from the list of leaded shades.

80

83

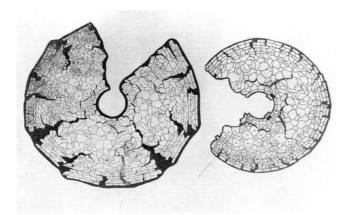

Working drawing for no. 83

81 Dogwood Hanging Shade, after 1902
H. 12 in (30.5 cm); DIAM. 28 in (71.1 cm)
Inscribed: *Tiffany Studios, New York*
CHMF 68-8
This conical shade is set with pink and white dogwood
blossoms and green foliage displayed against a ground of
variegated fractured glass. Catalogued by the Tiffany
Studios as a hanging shade, no. 605, a 28-in. "Dogwood,
straight sides, circular."

82 Black-eyed Susan Hanging Shade, after 1902
H. 11½ in (29.2 cm); DIAM. 25 in (63.5 cm)
Inscribed: *Tiffany Studios, New York*
CHMF 67-18
A shallow dome with a broad straight-sided band, this
shade depicts yellow and amber black-eyed Susans with
green foliage and lattice on a ground of fracture glass.
Catalogued by the Tiffany Studios as a leaded shade, no.
1518, a 25-in "Black-eyed Susan, like shade of No. 351."
No. 351 is an Appleblossom shade of similar configura-
tion. According to family tradition this shade was origi-
nally installed in the library at the Tiffany house on 72nd
Street and subsequently removed to Laurelton Hall.

83 Peony Table Lamp, after 1902
H. 32½ in (82.6 cm); DIAM. 22 in (55.9 cm)
Base inscribed: *Tiffany Studios/New York/6006*
Shade inscribed: *Tiffany Studios/New York*
CHMF 69-16
This domed shade, with an incurvate band at its lower
margin, depicts peony blossoms of crimson shaded to
pinkish white with green foliage against amber and blue.
An extant working drawing indicates that 960 precisely
cut pieces of glass were required for its production. The
four-footed, lobed base with tendril standard appears to
be identical with that of a Nasturtium lamp illustrated in
the 1904 booklet *Bronze Lamps* published by the Tiffany
Studios. The illustration is annotated "an extension
lamp" and "367." The entry for no. 367 in the Tiffany
Studios catalogue appears under "electric lamps" and is
noted "library, standard, cushion base, large, O'Brien."
This lamp descended with other personal property in the
estate of Louis Tiffany's son, Charles L. Tiffany.

84   Glass Panel Illustrating the Design for the Poppy Shade, 1900–1910
12½ x 16½ in (31.8 x 41.9 cm)
Inscribed upper left, on a metal plate: *16" con. poppy #1458*
CHMF 64-22
A flat section of a lamp shade depicting crimson poppies with amber scrolls on a light green ground is set into dark glass. This panel illustrates a single repeat of the design for the Poppy shade. The number on the panel conforms with an entry in the Tiffany Studios catalogue as a leaded shade, no. 1458, a 16-in "Poppy, conventional dome. . . ."

85   Glass Panel Illustrating the Design for a Leaded Shade, 1900–1910
12½ x 16½ in (31.8 x 41.9 cm)
Unmarked
CHMF 64-33
Like nos. 84 and 86, a study for a lamp depicting the pink blossoms and green foliage of a horse chestnut tree on a blue ground set into dark glass.

86   Glass Panel Illustrating the Design for a Leaded Shade, 1900–1910
14½ x 21 in (36.8 x 53.3 cm)
Unmarked
CHMF 64-25
Like nos. 84 and 85, a study for a lamp depicting amber and green tulips.

87   Dragonfly Table Lamp, after 1902
H. 27 in (68.6 cm); DIAM. 20 in (50.8 cm)
Base inscribed: *Tiffany Studios/New York/360/4478*
Shade inscribed: *Tiffany Studios, New York, 1495-36*
CHMF 66-5
This lamp has a conical shade of coppered Favrile glass depicting dragonflies, their wings overlaid with pierced metal and set against a ground of stylized leaves fitted with amber and green "jewels." The bronze standard with tendril design has a low, bulbous base supported on four legs. It is electric, fitted for three bulbs. The shade was catalogued by the Tiffany Studios as a leaded shade, no. 1495, a 20-in "Dragonfly, cone." The Dragonfly shade was designed by Clara Driscoll for the Tiffany Studios and was first exhibited at the exhibition staged by S. Bing at the Grafton Galleries in London in 1899. It was again exhibited at the Paris exposition of 1900.

87

88   Dragonfly Table Lamp, after 1902
H. 27 in (68.6 cm); DIAM. 20 in (50.8 cm)
Base inscribed: *262/Tiffany Studios New York*
Shade inscribed: *Tiffany Studios New York 1495*
CHMF 69-3
The bronze tendril-wrapped standard has a low bulbous base with ribbed and petaled detail. Electric, fitted with three bulbs, it is identical in design to no. 87, though the shades differ in the colors and juxtaposition of the Favrile glass selected for their production. As a result, each remains a unique object.

89   Wisteria Table Lamp, ca. 1902
H. 27 in (68.6 cm); DIAM. of shade 18 in (45.7 cm)
Base inscribed: *Tiffany Studios/New York/27770*, with the Tiffany Glass and Decorating Company monogram and the number *2076*
Shade inscribed: *Tiffany Studios/ New York*
CHMF 70-20
This domed shade with deep, straight sides and irregular lower border consists of a pattern of bronze branches, open at the top, supporting pendant wisteria blossoms and foliage in coppered, Favrile glass—the foliage in shades of green and the blossoms in tones ranging from roseate and dark purples through pale blue. The bronze standard is sculpted in the form of a tree trunk, rooted in a circular base. Electric, fitted for four bulbs, this lamp was catalogued by the Tiffany Studios as an electric lamp, no. 342, "Wistaria [sic] lamp and shade, large."

90

Although unsigned, this extremely rare lamp is unquestionably a product of the Tiffany Studios. A virtually identical lamp is illustrated in an original Tiffany Studios photograph and is annotated *L 146*. Likewise the entry for no. 146 in the Tiffany Studios catalogue under oil lamps, notes "Mosaic floral base, cobweb shade." This lamp has been converted from oil to electricity, possibly by the Studios themselves, and is fitted with three bulbs.

92 Bamboo Floor Lamp, after 1902
H. 63 in (160 cm); DIAM. overall 24½ in (62.2 cm)
Base inscribed: *Tiffany Studios/New York/10923*
Shade inscribed: *Tiffany Studios/New York*
CHMF 64-13
In an integrated design, the shade of this lamp depicts green bamboo foliage and ochre bamboo stalks on a ground of amber. The bamboo stalk is repeated in the naturalistically modeled stand—a design used for table lamps, candle lamps, and candlesticks (see no. 182).

93 Ten-Light, Drop Cluster Pond Lily Table Lamp,
after 1902
H. 21 in (53.3 cm)
Inscribed: *Tiffany Studios/New York/381*
CHMF 74-3
The high relief bronze base of this table lamp depicts pond lily pads, buds, and blossoms from which emerge ten looping stems supporting pendant Favrile glass blossoms. These lamps were extremely popular and the Tiffany Studios catalogue lists seven-light, ten-light, twelve-light, and eighteen-light models, the latter having been awarded a prize at the Turin Exposition in 1902.

94 Twelve-Light, Drop Cluster Pond Lily Floor Lamp,
after 1902
H. 55 in (139.7 cm)
Base inscribed: *Tiffany Studios/New York/685*
Shades inscribed: *L.C.T.*
CHMF 70-13
From the high relief bronze base of water lily pads, buds, and blossoms, twelve bronze stems emerge and entwine to form the column of this lamp before flaring out at the top to support pendant Favrile glass blossoms of ivory and green. Similar to no. 93.

90 Pony Wisteria Table Lamp, 1902–1918
H. 16¾ in (42.6 cm); DIAM. of shade 9½ in (24.1 cm)
Base inscribed: *Tiffany Studios/New York/7805*
Shade inscribed: *Tiffany Studios/ New York*
CHMF 69-8
Similar to no. 89, this lamp varies in its smaller size and in the greater articulation of detail on its standard. Electric, fitted for three bulbs, this lamp was catalogued by the Tiffany Studios as an electric lamp, no. 349, "Pony Wistaria [sic]."

91 Spider Web Table Lamp, ca. 1900
H. 30 in (76.2 cm); DIAM. 20½ in (52 cm)
Unmarked
CHMF 62-20
This lamp is remarkable for the total integration of its shade and base. The base is set with Favrile glass mosaics depicting narcissus between broad bronze ribs which flare out from the body and develop as branches. These branches, set with Favrile glass blossoms, support the shade which continues the design, incorporating spider webs, foliage, and additional blossoms.

92

94

95 Bronze Table Lamp with Damascene Favrile Blown Glass Shade, ca. 1920

H. 14¾ in (37.5 cm)
Base inscribed: *LCT* monogram/*Louis C. Tiffany Furnaces, Inc/Favrile 16A*
Shade inscribed: *L.C.T. Tiffany 5*
CHMF 73-3
Produced after Tiffany's retirement from active participation in the firm. Similar lamps were illustrated by the Tiffany furnaces en suite with desk sets and dressing table accessories.

96 Candle Lamp, ca. 1900

H. 16½ in (41.9 cm)
Base inscribed: *L.C.T. 9946*
Shade inscribed: *L.C.T. 1472*
CHMF 56-48
The base and shade of this lamp are of gold iridescent glass, the candle-shaped fuel holder is decorated with a green flame design, and the chimney is iridescent. Although this lamp burns oil, similar lamps made in various sizes were fitted for candles or for electricity.

98

Glass

Long before Tiffany had begun making windows and, in fact, long before he had begun his experiments with glass, he had collected glass. "From infancy his colourist's eye had passionately loved the rich effects produced in antique glass in the course of centuries. While as yet almost a child, he had greedily sought for a few of these magic relics of the past, and his search was greatly facilitated by his father's position."[1] In the acquisition of his collection he was also assisted and encouraged by his father's chief designer, Edward C. Moore, whose large collection of ancient Persian, Egyptian, Roman, and Syrian glass was bequeathed to the Metropolitan Museum of Art in 1891.[2] Efforts to duplicate the iridescence and brilliancy of this glass, which had resulted from centuries of age and decomposition, was, in fact, part of Tiffany's experimentation. Failing in those early attempts, he would on occasion use actual shards of ancient glass within the composition of some windows and mosaics. In his own home, he had placed above a fireplace a large panel "made up of little pieces of antique glass . . . whose pieces, all of irregular shape are set into a leaden framework, similar to that of a stained glass window."[3]

Tiffany was not the first to experiment with the problem of simulating iridescence in contemporary glass. In the 1870s glasshouses in Vienna and that of Thomas Webb in England were attempting to produce the same result.[4] Arthur Nash, a former employee of Webb's, came to the United States and, with Tiffany, established the glasshouse at Corona. Nash undoubtedly brought with him invaluable knowledge and skill and has been credited with having suggested the Tiffany trade name "Favrile."

Tiffany had spent more than twelve years in experimentation with and the production of stained glass and stained glass windows when the Corona glassworks began production. The success of his windows and the challenges presented by the glass being produced were to lead Tiffany into yet another venture; Samuel Bing reported that "having thus created a material which is admirable in every respect, possessing qualities quite unknown till now, Tiffany gave it the name of 'Favrile Glass,' and proposed to use it for other purposes than the making of stained-glass windows. His great ambition was to employ it in the manufacture of *objets d'art*."[5]

In the production of such objects, Tiffany was to confront a tradition more ancient than that he had encountered with windows. As Bing observed, "In view of the prestige of the old Venetian glassware, so elegant as to outline, but somewhat too frail and artificial; after the delicate jewellery of the Chinese glassworkers, who treated their curious material as they would the rarest cameos; after the wonderful progress realised in vitreous art in Bohemia; after the astonishing work produced by Emile Gallé; in presence of all these marvels, could inventive genius be expected to go farther?"[6] Tiffany himself had stated, "Copying what others have done helps us indeed to exercise our eyes; but merely to copy and not to employ our imagination—is to strangle our talent, our heritage! Styles are merely the copying of what others have done, perhaps done better than we. God has given us our talents, not to copy the talents of others, but rather to use our brains and imagination in order to obtain the revelation of True Beauty!"[7] Thus Tiffany the collector aware of the accomplishments of others, Tiffany the glassmaker who saw inherent beauty in his materials, and Tiffany the artist who saw in nature the true source of beauty began to create objects whose beauty was fixed in the molten metal of the furnace and whose form derived from the spontaneity of nature. The genesis of these objects was described by Samuel Bing following a visit to Tiffany's glassworks:

Look at the incandescent ball of glass as it comes out of the furnace; it is slightly dilated by an initial inspiration of air. The workman charges it at certain pre-arranged points with small quantities of glass, of different textures and different colours, and in the operation is hidden the germ of the intended ornamentation. The little ball is then returned to the fire to be heated. Again it is subjected to a similar treatment (the process being sometimes repeated as many as twenty times), and, when all the different glasses have been combined and manipulated in different ways, and the article has been brought to its definite state as to form and dimensions, it presents the following appearance: The motifs introduced into the ball when it was small have grown with the vase itself, but in differing proportions; they have lengthened or broadened out, while each tiny ornament fills the place assigned to it in advance in the mind of the artist.[8]

Tiffany's direct involvement in the production of these objects has been well chronicled. It is clear that he suggested the forms of some objects while Nash and others proposed or discovered the remainder. He retained control over the color, decoration, and form of the objects that were produced by the furnaces, and he encouraged his workmen to experiment freely within that production. This interaction was recalled by Jimmy Stewart, a former employee: "I was there the day that we hit the colors, that we made the first vase of Tiffany iridescent glass. That was in 1895. He, Mr. Tiffany himself, was down in his office with Mr. Nash and his chemist, and I am positive I was sent down to the office to bring Mr. Tiffany up to show him this new vase that he never saw before. When he came up he was so delighted—I can see him prancing around and dancing around there yet, and pulling his belt up. . . ."[9] Stewart also stated, "I recall when I went to work in that factory Mr. Nash was the boss—under Mr. Tiffany, of course—and I always understood that Mr. Tiffany was the man who accepted or rejected a shape."[10] After Tiffany had approved a form for production, his workmen were again free to express their own creative instincts in the production of that form. Stewart recalled, "Oh, we had so many ways of decorating vases. There were never two days alike in the Tiffany furnaces, never. . . . You know, this glass is a queer substance. It does everything only what you want it to do, so you have to be the boss and make it do what you want it to do to get the shape. . . . I could stop fifty different times and have fifty different vases."[11] The forms of the blown glass objects produced in these early years reflect both the organic evolution of the object itself and Tiffany's personal predilection for forms derived from nature. A Tiffany brochure published in 1898 stated that "the forms of Tiffany Favrile Glass are very largely derived from natural motives."[12] In responding to these objects and their decoration, Samuel Bing observed, "Never, perhaps, has any man carried to greater perfection the art of faithfully rendering Nature in her most seductive aspects, while subjecting her with so much sagacity to the wholesome canons of decoration."[13]

Samuel Bing, friend and patron of Louis Comfort Tiffany, also arranged the earliest recorded sale of a piece of Tiffany's glass.[14] The most outspoken proponent of Tiffany's new art, he ultimately became sole distributor for Tiffany in Europe. In 1895 Bing opened a new gallery which he called Le Salon de l'Art Nouveau. Within eight years the names of Bing and Tiffany were to become inexorably associated with what had become known as the Art Nouveau style. Ironically, the mantle of this designation rested uneasily, and in 1903 Bing wrote, "In the year 1895, the writer of these pages founded in the rue de Provence, Paris, a center open to all the forces of artistic innovation. In order to designate the tendencies of this enterprise, he devised the title of L'Art Nouveau, without suspecting then that this combination of words would gain the doubtful honor of serving as a label for miscellaneous creations, some of which were to reach the limits of license and folly."[15] Although Tiffany himself did not become involved in the philosophical and art historical debates that ensued, it is reasonable to assume that he concurred with Bing's assessment that Art Nouveau was not a style but a movement and that its proponents shared not in a prescribed style but rather in their lack of preconceived ideas, their freedom from restraint in the form of expression, and a mutual hatred of stagnation. Bing's objections notwithstanding, Art Nouveau was to become accepted as an international art style and much of the art of Louis Comfort Tiffany, particularly his blown glass, was to be judged among the finest expressions of that style in America.

The blown glass produced by Tiffany created a sensation and almost immediately became widely imitated and sought after by collectors and museums. Tiffany continued to experiment, introducing such diverse innovations as his lava glass, a heavy, rough-textured glass in free, almost accidental forms with thick trailings of iridescence; Cypriot glass, with rough, iridescent surfaces simulating the long sought-after decomposed surfaces of ancient glass; agate glass, produced by intermingling various colors of molten glass without mixing, and cutting or faceting the finished object to display its agate-like quality; and aquamarine glass, an extremely heavy form of cased glass with decorative inclusions of marine flora and/or fishes in clear or light green transparent glass. Additionally, forms were carved, cut, decorated with trailed overlays, or, as in the case of the superb floriforms and rosewater flasks, became sculptural entities simulating nature. In addition to the glasswares cited (in part) above, which were intentionally produced as objets d'art or cabinet pieces, the Tiffany Studios produced free-blown glass hollowware and more than a dozen stock patterns of tablewares.

The Tiffany Studios maintained strict control over the marketing of all glassware produced. In addition to their own showrooms, Tiffany Favrile glasswares were retailed by Tiffany & Company in New York and London and, by exclusive franchise, were consigned to Marshall Field and Company of Chicago, Shreve and Company of San Francisco, and Neiman-Marcus of Dallas. Each piece was carefully marked and numbered before leaving the Corona storerooms. Although the markings are helpful in identifying Tiffany glass, the numerical notations are not yet totally understood; they relate to an internal system of inventory control for which the index does not survive. Traditionally, a number prefixed with a small "o" indicated a special order; a number prefixed with an "x" indicated an experimental piece; a number prefixed with the letters "EX" indicated an exhibition piece; and a number prefixed with "A-Coll" indicated that the object had been reserved for the personal collection of Louis Comfort Tiffany. For the more frequently encountered numbers, Robert Koch has proposed a registry based upon the letter prefixes and suffixes and a numerical sequence that does not exceed 9999; however, as he has pointed out, "the numbers on Tiffany vases can be an aid to dating, but only as a *terminus ante quem*."[16] Stuart Feld in his study of the documented Tiffany glass in the collection of the Metropolitan Museum of Art has suggested a correlation between the numbers and design.[17] Hugh McKean, in noting that both the marks and marking systems changed over the years, has observed that "some are clear, but others are obscure and may remain so since exceptions seem to abound for every proposed explanation."[18]

1. Samuel Bing, from *Kunst und Kunsthandwerk*, Vol. 1 (1898); translation published by The MIT Press in *Artistic America, Tiffany Glass, and Art Nouveau* (Cambridge, 1970), p. 204.

2. Charles H. Carpenter, Jr. with Mary Grace Carpenter, *Tiffany Silver* (New York, 1978), pp. 27–28.

3. Bing, p. 204.

4. Diane Chalmers Johnson, *American Art Nouveau* (New York, 1979), p. 107.

5. Bing, p. 202.

6. Ibid.

7. Louis C. Tiffany, "Color and Its Kinship to Sound," address before the Rembrandt Club of Brooklyn, 1917, reprinted by Robert Koch, *Louis C. Tiffany's Art Glass* (New York, 1977), p. 39.

8. Bing, pp. 208–211.

9. Robert Koch, "An Interview with Jimmy Stewart," *Louis Tiffany's Glass-Bronzes-Lamps*, p. 64. Stewart's comment regarding the "first vase of Tiffany iridescent glass" referred to a technical breakthrough in reference to securing the proper iridescence on the red-lead glass used for blowing.

10. Ibid.

11. Ibid., pp. 69–70.

12. Robert Koch, *Louis C. Tiffany's Art Glass* (New York, 1977), p. 11.

13. Bing, p. 211.

14. Koch, *Art Glass*, p. 10.

15. Bing, footnote, p. 227.

16. Koch, *Art Glass*, p. 12. The registry appears on p. 40.

17. Stuart P. Feld, "Nature in Her Most Seductive Aspects: Louis Comfort Tiffany's Favrile Glass," *The Metropolitan Museum of Art Bulletin* 21 (November 1962), p. 108.

18. Hugh F. McKean, *The "Lost" Treasures of Louis Comfort Tiffany* (Garden City, N.Y., 1980), p. 279.

99, 100

97 Panel of Twelve Glass Tiles Set in Lead Cames,
after 1881
H. overall 13 ¼ in (33.7 cm); H. of each tile 3 in (7.6 cm)
Inscribed: *PAT. FEB 8th 1881/L.C.T. & Co.*
CHMF 79-534
The twelve, square, pressed glass tiles mounted in this panel illustrate but a few of the many designs, colors, and combinations of colors produced by Tiffany.

98 Vase, possibly 1885–1892
Favrile glass; H. 10 in (25.4 cm)
Inscribed: Tiffany Glass Company monogram (acid etched)
CHMF 62-19
Baluster-shaped vase of opaque white glass with two bands of irregular, flame-shaped iridescence in two shades of gold.

99 Cabinet Piece, possibly 1885–1892
Favrile glass; H. 2¾ in (7 cm)
Inscribed: Tiffany Glass Company monogram (acid etched)
CHMF 72-1
Small pyriform body of dark blue Favrile glass with thick irregular trailings of iridescent glass. Although the latter is similar to that found on lava glass, the overall form here is more conventional.

100 Vase, ca. 1913
Lava glass; H. 7½ in (19 cm)
Inscribed: *9771K/L.C. Tiffany-Favrile*
CHMF 65-29
Freeform vase of dark blue translucent glass with irregular trailings of thick gold and a gold iridescence.

101 Vase, ca. 1896
Cypriot glass; H. 7¾ in (19.7 cm)
Base inscribed: *LCT E1771*; and on side of base: *Louis C. Tiffany*
Retains original paper label with Tiffany Glass and Decorating Company monogram
CHMF 56-24
Irregular ovoid body of orange and red translucent glass with heavily pitted surface and gold iridescence.

102 Vase, ca. 1899
Cypriot glass; H. 8½ in (21.6 cm)
Inscribed: *L.C.T./K1462/2461*
CHMF 62-40
Dark brown Cypriot glass with gold and green iridescent flames.

104

Iridescent gold at the top shading to peacock hues at the base. Lower surfaces of the sides have been tooled (while molten) into a series of swirled designs.

106 Vase, ca. 1905
Favrile glass; H. 11⅛ in (28.3 cm)
Inscribed: *L.C.T. Y3356*
CHMF 52-5
Stemmed, trumpet-shaped vase on a domed base of transparent gold iridescent glass.

107 Perfume Bottle, ca. 1912
Favrile glass; H. 4½ in (11.4 cm)
Inscribed: *L.C. Tiffany-Favrile 5144H*
CHMF 54-31
Iridescent gold and applied "lily pads" of alternating height. The interior of the neck has been ground to receive a stopper (now missing).

108 Vase, ca. 1914
Favrile glass; H. 6½ in (16.5 cm)
Inscribed: *L.C. Tiffany-Favrile/1564J*
CHMF 52-4
Low bulbous base with long, narrow neck with flared rim and gold iridescence. The form of this vase may have been suggested by Tiffany's collection of ancient glass.

109 Vase, after 1894
Favrile glass; H. 12 in (30.5 cm)
Inscribed: *100K/L.C. Tiffany-Favrile/Exhibition Piece*
CHMF 66-54
Bulbous vase with an elongated neck of translucent opal glass cased in red with subtle vertical trailings in the red on a dark red flared foot.

110 Vase, ca. 1914
Favrile glass; H. 6½ in (16.5 cm)
Inscribed: *L.C. Tiffany, Inc. Favrile 39904* (in script)
CHMF 64-4
Vase of red glass cased in dark blue-black glass with mottled inclusion of lighter blue. The vertical bands of the surface have been polished to reveal the red body.

111 Vase, ca. 1900
Favrile glass; H. 8½ in (21.6 cm)
Inscribed: *L.C.T. K2973*
CHMF 54-103
Baluster-shaped vase with flattened shoulder, high neck, and flared rim of green iridescent glass with tendril decoration in gold iridescence. The interior is a whitish gold.

103 Cabinet Piece, 1899–1900
Cypriot glass; H. 3 in (7.6 cm)
Inscribed: *03167*
Retains paper label of Tiffany Glass and Decorating Company and paper label of S. Bing's Salon de l'Art Nouveau, Paris
CHMF 78-229
This small bowl with swirling bands in iridescent Cypriot glass was a special order to be sold at S. Bing's Salon de l'Art Nouveau in Paris.

104 Vase, ca. 1896
Cypriot glass; H. 21¼ in (54 cm)
Inscribed: *L.C.T. E161 2217*; the number 1709 has been overstruck
Retains original paper label
CHMF U-6
Of unusually large proportion, this vase is of a dull green Cypriot glass with brown and gold variegated iridescence.

105 Cabinet Piece, ca. 1899
Favrile glass; H. 3¾ in (9.5 cm)
Inscribed: *L.C.T. L1802*
CHMF 56-34

103, 102, 101

110

113, 111, 112

112 Vase, after 1900
Favrile glass; H. 10½ in (26.7 cm)
Inscribed: *Louis C. Tiffany/010515*
CHMF 54-1
Having a bulbous body with flattened shoulder and broad, flared neck, this vase is a yellow-ochre with plain and damascene bands of iridescent silvery blue.

113 Vase, ca. 1912
Favrile glass; H. 13¼ in (33.7 cm)
Inscribed: *L.C. Tiffany-Favrile x204/3772G/ L.C. Tiffany-Favrile*
CHMF 70-24
Modified pyriform vase with wide, elongated neck and broad flat rim in opalescent white with a damascene band of iridescent gold at the neck.

114 Vase, ca. 1910
Favrile glass; H. 5¾ in (14.6 cm)
Inscribed: *L.C. Tiffany Favrile 5973E*
CHMF 54-14
Highly polished transparent red body on a lustrous green flared foot. The iridescent green band at the neck is centered with a zig-zag detail in polychrome.

115 Vase, ca. 1912
Favrile glass; H. 10¼ in (26 cm)
Inscribed: *L.C. Tiffany-Favrile 2301H*
CHMF 56-40
Gold-brown iridescent vase with interlaced zigzag band of green and ivory at the neck.

116 Vase, ca. 1915
Favrile glass; H. 7 in (17.8 cm)
Inscribed: *2400 J L.C. Tiffany Favrile/Panama-Pacific Ex*
CHMF 70-23
Iridescent green double baluster vase, the upper portion of iridescent gold with interlaced zig-zags of green and ochre. Exhibited at the Panama-Pacific International Exposition, San Francisco, 1915.

117 Wall Plaque, ca. 1895–1900
Favrile glass; H. 15¼ in (38.7 cm)
Inscribed: *Louis C. Tiffany 010128*
CHMF 78-8
Iridescent, translucent green with gold. The convex pontil has been polished and cut in an arabesque design. This is a special order piece, and the signature appears to be by Louis Tiffany's own hand.

116, 118, 114

118 Plate, ca. 1918
Favrile glass; DIAM. 8⅞ in (22.4 cm)
Inscribed: *L.C. Tiffany Inc. Favrile x87 397OM*
CHMF 52-2
Iridescent green plate with gold decoration at rim. The *x87* inscription is traditionally thought to indicate an experimental piece.

119 Flower Bowl with "Frog," 1918–1928
Favrile glass; Bowl: DIAM. 10³⁄₁₆ in (26.5 cm);
Frog: H. 3⅛ in (8 cm)
Bowl inscribed: *1807 9191M Louis C. Tiffany/Furnaces, Inc.* and *543/C63*
Frog inscribed: *1685 L.C.T. Favrile*
CHMF 79-255a (bowl)
CHMF 79-255b (frog)
Shallow bowl of iridescent blue with vines and lily pads of golden green. Frog of iridescent blue.

120 Vase, ca. 1902
Favrile glass; H. 11 in (27.9 cm)
Inscribed: *Louis C. Tiffany/R4017*
CHMF 57-5
Globular vase tapering at the shoulder to a narrow, folded rim, the opaque gray-green body decorated with small pendant blossoms of yellow and black above leaf forms and trailings of iridescent silver-blue.

121 Inkwell, ca. 1897
Favrile glass and silver; H. 4¾ in (12 cm)
Glass inscribed: *LCT 08476*
Silver inscribed: *Tiffany & Co./Maker/Sterling Silver*
CHMF 54-16
Lobed and stepped bulbous body of iridescent blue-green
with overall damascene decoration. The collar of the
silver top repeats the pattern of the glass. This was a
special order piece and demonstrates the cooperation
between Louis Comfort Tiffany and Tiffany & Co.

122 Peacock Decanter, ca. 1895
Favrile glass, silver, and precious stones; H. 14¼ in
(36.2 cm)
Inscribed: *LCT/D689*
Retains original paper label of the Tiffany Glass and
Decorating Company
CHMF 66-10
Pyriform bottle of iridescent translucent blue-brown
glass with intersecting zig-zag bands of iridescent gold,
the elongated neck mounted with an interlaced collar of
silver flanked by fully modeled silver peacocks. The collar
and the silver stopper are set with diamonds, pearls,
sapphires, and garnets.

123 "Rosewater" Vase, after 1902
Favrile glass; H. 17 in (43.2 cm)
Inscribed: *#04163*
Retains part of a paper label printed with the conjoined
LCT monogram
CHMF 66-13
Of a form derived from ancient rosewater droppers, this
vase is of violet Favrile glass shaded to pink with a gold
iridescence.

124 Compote, ca. 1900–1920
Favrile glass; H. 12 in (30.5 cm)
Inscribed: *L.C. Tiffany-Favrile 1251*
CHMF 54-33
Iridescent gold and ivory with bands of green at the stem
developing as stylized leaves on the underside of the
bowl.

125 Floriform Vase, ca. 1905
Favrile glass; H. 13½ in (34.3 cm)
Inscribed: *L.C.T. Y6535*
Retains original paper label with *LCT* monogram
CHMF 54-56
Of the so-called calyx form, the vase features stylized
green leaves or sepals on the white opalescent body and
clear glass base.

120

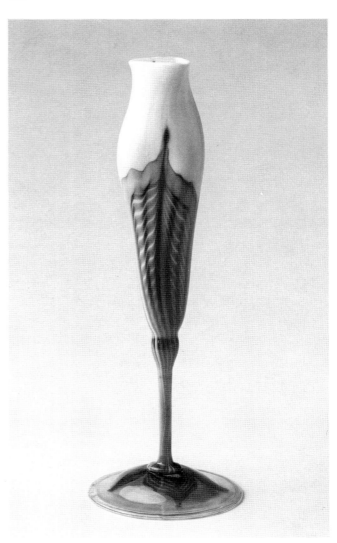

125

121

126 Floriform Vase, ca. 1907
Favrile glass; H. 18 in (45.7 cm)
Inscribed: *L.C.T.-3699B*
CHMF 54-52
Iridescent gold vase with deeply ruffled bowl on a narrow stem with a low, bulbous base.

127 Floriform Vase, ca. 1900
Favrile glass; H. 13 in (33 cm)
Inscribed: *L.C.T. M2068*
Retains paper label of the Tiffany Glass and Decorating Company
CHMF 56-32
Creamy white opaque vase, the stem of which has been polished to reveal vertical green stripes. The iridescent gold-orange of the inside surface becomes a red-orange at the rim.

128 Floriform Vase, ca. 1903
Favrile glass; H. 19 in (48.3 cm)
Inscribed: *L.C.T./T1146*
CHMF U-12
With a broad ruffled rim above a slender stem on a low bulbous base, the vase has a surface of semi-opaque white over iridescent chartreuse with stripes of green.

129 "Jack-in-the-Pulpit" Vase, ca. 1912
Favrile glass; H. 18½ in (47 cm)
Inscribed: *3918G L.C. Tiffany-Favrile*
CHMF 54-26
74

Iridescent gold floriform with depressed, bulbous base, slender stem, and broadly flaring rim.

130 Vase, 1892–1900
Favrile glass; H. 4½ in (11.4 cm)
Inscribed: *Louis C. Tiffany-Favrile* (engraved script)
CHMF 56-3
Cased glass vase with non-transparent, blue-green damascene iridescence, with a median band of lozenge-shaped windows cut and polished into the surface to reveal the clear glass interior.

131 Vase, ca. 1918
Favrile glass; H. 9¼ in (23.5 cm)
Inscribed: *3301P L.C. Tiffany-Favrile*
CHMF 70-22
Pyriform vase of iridescent gold Favrile glass with inclusions of fracture glass, the whole having been cased in clear glass surfaced with a dark blue-brown iridescence. The flame-shaped reserves (or windows) form a median band outlined with two conforming bands of silver iridescence.

132 Vase, 1900–1910
Agate Favrile glass; H. 3¼ in (8.3 cm)
Inscribed: *L.C. Tiffany-Favrile 104A-Coll*
CHMF 66-51
Ovoid vase, the surfaces faceted to reveal the random color and pattern of the green and yellow agate glass. From Tiffany's personal collection.

133 Vase, ca. 1910
Agate Favrile glass; H. 7½ in (19 cm)
Inscribed: *L.C. Tiffany-Favrile/7008D*
CHMF 66-11
Modified baluster form of layered milky green and amber glass, the surface cut and polished in a diamond pattern displaying the strata of colored glass.

134 Vase, ca. 1913
Favrile glass; H. 7¾ in (19.7 cm)
Inscribed: *L.C. Tiffany Favrile Paris Salon/1914 8568H*
CHMF 66-3
Baluster-shaped vase of red-gold iridescence with irregular inclusions of green and blue cased in clear glass.

135 Vase, after 1892
Favrile glass; H. 6¾ in (17.1 cm)
Inscribed: *L.C. Tiffany Favrile 111A-Coll*
CHMF 66-53
Pyriform vase of iridescent glass with irregular broad trailings of greens, grays, and ochre suspended in clear glass. From Tiffany's personal collection.

123

128

136 Vase, 1902
Favrile glass; H. 8⅛ in (20.7 cm)
Inscribed: *R 2401/Louis C. Tiffany*
CHMF 66-47
Ovoid vase with overall decoration of white flowers with
yellow centers amid stylized green stems suspended in
clear glass. The inside of the vase has a gold iridescence.
Exhibited at Turin in 1902 and illustrated in the catalogue
of the Exposition.

137 Vase, ca. 1917
Favrile glass; H. 13½ in (34.3 cm)
Inscribed: *1146/L.C. Tiffany/Favrile/Exhibition Piece*
CHMF 55-3
Baluster-shaped vase decorated with vertical stalks of
green-brown leaves and blossoms of red, yellow, and
white cased in a translucent brown glass with an irides-
cent inner surface.

130, 131

138 Vase, ca. 1905
Favrile glass; H. 6⅝ in (16.8 cm)
Inscribed: *L.C.T. Y3193*
CHMF 79-531
Six Favrile glass morning glory blossoms and random
green leaves are suspended in clear glass with a gold
iridescence on the inner surface.

139 Vase, ca. 1905
Favrile glass; H. 5½ in (14 cm)
Inscribed: *EX 1024/Louis C. Tiffany Favrile*; additional
inscription: *Paris/Salon/1st award/L. C. Tiffany* (applied
with red paint)
CHMF 56-1
Ovoid vase narrowing at the shoulder to a short cylindrical neck. The upper portion decorated with blue morning glories amid green foliage cased in clear glass with a
gold iridescence on the inner surface.

140 Vase, ca. 1915
Aquamarine Favrile glass; H. 7½ in (19 cm)
Inscribed: *Louis C. Tiffany-Favrile Special Exhibition
1335H*
CHMF 67-11
Pendant sprays of Favrile glass dogwood blossoms with
dark green foliage and brown branches are suspended in
transparent aquamarine glass.

133, 132

141 Vase, ca. 1915
Aquamarine Favrile glass; H. 12 in (30.5 cm)
Inscribed: *L.C. Tiffany, Inc. Favrile, 5399M
Panama-Pacific Ex*
CHMF 62-5
Favrile glass flowers of white and yellow with green
foliage cased in the bulbous base of clear glass. Exhibited
at the Panama-Pacific International Exposition in San
Francisco, 1915.

142 Vase, after 1902
Rock crystal; H. 7 in (17.8 cm)
Inscribed: *L.C. Tiffany 115*
CHMF 59-1
Natural, translucent rock crystal carved with flower and
leaf motifs.

143 Paperweight, after 1892
Favrile glass; H. 2½ in (6.4 cm)
Inscribed: *L.C. Tiffany Favrile 97A-Coll*
CHMF 68-9
Pyramidal weight of highly polished, faceted glass shad-
ing from a deep, translucent olive to an opaque ochre.
From Tiffany's private collection.

144 Vase, ca. 1895
Favrile glass; H. 7 in (17.8 cm)
Inscribed: *L.C. Tiffany/Favrile C251*
CHMF 57-3
Baluster-shaped vase of marbled, cream-colored translu-
cent glass. The highly polished surfaces have been cut to
form vertical flutes or panels.

145 Vase, ca. 1907
Favrile glass; H. 6 in (15.2 cm)
Inscribed: *L.C. Tiffany-Favrile 4732B* and *7171*
CHMF U-17
Ovoid vase with flared rim of red glass, the surface carved
in a leaf motif.

146 Vase, ca. 1895
Favrile glass; H. 8¼ in (21 cm)
Inscribed: *E752 L.C. Tiffany Favrile*
CHMF 65-24
Iridescent trailed decoration of branches and leaves on a
caramel-colored ground etched and engraved with birds,
insects, and blossoms.

139, 134, 136

137, 135

138

140

141

145, 143, 144

147 Bowl, 1892-1901
Glass marquetry; H. 7 in (17.8 cm)
Inscribed: *Louis C. Tiffany 03440*
Retains original label with Tiffany Glass and Decorating
Company monogram
CHMF 64-31
Clear glass bowl inlaid (while still molten) with translucent red and green glass. Inlaid surfaces have been cut to enhance the naturalistic effect of the floral forms. Surfaces of the clear glass have been cut in designs in the manner of the rococo. The small *o* prefix indicates that this bowl was made as a special order.

148 Two Punch Cups, ca. 1907
Favrile glass; H. 2½ in (6.4 cm)
Both inscribed: *L.C. Tiffany-Favrile 7459B*
CHMF 56-50 a and b
Globular cups of clear glass with green and red detail on
etched and cut design of grapes, leaves, and tendrils.
Originally part of a larger set.

149 Bowl, 1900-1920
Favrile glass; H. 2½ in (6.4 cm)
Inscribed: *L.C. Tiffany-Favrile*
CHMF 66-59
Transparent pink bowl with radial bands of opaque pink
on a raised foot of light blue-green.

150 Goblet, 1900-1920
Favrile glass; H. 8 in (20.3 cm)
Inscribed: *L.C. Tiffany-Favrile*
CHMF 66-64
The bowl of the goblet is of opaque turquoise-to-clear
glass on a clear stem with an opaque white base.

151 Set of Four Stemmed Glasses, 1900-1920
Each with a lime-green bowl on an iridescent gold stem
a. Water Goblet; H. 5⁵⁄₁₆ in (13.5 cm)
Inscribed: *L.C. Tiffany-Favrile 667*
CHMF 55-13a

b. Champagne Glass; H. 5½ in (11.4 cm)
Inscribed: *L.C. Tiffany-Favrile 211*
CHMF 55-13b

c. Wine Glass; H. 4½ in (11.4 cm)
Inscribed: *L.C. Tiffany-Favrile 211*
CHMF 55-13c

d. Liqueur Glass; H. 4¾ in (12 cm)
Inscribed: *L.C. Tiffany-Favrile 658*
CHMF 55-13d

152 Four Goblets, ca. 1895
Favrile glass; H. 6¾ in (17.1 cm)
Inscribed respectively: *L.C.T./D2607; L.C.T./D2070;
L.C.T./D2073;* and *L.C.T./D2077*
CHMF 67-3 through 67-6
From a larger set, each of these free-blown goblets of
translucent gold iridescent glass has a cylindrical bowl
tapering above a knopped baluster stem on a circular
foot.

147

152

158

Ceramics

Like other American decorative arts exhibited at the Centennial in Philadelphia, the American ceramics were faulted for their lack of originality. One critic observed that they had been "unable to approach even the lower grades of European wares" and that "American attempts at artistic decoration were such as to make the judicious grieve."[1] Curiously, one small group of ceramics was favorably if barely noted. It was a collection of china that had been painted by a society of affluent ladies in Cincinnati, Ohio. In discussing the origin and purposes of their society one member stated that "tidings of the veritable renaissance in England under the leadership of William Morris and his associates had reached this country."[2] The American response to the crafts revival that Morris was championing in England was most clearly evident in the establishment of numerous such craft-oriented societies. Although many of these groups intended to promote a "promising field for the lucrative employment of women" they were more frequently viewed as nothing more than an "amusement of the idle rich."[3]

In 1877 Candace Wheeler established the Society of Decorative Arts in New York which she modeled after London's Kensington School of Art Needlework. She proposed that the society's goal was to "encourage women who possess artistic talent and to furnish . . . a market for their work." To this end, courses were offered in art needlework, medieval embroidery, and china and tile painting.[4] In 1878 the curriculum was expanded and "under the direction of Mr. Tiffany and Mr. Lockwood de Forest . . . a class was offered in unbaked pottery."[5] Wheeler solicited the assistance of artists like Tiffany and de Forest in an attempt to improve the amateurish level of the work being produced; so it can be assumed that each had more than an amateur's familiarity with the craft. Lockwood de Forest's credentials for instructing such a course can only be speculated, and Louis Tiffany's remain totally unexplained.[6] However, it was noted that during this time, for someone of Tiffany's circumstances, it had "become a mark of inculture to be wholly ignorant of ceramic art."[7]

In 1879 Tiffany discontinued his instruction with the Society and invited Candace Wheeler to join him in the Associated Artists stating that he intended to pursue ". . . the real thing, you know; a business, not a philanthropy or any amateur educational scheme."[8] In the next two decades, in fact, many such philanthropies and amateur societies were themselves to become the real thing. One of the "affluent ladies" from Cincinnati established the important and influential Rookwood Pottery. Eventually, the women from these schools and societies developed an art pottery industry that by the end of the century represented the highest achievement of American ceramic production. Tiffany, however, had become preoccupied with other matters, and there is no evidence to suggest that he produced or experimented with ceramics during this period.

By 1900 his interest evidently had been renewed, and the December issue of *Keramic Studio* reported that "Mr. Louis Tiffany is busy experimenting in pottery which no doubt means that he will finally produce something as artistic as his Favrile glass."[9] In June of 1902 the same publication again reported "that Mr. Tiffany, the maker of the beautiful Favrile glass, is experimenting in pottery, and it is very probable that he is not following beaten paths and that we will see sooner or later some striking and artistic potteries come out of his kilns."[10] While the public waited, Tiffany became directly involved in the experimentation; as a former employee claimed, ". . . some of the first master pots were handthrown on the wheel by Mr. Tiffany."[11] The results of his years of experimentation were finally unveiled in 1904 when he exhibited three pieces of Favrile pottery at the St. Louis Exposition. The following year other examples were shown at the New York Keramic Society and at Tiffany & Company. By 1906 the pottery was in production and examples were exhibited in Europe and illustrated in *Dekorative Kunst*.[12] These illustrations revealed a full maturation of Tiffany's style. Among the forms already being produced were the fern tendril, calla lily, and cornstalk vases and the cattail pitcher.

Unlike many of his other artistic ventures, Favrile pottery was introduced into a market that was already distinguished by the achievements of established art potteries. Tiffany & Company had carried both American and European art pottery and Louis Tiffany's own studio had produced lamps on bases supplied by Grueby and had exhibited examples of the work of French art potters. As had been predicted, Tiffany, though familiar with the work of his contemporaries, chose not to follow "beaten paths." Martin Eidelberg observed that "while the novel forms and colorations are part of the general 1900 *zeitgeist*, still the specific qualities of Tiffany pottery show little external influence."[13] Favrile pottery like Favrile glass derived its forms from nature and from Tiffany's sensitivity to the properties of the medium. In the creation of a master pot, Tiffany wrought the clay into a form which he perceived as beautiful and then fixed that beauty in the fire of the kiln. The object thus created was, like his glass, beautiful in its own right. In the replication of that object, through slip-casting, its beauty was transmitted by the mold to the new pot and was again fixed in the fire of the kiln. Through the interaction of the application of glazes and the vagaries of the kiln, these pots were imbued with the added beauty of color and uniqueness. As a consequence, like his lamps, no two pots were ever identical (see nos. 170, 171 and 172).

Tiffany already had developed a mature repertoire during the experimentation period of his pottery production, but he continued to introduce new forms and to explore the potential of ceramic technology. In 1910 he introduced Favrile Bronze Pottery which is characterized by a seamless surface of bronze over a slip-cast piece of pottery.[14] For the creation of these objects, Tiffany drew upon the talents of both his pottery and metal departments; in the application of the metal, the potter imparted form, then the palette of the metalsmith provided the patina on the bronze.

Although his pottery was never a commercial success, Tiffany's personal interest in it appears to have been considerable. Like the many other ventures that required so great an investment of his time and money, the production of Favrile pottery ceased with his retirement from active participation in the operation of the Tiffany Furnaces. Little appreciated in its own time and overshadowed by the success of Favrile glass, Tiffany's pottery was a major manifestation of an important period in America's ceramic history and is now considered among the finest achievements of American ceramic art.[15]

1. Garth Clark, *A Century of Ceramics in the United States 1878–1978* (New York, 1979), p. 2.

2. Martin Eidelberg, "Art Pottery, *The Arts and Crafts Movement in America*, exhibition catalogue, Art Museum, Princeton University and the Art Institute of Chicago (Princeton, 1972), p. 119.

3. Herbert Peck, *The Book of Rookwood Pottery* (New York, 1968), p. 5.

4. Virginia Williams, "Candace Wheeler, Textile Designer for Associated Artists," *Nineteenth Century* 6 (Summer 1980), p. 60.

5. Robert Koch, *Louis C. Tiffany, Rebel in Glass* (New York, 1964), p. 11.

6. Anne Suydam Lewis, *Lockwood de Forest: Painter, Importer, Decorator*, exhibition catalogue, Heckscher Museum (Huntington, New York, 1976) p. 12 and n. 4. Lewis has proposed that de Forest had at least an association with ceramics through his friend Walter Palmer and his sister Julia de Forest.

7. Peck, p. 5.

8. Louis C. Tiffany, quoted by Candace Wheeler; cited by Hugh F. McKean, *The "Lost" Treasures of Louis Comfort Tiffany* (Garden City, N.Y., 1980), p. 101.

9. Adelaide Alsop Robineau in *Keramic Studio* (December 1900); cited by McKean, p. 205.

10. "French Pottery," *Keramic Studio* 4 (June 1902), p. 30; quoted by Martin Eidelberg, "Tiffany Favrile Potter," *Connoisseur* 169 (September 1968), p. 61, n. 7.

11. Robert Koch, *Louis C. Tiffany's Glass-Bronzes-Lamps* (New York, 1971), p. 149.

12. Eidelbert, "Tiffany Favrile Pottery." Illustrations reprinted from *Dekorative Kunst* appear on pp. 59–60.

13. Ibid., p. 60.

14. Koch, *Glass-Bronzes-Lamps*, p. 152; McKean, p. 210.

15. Clark, p. 334.

153 Cabinet Piece, ca. 1910
Favrile pottery; H. 4 in (10.2 cm)
Inscribed: *127 A-Coll L.C. Tiffany Favrile Pottery*
CHMF 69-11
Cabinet piece with thick flowing glazes in turquoise, blue, and dark blue. From Tiffany's personal collection.

154 Vase, ca. 1906
Favrile pottery; H. 14¾ in (37.5 cm)
Inscribed: *84-A-Coll L.C. Tiffany Favrile Pottery* with *LCT* monogram, and *T*
CHMF 77-42
Large, elongated ovoid vase with a blue-black iridescent glaze marked by runs of green, brown, and yellow. From Tiffany's personal collection.

155 Vase, 1900-1910
Favrile pottery; H. 9½ in (24.1 cm)
Inscribed: *LCT* monogram, and *L.C. Tiffany Favrile Pottery*
CHMF 69-7
Classic baluster form with elongated, flared neck. The vase has an iridescent glaze of blue and ochre, reminiscent of Roman glass.

156 Vase, ca. 1910
Favrile pottery; H. 11 in (27.9 cm)
Inscribed: *201 A-Coll L.C. Tiffany Favrile Pottery,* and with the *LCT* monogram
CHMF 79-532
Three-handled, bulbous body with high, broad neck, glazed with blue-green and silver-blue. Reminiscent of Roman glass. From Tiffany's personal collection.

157 Vase, 1900-1910
Favrile pottery; H. 12½ in (31.8 cm)
Inscribed: *LCT* monogram (incised)
CHMF 78-11
Three-handled, bulbous body with raised neck and a variegated green, textured glaze. A similar vase appears in photographs of the living room at Laurelton Hall.

158 Fern Tendril Vase, ca. 1906
Ceramic; H. 10¼ in (36.2 cm)
Inscribed: *LCT* monogram (incised)
CHMF 63-1
White bisque vase in form of opening fern fronds, pale green glaze on the interior.

157

159   Celery Vase, ca. 1906
Ceramic; H. 11¼ in (28.6 cm)
Inscribed: *LCT* monogram (incised)
Painted: *P1343/L.C.Tiffany-Favrile Pottery*
CHMF 74-26
Vase in the naturalistically modeled form of a stalk of
celery, with pale green, ivory, and cream-colored glazes.

160   Pitcher, 1900-1910
Favrile pottery; H. 12⅜ in (31.5 cm)
Inscribed: *LCT* monogram, and *P1157 L.C.Tiffany Inc.*
Favrile Pottery
CHMF 79-527
Cylindrical pitcher pinched to form the handle, the whole
having been modeled with cattails in low relief; mottled
yellow-green and green glazes.

161   Vase, ca. 1900-1910
Ceramic; H. 16¼ in (41.3 cm)
Inscribed: *LCT* monogram, and *L.C.Tiffany Favrile*
Pottery 82 A-Coll
CHMF 66-55
Large, melon-ribbed vase with shaded glazes of green
and chartreuse. This vase appears in photographs of the
second-floor gallery surrounding the court at
Laurelton Hall.

162   Vase, 1900-1910
Favrile pottery; H. 5 in (12.7 cm)
Inscribed: *LCT* monogram (incised)
CHMF 62-11

161

Ovoid body naturalistically modeled as a magnolia seed
pod. Glazed with a transparent dark brown over cream.

163   Vase, ca. 1914.
Favrile pottery; H. 8⅞ in (22.5 cm)
Inscribed: *LCT* monogram (incised)
CHMF 64-2
Gourd-shaped vase with surfaces modeled in pendant
peapods and tendrils glazed in a pale, transparent green.
A similar vase appears in photographs of the court at
Laurelton Hall.

164   Vase, 1900-1910
Favrile pottery; H. 7¹³⁄₁₆ in (19.3 cm)
Inscribed: *LCT* monogram (incised)
CHMF 76-4
High ovoid body on a cylindrical base with lobed foot,
modeled with grasses in low relief; green and yellow-
green glazes.

163

164

165 Vase, ca. 1910
Favrile pottery; H. 5⅜ in (13.7 cm)
Inscribed: *LCT* monogram (incised); another mark may
be either a 7 or an *L*
CHMF 80-16
Vase in form of a hollow tree stump surrounded by
mushrooms in high relief. Exterior glazed in a streaked
brown-ochre, the interior in a splotchy white-and-tan.

166 Vase, ca. 1906
Ceramic; H. 10 in (25.4 cm)
Inscribed: *LCT* monogram (incised), and the letters *P*
and *AG*
CHMF 76-13
Freeform vase modeled as a cluster of milkweed. The
pods and stems are glazed in bluish greys, greens,
browns, and white against a textured purple ground.

167 Vase, ca. 1906
Favrile pottery; H. 11¼ in (28.6 cm)
Inscribed: *LCT* monogram (incised)
CHMF 74-30
Cylindrical bisque vase modeled with calla lilies, the
stems in low relief against the body and the blossoms and
leaves in high relief against the pierced top; green glazed
interior.

168 Vase, ca. 1910
Favrile pottery; H. 5⅝ in (14.2 cm)
Inscribed: *LCT* monogram (incised)
CHMF 77-39
Bulbous body with elongated, pierced neck natural-
istically modeled with flowers and foliage. Blue-green
glaze with slight iridescence.

169 Bowl, ca. 1910
Favrile pottery; DIAM. 7¼ in (18.4 cm)
Inscribed: *LCT* monogram (incised)
CHMF 74-28
Low circular bisque bowl with incurvate sides, modeled
with flower and foliage, possibly periwinkles, the upper
portion pierced between the blossoms. This bowl was
also produced in bronze pottery.

170 Bowl, ca. 1910
Ceramic; H. 4½ in (11.4 cm)
Inscribed: *LCT* monogram (incised)
CHMF 66-18
Of irregular contour, the bisque body is modeled with
fish and waves. The interior has a green glaze.

172

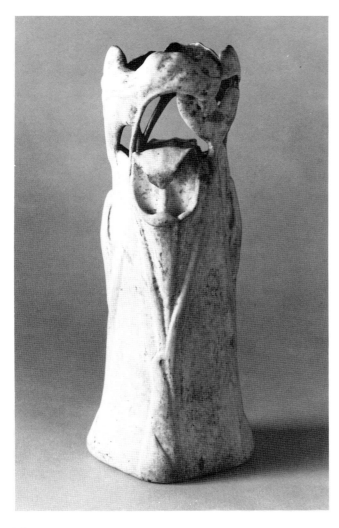

167

171 Bowl, ca. 1910
Ceramic; H. 4½ in (11.4 cm)
Inscribed: *LCT* monogram (incised), and the letters *P* and *EL*
CHMF 74-27
Identical with nos. 170 and 172, but with blue, green, pink, and white glazes.

172 Bowl, ca. 1910
Ceramic and bronze; H. 4½ in (11.4 cm)
Inscribed: *L.C. Tiffany-Favrile Bronze Pottery—B.P. 392*
CHMF 55-9
Identical with nos. 170 and 171, except cased in bronze.

173 Vase, ca. 1910
Ceramic and bronze; H. 7¼ in (18.4 cm)
Inscribed: *L.C. Tiffany-Favrile Bronze Pottery,* with *LCT* monogram, and *B.P. 325 40 A-Coll*
CHMF 65-26
Cylindrical vase with flared foot, the surface modeled with nasturtium blossoms and foliage. The interior with a green glaze, the exterior with bronze. From Tiffany's personal collection.

174 Vase, 1900-1910
Favrile bronze pottery; H. 13 in (33 cm)
Inscribed: *LCT* monogram, with *L.C. Tiffany Favrile Bronze Pottery BP279 6262*
CHMF 77-26
Tall, cylindrical ceramic vase modeled in low relief with stalks and ears of corn. Cased in bronze; dark green glazed interior.

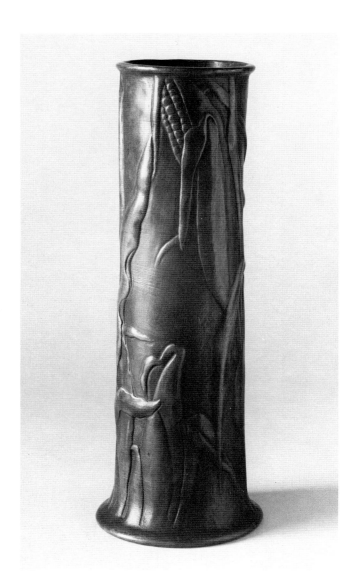

174

175 Covered Jar, ca. 1900-1910
Favrile pottery; H. overall 9 in (22.9 cm)
Jar inscribed: *LCT* monogram and, in pencil, *LCT P-15*
Cover unmarked
CHMF 76-8 a and b
The jar, of elongated ovoid form, and its cover have low relief floral surface modeling with soft yellow-green glazes accented with darker green.

176 Bowl, 1910-1915
Favrile pottery; H. 6⅜ in (16.3 cm)
Inscribed: *LCT* monogram (incised)
CHMF 76-14
Bulbous bowl with raised, molded rim. The surfaces decorated with a raised stippling of lions and highly stylized floral motifs. The yellow-brown transparent glaze has trailings of red-brown.

176

154 Vase, Favrile pottery, ca. 1906.

177, 189, 178

Metals, Enamels, and Jewelry

Louis Comfort Tiffany demonstrated an appreciation for the art of the metals craftsman as a young man when, with the encouragement of Edward C. Moore, he began to collect Japanese sword guards (tsuba). He was undoubtedly aware of the Japanese influence reflected in Moore's designs for silver, which had helped to establish the Tiffany & Company's reputation as silver manufacturers.[1] Tiffany had made use of iron in some of his earliest interior designs, including the chandeliers and various decorative elements for the 7th Regiment Armory. In some of his early windows, the Magnolia for example, he explored the sculptural properties of the lead cames, though this exploration was ancillary to his primary composition in glass. In work such as the canonical candlesticks and tabernacle door for the Columbian Exposition chapel, Tiffany made extensive use of metal, but here again its function was subordinated to the mounting of quartz pebbles and semi-precious stones which predominate in the design. In describing the original cross (now lost) for the chapel, Tiffany pointed out that there was "just enough metal to carry an enormous quantity of white topazes."[2] In creating these objects Tiffany used metal as a jeweler would, and in fact he stated that "the cross and candlesticks, taken together, give a very good idea of our decorative church jewelry work."[3]

This jeweler's approach to metals was sufficient for these early exhibition and custom pieces, but when he began to produce and market lamps, structural and functional requirements coupled with the need for standardization dictated a different approach. For the lamps first offered, Tiffany relied upon other manufacturers for bases and fittings. Tiffany, however, was a man who had determined that in order to obtain the results that he wanted, he had to control and direct production. Consequently, when the glasshouse at Corona was expanded in 1897, a foundry was established. Alvin J. Tuck was hired to supervise the new metals department and, working directly with Tiffany, became the principal designer of the metal wares produced. The first of these appear to have been lamps, but by the time of Tiffany's exhibition at the Grafton Galleries in 1899, it was apparent that production had begun to diversify. In addition to the lamps (see previous discussion), the catalogue of that exhibition notes three candelabra, four inkstands, a paperweight, a letter box, two plaques, and three powder-boxes.[4] Each of these items was described as being "in metal," and some bore the additional descriptions "with glass blown inside" or "in metal inlay."[5] The metal referred to was bronze and, like Tiffany's work in other media, was fashioned in designs derived from nature.

In executing these designs, as he had with glass, Tiffany respected the integrity of his medium while exploiting its inherent properties. His bronze candlesticks display designs that both replicate and stylize natural forms. He also created forms that derive from the potential of the metal as well as designs that reflect his awareness of the jeweler's art. By blowing molten glass into pierced bronze he exploited the inherent properties of each material and produced an object whose final form depended upon the unique reaction between these materials. Glass, in the form of mosaics, was also used to decorate the surfaces of bronze objects such as lamp bases and planters.

As the production of the Tiffany metal department expanded and as more utilitarian objects were added to the inventory, Tiffany was at last able to offer objects of high artistic quality that could reach a broader segment of the American public. Although his strict maintenance of high standards of craftsmanship and use of costly materials precluded a true mass market for these objects, many Americans unable to commission a Tiffany window or purchase an expensive lamp were able to acquire a candlestick, an inkstand, a paperweight, or even some elements of a desk set. The latter were not, in fact, created as sets but rather consisted of coordinated patterns for a variety of desk furnishings. Crafted in bronze and available in a variety of finishes, their designs often incorporated glass or abalone shell. In 1906 four such patterns were available and by 1910 there were eight. No less than fifteen had been created by 1920 and the individual items available in a pattern could number as many as thirty.[6] Other objects for domestic use were produced at the foundry in Corona. By 1906 the Tiffany Studios price book carried 210 entries for fancy goods as diverse as a $1 pencil holder, a $40 table with "fluted metal legs, wood top, 14" square" (no. 188), and a $150 mirror described as "three-fold, metal and inlaid glass, 11½" square." Castings were also made from actual antique originals; the cast bronze Romanesque cup in this exhibition is a rare example of that production.

Although bronze was the principal metal employed at the Tiffany Furnaces, others were also used and among the rarest of these is silver.[7] Although some silver can be attributed to Louis Comfort Tiffany, little appears to have been made, and curiously the catalogue of the sale that disposed of the contents of Laurelton Hall carried but one entry for silver: "1079. Repoussé Sterling Silver Tea Service *Tiffany Studios, New York* Teapot, hot-water kettle on stand with spirit burner, sugar bowl, and creamer; squat pear-shaped bodies in plain silver *repoussé* to simulate floral petals."[8] This service, which appears in photographs of the dining room at Laurelton Hall, was displayed and apparently used en suite with a tray, also marked by the Tiffany Studios but made of hammered

197 **Vase**, enamel on copper, after 1904.

206 The Peacock Necklace, ca. 1906.

206 The Peacock Necklace, reverse.

copper. The silver powder box (no. 178) is not only a rare example of marked Tiffany Studios silver but is also significant in its use of turquoise enamel in conjunction with its repoussé decoration.

When Samuel Howe described enamel as "a strong, active force for color, which requires great care in use . . . it is, by nature, assertive and capricious," he came close to describing his friend Louis Comfort Tiffany.[9] There is no doubt that Tiffany was a strong active force for color or that he was assertive. In his creation of superb enamels, however, one might incorrectly perceive him as capricious. His entire career in stained glass had involved the avoidance of the use of enamels, the practice of which he felt had marked "the beginning of deterioration in glass windows from the stand point of art."[10] In this context, Tiffany saw enamel as compromising the inherent property of the pot metal by obfuscating its translucent color. The issue, though, was not one of enamels per se; it was in their use in conjunction with stained glass. Enamel, applied to copper, silver, or gold represented a medium in its own right, possessing its own inherent properties and the potential to approach the gem-like purity of color and brilliance that Tiffany loved.

Edward C. Moore had experimented with enamels on silver at Tiffany & Company, and when the metal furnaces were opened at Corona, Tiffany, too, began to experiment. This began in 1898, and the work of the new enameling department, headed by Julia Munson, was first seen on a copper lamp base exhibited at Paris in 1900. Exhibited at Buffalo in 1901 and Turin in 1902, Tiffany's enamels were well received. The enamels department, composed entirely of women, operated like all other departments within the Tiffany Studios and produced works of art whose designs were either originated or approved by Tiffany. The designs were worked up in repoussé copper (or silver), the powdered glass with metallic oxides was applied, and the whole was heated in a kiln to fuse the enamel to the metal object.[11] The application of multiple layers of enamel increased not only the risk of ruining the enamels already applied but also the cost. As a consequence, the enamels constituted one of the most limited productions of the Tiffany Studios. The Tiffany & Company *Blue Book* for 1910 noted a small number of objects ranging in price from $10 to $99 and provided a description of Tiffany enamels: "Made under the personal supervision of Mr. Louis C. Tiffany/An enamel with and without iridescent lustre, on plain and repoussé surfaces. By placing translucent colors one upon another and applying fire-art treatment, effects are obtained similar to those of Tiffany Favrile Glass and equally unique and distinctive in character."[12] Tiffany, whose private collection of these enamels consisted of ninety-three objects,[13] saw yet another similarity. In 1902 he exhibited one of his enameled vases in the window of Tiffany and Company surrounded by precious and semi-precious stones that corresponded in color to his enamels. Samuel Howe, after having seen this

display, reported that "in the results of the test, the enamels proved equally fine in quality and tone of color with the gems; due allowance being made for the scintillation and counter lights cast by the latter."[14]

Julia Munson, who had headed the enamel department at the Tiffany Furnaces, was selected by Tiffany to head a new experimental art venture; with her experience in enameling she was ideally suited to direct Tiffany's exploration of the creative possibilities of artistic jewelry. Her selection for this project was also in keeping with Tiffany's acceptance and encouragement of women in his business.[15] The success of their joint efforts was later recalled by Miss Munson when she observed that "in no craft is the technical soundness of Mr. Tiffany's craftsmanship more apparent than in the little pieces he created in this venture. I can trace a decided influence in the best jewelry of today back to his strenuous effort to apply art to jewelry, which we all know is most difficult."[16]

It is curious that Tiffany, the son of one of the world's most distinguished jewelers, a painter whose work was referred to as early as 1873 as "art jewelry," an artist in stained glass who created windows in the form of renaissance brooches and whose early work in metals was compared with Gaulish jewelry, should have waited so long in his career to work in this medium. Hugh McKean offers an explanation: "Louis Tiffany's refreshing jewelry, whether intentionally so or not, may have been a gentle response to his father's unabashed commercialism."[17] It is probably no accident that this activity was coincident with the death of Charles L. Tiffany and Louis Comfort Tiffany's appointment as vice-president and art director of Tiffany & Company.

Gertrude Speenburgh has noted that "as was his usual habit when engaged in developing a new venture still in the experimental stage, he carried on the work in a most secretive manner."[18] These experiments continued for two years, and in 1904 Tiffany & Company exhibited twenty-five pieces of jewelry "designed by Louis C. Tiffany" at the St. Louis World's Fair.[19] For those who had expected lavish assemblages of rare and precious stones like those which had come to be associated with the name of Tiffany & Company, the productions of the new artistic jewelry department were to prove disappointing. On page 650 of the 1910 edition of the Tiffany *Blue Book*, beneath the entry for Diamond Tiaras ". . . many crowned and surmounted by large diamonds or pear-shape pearls $1,800. upward," appears the entry for Tiffany art jewelry: "Designed and made under the personal supervision of Mr. Louis C. Tiffany. No pieces duplicated. Among the features of this work are the remarkable color effects obtained in the combinations of gold and enamel with precious and semi-precious stones."[20] In the nine categories of objects listed, the prices ranged from $8 to $3,500. As could be expected, the design of Tiffany's artistic jewelry derived from nature; jewels were produced in the forms of clover and wild carrot blossoms, blackberries, insects, and the inevitable peacock. The latter was selected for the design of what has generally been considered Tiffany's masterpiece in this medium (see no. 206). The "Peacock Necklace," first shown in Paris in 1906, was Tiffany's favorite exhibition piece, and he selected it to be illustrated in *The Art Work of Louis C. Tiffany*. In the production of less ambitious pieces of artistic jewelry Tiffany selected stones for the beauty of their color rather than their value and, as he had done with his glass, mounted them in simple settings designed only to enhance and maximize that beauty. In speaking of his jewelry Tiffany observed, "One may say that the quality, the artistic quality, of the jewelry which is found among a people goes far to measure that people's level in art. Hence the importance of having artists instead of untrained artisans to supply jewelers with designs; . . . to supply a class of jewelry not only original and individual, but often very beautiful."[21] Unfortunately, the American people's "level in art" was not to meet with Tiffany's expectations, and with his death Tiffany & Company closed the department in 1933.

1. This influence is discussed by Charles H. Carpenter, Jr., in *Tiffany Silver* (New York, 1978) and was observed by Samuel Bing in *Artistic America, Tiffany Glass, and Art Nouveau*, pp. 121–123.

2. *A Synopsis of the Exhibit of the Tiffany Glass and Decorating Company in the Section of the Manufactures and Liberal Arts Building at the World's Fair* . . .(New York, 1893), p. 11.

3. Ibid.

4. Robert Koch, *Louis Comfort Tiffany's Glass-Bronzes-Lamps* (New York, 1971), p. 88.

5. Ibid.

6. Ibid., p. 89. See also *Tiffany & Company Blue Book* (New York, 1910), pp. 215–219.

7. Charles H. Carpenter, Jr., "The Silver of Louis Comfort Tiffany," *Antiques* 117 (February 1980), pp. 390–397.

8. Parke-Bernet Galleries, Inc., sale catalogue, *Objects of Art . . . The Extensive Collection of the Louis Comfort Tiffany Foundation* (New York, 1946), p. 199.

9. Hugh F. McKean, *The "Lost" Treasures of Louis Comfort Tiffany* (Garden City, N.Y., 1980), p. 237.

10. Louis C. Tiffany, "Color and its Kinship to Sound," address before the Rembrandt Club of Brooklyn, 1917, reprinted by Robert Koch, *Louis C. Tiffany's Art Glass* (New York, 1977), p. 36.

11. McKean, p. 238; Koch, *Glass-Bronzes-Lamps*, pp. 152–153.

12. *Tiffany & Company Blue Book*, pp. 311–312.

13. Parke-Bernet Galleries sale catalogue, pp. 48–51.

14. McKean, p. 242.

15. Clara Driscoll, one of the most accomplished of his designers, had worked for Tiffany since 1887; by 1904, earning a salary of more than $10,000 a year, she was one of the highest paid female employees in the United States. See Robert Koch, *Louis C. Tiffany, Rebel in Glass* (New York, 1964), p. 130.

16. Gertrude Speenburgh, *The Arts of the Tiffanys* (Chicago, 1956), p. 73.

17. McKean, p. 243.

18. Speenburgh, p. 74.

19. Koch, *Glass-Bronzes-Lamps*, p. 156.

20. *Tiffany & Company Blue Book*, p. 650.

21. Louis C. Tiffany, quoted by McKean, p. 243.

43 The Entombment, stained glass, 1892.

177 Cream Pitcher, after 1902
Repoussé copper with gold, silver, and ebony;
H. 3¼ in (8.3 cm)
Inscribed: *Tiffany Studios/New York*
CHMF 70-11
Of oval section, the pitcher has straight sides which swell
out at the top. The surfaces depict trillium plants and
blossoms in repoussé picked out in gold, silver, and
patinated copper. The simple curved handle is of ebony.

178 Box, 1902-1920
Silver and enamel; H. 1⅞ in (4.6 cm); DIAM. 4⅛ in
(10.5 cm)
Box inscribed: *Tiffany Furnaces/Sterling/239* and *9/289*
Cover inscribed: *239* (twice)
CHMF 78-1
Octagonal covered box with borders of pebbled decora-
tion in repoussé and turquoise enamel.

179 Planter, ca. 1900
Bronze, Favrile glass mosaic, and copper; H. 4 in
(10.2 cm); DIAM. 12 in (30.5 cm)
Planter inscribed: *Tiffany Studios/New York/29117B/S/
C305/S/C5407*
Liner inscribed: *Tiffany Studios/New York/29117/S/C
305/S/C 5407*
Both inscribed with the Tiffany Glass and Decorating
Company monogram
CHMF 58-2
Shallow, rounded body of cast bronze features blossoms
and foliage in relief against a ground of translucent,
iridescent mosaic in blue and green. The liner is of copper.

180 Candlestick, ca. 1900
Bronze; H. 8 in (20.3 cm)
Inscribed: *Tiffany Studios/New York/1203,* with *TS*
monogram
CHMF 54-101
A flat, stylized leaf supports two tendril forms, one of
which is mounted with a globular candle cup with flared
bobêche.

181 Candlestick, after 1902
Bronze; H. 16¾ in (42.5 cm)
Inscribed: *Tiffany Studios/New York/1213 V605*
CHMF U22-1
Globular candle cup supported by three prongs atop a
simple, slender stem with flat, circular base.

179

182 Candlestick, after 1902
Bronze; H. 10¼ in (26 cm)
Inscribed: *Tiffany Studios/New York, 1205*
CHMF 58-3-1
Naturalistically modeled as a stalk of bamboo, the
lower portion of which has been split and flared to form
the base.

183 Candlestick, after 1902
Bronze and Favrile glass; H. 19½ in (49.5 cm)
Inscribed: *Tiffany Studios/New York/D884*
CHMF 67-16
The goblet-shaped candle cup of iridescent gold Favrile
glass with applied lily pads rests atop the stem of an
inverted blossom of Queen Anne's lace.

184 Candlestick, after 1902
Bronze and Favrile glass; H. 16¼ in (41.3 cm)
Inscribed: *Tiffany Studios/New York/1223*
CHMF 66-27
The feathered Favrile glass candle cup is supported
on a bronze stem and open base set with spheres of
Favrile glass.

185 Candlestick, after 1902
Bronze and Favrile glass; H. 8½ in (21.6 cm)
Inscribed: *Tiffany Studios/New York/29117 29117/6104*
CHMF 54-102
Globular candle cup set with green-blue iridescent glass
supported on three splayed legs which terminate in
bronze spheres.

180, 186, 182, 185, 183, and 181

186 Candlestick, after 1902
Bronze and Favrile glass; H. 20¾ in (52.7 cm)
Inscribed: *Tiffany Studios/New York/5393*
CHMF 59-3
A simple circular base and slender stem support a
reticulated candle cup into which opaque green glass
has been blown.

187 Candelabrum, after 1902
Bronze and Favrile glass; 15 x 21 in (38.1 x 53.3 cm)
Inscribed: *Tiffany Studios/New York 10088,* with
Tiffany Studios monogram
CHMF U-21
The six reticulated candle cups with blown opaque green
glass are aligned along organically conceived branches
which "grow" from a low stem with circular base. A
central tendril has a recess fitted with a candle snuffer.

188 Table, after 1902
Oak and bronze; H. 30 in (76.2 cm)
Inscribed: *Tiffany Studios/New York*
CHMF 78-235
Square oak top supported on a bronze frame with four
shaped and reeded legs and diagonal stretchers. This table
is illustrated in a damaged glass plate negative from the
Tiffany Studios.

189 Teapot on Stand, undated
Silver-plated bronze; H. 10¼ in (26 cm)
Inscribed: *Tiffany Studios/New York*
CHMF 80-18
Although a variety of finishes were available on bronzes
cast at the Tiffany Studios, silver-plated wares are rare in
their survival. The design of this teapot and its stand
integrates the organic quality that characterizes much of
Tiffany's work in metal and the functional relationship
between the pot, stand, and burner.

187

190   Pen-and-Ink Stand, ca. 1910
Silver-plated bronze and Favrile glass; L. 8 in (20.3 cm)
DIAM. 4 in (10.2 cm)
Stand inscribed: *Tiffany Studios/New York 10388*;
Tiffany Studios/New York 3664
Cover inscribed: *3664*
Glass inkwell inscribed: *L.C.T.*
CHMF 53-6
Rectangular silvered bronze box set with blue-green
iridescent turtleback tiles. The interior is fitted with ink-
wells and hooks for pens.

191   Inkstand, Zodiac Design, 1902-1918
Bronze; H. 3¼ in (8.3 cm)
Inscribed: *Tiffany Studios/New York 1072*
CHMF 75-4
Pyramidal form with rounded contours, the six panels
decorated with signs of the zodiac. A glass insert held
the ink.

188

190

192 Booklet, *The Zodiac Desk Set,* after 1902
6¼ x 3½ in (15.9 x 8.9 cm)
Retains paper label: *Whitmore's/New Art Gallery/1517 Dodge St./Omaha*
CHMF 79-522
A fifteen-page promotional booklet on the Zodiac Desk Set published by Tiffany Studios.

193 Desk Set, Abalone Pattern, 1902-1918
Gilded bronze with disks of abalone shell.
All pieces inscribed: *Tiffany Studios/New York*
Individual pieces inscribed as listed below:

a. Paper rack	*1151/2949*
b. Blotter ends	*1152/2812*
c. Inkstand	*1157/2780*
d. Stamp box	*1158/5307*
e. Pen tray	*1159/2020*
f. Pen brush	*1160/ 863*
g. Paper knife	*1163/3196*
h. Rocker blotter	*1164/7119*
i. Letter clip	*1165/1296*
j. Calendar frame	*1166/1390*
k. Thermometer	*1167/ 925*
l. Memoranda pad	*1169/1376*
m. Letter scales	*1170/2371*
n. Utility box	*1176/1845*
o. Reading glass	*1178/1368*
p. Lamp shade	*1928/1855*
q. Lamp base	*604/4456*

CHMF 68-3-1 through 68-3-15
and 68-3-17 b, c

194 Inkstand, 1920-1928
Enameled metal with Favrile glass; 2½ x 3¾ x 3¾ in (6.4 x 9.5 x 9.5 cm)
Inkstand inscribed: *LCT* monogram/*Louis C. Tiffany Furnaces, Inc./347/3510*
Glass inkwell inscribed: *LCT Favrile*
CHMF 58-17
Square metal box with bold geometric designs in pink and blue enamel. The interior is fitted with a gold iridescent Favrile glass inkwell with a floriform lip.

195 "Romanesque" Cup, after 1902
Bronze; H. 3⅞ in (9.7 cm)
Inscribed: *S113 Tiffany Studios/From the Antique*
CHMF 78-1053 a, b (model), c (photograph)
Cylindrical bronze cup with frieze of Roman figures; cast from a mold taken from an antique cup. The ceramic model (inscribed with the monogram of the Tiffany Studios) used to cast the cup and a Tiffany Studios photograph of the original "Romanesque" cup with the reproduction survive and accompany this piece.

196 Desk Tray, after 1900
Enamel on repoussé copper; 11¼ x 6 in (28.6 x 15.2 cm)
Inscribed: *Louis C. Tiffany EL 169*
CHMF 70-16
Of irregular outline, the tray depicts milkweed pods in
lustrous green, red, gold, and transparent enamels. One
of the pods opens to reveal a small compartment.

197 Vase, after 1904
Enamel on repoussé copper; H. 7½ in (19 cm)
Inscribed: *162 A Coll L.C. Tiffany SG 123*
CHMF 66-1
Urn-shaped vase of repousséd copper enameled with
green foliage and red-gold blossoms on a ground shaded
from blue to violet. The flower depicted has been called
"Dutchman's pipes." From Tiffany's personal collection.

198 Vase, after 1904
Enamel on repoussé copper; H. 9 in (22.9 cm)
Inscribed: *Louis C. Tiffany SG 80 SC 249*
CHMF 65-3
Cylindrical vase decorated with clusters of tightly coiled
fern tendrils in green and gold enamel on a ground of
iridescent mauve.

199 Lady's Ring, 1902-1915
Inscribed: *Tiffany & Co.*
CHMF 71-14
Lapis lazuli set in 18-karat gold modeled with interlacing
leaves and berries.

200 Lady's Ring, 1902-1915
Inscribed: *14K Tiffany & Co.*
CHMF 71-16
Large emerald-cut topaz set in 14-karat gold with enamel.

201 Lady's Ring, 1902-1915
Inscribed: *18K Tiffany & Co.*
CHMF 71-19
Dark green tourmaline set in 18-karat gold.

198

202 Lady's Pin, 1902-1915
DIAM. 1¼ in (3.2 cm)
Inscribed: *Tiffany & Co.*
CHMF 71-13
Circular pin of gold filigree set with a large center topaz and four pale cabochon stones. The design of this pin may have been derived from Gaulish jewelry, a source that has been suggested as having influenced the filigree metalwork of the Columbian Exposition Chapel.

203 Brooch, 1902-1915
L. 2¹³/₁₆ in (6.7 cm)
Inscribed: *Tiffany & Co.*
CHMF 62-21
Large translucent opal mounted over a filigree of gold flanked by demantoids and sapphires set in tapering strands of gold.

204 Pin, 1902-1915
L. 1¼ in (3.2 cm)
Inscribed: *Tiffany & Co.*
CHMF 74-4
Large oval cabochon of lapis lazuli surrounded by scrolling bands of gold.

205 Bracelet, 1902-1915
L. 7½ in (19.1 cm)
Inscribed: *Tiffany & Co.*
CHMF 77-19
Double strand of gold with dark blue enamel centered with an oval medallion set with five cabochons of lapis lazuli surrounded by small lapis beads.

206 The Peacock Necklace, ca. 1906
L. 10 in (25.4 cm)
Unsigned; designed by Louis Comfort Tiffany, made by Julia Sherman. Exhibited at the Paris Salon of 1906.
CHMF 58-1
The large peacock medallion with its mosaic of opals, emeralds, and other precious stones surrounded by amethysts and sapphires is flanked by pairs of rosettes set with topaz and demantoids and is suspended from tulip-shaped plaques of gold enameled with a pair of peacocks facing each other across cabochon emeralds and surrounded by sapphires, amethysts, and rubies. A chain of gold, pearls, and demantoids drapes beneath the central medallion and above a wreath of enameled gold centered with a topaz. Beneath the wreath is a single pendant ruby which was "selected not for its costliness but for the exact shade of red." The reverse is enameled gold depicting flamingos surrounded by flowers. The necklace is secured by a silk cord.

205, 203, 202

207

World's Columbian Exposition Chapel

In 1892 Louis Comfort Tiffany began work on an ambitious project to be exhibited at the World's Columbian Exposition. Staged in a vast, ideal city of neo-classical "palaces" rising on the banks of Lake Michigan at Chicago, the fair was to be the grandest of all of the International Expositions. Tiffany, who was creating chandeliers for the Women's Building and preparing six paintings for the fair, saw it as an opportunity to showcase the achievements of his newly reorganized Tiffany Glass and Decorating Company. In a portion of the space reserved by his father's firm in the Manufactures and Liberal Arts Building, Tiffany installed his exhibition, which consisted of two decorated rooms and a chapel. The rooms, one designated as "light" and the other "dark," displayed his mastery of domestic interior design. The chapel was a tour de force in the application of his glass to an ecclesiastical interior and was immediately hailed internationally as one of the highest achievements of original American design.

Variously described as Romanesque and/or Byzantine "but entirely original in its decorative details," the chapel "was made from a design by Mr. Louis C. Tiffany . . . and executed under his supervision."[1] The chapel, as described by a visitor to the fair, consisted of "a superb altar set under triple mosaic arches. The floor of the sanctuary is of the most intricately wrought glass mosaic, as are the chancel steps and the front of the altar itself. The heavy columns, too, are of iridescent mosaic. The lectern is of the same exquisite work, as is also the font which has a finely wrought cover of glass. . . . There are exhibited some surpassingly fine vestments, an altar cross spangled with jewels, and some fine candlesticks of Connemara [sic] marble. The entire effect of this little chapel . . . is exceedingly rich."[2] Tiffany's exhibit, particularly the chapel, was enthusiastically received and reviewed, and for his efforts the Tiffany Glass and Decorating Company was awarded fifty-four medals.

Following the fair, the chapel was dismantled; and on February 15, 1894, the New York Times announced that "this extraordinary exhibit, which won a host of medals for the Tiffany Glass Company, is shown this week at the offices in Fourth Avenue, near Twenty-fifth Street." It was subsequently purchased by Celia Whipple Wallace, a wealthy Chicago philanthropist, who presented it to the Cathedral of Saint John the Divine, then under construction in New York City. Installed in the Romanesque crypt of the cathedral, the chapel was used for services until 1911. Regrettably, when the decision was made to abandon the Romanesque style and complete the cathedral in the more "fashionable" Gothic style, the chapel was abandoned and allowed to fall into disrepair. Tiffany himself entered into negotiations with the cathedral au-

thorities for the preservation of the chapel noting that "as I consider it some of my best work it is but natural that I should feel that some immediate action should be taken for its permanent preservation."[3]

In 1916, the Cathedral authorities granted permission for Tiffany to remove the chapel, and he installed it in a building that had been built for it on the grounds of Laurelton Hall. When the Trustees of the Tiffany Foundation disposed of the estate in 1946, the altar, the furnishings, and most of the windows were dispersed, leaving the building with its mosaics and some windows exposed to the elements. Following the fire that destroyed much of Laurelton Hall in 1957, the remaining elements of the chapel were acquired by Mr. and Mrs. Hugh F. McKean, who subsequently reassembled the elements that had been dispersed. Its survival now secure, the chapel in its entirety is part of the collection of the Charles Hosmer Morse Foundation.

1. "Tiffany Glass and Decorating Company's Exhibit at the Columbian Exposition," *The Decorator and Furnisher* 23 (October 1893), p. 10.
2. Major Ben C. Truman, *The History of the World's Fair* (Philadelphia, 1893), p. 219.
3. Letter from Louis C. Tiffany to Cathedral of St. John the Divine, 27 May 1916; cited by McKean, p. 144.

208

207 World's Columbian Exposition Chapel
Facsimile of watercolor rendering; original by Joseph Lauber, ca. 1893
Chromolithograph; 10⅜ x 12¾ in (26.4 x 32.4 cm)
Unsigned
CHMF 68-F
The Lauber watercolor is the principal depiction of the chapel as it was originally installed. The Field of Lilies window (no. 42) with its original angel panel can be seen at left.

208 Chapel Door, ca. 1916
Oak and iron; 77 x 50 in (195.6 x 127 cm); with surround: 96 x 65½ in (243.8 x 166.4 cm)
Unsigned; from the chapel building at Laurelton Hall
CHMF 58-22
The door, of heavy oak timbers, is centered with a large cross of pierced and overlaid wrought iron similar in design to that of the altar cross, also made in 1916. Three large hinges of similar iron work support the door in an oak surround. A carved inscription reads: *Knock/ and it shall be opened/ unto thee.*

209 The Peacock Reredos, ca. 1892
Glass mosaic on plaster; 90 x 72 in (228.6 x 182.9 cm)
Unsigned; from the World's Columbian Exposition Chapel
CHMF U-75
Described by the Tiffany Glass and Decorating Company in 1893: "The Reredos itself is made of polished black marble and iridescent glass mosaics, these mosaics giving forth deep blue and pearl-like lights. The design employed is the Vine, symbolical of the Sacrament of the Eucharist, and among these vines there are portrayed peacocks, used here after the manner of the Primitive Christians, as symbolizing immortality, for it was believed in the early ages that the flesh of the peacock was incorruptible. The aim of the designer was two-fold: first, to convey to the minds of the spectators that the joys of immortality are dependent upon the Vine of the New Testament, and, secondly, to illustrate by symbols the sacred texts which are inscribed upon the retables."
Seven large garnets originally set into the crown were stolen in 1902 and were replaced with glass.

210 Elements of the Ciborium, ca. 1892
Glass mosaic, plaster, and gilded plaster
Unsigned; from the World's Columbian Exposition Chapel
CHMF CHAPEL
In a pamphlet on their exhibit, the Tiffany Glass and Decorating Company described the ciborium as "composed of a series of arches, the soffit of each arch falling a considerable distance below the one immediately next to it, in that way exposing a series of faces which are covered with ornaments in relief and made brilliant by overlays of gold, settings of jewels and inlays of mosaic inscriptions. A very effective perspective is obtained by this method of construction and ornamentation. These arches rest upon columns, whose capitals are heavy with relief ornament, upon a background of mosaic, and having astragals of jewels set in gold. The shafts are composed of 200,000 squares of transparent glass mosaic, of red, green, and brownish tones, a species of decoration and construction never before used for this purpose. The shafts rest upon bases of black marble."

211 Altar, with Retables and Tabernacle, ca. 1892
Marble, glass mosaic, glass jewels, and semi-precious stones; 39 x 94 x 50 in (99 x 238.8 x 127 cm)
Unsigned; from the World's Columbian Exposition Chapel
CHMF 75-23
In 1893 the Tiffany Glass and Decorating Company described the altar with its retables and tabernacle as follows: "The mensa is a single slab of Carrara marble resting upon a frontal of white glass mosaic, made of 150,000 pieces, relieved and ornamented with the Apo-

calyptic emblems of the four Evangelists, worked out in mother-of-pearl mosaics, in four circles immediately beneath the edge of the mensa and either side of the centre line, where there is a larger circle containing a monogram of the Holy Name, imbedded in a background of Rosary beads and enriched by inlays of gold and precious stones, and made iridescent with mother-of-pearl. Back and above the mensa there are two retables, the treads of which are made with slabs of the same marble as used in the mensa, while the risers are filled with gold mosaic, carrying an inscription in white mosaic letters, taken from the sixth chapter of the Gospel, according to St. John, and directly relating to the Eucharistic office. Dividing the retables, immediately in the centre of the altar, and two feet back from the edge of the mensa, there is a low tabernacle, the door of which is a mass of semi-precious marbles, made more precious here and there by real gems."

212, 213

212 Altar Cross, ca. 1916
Brass, Favrile glass, and mother-of-pearl; H. 24 in (61 cm)
Unsigned; from the chapel as reconstructed at Laurelton Hall
CHMF 75-16
Of simple profile, the cross—faced with large glass jewels set into a jeweled filigree surrounded by tesserae of mother-of-pearl—rests on a stepped base which is inscribed *Sanctus*. Electrified, the large jewels glow when illuminated. This cross was made by Tiffany to replace the original one made for the Columbian Exposition. Described as having "just enough metal to carry an enormous quantity of white topazes," it was stolen while at the Cathedral of St. John the Divine.

213 Four Altar Candlesticks, ca. 1892
Gilded metal filigree, semi-precious stones; H. 36 in (91.4 cm)
Unsigned; from the World's Columbian Exposition Chapel
CHMF 75-18 through 75-21
All conform in form and size, but each candlestick differs in the detail of its filigree and use of polished semi-precious stones. There were originally six "canonical candlesticks" on the altar at the exhibition; however, two are now lost. The candles are electrified.

214 Baptismal Font, ca. 1892
Marble, glass, and glass mosaic; 63 x 42 in (160 x 106.7 cm)
Unsigned; from the baptistry of the World's Columbian Exposition Chapel
CHMF 75-25
The font and its cover form a sphere, which is supported by seven marble columns inlaid with glass tesserae and rests on a two-tiered platform of marble and glass mosaic. The hemispherical font is surfaced with opalescent glass mosaics of interlaced bands and circles set with glass jewels. Opalescent glass spheres encircle the lower margin and the rim has a band of marble dentils set with glass jewels. The domed cover (possibly the prototype for the later lampshades) is of silver-backed glass and glass jewels mounted in lead cames and soldered copper foil.

215 Lectern, ca. 1892
Marble and glass mosaic; H. 54 in (137.2 cm)
Unsigned; from the World's Columbian Exposition Chapel
CHMF 75-26
Of simple line, the lectern rests on three mosaic columns and a mosaic frontal centered with a circumscribed cross and sacred emblems. In describing it, the Tiffany Glass and Decorating Company noted: "In this *Instrumenta Ecclesiastica*, as in all other objects in the chapel, we have attempted to produce something out of the usual line, but at the same time in union with the laws of the Church and in harmony with ecclesiastical traditions. In order that the Lectern should be in harmony with the rest of the chapel furniture, it is made of white marble with inlays of glass mosaic."

216 Standing Candlestick, ca. 1892
Marble and glass mosaic; H. 60 in (152.4 cm)
Unsigned; from the World's Columbian Exposition Chapel
CHMF 75-17
One of a pair of lectern lights that were noted as being "richly inlaid with glass mosaics and marble."

217 Elements from the Electrolier, ca. 1892
Gilded metal and glass
Unsigned; from the World's Columbian Exposition
Chapel
CHMF 74-25

In its original configuration, this extraordinary electrified chandelier was in the form of a Latin cross mounted with panels of stained glass and set with glass turtleback tiles illuminated by concealed lights. The four arms of the cross intersected below a crown of gilded metal set with turtleback tiles, glass spheres, and lightbulbs in floriform sockets. A screen of chains set with opalescent spheres of glass descended from the crown terminating in a circle of pendant light bulbs. Tiffany, who had worked with Thomas Edison on the design of the lighting for the Lyceum Theatre in New York in 1885, was widely acclaimed for this electrolier and for the harmonious integration of the technology of electricity into its design.

222

Laurelton Hall

With the death of his father in 1902, Louis Tiffany inherited his share of the vast fortune that Charles L. Tiffany had amassed through Tiffany & Company. From the estate, Louis purchased the house he occupied at 72nd and Madison Avenue and, in the same year, aquired additional property on Long Island comprising 580 acres and an old resort hotel named Laurelton Hall. Upon completion of the latter transaction, the resort was closed to the public, the hotel was demolished, and Tiffany began planning a new house to occupy the imposing site overlooking Cold Spring Harbor and Long Island Sound. Designing a house was not a new experience for Tiffany who, in addition to the numerous interior design commissions he had executed, had already designed the mansion at 72nd and Madison Avenue and The Briars on Long Island. In approaching this project, however, Tiffany was to direct his now mature mastery of his diverse talent into the creation of a complete artistic environment that was to encompass not only the architecture of the house but the modeling of the surrounding landscape as well. Although the working drawings for the house were prepared by a young architect employed by the Tiffany Studios, the design was exclusively Tiffany's. A contemporary reporter noted that Tiffany "refused to yield to the imprisonment of historic style . . . so false to the ideals of our civilization . . . the painter determined to work alone and fight out the problem in his own way."[1]

Tiffany's initial approach to the design of his new estate began with a careful study of the site, its topography, its soil, and its surrounding woodlands. His study of the topography dictated his planning for the placement of the house, roads, water courses, lakes, and gardens. The local soil yielded the sand and gravel with which he was to build, and his attention to the woodlands directed the careful integration of his design into the landscape. Of this process, Samuel Howe reported in *Appletons Magazine* that "for a long time the problem resided in models of clay and portfolios of strange and interesting sketches added to and worked over as the spirit moved. They illustrated the position of the trees, the undulating nature of the ground, the actual levels, the outline of the small ponds, and the general character of everything. The most important points were of course settled on the spot, of which the drawing office knew so little that measurements had often to be taken to render possible the completion of that section of the scheme. The place literally grew from the ground up, not from the drawing office down."[2]

The main house, completed in August of 1904, represented the embodiment of Tiffany's unique perception of art and beauty and, like every other manifestation of that perception, was unlike anything that had ever been seen

before. Masterfully situated against the hillside, the house of warm grey stucco with its horizontal bands of windows was capped by a molded copper roof patinated a bluish green. The roof was pierced by a great clock tower fitted with a replica of the Westminster chimes. The house with its attached ancillary structures extended for more than 280 feet. Conforming with the topography of its site, the eighty-four-room complex was constructed on multiple levels and, in addition to a three-story octagonal court with a central fountain and domed ceiling of iridescent glass, a 38-foot-long dining room, and a remarkable living room with several levels, "the complex included ten or so bedrooms, a pipe organ, hanging gardens, terraces, a bowling alley, a squash court, a large conservatory, and an assortment of other subdivisions that defy classification."[3] As an added convenience, "a cork-lined tunnel provided electric-lighted access to the swimming beach."[4] There has been considerable speculation concerning the cost of Laurelton Hall's construction and although Tiffany never revealed the actual cost, McKean has noted that in 1904 the property taxes on the estate were as much as $157,000. The originality of the structure is thus implicit in Samuel Howe's observation that "by no means is it a rich man's house as we understand it to-day, because the dollar does not appear . . . as to beauty, the central court is a gem; . . . the rest of the house is plain."[5]

The emergence of an architectural statement as unique as Laurelton Hall also stimulated interest in the source and influence for its design. Hugh McKean has commented that "the main masses of Laurelton Hall had the molded look of a Pullman car,"[6] and Robert Koch pointed out that "similarly daring and unconventional forms can be found in the works of Gaudi in Spain and of Taut in Germany. . . ."[7] The similarities found in some of the architectural designs of the Belgian architect and designer Henry Van de Velde should also be mentioned. Tiffany was familar with Van de Velde through Samuel Bing, as both had exhibited and executed commissions for Bing's gallery. Tiffany's work was exhibited with furniture, fabrics, and lamps by Van de Velde in 1896 and again in 1898 at the gallery of La Libre Esthétique in Brussels. Herwin Schaefer, noting similarities in windows designed by Tiffany and Van de Velde, observed the "close resemblance in inspiration and intent."[8] The possibility of an aesthetic link between these two important proto-modern designers relative to Laurelton Hall is particularly interesting given Van de Velde's appointment in 1904 as director of the Arts School and School of Arts and Crafts at Weimar, the predecessor of the now famous Bauhaus. Perhaps it was Samuel Howe who most clearly perceived the genesis of Laurelton Hall's design when he noted that the house represented to Tiffany "the desire of his heart on which he centered so many hopes and dreams" and that "the perfume of the Orient and the horse sense of America . . . are seen everywhere."[9]

In the years that followed the construction of Laurelton Hall, Tiffany, having created a living statement of his art ideal, began bringing together the finest examples of his own work and installing his collection there. In 1916 his chapel from the World's Columbian Exposition was salvaged from neglect in the Cathedral of St. John the Divine and installed in a building he had constructed for it on the grounds of the estate.

In 1918 Tiffany created the Louis Comfort Tiffany Foundation with an endowment of $1.5 million and entrusted to it the care and maintenance of Laurelton Hall, its gardens, and his collections, all to be operated as a museum and an art institute. This foundation, through the award of fellowships, invited promising young American artists to spend a season as Mr. Tiffany's guests on the estate. Although the Tiffany Fellows were referred to as students, there was no formal instruction offered. Tiffany, who had stated that "it is my dearest wish to help young artists of our country to appreciate more the study of nature and to assist them in establishing themselves in the art world," proposed that his guests, free of financial pressures and under the patronage of his foundation, pursue their various arts surrounded by the beauty of nature and within an environment that was itself the incarnation of his perception of beauty based upon nature.[10] For at least one of Tiffany's students the "lesson" was not lost; Hugh McKean recalled, "Under one set of circumstances, and perhaps only then, Laurelton Hall seemed to explain itself. At night when the lights in the court hung like Japanese lanterns in a garden, and the slender fountain was changing color slowly, and the globe over it glowed with a soft yellow light, and the organ was playing, and palm trees and flowers were everywhere, and with Louis Tiffany sitting benign and content on a divan among young people whose lives he wanted so much to touch with beauty, Laurelton Hall made a great deal of lovely sense. Then it seemed to state its purpose in clear terms."[11]

It became evident, however, that Tiffany's vision, manifest in both Laurelton Hall and his foundation, was to be realized only through the sheer strength of his own personality; following his death in 1933, change was rapid and inexorable. The house was closed in 1938, and with the United States' entry into World War II the school was closed. In 1946 the trustees of the foundation asked the courts to set aside Tiffany's original plan for the foundation. Permission was granted for the reorganization of the trust, whereupon the trustees declared Laurelton Hall and its collections to be a liability. From September 24th through the 28th of 1946, Parke-Bernet Galleries in New York dispersed the collections at public auction. The remaining land and buildings were sold in 1949; the four-acre tract which contained Laurelton Hall, its gar-

dens, fountains, and yacht harbor sold for only $10,000. At 5:30 p.m. on March 6, 1957, fire was discovered on the top floor of Laurelton Hall. Firemen, hindered by the difficult access through the narrow lane that approached the house and by a shortage of water, were helpless to contain the flames. By midnight the fire was still raging out of control.[12]

Hugh and Jeanette McKean later visited the ruins of Laurelton Hall, and Hugh later recalled, "The view of Cold Spring Harbor and the land running out to the Sound was still beautiful, but charred timbers and twisted pipes made bizarre patterns against the sky, and jagged holes stared where windows should have been."[13] Fortunately, some of the finest parts of the great house escaped destruction, and the McKeans were able to acquire the surviving windows and "everything else the fire and vandals had spared."[14] Much of this material, now safely in the care of the Charles Hosmer Morse Foundation, is included in this exhibition.

1. Samuel Howe, "The Dwelling Place as an Expression of Individuality," *Appletons Magazine* (February 1907), p. 157.

2. Ibid.

3. Hugh F. McKean, *The "Lost" Treasures of Louis Comfort Tiffany* (Garden City, N.Y., 1980) p. 113.

4. Ibid.

5. Howe, p. 156. This observation was by no means derogatory. Howe also mentions that although the house was notable for many things, these could be expressed in the three words modernity, utility, and beauty. As regarded modernity, Howe was obviously delighted by Tiffany's "absence of cornices to passages and bedrooms; the preserving of the best views from the windows, even though it entailed a breach in an architectural law; the substitution of cement for tiles or mosaic in the floors and on the side walls of the bathrooms; and the large number of these practical luxuries; and the great whole-souled handling of primitive materials in almost a primitive manner. . ." (p. 161).

6. McKean, p. 113.

7. Robert Koch, *Louis C. Tiffany, Rebel in Glass* (New York, 1964), p. 144.

8. Herwin Schaefer, "Tiffany's Fame in Europe," *Art Bulletin* 44 (December 1962), p. 316. Schaefer discusses at some length Tiffany's association with Van de Velde and Van de Velde's little-known use of stained glass.

9. Howe, p. 156.

10. Louis Comfort Tiffany, quoted by McKean, p. 265.

11. Ibid., p. 125.

12. *New York Herald Tribune*, March 6, 1957.

13. McKean, p. xi.

14. Ibid., p. 144.

224

218   Seven Architectural Drawings for Laurelton Hall,
ca. 1903
a. First floor plan, 27 x 49⅜ in (68.6 x 125.3 cm)
b. Second floor plan, 27 x 49 in (68.6 x 124.5 cm)
c. Third floor plan, 20⅛ x 37⅛ in (51.1 x 94.3 cm)
d. Elevation looking north, 24 x 52⅜ in (70 x 132.9 cm)
e. Elevation looking east, 24 x 28½ in (70 x 72.4 cm)
f. Elevation looking west, 24 x 28½ in (70 x 72.4 cm)
g. Elevation looking south, 23 x 51½ in (58.4 x 130.8 cm)
Ink on linen
Each drawing inscribed: *Residence for L.C. Tiffany/Cold
Springs Harbor/R.L. Pryor/Architect/341 4th Avenue
New York; Scale 3/16 = 1 foot*
CHMF ARCHIVE
Louis Comfort Tiffany designed Laurelton Hall; however, Robert L. Pryor, who was employed by Tiffany Studios, provided technical details and working drawings.
The address noted on the drawings is that of the Tiffany
block: 333-341 4th Avenue, New York.

**219   A Model for the Smokestack,
Laurelton Hall,** after 1904
Wood; H. 60 in (152.4 cm)
Unsigned
CHMF 60-9
The smokestack was for a remote power plant located on
the estate. As constructed, it rose sixty feet high and was
set with iridescent blue mosaics.

220   View from the Stables, Laurelton Hall, by Alan
Dunn (b. 1900), ca. 1925
Watercolor; 14¾ x 20¾ in (37.3 x 52.6 cm)
CHMF P-5-73-O

221   The Garden Side of Laurelton Hall, by Alan Dunn
(b. 1900), ca. 1925
Watercolor; 14¾ x 20¾ in (37.3 x 52.6 cm)
CHMF P-5-73-P

222   The Garden Facade of Laurelton Hall, by Alan
Dunn (b. 1900), ca. 1925
Watercolor; 13¾ x 20½ in (34.8 x 52 cm)
CHMF P-5-73-L
This watercolor illustrates the Poppy Loggia, now
installed in the American Wing at the Metropolitan
Museum of Art, New York.

225

223   View of the Daffodil Terrace, Laurelton Hall,
by Alan Dunn (b. 1900), ca. 1925
Watercolor; 13¾ x 20¾ in (34.8 x 52.6 cm)
CHMF P-5-73-1

224   Daffodil Capitals from the Daffodil Terrace,
after 1904
Cement and Favrile glass; Each H. 22¼ in (56.5 cm)
Unsigned
CHMF 57-23K, 57-23L
These cement capitals are set with green Favrile glass
tesserae which form stems that intersect and flare outward above a rope-shaped cement collar and terminate in
fully modeled daffodil blossoms of yellow Favrile glass.
The capitals crowned the elegant sixteen-sided columns
that supported the polychromed, cross-timbered roof of
the Daffodil Terrace, adjacent to the dining room.

225   Two Pear Tree Panels from the Daffodil Terrace,
after 1904
Favrile glass tiles and wood; Each 25¼ x 59½ in (64.1 x
151.1 cm)
Unsigned
CHMF 59-4 and 59-7
The foliage, fruit, branches, and twigs of a pear tree are
depicted in the Favrile glass of these iridescent, opaque
plaques set into a wooden lattice. Designed to be viewed
from below, and against the sky, the panels filled the
fascias of an opening through the roof of the Daffodil
Terrace. This opening was provided to accommodate
a pear tree growing on the site when the terrace
was constructed.

226　Wall Covering from the Court at Laurelton Hall,
ca. 1904
Oil on canvas; 136½ x 48 in (346.7 x 121.9 cm)
Unsigned
CHMF 58-20
The design for this stenciled polychrome wall covering
and its border was taken from a ceramic tile mural in the
Topkapi Palace, Istanbul, Turkey.

**227　Ornamental Plaque Found in the Ruins of
Laurelton Hall,** ca. 1900
Painted plaster and glass; 24 x 23 in (60.9 x 58.4 cm)
Unsigned
CHMF 57-33
Relief plaster of foliate forms on a ground of blue and
green and set with glass jewels.

**228　Ornamental Plaque Found in the Ruins of
Laurelton Hall,** 1922
Painted plaster; 28¾ x 23½ in (72.9 x 59.7 cm)
Signed: *E. Novara* (?)
CHMF 57-32
Relief plaster panel depicting philodendron leaves.

**229　Ornamental Plaque Found in the Ruins of
Laurelton Hall,** ca. 1900
Painted plaster and glass; 33½ x 24¾ in (85.1 x 62.7 cm)
Unsigned
CHMF 57-29
The plaster surface, modeled in low relief floriform
designs, is painted and set with blue and green glass.
Possibly predating Laurelton Hall, the original context
for this panel and nos. 227 and 228 is unknown.

**230　Medallion Carpet from the Dining Room at
Laurelton Hall,** after 1908
Wool; 25 ft 7 in x 8 ft 8 in (779.8 x 238.7 cm)
Unsigned
CHMF 67-12
On a ground of mazarine blue, a central white medallion
of floral and arabesque detail, surrounded by stylized
cranes with out-stretched wings, is flanked by two
smaller medallions of similar design. A broad border at
each end repeats the designs of cranes and arabesques.
This carpet is one of three that, placed side by side,
covered the floor of the dining room. Two semi-octagonal
carpets of similar design in mazarine blue on a white
ground filled the bays at each end of the room. The design
of the medallions was repeated overhead in the leaded
glass shade (no. 234).

226

231

231 Dining Table, ca. 1904
Painted wood; H. 29½ in (74.9 cm) DIAM. 71 in
(180.3 cm)
Unsigned; designed by Louis Comfort Tiffany and
probably made by Schmitt Brothers
CHMF 58-10-1
Painted in a warm grey enamel; the top of the octagonal
table rests on a recessed drum with a flared skirt that
conforms to the eight angular cabriole legs which
terminate in round pad feet. This is one of three similar
tables made for the room, its design brilliantly integrating
elements of the Arts and Crafts style with those of the
Orient.

232 Three Side Chairs, ca. 1904
Painted wood; 43½ x 15 x 17 in (110.5 x 38.1 x 43.2 cm)
Unsigned; designed by Louis Comfort Tiffany and
probably made by Schmitt Brothers
CHMF 58-10-3, 58-10-6, 58-10-7
En suite with the table (no. 231) and painted the same
warm grey; the chair backs have a simple, deep crest rail
above three flat columnar slats between tapered stiles.
The rounded skirt rails conform to the knees of the four
H-stretchered cabriole legs that terminate in round pad
feet. The fabric on the seats is not original.

233 Arm Chair, ca. 1904
Painted wood; 45 x 18 x 18½ in (114.3 x 45.7 x 47 cm)
Unsigned; designed by Louis Comfort Tiffany and
probably made by Schmitt Brothers
CHMF 58-10-2
En suite with the table (no. 231) and the chairs (no. 232);
this chair is larger and fitted with arms.

**234 Ceiling Light from the Dining Room at Laurelton
Hall,** after 1904
Favrile glass and iron; DIAM. 66 in (167.6 cm)
Unsigned
CHMF 70-21
The shade, in the form of a medallion of Favrile glass in
shades of pink, blue, purple, and amber, repeats the
design of the medallions in the carpets (see no. 230).
The soldered copper foil joints have been silvered.

232, 233

Awards and Decorations

Louis Comfort Tiffany exhibited his art at the American Centennial Exhibition in Philadelphia in 1876 and at every major international exposition for the next forty years. For his efforts, he received innumerable awards and decorations, ranging from an incredible fifty-four medals at Chicago in 1893 to being named a chevalier of the Ordre National de la Légion d'Honneur, Paris, 1901.

235 Gold Medal
Internationale Kunstausstellung
Dresden, 1901
CHMF 68-51

236 Gold Medal
Panama-Pacific International Exposition
San Francisco, 1915
CHMF 68-56

237 Silver Medal
Panama-Pacific International Exposition
San Francisco, 1915
CHMF 68-58

238 Certificate to Accompany the Silver Medal
Pan-American Exposition
Buffalo, 1901
CHMF ARCHIVE

239 Gold Medal
Louisiana Purchase Exposition
St. Louis, 1904
CHMF 68-53

240 Gold Medal
Exposition Universelle Internationale
Paris, 1900
CHMF 68-46

241 Certificate, Medal for Specific Merit
The World's Columbian Exposition
Chicago, 1893
CHMF 68-60-5

242 Certificate, Medal for Specific Merit
The World's Columbian Exposition
Chicago, 1893
CHMF 68-60-4

243 Medal
Ordre National de la Légion d'Honneur
Paris, January 30, 1901
CHMF 68-50

244 Certificate
Ordre National de la Légion d'Honneur
Paris, January 30, 1901
CHMF 68-60-27

Tiffany's Contemporaries

In addition to the art of Louis Comfort Tiffany, a representative sampling of works by contemporary artists and artisans has been included in the exhibition.

245 Emile Gallé (French, 1846–1904)
Vase, ca. 1900
Glass; H. 21 in (53.3 cm)
Inscribed: *Gallé*
CHMF GL-28-69
Tall, cylindrical vase with glass marquetry in purple and green cut to designs of iris blossoms, stems, and foliage.

Emile Gallé was the leading exponent of French Art Nouveau glass, as well as a designer of furniture in the same style. Well known throughout Europe and the United States by 1900, he ran a large factory that turned out a considerable quantity of unique glassware. Many of these were sold by the noted art dealer, S. Bing, in his Salon de l'Art Nouveau, where Tiffany glass was also exhibited. Gallé's work was also sold by Tiffany & Company in New York by 1893.

245, 246

246 Emile Gallé (French, 1846–1904)
Vase, ca. 1900
Glass; H. 14½ in (36.8 cm)
Inscribed: *Cristallerie Emile Gallé, A Nancy/Modèle et Décor Déposés* (acid etched)
CHMF GL-3-69
Vase with low, globular body and a tall, cylindrical neck decorated with etched and raised flowers and foliage; enameled in yellow, orange, brown, green, and purple highlighted with gold.

Tiffany was well aware of Gallé's glass, having seen it both in New York and Paris at the time that Tiffany was developing his own art glass. Parallels may be seen in the selection of motifs from nature, the skillful exploitation of imperfections in the glass, the eclectic nature of their sources, and the emphasis on the ductility and translucency of the medium. In contrast to Gallé, Tiffany preferred more brilliant, saturated colors, simpler ornamentation, and a more abstract overall design. Tiffany went far beyond Gallé in his desire to see the decorative elements evolve within the initial formation of the glass vessel itself.

247

247 Steuben Glass Works, Corning, New York
Vase, ca. 1905
Aurene glass; 8½ x 7 in (21.6 x 17.8 cm)
Inscribed: *Steuben Aurene 6297*
CHMF U-81
Flat, fan-shaped vase on a flat circular foot, iridescent blue with iridescent gold and white.

The Steuben Glass Works was founded in 1903 and functioned independently until 1918 when it was absorbed by Corning Glass Works. Steuben was managed by the innovative glass artist Frederick Carder (1864–1963) who developed the iridescent glass called Aurene, one of a number of modern decorative styles in which the firm specialized. Aurene glass was registered with the patent office in 1904, but was only fully developed for production in 1905. In some cases the Steuben glass so closely resembled Tiffany's glass that Tiffany, fearing such competition in the market place, threatened in 1913 to file suit against Carder. Among other things, he charged that Carder had learned of Tiffany's methods by employing a workman who had been trained in Tiffany's own studios. Tiffany's action was discontinued in 1914.

248 Maria Longworth (Nichols) Storer (American, 1849–1932)
Rookwood Pottery, Cincinnati
Vase, ca. 1900
Ceramic, bronze, and semi-precious stones; H. 15½ in (39.4 cm)
Inscribed: *M.L.S.* for Maria Longworth Storer
CHMF M-52-66
Glazed ceramic ovoid vessel mounted in "ropes" of bronze which trail down the bronze standard, modeled as waves of the sea and including seahorses and an octopus. The whole is set with pearls, tiger's eyes, and moonstones.

More famous as the founder of the Rookwood Pottery, Storer also worked in metals. She received a gold medal for her pottery and metal work at the Paris Exposition of 1900.

249 Kataro Shirayamadani (Japanese, 1865–1948)
Rookwood Pottery, Cincinnati
Vase, dated 1900
Ceramic and silver-plated copper on ceramic; H. 18½ in (47 cm)
Inscribed: K. Shirayamadani (in Japanese characters)
Rookwood 1900/S1537
CHMF PO-60-66
Conical ceramic vase with glaze of ochre and raw umber, mounted in silver in the form of an octopus resting on base of sand and sea shells.

A native of Japan, Kataro Shirayamadani was invited to join the decorating staff of Rookwood Pottery in 1877, and worked for them almost continuously until the end of his life. He was tremendously influential in introducing many of the decorative Japanese motifs which characterize much of the Rookwood pottery; he also designed many of the standard Rookwood pottery shapes.

250 Artus Van Briggle (American, 1869–1904)
Rookwood Pottery, Cincinnati
Vase, 1892
Ceramic; H. 12 in (30.5 cm)
Inscribed: Rookwood monogram *RP* with six flames
Incised: *A.V.B.* for Artus Van Briggle
CHMF PO-57-67
Bulbous body with swirling, concentric ridges and a high neck flared at the lip. Decorated with under-the-glaze slip-painted sprigs of cherries and foliage in yellow, orange, and brown on a high gloss ground shaded from dark brown to light orange.

Van Briggle was associated with the Rookwood Pottery between 1887 and 1899. Two years after the production of this vase, the Pottery sent him to Paris on a scholarship to study painting and clay modeling. His subsequent exposure to Art Nouveau played an important role in his later work at the Rookwood Pottery and had an additional impact on his colleagues there.

251 Albert Valentien (American, 1862–1925)
Rookwood Pottery, Cincinnati
Vase, 1890
Ceramic; H. 11¼ in (28.6 cm)
Inscribed: *Rookwood 1890/488F/W* and *A.R.V.* for Albert R. Valentien
CHMF PO-59-66
Ovoid vase with flared neck, the surfaces modeled with pitcher plants, the exterior glazed in brown and burnt orange, the interior in yellow.

Albert Valentien joined the Rookwood Pottery in 1881 as their first full-time decorator, became head of the decorating department, and remained there until 1903. A 1907 commission from Miss Ellen Scripps to paint all of the California wild flowers prompted Valentien to move to San Diego where he and his wife established the Valentien Pottery.

252   A. F. Best
J. B. Owens Pottery, Zanesville, Ohio
Vase, undated
Ceramic; H. 12 in (30.5 cm)
Vase inscribed: *J. B. Owens/Utopian/1025*
Portrait inscribed: *A. F. Best*
CHMF PO-7-65
Ovoid vase with short, narrow neck, decorated under the glaze with a slip-painted portrait identified by an inscription under the glaze: *Wanstall/Arapahoe*.

The J. B. Owens Pottery Company, which operated between 1896 and 1906, was one of a number of successful potteries established in Zanesville, Ohio. A considerable corps of decorators was employed, including A. F. Best. The mark "Utopian" refers to a distinct variety or style of ware produced by J. B. Owens of which this vase is an example.

253   Jacques Sicard (American, 1865–1923)
S. A. Weller Pottery, Zanesville, Ohio
Vase, 1901–1907
Ceramic; H. 5 ½ in (14 cm)
Inscribed: *Weller Sicard*; impressed: 29
CHMF PO-47-69
Low, four-lobed vase with tapered body and two handles, decorated with flowers and foliage on a spotted ground in iridescent amber, magenta, purple, and blue.

Before coming to the S. A. Weller Pottery, Jacques Sicard had worked at the French pottery of Clement Massier where he experimented with lustre glazes inspired by Hispano-Moresque pottery. At Weller, Sicard was noted for his decoration in metallic lustres on an iridescent ground.

254   Ruth Erickson (American)
Grueby Pottery, Boston
Vase, 1905
Ceramic; H. 16¾ in (42.4 cm)
Inscribed: *Grueby Pottery, Boston, U.S.A.*, with the Ruth Erickson monogram, and *8/17/05*
CHMF PO-9-66
Large, elongated oval vase, the surface modeled in low relief with stylized daisy blossoms and attenuated foliage; apple green matte glaze with the blossoms in yellow and white.

Ruth Erickson was one of a number of artists, primarily young women, who decorated pottery for Grueby.

255   Grueby Pottery, Boston
Vase, ca. 1899–1910
Ceramic; H. 11 in (27.9 cm)
Inscribed: *Boston, U.S.A.*
Retains original paper label of the Grueby Pottery, Boston
CHMF PO-72-66

249, 251, 250

Ovoid body with flared, ruffled lip, the surfaces modeled in low relief with narcissus blossoms and foliage; rough textured green glaze with matte finish, the blossoms picked out in color.

The Grueby Faience Company, Inc. began producing art pottery in 1897, and continued under the name of Grueby Pottery from 1898 until around 1909 to 1911. Grueby's wares won considerable acclaim, including one silver and two gold medals at the Paris Exposition in 1900.

256   Pewabic Pottery, Detroit
Vase, ca. 1903
Ceramic; H. 19 in (48.3 cm)
Inscribed: *Pewabic Detroit* (circular mark)
CHMF PO-22-71
Baluster-shaped vase with marbled pattern of iridescent glazes of green, blue, purple, brown, and ochre.

Mary Chase Perry (1867–1961) opened the Pewabic Pottery in Detroit in 1903. Her early wares showed the influence of the pioneer French potter Auguste Delaherche as well as the styles of the French Art Nouveau movement. Perry concentrated on glaze chemistry, producing the much-sought-after "Egyptian blue," a superb iridescent glaze.

254, 255

257   George E. Ohr (American, 1857–1918)
Pitcher, undated
Ceramic; H. 4 ½ in (11.4 cm)
Inscribed: *G.C. Ohr* (in script)
CHMF PO-18-75
Freeform cream pitcher with "pinched" handle and a violet glaze.

After making a two-year, sixteen-state tour of the nation's potteries, George Ohr returned to his hometown of Biloxi, Mississippi, and set up his own workshop. The initial shop, which burned in 1893, was rebuilt and operated until 1909. Ohr's work is characterized by innovative, gestural play as exemplified in this vase. In addition, Ohr was involved in an expression which included erotic-humorous subjects where words were played with as freely as clay. This expression was strangely prophetic of the ceramic work of the 1960s and 1970s.

258   Rozenberg near The Hague
Vase, 1900–1913
Porcelain; H. 6¾ in (17 cm)
Inscribed: with the Rozenberg den Haag mark
CHMF PO-2-71
Baluster-shaped vase of square section and narrow neck, painted decoration of stylized flowers and swirls.

About 1900 this faience factory began producing an eggshell porcelain. It was often painted from designs by J. Schelling and R. Stehren in the Art Nouveau style, with a preference for yellow, green, and purple.

259   Riessner and Kessel, Bohemia
Statuette, ca. 1892
Ceramic; H. 21 in (53.3 cm)
Inscribed: *Imperial Amphora Turn*, with the crowned Amphora/Austria mark, and *775/G21*
CHMF PO-6-70
Figure of a woman in gilt gown with arms extended and resting upon large leaves which serve as trays—the base having a female head, the hair of which evolves as water forms.

Reissner and Kessel's "Amphora" porcelain factory was established in 1892 at Turn-Teplitz in Bohemia. Its products won prizes at several international exhibitions, including the World's Columbian Exposition in Chicago in 1893 and the California Midwinter Fair in San Francisco in 1893-4. Earthenware vases of highly imaginative Art Nouveau forms with stylized leaf and flower motifs were a specialty, and porcelain figures along the same lines were also produced.

260   Globe attributed to Witwe Löetz Glasshouse
Base attributed to **Peter Behrens** (German, 1868–1940)
Table Lamp, ca. 1900
Glass and silvered pewter; H. 23 in (58.4 cm)
Unmarked
CHMF M-27-69
Globe of yellow decoration in gold, blue, and silver. Base is silverplated cast pewter in the highly stylized form of two female figures, each holding large moonstones and wearing headdresses set with moonstones.

At one time as well known as Tiffany in the United States and Gallé in France, Löetz glass was produced in Klostermühle, Bohemia. Shortly before 1900 the Löetz glasshouse began producing iridescent Art Nouveau glass vessels similar to, and probably inspired by, Tiffany Favrile glass. In contrast to Tiffany's production, Löetz glass remains anonymous, as it relates to corporate rather than individual production.

The great German architect and industrial designer Peter Behrens was perhaps the first to design for mass production. Initially a designer of glass, porcelain, metal work, and jewelry, he experimented briefly with the elaborate curvilinear forms of Art Nouveau. Soon, however, Behrens evolved a more enduring style of monumental simplicity, characterized by an unprecedented honesty of function and materials.

261   Charles Ashbee (English, 1863–1942)
Coffret, undated
Wood and silvered metal with enamel; 3 x 5¼ x 3⅞ in (7.6 x 13.3 x 9.7 cm)
Inscribed: the *CA* monogram and the number *5*
CHMF 70-3
Small rectangular wooden box, covered with silver, raised on four splayed feet. The top bears decoration in the form of a tree branch over blue, green, yellow, and pink enameling, surrounded by curvilinear designs.

Charles Robert Ashbee designed furniture in a lighter version of the style originated by William Morris, and silver and metalwork in a style which would now be called Art Nouveau, although Ashbee himself would have denied the name. A principal organizer of the Arts and Crafts movement in England, Ashbee founded the Guild and School of Handicraft. His own work and that of the School was exhibited widely in England and on the continent.

262   Liberty, London
Carriage Clock, after 1903
Metal, glass, and enamel, with French movement; 5½ x 4¼ x 4 in (8 x 10.8 x 10.2 cm)
Inscribed: *Tudric/0721/04boe 5530*
CHMF 70-4
Metal cased clock with carrying handle, with designs of ivy at the corners of the glazed front, the face enameled on copper in blue and green with Roman numerals in black.

Like S. Bing, Sir Arthur Lasenby Liberty (1843–1917) was a producer and dealer in Art Nouveau, but not a designer. He was both Bing's forerunner and his English counterpart. In 1903, he introduced a new type of pewter, with a high proportion of silver in the alloy, which he called "Tudric" and of which this clock is made. The organic motif and enamel work on this clock are also characteristic of many of the objects marketed by Liberty, both in London and in Paris, after 1899.

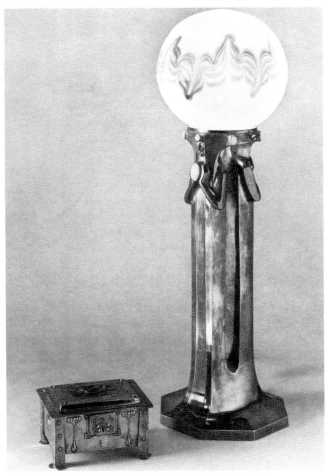

261, 260

263   Alf. Daquet (French)
Shelf Clock, after 1895
Wood, copper and colored glass "jewels"; H. 16¼ in (41.3 cm)
Inscribed: *Cuivres S. Bing/Alf. Daquet* (in repoussé)
CHMF M-45-66
Arrow-shaped clock covered with copper sheeting; overall thorn design set with opalescent and colored glass jewels.

Daquet was most likely the designer of this clock, which was marketed by the Paris dealer S. Bing in his Salon de l'Art Nouveau. The shop was opened in 1895 and carried the works of the leading Art Nouveau craftsmen, including Tiffany, and the paintings of Bonnard, Toulouse-Lautrec, Vuillard, and Munch, among others.

264　E. Maurel (French)
Vase, undated
Gilt bronze; H. 12¼ in (31.1 cm)
Inscribed: *E. Maurel*
CHMF 60-5
Flattened bulbous body with incurvate, elongated neck
and sinuous conforming open handles terminating in a
woman's face at the top. The base is decorated with a
cluster of flowers.

265　Joseph J. Emmanuel Descombs (French,
1869–1950)
Statuette, ca. 1925
Bronze and ivory; H. 15¼ in (38.7 cm)
Inscribed: *Joe Descomps*
CHMF MET-5-71
Standing female figure of bronze and ivory on a
marble base.
　The artist, Joseph Descombs, whose name was actually
Cormier, exhibited regularly at the Paris Salons where he
received medals in 1921, 1925, and 1928.

266　Quezal Art Glass and Decorating Company
Vase, ca. 1905
Quezal glass; H. 3¾ in (9.4 cm)
Inscribed: *Quezal*
CHMF GL-59-79
Low, bulbous body with raised and flared neck. The gold
iridescent glass is cased in green with iridescent gold.
　Established in Brooklyn, New York, by two former
employees of Louis Comfort Tiffany, the Quezal Art
Glass and Decorating Company was one of the first firms
to imitate his iridescent glass. The firm took its name from
the gaily colored quezal bird of Central America.

267　Joseph Fortune Meyer (American, 1848–1931)
Vase, ca. 1900
Ceramic; H. 6⅝ in (16.7 cm)
Inscribed: *NC* monogram (incised); *L.H.T.*; the Joseph
Meyer monogram; and *AK88*
CHMF PO-48-67
Pyriform vase with engraved, geometric, and stylized
floral forms with high gloss glazes in blues, white,
and green.
　Joseph Meyer was born in France and emigrated to
Biloxi, Mississippi. In 1886 he became one of the first
potters at the New Orleans Art Pottery Company, where
he was joined for a time by artist potter George E. Ohr
(see no. 257). In 1896 Meyer joined the Newcomb Pottery, a unique experiment by the Sophie Newcomb
Memorial College, the women's division of Tulane University in New Orleans. Meyer remained the primary
thrower at the Pottery until 1928.

Selected Bibliography

Books

Amaya, Mario. *Tiffany Glass.* New York: Walker and Co., 1976.

Arwas, Victor. *Glass: Art Nouveau to Art Deco.* New York: Rizzoli International Publications, 1977.

Bing, Samuel. *Artistic America, Tiffany Glass, and Art Nouveau.* Cambridge, Massachusetts: The MIT Press, 1970.

Carpenter, Charles H., Jr., with Mary Grace Carpenter. *Tiffany Silver.* New York: Dodd, Mead & Company, 1978.

Clark, Garth. *A Century of Ceramics in the United States 1878–1978.* New York: E. P. Dutton, 1979.

DeKay, Charles (anonymous author). *The Art Work of Louis Comfort Tiffany.* New York: Doubleday, Page & Company, 1914.

Doros, Paul. *The Tiffany Collection of the Chrysler Museum at Norfolk.* Norfolk, Virginia: The Chrysler Museum at Norfolk, 1978.

Duncan, Alistair. *Light and Landscape in Tiffany Windows.* New York: Simon and Schuster, 1980.

Glover, Ray and Lee. *Art Glass Nouveau.* Rutland, Vermont: Charles E. Tuttle Co., Inc., 1967.

Johnson, Diane Chalmers. *American Art Nouveau.* New York: Harry N. Abrams, Inc., 1979.

Koch, Robert. *Louis Comfort Tiffany's Glass-Bronzes-Lamps: A Complete Collector's Guide.* New York: Crown Publishers, Inc., 1971.

Koch, Robert. *Louis C. Tiffany's Art Glass.* New York: Crown Publishers, Inc., 1977.

Koch, Robert, *Louis C. Tiffany, Rebel in Glass.* New York: Crown Publishers, Inc., 1964.

McKean, Hugh F. *Revolt in the Parlor.* Winter Park, Florida: Parlor Press, 1969.

McKean, Hugh F. *The "Lost" Treasures of Louis Comfort Tiffany.* Garden City, New York: Doubleday & Co., Inc., 1980.

Neustadt, Egon. *The Lamps of Tiffany.* New York: The Fairfield Press, 1970.

Paton, J. *Lamps: A Collector's Guide.* London: Souvenir Press, 1978.

Peck, Herbert. *The Book of Rookwood Pottery.* New York: Crown Publishers, Inc., 1972.

Polak, A. *Glass: Its Maker and Its Public.* London: Weidenfeld and Nichols, 1975.

Purtell, Joseph. *The Tiffany Touch.* New York: Random House, Inc., 1971.

Revi, Albert Christian. *American Art Nouveau Glass.* Camden, New Jersey: Thomas Nelson and Sons, 1968.

Speenburgh, Gertrude. *The Arts of the Tiffanys.* Chicago: Lightner Publishing Corporation, 1956.

A Synopsis of the Exhibit of the Tiffany Glass and Decorating Company in the Section of the Manufactures and Liberal Arts Building at the World's Fair. . . . New York: Tiffany Glass and Decorating Company, 1893.

Tiffany & Co. Blue Book. New series, vol. XVII. New York: Tiffany & Co., Publishers, 1910.

Truman, Ben. C. *History of the World's Fair.* Philadelphia: Mammoth Publishing Company, 1893.

Wheeler, Candace. *Yesterdays in a Busy Life.* New York: Harper Brothers, 1918.

Articles

Bordes, Marilynn Johnson. "Stained Glass of Tiffany and La Farge in The Met's New Wing." *Nineteenth Century* (Autumn 1980): 36–38.

Carpenter, Charles H. "The Silver of Louis Comfort Tiffany." *Antiques* 117 (February 1980): 390–7.

Craven, Wayne. "Samuel Colman (1832–1980): Rediscovered Painter of Far-Away Places." *The American Art Journal* 8, no. 1 (May 1976): 16–37.

Deisroth, Barbara. "Tiffany Today." *Nineteenth Century* 4, part 1 (Spring 1978): 62–9.

Doros, Paul E. "Tiffany Glass at the Chrysler Museum, Norfolk, Va." *Antiques* 111 (April 1977): 746–50.

Duncan, Alistair. "Light and Landscape in Tiffany Windows." *Connaissance des Arts* (November 1980): 105–112.

Eidelberg, Martin P. "Tiffany Favrile Pottery, A New Study of a Few Known Facts." *Connoisseur* 169 (September 1968): 57–61.

Faude, Wilson H. "Associated Artists and the American Renaissance in the Decorative Arts." *Winterthur Portfolio* 10 (1975): 101–130.

Feld, Stuart P. "Nature in Her Most Seductive Aspects: Louis Comfort Tiffany's Favrile Glass." *The Metropolitan Museum of Art Bulletin* 21 (November 1962): 101–12.

Hamlin, A. D. F. "L'Art Nouveau, Its Origin and Development." *The Craftsman* 3, no. 3 (December 1902): 129–143.

Howe, Samuel. "The Dwelling Place as an Expression of Individuality, The House of Louis C. Tiffany." *Appletons Magazine* (February 1907): 157–163.

——. "An American Country House." *The International Studio* (February 1908): 294–296.

Koch, Robert. "Glass as Ornament: From Richardson to Wright." *Record of The Art Museum, Princeton University* 34, no. 2 (1975): 28–35.

Koch, Robert. "Louis C. Tiffany's Collection of Japanese Art." *Society for Architectural Historians Journal* 35 (December 1976): 300–308.

Koch, Robert. "Tiffany's Abstractions in Glass." *Antiques* 105 (June 1974): 1290–94.

McKean, Hugh F. "Tiffany Windows." *American Craft* (October/November 1980): 29–33.

O'Neal, William B. "Three Art Nouveau Glass Makers." *Journal of Glass Studies* 2 (1960): 125–137.

Saks, Judith. "Tiffany's Household Decoration—A Landscape Window." *The Bulletin of the Cleveland Museum of Art* (October 1976) 227–234.

Schaefer, Herwin. "Tiffany's Fame in Europe." *Art Bulletin* 44 (December 1962): 309–28.

Schopfer, Jean. "L'Art Nouveau." *The Craftsman* 3, no. 4 (July 1903): 229–238.

"Tiffany Glass and Decorating Company's Exhibit at the Columbian Exposition." *The Decorator and Furnisher* 23 (October 1893): 9–12.

Tiffany, Louis C. "What is the Quest of Beauty?." *The International Studio* 58 (April 1916): lxiii.

"The Unexpected Art of Louis Comfort Tiffany." *American Heritage* (October/November 1979): 54–61.

Weinberg, Helene Barbara. "The Early Stained Glass Works of John La Farge (1835–1910)." *Stained Glass* 67 (Summer 1972): 4–16.

Weinberg, Gabriel P. "Samuel Bing: Patron of Art Nouveau." *Connoisseur* 172 (December 1969): 296–299.

Williams, Virginia. "Candace Wheeler, Textile Designer for Associated Artists." *Nineteenth Century* 6, no. 2 (Summer 1980): 60–61.

Exhibition Catalogues

The Art of Louis Comfort Tiffany. The Toledo Museum of Art, Toledo, Ohio, November 12–December 17, 1978.

The Arts of Louis Comfort Tiffany and his Times. John and Mable Ringling Museum of Art, Sarasota, Florida, February 7–June 1, 1975.

Beauty Fixed in Many Mediums; an Exhibition of the Works of Louis Comfort Tiffany from the Collection of Hugh and Jeanette McKean. Art Gallery, Florida State University, Tallahassee, Florida, 1972.

Clark, Robert Judson, ed. *The Arts and Crafts Movement in America.* The Art Museum, Princeton University, Princeton, New Jersey, 1972.

Koch, Robert, Thomas S. Tibbs, and Robert Laurer. *Louis Comfort Tiffany.* Museum of Contemporary Crafts of the American Craftsmen's Council, New York, January 24–April 6, 1958.

Lewis, Anne Suydam. *Lockwood de Forest: Painter, Importer, Decorator.* Heckscher Museum, Huntington, New York, 1976.

Reynolds, Gary A. *Louis Comfort Tiffany: The Paintings.* The Grey Art Gallery and Study Center, New York University, March 20–May 12, 1979.

Tiffany's Tiffany. The Corning Museum of Glass, Corning, New York, June 1–November 2, 1980.

Tracy, Berry B. *19th Century America, Furniture and Other Decorative Arts.* The Metropolitan Museum of Art, New York, 1970.

Works of Art by Louis Comfort Tiffany. Morse Gallery of Art, Rollins College, Winter Park, Florida, February 21–March 31, 1955.

Claire Thacker

with Herbert Puchta and Jeff Stranks

English in Mind

* Teacher's Book 2

CAMBRIDGE
UNIVERSITY PRESS

PUBLISHED BY THE PRESS SYNDICATE OF THE UNIVERSITY OF CAMBRIDGE
The Pitt Building, Trumpington Street, Cambridge, United Kingdom

CAMBRIDGE UNIVERSITY PRESS
The Edinburgh Building, Cambridge CB2 2RU, UK
40 West 20th Street, New York, NY 10011–4211, USA
477 Williamstown Road, Port Melbourne, VIC 3207, Australia
Ruiz de Alarcón 13, 28014 Madrid, Spain
Dock House, The Waterfront, Cape Town 8001, South Africa

http://www.cambridge.org

© Cambridge University Press 2004

First published 2004
Third printing 2005

Printed in the United Kingdom at the University Press, Cambridge

Typefaces Agenda, Celeste. *System* QuarkXPress® [Pentacor]

A catalogue record for this book is available from the British Library

Library of Congress Cataloguing in Publication data

ISBN 0 521 75060 1 Teacher's Book
ISBN 0 521 75055 5 Student's Book
ISBN 0 521 75059 8 Workbook with Audio CD / CD-ROM
ISBN 0 521 75061 X Teacher's Resource Pack
ISBN 0 521 75062 8 Class Cassettes
ISBN 0 521 54505 6 Class Audio CDs

Contents

Map of Student's Book   4
Introduction   6

Teacher's notes and keys

Module 1   Take it to the limit   10
            1   Explorers   11
            2   That's an idea!   18
            3   She jumped well   23
            4   Our world   30
            Module 1 Check your progress   36

Module 2   Different lives   37
            5   Canada and the USA   38
            6   Growing up   45
            7   Have a laugh   50
            8   A great film!   55
            Module 2 Check your progress   61

Module 3   Weird and wonderful   62
            9   Disaster!   63
            10 A place to stay   68
            11 Your mind   74
            12 Music makers   80
            Module 3 Check your progress   86

Module 4   Dreams and reality   87
            13 Doctor's orders   88
            14 If I had ...   94
            15 Lost worlds   99
            16 Good or bad luck?   105
            Module 4 Check your progress   111

Projects   112

Workbook key   114

Acknowledgements   128

	Unit	Grammar	Vocabulary	Pronunciation
Module 1 **Take it to the limit**	1 Explorers	Present simple / continuous & past simple review.	Guessing meaning from context. Everyday English.	Linking sounds in the past simple.
	2 That's an idea!	Past continuous. Past continuous vs. past simple. *when/while*.	Phrases with *get*.	*was & were*.
	3 She jumped well	Comparative & superlative adjectives. Intensifiers with comparatives. *(not) as … as*. Adverbs/comparative adverbs.	Antonyms. Everyday English.	*than & as*.
	4 Our world	*will/won't & might / may (not)* for prediction. First conditional, *unless*.	The environment.	/əʊ/ (w*o*n't).
	Module 1 Check your progress			
Module 2 **Different lives**	5 Canada and the USA	Question tags. Present perfect simple, *just/already/yet*.	North American & British English. Everyday English.	Intonation in question tags.
	6 Growing up	Present simple passive. *let / be allowed to*.	Describing a person's age.	/aʊ/ (all*ow*ed).
	7 Have a laugh!	Present perfect simple, *for* vs. *since*.	Verb & noun pairs. Everyday English.	*have, has & for*.
	8 A great film!	Verbs + *-ing* / verbs + infinitive.	Film.	Consonant clusters.
	Module 2 Check your progress			
Module 3 **Weird and wonderful**	9 Disaster!	Past simple passive. *a, an* or *the*.	Disasters. Everyday English.	'Silent' letters.
	10 A place to stay	*too much / many & not enough*. *will* vs. *be going to*.	Homes.	Sound and spelling: *-ough*.
	11 Your mind	Determiners (*everyone / no one* etc.). *must/mustn't* vs. *don't have to*.	Remembering & forgetting. Everyday English.	*must*.
	12 Music makers	Present perfect continuous. Present perfect simple and continuous.	Music.	Sentence stress: rhythm.
	Module 3 Check your progress			
Module 4 **Dreams and reality**	13 Doctor's orders	Defining relative clauses. *used to*.	Medicine. Everyday English.	/z/ or /s/ in *used*.
	14 If I had …	Second conditional.	Information technology & computers.	*'d*.
	15 Lost worlds	Past perfect.	Noun suffixes: *-r, -er, -or & -ist*. Everyday English.	*had & 'd*.
	16 Good or bad luck?	Reported statements & questions. Third conditional.	Noun suffixes: *-ation & -ment*.	*would've / wouldn't have*.
	Module 4 Check your progress			
	Projects ● Pronunciation ● Speaking: additional material ● Irregular verbs and phonetic chart ● Word list			

4

Speaking & Functions	Listening	Reading	Writing
Describing temporary & permanent activities, past & present situations. Interview about free time.	Story about the Oregon Trail.	At the bottom of the sea. The Oregon Trail. Story: Here's my phone number.	Filling in forms.
Describing past activities. Discussion: jeans.	Stories about famous inventions. Part of a ghost story.	Young girl gets prize. Culture: Jeans.	Story about an invention.
Making comparisons. Describing a sports event. Comparing yourself with others.	Information about record-breaking sports people.	Tara's last minute win. Story: Was she pretty?	Magazine report of a sports event.
Discussing environmental problems. Predicting future events. Discussion: renewable forms of energy.	Radio interview about different forms of energy.	Our fragile planet. Culture: Energy around the world.	Website article about your town/environment.
Checking information. Talking about recently completed activities.	Quiz about Canada & the USA.	Quiz about Canada and the USA. $1000 for young Vancouver poet. Poem: Whale song. Story: You said 6.30, didn't you?	Email about a holiday.
Describing a ceremony. Retelling a story. Talking about permission. Discussion: minimum age limits.	Story about a coming of age ceremony. Dialogue about minimum ages.	From teenager to adult. Culture: Call yourself an adult?	Magazine article about a special day or ceremony.
Talking about unfinished situations. Questionnaire: Are you fun to be with? Talking about having fun.	Song: Don't worry, be happy.	An interview with a clown doctor. Questionnaire: Are you fun to be with? Story: Who's going to sing?	Email about how you have fun.
Expressing likes/dislikes & preferences. Talking about films. Discussion: film stars & fame.	Dialogue about a film. Dialogue about a Hollywood star.	It was really terrifying … . Short film reviews. Culture: Hollywood lives.	Film review.
Exchanging information. A quiz. Describing a dream.	Interview about a famous earthquake.	Tsunami – the giant wave. Story: Let's talk about it later.	Newspaper story about a forest fire.
Describing quantity. Talking about your home. Discussion: stereotypes.	Descriptions of homes.	Want an adventure? Spend ten days in Borneo! An email about a holiday. Culture: Life 'down under'.	Email about a plan for a holiday.
What's your strongest intelligence? Discussing memory.	Interview about 'multiple intelligences'.	How to improve your memory. Story: The winners are … .	Competition entry.
Describing recently completed & unfinished actions. Talking about music & instruments. Discussion: pop music & fashion.	People talking about music & musical instruments.	A young winner. Culture: Pop music in Britain & the USA – a brief history.	Letter about your favourite type of music.
Expressing past habits. Exchanging information.	Dialogue at the doctor's. Dialogue about Joseph Lister.	Medicine in the past – treating headaches. Story: I used to like Joanne.	Magazine article about a famous scientist.
Giving advice. Talking about unreal situations. Discussion: computers & the Internet.	Descriptions of problems caused by computers.	Computers – good for learning, or just for fun? The Goosehead Guide to Life. Culture: Just how great are computers?	Competition entry.
Describing events in the past & earlier past. Telling a picture story.	Radio programme about the 'army of Xi'an'.	The discovery of Machu Picchu. Story: I don't think so.	Short story.
Reporting statements & questions. Discussion: superstitions.	Dialogue about an unlucky day. Dialogue about superstitions in Britain.	A lucky break for the shoeshine boy. Culture: Where do superstitions come from?	Email to apologise for something.

Introduction

'If you can teach teenagers, you can teach anyone.' Michael Grinder

Teaching teenagers is an interesting and challenging task. A group of adolescents can be highly motivated, cooperative and fun to teach on one day, and the next day the whole group or individual students might turn out to be truly 'difficult' – the teacher might, for example, be faced with discipline problems, disruptive or provocative behaviour, a lack of motivation, or unwillingness on the students' part to do homework assigned to them.

The roots of these problems frequently lie in the fact that adolescents are going through a period of significant changes in their lives. The key challenge in the transition period between being a child and becoming an adult is the adolescent's struggle for identity – a process that requires the development of a distinct sense of who they are. A consequence of this process is that adolescents can feel threatened, and at the same time experience overwhelming emotions. They frequently try to compensate for the perceived threats with extremely rude behaviour, and try to 'hide' their emotions behind a wall of extreme outward conformity. The more individual students manage to look, talk, act and behave like the other members of their peer group, the less threatened and insecure they feel.

Insights into the causes underlying the problems might help us to understand better the complex situation our students are in. However, such insights do not automatically lead to more success in teaching. We need to react to the challenges in a professional way.[1] This includes the need to:

- select content and organise the students' learning according to their psychological needs;
- create a positive learning atmosphere;
- cater for differences in students' learning styles and intelligence(s), and facilitate the development of our students' study skills.

English in Mind has been written taking all these points into account. They have significantly influenced the choice of texts, artwork and design, the structure of the units, the typology of exercises, and the means by which students' study skills are facilitated and extended.

The importance of the content for success

There are a number of reasons why the choice of the right content has a crucial influence over success or failure in the teaching of adolescents. Teachers frequently observe that teenagers are reluctant to 'talk about themselves'. This has to do with the adolescent's need for psychological security. Consequently, the 'further away' from their own world the content of the teaching is, the more motivating and stimulating it will be for the students. The preference for psychologically remote content goes hand in hand with a fascination with extremes and realistic details. Furthermore, students love identifying with heroes and heroines, because these idols are perceived to embody the qualities needed in order to survive in a threatening world: qualities such as courage, genius, creativity and love. In the foreign language class, students can become fascinated with stories about heroes and heroines to which they can ascribe such qualities. *English in Mind* treats students as young adults, offering them a range of interesting topics and a balance between educational value and teenage interest and fun.

As Kieran Egan (see footnote 1) stresses, learning in the adolescent classroom can be successfully organised by starting with something far from the students' experience, but also connected to it by some quality with which they can associate. This process of starting far from the students makes it easier for the students to become interested in the topic, and also enables the teacher finally to relate the content to the students' own world.

A positive learning atmosphere

The creation of a positive learning atmosphere largely depends on the rapport between teacher and students, and the one which students have among themselves. It requires the teacher to be a genuine, empathetic listener, and to have a number of other psychological skills. *English in Mind* supports the teacher's task of creating of positive learning experiences through: clear tasks; a large number of carefully designed exercises; regular opportunities for the students to check their own work; and a learning process designed to guarantee that the students will learn to express themselves both in speaking and in writing.

Learning styles and multiple intelligences

There is significant evidence that students will be better motivated, and learn more successfully, if differences in learning styles and intelligences are taken into account in the teaching-learning process.[2] The development of a

---

[1] An excellent analysis of teenage development and consequences for our teaching in general can be found in Kieran Egan: *Romantic Understanding*, Routledge and Kegan Paul, New York and London, 1990. This book has had a significant influence on the thinking behind *English in Mind*, and the development of the concept of the course.

[2] See for example Eric Jensen: *Brain-Based Learning and Teaching*, Turning Point Publishing, Del Mar, CA, USA, 1995, on learning styles. An overview of the theory of multiple intelligences can be found in Howard Gardner: *Multiple Intelligences: The Theory in Practice*, Basic Books, New York 1993.

number of activities in *English in Mind* have been influenced by such insights, and students find frequent study tips that show them how they can better utilise their own resources.[3]

The methodology used in *English in Mind*

Skills: *English in Mind* uses a communicative, multi-skills approach to develop the students' foreign language abilities in an interesting and motivational way. A wide range of interesting text types is used to present authentic use of language, including magazine and newspaper clippings, interviews, narratives, songs and engaging photo stories.

Grammar: *English in Mind* is based on a strong grammatical syllabus and takes into account students' mixed abilities by dealing with grammar in a carefully graded way, and offering additional teaching support (see below).

Vocabulary: *English in Mind* offers a systematic vocabulary syllabus, including important lexical chunks for conversation.

Culture: *English in Mind* gives students insights into a number of important cross-cultural and intercultural themes. Significant cultural features of English-speaking countries are presented, and students are involved in actively reflecting on the similarities and differences between other cultures and their own.

Consolidation: Four Check your progress revision units per level will give teachers a clear picture of their students' progress and make students aware of what they have learned. Each revision unit is also accompanied by a project which gives students the opportunity to use new language in a less controlled context and allows for learner independence.

Teacher support: *English in Mind* is clearly structured and easy to teach. The Teacher's Book offers step-by-step lesson notes, background information on content, culture and language, additional teaching ideas and the tapescripts. The accompanying Teacher's Resource Pack contains photocopiable materials for further practice and extra lessons, taking into consideration the needs of mixed-ability groups by providing extra material for fast finishers or students who need more support, as well as formal tests.

Student support: *English in Mind* offers systematic support to students through: Study help sections and Skills tips; classroom language; guidance in units to help with the development of classroom discourse and the students' writing; a wordlist including phonetic transcriptions and lists of irregular verbs and phonetics (at the back of the Student's Book); and a Grammar reference (at the back of the Workbook).

English in Mind: components

Each level of the *English in Mind* series contains the following components:

- Student's Book
- Class CDs or Class Cassettes
- Workbook with accompanying Audio CD / CD-ROM
- Teacher's Book
- Teacher's Resource Pack
- Website resources

The Student's Book

Modular structure: The *English in Mind* Student's Books are organised on a modular basis – each contains four modules of four units per module. The modules have broad themes and are organised as follows: a) a two-page module opener; b) four units of six pages each; c) a two-page Check your progress section.

Module openers are two pages which allow teachers to 'set the scene' for their students, concerning both the informational content and the language content of what is to come in the module itself. This helps both to motivate the students and to provide the important 'signposting' which allows them to see where their learning is going next. The pages contain: a) a visual task in which students match topics to a selection of photographs taken from the coming units; b) a list of skills learning objectives for the module; c) a short matching task which previews the main grammar content of the coming module; and d) a simple vocabulary task, again previewing the coming content.

The **units** have the basic following structure, although with occasional minor variations depending on the flow of an individual unit:

- an opening **reading** text
- a **grammar** page, often including pronunciation
- two pages of **vocabulary** and **skills** work
- either a **photo story** or a **Culture in mind** text, followed by **writing skills** work.

The **reading texts** aim to engage and motivate the students with interesting and relevant content, and to provide contextualised examples of target grammar and lexis. The texts have 'lead-in' tasks and are followed by comprehension tasks of various kinds. All the opening texts are also recorded on the Class CD/Cassette, which allows teachers to follow the initial reading with a 'read and listen' phase, giving the students the invaluable opportunity of connecting the written word with the spoken version, which is especially useful for auditory learners. Alternatively, with stronger classes, teachers may decide to do one of the exercises as a listening task, with books closed.

---

[3] See Marion Williams and Robert L. Burden: *Psychology for Language Teachers*, Cambridge University Press, 1997 (pp. 143–162), on how the learner deals with the process of learning.

Grammar usually follows the initial reading. The emphasis is on active involvement in the learning process. Examples from the texts are isolated and used as a basis for tasks, which focus on both concept and form of the target grammar area. Students are encouraged to find other examples and work out rules for themselves. Occasionally there are also Look boxes which highlight an important connected issue concerning the grammar area, for example, in Unit 8, work on *prefer* has a Look box which highlights the use of the preposition *to* used after *prefer* (I prefer writing emails **to** talking on the phone). This is followed by a number of graded exercises, both receptive and productive, which allow students to begin to employ the target language in different contexts and to produce realistic language. Next, there is usually a speaking activity, aiming at further personalisation of the language.

Each unit has at least one **Vocabulary** section, with specific word fields. Again, examples from the initial text are focused on, and a lexical set is developed, with exercises for students to put the vocabulary into use. Vocabulary is frequently recycled in later texts in the unit (e.g. photo stories or Culture in mind texts), and also in later units.

Pronunciation is included in every unit. There are exercises on common phoneme problems such as /əʊ/ in *won't* as well as aspects of stress (within words, and across sentences) and elision. Vital areas such as the use of schwa /ə/ are dealt with on more than one occasion, and often in relation to a grammar area, for example, the pronunciation of *have*, *has* and *for* when the present perfect is taught.

Language skills are present in every unit. There is always at least one **listening skills** activity, with listening texts of various genres; at least one (but usually several) **speaking skills** activity for fluency development; **Reading skills** are taught through the opening texts and also later texts in some units, as well as the Culture in mind sections. There is always a **writing skills** task, at the end of each unit.

The final two pages of each unit have either a **photo story** (odd-numbered units) or a **Culture in mind** text (even-numbered units). The **photo stories** are conversations between teenagers in everyday situations, allowing students to read and listen for interest and also to experience the use of common everyday language expressions. These Everyday English expressions are worked on in exercises following the dialogue. The **Culture in mind** texts are reading and/or listening texts which provide further skills practice, and an opportunity for students to develop their knowledge and understanding of the world at large and in particular the English-speaking world. They include a wide variety of stimulating topics, for example, the history of jeans, different legal age limits around the world, life in Australia and the history of pop music in Britain and the USA.

The final activity in each unit is a **writing skills** task. These are an opportunity for students to further their control of language and to experiment in the production of tasks in a variety of genres (e.g. letters, emails, reports, etc.). There are model texts for the students to aid their own writing, and exercises providing guidance in terms of content and organisation. Through the completion of the writing tasks, students if they wish, can also build up a bank of materials, or 'portfolio', during their period of learning: this can be very useful to them as the source of a sense of clear progress and as a means of self-assessment. A 'portfolio' of work can also be shown to other people (exam bodies, parents, even future employers) as evidence of achievement in language learning. Many of the writing tasks also provide useful and relevant practice for examinations such as Cambridge ESOL PET or Trinity Integrated Skills Examinations.

When a module of four units closes, the module ends with a two-page **Check your progress** section. Here the teacher will find exercises in the Grammar, Vocabulary and Everyday English expressions that were presented in the module. The purpose of these (as opposed to the more formal tests offered in the Teacher's Resource Pack) is for teachers and students alike to check quickly the learning and progress made during the module just covered; they can be done in class or at home. Every exercise has a marking scheme, and students can use the marks they gain to do some simple self-assessment of their progress (a light 'task' is offered for this).

Beyond the modules and units themselves, *English in Mind* offers at the **end of the Student's Book** a further set of materials for teachers and students. These consist of:

- **Projects**: activities (one per module) which students can do in pairs or groups (or even individually if desired), for students to put the language they have so far learned into practical and enjoyable use. They are especially useful for mixed-ability classes, as they allow students to work at their own pace. The projects produced could also be part of the 'portfolio' of material mentioned earlier.
- An **irregular verb** list for students to refer to when they need.
- A listing of **phonetic symbols**, again for student reference.
- A **wordlist** with the core lexis of the Student's Book, with phonetic transcriptions. This is organised by unit, and within each unit heading there are the major word-fields, divided into parts of speech (verbs, nouns, adjectives, etc.). The wordlists are a feature that teachers can use in classrooms, for example, to develop students' reference skills, or to indicate ways in which they themselves might organise vocabulary notebooks, and by students at home, as a useful reference and also to prepare for tests or progress checks.

The Workbook

The Workbook is a resource for both teachers and students, providing further practice in the language and skills covered in the Student's Book. It is organised unit-by-unit, following the Student's Book. Each Workbook unit has six pages, and the following contents:

Exercises: an extensive range of supporting exercises in the grammatical, lexical and phonological areas of the Student's Book unit, following the progression of the unit, so that teachers can use the exercises either during or at the end of the Student's Book unit.

Everyday English and **Culture in mind**: extra exercises on these sections in alternating units, as in the Students Book.

Study help: these sections follow a syllabus of study skills areas, to develop the students' capacities as independent and successful learners. After a brief description of the skill, there are exercises for the students to begin to practise it.

Skills in mind page: these pages contain a separate skills development syllabus, which normally focuses on two main skill areas in each unit. There is also a skill tip relating to the main skill area, which the students can immediately put into action when doing the skills task(s).

Unit check page: this is a one-page check of knowledge of the key language of the unit, integrating both grammar and vocabulary in the three exercise types. The exercise types are: a) a cloze text to be completed using items given in a box; b) a sentence-level multiple choice exercise; c) a guided error correction exercise.

At the end of the Workbook, there is a **Grammar reference** section. Here, there are explanations of the main grammar topics of each unit, with examples. It can be used for reference by students at home, or the teacher might wish to refer to it in class if the students appreciate grammatical explanations.

The Workbook includes an **Audio CD / CD-ROM**, which contains both the listening material for the Workbook (listening texts and pronunciation exercises) and a CD ROM element, containing definitions for the wordlist items with a spoken model for each one. A range of carefully graded grammar and vocabulary exercises provide further practice of language presented in each module.

The Teacher's Book

The Teacher's Book contains:

- clear, simple, practical teaching **notes** on each unit and how to implement the exercises as effectively as possible
- complete **tapescripts** for all listening and pronunciation activities

- complete **answers** to all exercises (grammar, vocabulary, comprehension questions, etc.)
- **optional further activities**, for stronger or weaker classes, to facilitate the use of the material in mixed-ability classes
- **background notes** relating to the information content (where appropriate) of reading texts and Culture in mind pages
- **language notes** relating to grammatical areas, to assist less-experienced teachers who might have concerns about the target language and how it operates (these can also be used to refer to the Workbook Grammar reference section)
- a complete **answer key** and **tapescripts** for the **Workbook**.

The Teacher's Resource Pack

This extra component, spiral bound for easy photocopying, contains the following photocopiable resources:

- an **Entry** test which can be used for diagnostic testing or also used for remedial work for the Starter section
- **module tests** containing separate sections for: Grammar, Vocabulary, Everyday English, Reading, Listening (the recordings for which are on the Class Cassettes/CDs), Speaking and Writing. A key for the Tests is also provided
- **photocopiable communicative activities**: one page for each unit reflecting the core grammar and/or vocabulary of the unit
- **photocopiable extra grammar exercises**: one page of four exercises for each unit, reflecting the key grammar areas of the unit
- **teaching notes** for the above.

Web resources

In addition to information about the series, the *English in Mind* website contains downloadable pages of further activities and exercises for students as well as other resources. It can be found at this part of the Cambridge University Press website:

www.cambridge.org/elt/englishinmind

Module 1
Take it to the limit

YOU WILL LEARN ABOUT ...

Ask students to look at the pictures on the page. Ask students to read through the topics in the box and check they understand each item. You can ask them the following questions, in L1 if appropriate:

1 *Where is the person in picture 6 and what is he doing?*
2 *Where are the people travelling to?*
3 *Who is the person in picture X?*
4 *Do you wear jeans?*
5 *What is the person in the snow doing?*
6 *What kind of energy do you use at home/ in the classroom?*

In pairs or small groups, students discuss which topic area they think each picture matches.

Check answers.

Answers
1 Famous inventions
2 Levi Strauss and the history of jeans
3 The Oregon trail
4 The environment and different kinds of energy
5 A snowboarder's dramatic win
6 An underwater explorer

YOU WILL LEARN HOW TO ...

See Introduction.

Use grammar

Students read through the grammar names and examples. Go through the first item as an example.
Weaker classes: Put the grammar headings on the board and ask students to look for an example of each in the list on the books. Elicit each one and if necessary write them on the board or ask a student to write the sentence on the board. Check answers.

Answers
Present simple vs. past simple: I usually walk to work, but yesterday I drove.
Past continuous vs. past simple: While we were working, we heard a loud noise.
Comparative and superlative adjectives: It's a bigger house than mine.
as ... as comparison: These books aren't as expensive as those ones.
Adverbs/comparative adverbs: I can write more quickly than my sister.
Modal verbs for future prediction: James won't go, but Mary might be there.
First conditional and *unless*: She won't know unless you tell her.

Use vocabulary

Write the headings on the board. Go through the items in the Student's Book and check understanding. Now ask students if they can think of one more item for the *Phrases with get* heading. Elicit some responses and add them to the list on the board. Students now do the same for the other headings. Some possibilities are:

Phrases with *get*: *get in, get out* (SB1, Unit 5); *get on*; *get off*; *get better*

Adjectives and their opposites: *honest – dishonest*; *polite – rude* (SB1, Unit 14); *good – bad*

The environment: *ozone layer*; *protect*; *recycle*; *rainforests*

1 Explorers

TOPIC: Explorers

TEXTS

Reading and listening: a text about underwater exploration
Reading and listening: a story about the Oregon Trail
Reading and listening: story: *Here's my phone number*
Writing: filling in forms

SPEAKING AND FUNCTIONS

Describing temporary and permanent activities
Exchanging information about past and present situations
Interviewing someone about their free time

LANGUAGE

Present simple and present continuous; past simple review
Vocabulary: guessing meaning from context
Pronunciation: linking sounds in the past simple
Everyday English: *Too right!*; *round here*; *bloke*; *Actually*

1 Read and listen

If you set the background information as a homework research task, ask students to tell the class what they found out.

BACKGROUND INFORMATION

Dr Robert Ballard: Has been researching for 29 years at the Woods Hole Oceanographic Institution (WHOI), Massachusetts. He was one of the first people to suggest using submersibles to do research work. He developed a system in the 1980 called The Argo which could transmit pictures in real time from under the sea. It was with this system that he found the wreck of the Titanic.

Submarine: Is part of the system of submersibles pioneered by Robert Ballard. It enables live photos from under the oceans to be transmitted to ships or computers around the globe. The robot submarine that Dr Ballard uses is called 'Jason' and is part of the Jason Project, an interactive science project for school children. Jason has floodlights, TV cameras and a mechanism for retrieving things from the sea bed. Signals from Jason can be broadcast to classrooms all over the world so that students everywhere can share in the live exploration of the sea bed.

Titanic: Was an English passenger ship which set sail on 10 April 1912, heading for New York. There were 2,227 people on board. The ship struck an iceberg on the night of 14–15 April and sank; 1,522 people died. The wreck is at the bottom of the Atlantic.

Warm up

Ask students to look at the photos. Ask them where they think they were taken (*under the sea*) and what Dr Ballard's job is (*an underwater explorer*). This can be done in L1 if necessary. Do not give answers at this point.

a Read through the questions as a class and ask students to read the text quickly to find the answers and check their answers to the *Warm up* questions. Remind them that they don't need to understand every word in the text. Students can compare answers in pairs before a whole class check. You can discuss the answers to question 2 as a class and see if students agree on the sort of things they think he finds.

Answers

1 He looks for shipwrecks, ancient cities and settlements.
2 Students' own answers.

b Students now listen to the recording of the story as they read. Students could be given the optional activity to do while they are listening.

TAPESCRIPT

See the reading text on page 6 of the Student's Book.

OPTIONAL ACTIVITY

🔊 Play the recording while students read the text (stronger classes could listen with books closed) and ask them to answer the following True/False questions:

1 Dr Ballard is French. (**False; he's American.**)
2 He is famous for finding The Titanic. (**True**)
3 Dr Ballard went to the Black Sea in 1999. (**False; he went in 2000.**)
4 The site they found is 7,000 or 8,000 years old. (**True**)

Check answers and ask students to correct the false answers. Play and pause the recording again as necessary.

2 Vocabulary
Guessing meaning from context

a Students read through sentences 1 to 5. Draw students' attention to the example and elicit that *small* is an adjective. Ask students how they know (because it goes before the noun and describes it). Explain that students must now identify the underlined words in the other items (nouns, adjectives, verbs, adverbs or prepositions). Students complete the exercise. Check answers. Ask students how they worked out which part of speech each word was.

Weaker classes: Books closed. Write the following example sentence on the board, leaving the space for the adjective blank (Dr Ballard uses a .... submarine). Ask students what sort of word could go in the gap and elicit *adjective*. Ask students if they can remember how the submarine was described in the text (small) and ask a student to come out and fill in the correct adjective on the board. Students then open their books at page 7. Follow the Stronger classes procedure from this point.

Answers
2 noun   3 verb   4 preposition   5 adverb

b Ask students what they do if they find a word in a text which they don't understand. Elicit their responses. Now ask them to read through words 1 to 5. Do the first item with them as an example. Once students have located the word in the text, ask them to identify which part of speech they think it might be. Elicit *noun* and ask them why (because it has a plural ending and an adjective before it). Students now work through the rest of the exercise, locating the words and identifying them. Check answers. Make sure students are clear at this point which part of speech each word is.

Answers
1 noun   2 adjective   3 verb   4 adjective
5 noun

Look at the first item again with students and see if they can work out the meaning only by using the information in the text. If students are having problems with this, they can use dictionaries. However, students should be encouraged only to use dictionaries if they cannot figure out the word. Remind them when using dictionaries that a word may have several different meanings and that they should look for the part of speech they need. Check answers.

Answers
1   places where a group of people live
2   very old
3   look or travel around to learn about a place
4   seen or heard as it is actually happening (e.g. a live concert)
5   things that are left behind when other parts are lost or taken away

Vocabulary notebook
Encourage students to note down the strategies for guessing meaning from context and to note down a few examples of their own or from the exercise. Students can write translation in their own language if it helps them remember.

Remind students that when they are reading a text and they find a word they don't know they should always try to continue reading and look at the other words around the word they don't know to help them try and work out its meaning.

3 Grammar
Present simple and present continuous

a **Stronger classes:** Students read through the examples from the text. Ask them to identify the tense in each sentence (Sentence 1: present simple; Sentence 2: present continuous).

Weaker classes: Books closed. Write the following examples (or some of your own) on the board: *I teach English. / I'm talking to you now.* Ask students to identify the verb in each sentence and to tell you which tense is being used and elicit the reason (you teach English as a job, you do it every day / you are talking to them now, it is an action happening at the time of speaking). Students now open their books at page 7 and look at the examples from the reading text. Go through the same procedure with these examples.

Students now read through the rule and try and complete it. Remind them to think about when the actions are done in each sentence. Ask them: Is it something that he always does? Is it happening now? Check answers.

Answers
simple
continuous

To check understanding of form and meaning at this point, you can ask students a few more questions of your own. For example:

T: *Alicia, what do you do at weekends?*
S1: *I (see my friends, etc.)*
T: *Paola, what are you doing now?*
S2: *I'm listening to you/studying English*, etc.

> **Language notes**
> 1 Students may have problems with these tenses in contrast because of the way their own language works. Students may produce statements like: **I am doing my homework every day. *My brother is work in a hospital.* Remind them again, if necessary, of the use of each tense and clarify any further problems.
> 2 It may be useful for students to translate some example sentences into their own language.

(b) Students read through the gapped text. Check any problems. Remind them to ignore the gaps for the moment. Go through the example with students asking them to explain why the verb is in the present simple (because this is his job, it is what he does, it is a regular routine). Students now complete the exercise, using the present simple or continuous forms of the verbs in brackets. Students can compare answers in pairs. Check answers, making sure students can justify their choice of tense.

Answers

1 doesn't go   2 uses   3 sends   4 isn't looking
5 is exploring   6 is/working

(c) This exercise can be set for homework. Students read through answers 1 to 7. Check any problems. Go through the example with them, reminding them of question forms and word order if necessary. Students complete the exercise. Check answers.

Weaker students: You can tell them that all the questions, except number 6, are *Wh*-questions. They can refer back to the text on page 6 to help them if necessary.

Answers

2   What does Dr Ballard do?
3   What does he find?
4   What does he use?
5   What does it do?
6   Is he looking for?
7   What is he working on at the moment?

Grammar notebook

Remind students to note down the rules for the use of present simple and present continuous and to put any examples they want down and translate them into their own language.

━━ **OPTIONAL ACTIVITIES** ━━━━━━━━━━

Different for a day

Stronger classes

Students choose a favourite popstar, football player, actor/actress, etc. They must think about what their own usual routine is and make some notes and then think about what they would do if they spent a day with their favourite star.

For example: *I usually eat breakfast at 7 o'clock. I have ...*

Today I'm having breakfast with (favourite star) and we're sitting in the (name of top hotel), etc. Students can then interview a partner and find out about the person they chose. Ask pairs to feedback to the class.

Weaker classes

They can do the same exercise but provide them with the following prompts:

- Breakfast: what I usually have and where I have it; where I am today and who I'm with, what I'm having.
- Travel to school: how I usually travel to school; how I'm getting there today.
- Lunchtime: what I eat, who I eat with and when I eat; where I'm having lunch today and who I'm having lunch with.

- After school: what time I usually go home, what I usually do when I get home; what I'm doing today, who I'm spending time with and what we're doing.

Encourage pairs to read out their usual and new routines to the class.

4   Speak

Read through the instructions as a class, making sure students understand what they have to do. Divide the class into Student A and Student B pairs. Tell all Student Bs to turn to page 122 and look at their information. Ask a stronger pair to demonstrate the example questions and answers, starting with Student A. Do another example yourself with another student, if necessary. Students complete the exercise. Remind students to look at the other words around the gap to help them think about the sort of questions they need to ask and the verb they need to use (present simple or continuous). Monitor and help as necessary, making sure students are using the question and answer forms correctly. Make a note of any repeated mistakes to go through as a class after they finish the exercise.

Answers
Student A: New York; winter; a trip; doing a lot of exercise; to the gym
Student A questions:
Where does Kevin live?
When does he climb?
What is he planning?
What is he doing this month?
Where does he go every day?
Student B: sport; making plans; climb a big waterfall; crazy
Student B questions:
What does Kevin love?
What is Kevin doing at the moment?
What does he want to do there?
What do people think about Kevin?

5   Read and listen

If you set the background information as a homework research task, ask students to tell the class what they found out.

BACKGROUND INFORMATION

Oregon Trail: This was the route used from the 1840s to 1870s by western settlers in the USA. The trail usually started in Missouri, heading north west towards the Rocky Mountains and ending in Oregon. It was approximately 3,200 kilometres long and could take at least six months to travel.

California Gold Rush: This started in 1848 when many settlers and prospectors travelled to

California in search of gold. Gold was apparently discovered there and within two years more than 40,000 hopefuls had flocked to California in the hope of striking it rich.

Native Americans: Are the tribes of people who are said to have first settled in the USA.

Cholera: Is a disease caused by contaminated water. It can occur in epidemics and if left untreated can be fatal.

Warm up

Ask students to look at the title of the text, the pictures and the map and to guess where the people are going (from New York to the west of the USA) and when this took place (in the 19th century). You could use the pictures to pre-teach *barefoot, wagon/wheels, carry.*

(a) Ask students to read through questions 1 to 4. Check any problems. Students now use the pictures and the map to help them answer the questions. If you have done the *Warm up*, students may already have an idea of some of the answers. Students can compare answers in pairs but do not give answers at this point, they will be dealt with in Exercise 5b.

(b) Students read the text quickly and check their answers to Exercise 5a. Remind students that they don't need to understand every word in the text and encourage them to use the techniques they discussed in Exercise 2 for guessing meaning from context.

Weaker students: You may want to pre-teach the following vocabulary: *emigrate; farmland; settler; mountain; gold; journey; western; attack; kill; helpful; temperatures; illness; gunshot; accidental.*

Check answers as a class.

Answers
1 Missouri, Kansas, Nebraska, Wyoming, Idaho, Oregon
2 3,200 kilometres
3 Sometimes more than a year.
4 They walked barefoot and caught illnesses such as cholera from drinking dirty water.

(c) (🔊) Read through the instructions and questions as a class and ask students to think about the sort of vocabulary they may hear. Write any suggestions on the board. Encourage them at this point to think about when the people were travelling, the dangers people faced and the problems they experienced. Play the recording for students to listen and note down the answers. Check answers and see if any of their predictions were correct. Play the recording again, pausing as necessary to clarify any problems.

TAPESCRIPT

Karen Hi Mark. How are you?
Mark Fine, thanks. I'm studying hard at the moment. I'm reading about the settlers on the Oregon Trail. It's really interesting.

Karen So what kind of things are you reading about?
Mark Well, for example, the story of the settlers on the Oregon Trail. It was a really difficult journey. It's fascinating to read. So many of the settlers died on the way.
Karen Why?
Mark Well, there are many reasons. For example, there were some big rivers on the way, and the settlers had to cross them: the Columbia River, for example, or the Green River. I read a story about that last night.
Karen About people crossing the Green River?
Mark Yes. It happened in the year 1850. The settlers wanted to cross the river, but an awful accident happened. Erm ... there were too many people on the boat, you know, and, ... in the middle of the river, the boat turned over and ... it sank in ten minutes. 37 people died.
Karen Really? Thirty-seven! Why did so many people get on the boat?
Mark Well, because the people who had the boats wanted to make a lot of money. You know, they wanted a lot of people on every trip. So they tried to get lots and lots of people on the boats. And crossing the Green River was very expensive anyway. It cost $16 per person, almost as much as a horse cost.
Karen How sad! So 37 people died, only because ...

Answers
1 A boat crossing the Green River sank.
2 Because there were too many people in the boat. The people who owned the boats wanted to make as much money as they could so they took money from as many people as they could which meant there were too many people to fit into the boat.

(d) (🔊) Students now read through the gapped text. Remind them to ignore the gaps for the moment. Check any problems. Students complete the text. Remind them to look at the context around each gap to help them try and guess the words or to use the information on the board. Play the recording again while students listen and check or change their answers. Play it again, pausing as necessary for students to clarify any problems.

Weaker classes: Ask students what other details they can remember about the story on the recording from Exercise 5c. Elicit their responses and put them on the board. If necessary, go through the first item as an example, encouraging students to think about what kind of information is missing.

Answers
1 1850   2 cross a river/the Green River
3 37   4 money   5 $16

6 Grammar

Past simple: regular and irregular verbs

a) Students covered this area in Student's Book 1, Unit 6.

Stronger classes: Students read through the instruction and find the verbs in the text. Students now read through the rule box and complete it. Check answers.

Weaker classes: Books closed. Put the following base forms on the board (*work*; *go*). Elicit the past simple of each verb and ask students which one is regular and which one is irregular. Ask students how they know which one is regular (*add* -ed *to the end of the base form*) and which one is irregular (*doesn't have* -ed *ending*). Students now open their books at page 9 and read through the instructions. Go through the first paragraph of the text with them if necessary and help them locate the first past simple regular verb. Remind them they should be looking for verbs ending in -*ed*. Tell them there are seven examples. Check answers.

Answers
Regular verbs
Para 1: emigrated; wanted; called; travelled
Para 2: hoped
Para 3: walked
Para 4: died

Answers

-ed; -ied; base form

b) Give students a few minutes to complete the table. Students can check their answers on page 124. Check answers with the class.

can – could
catch – caught
come – came
find – found
go – went
have – had
leave – left
see – saw
sink – sank
take – took
write – wrote

> **Language notes**
> 1 Remind students that past simple irregulars just have to be memorised. Students may still produce statements like: **I finded the answer*.
> 2 You may find it useful to revise the pronunciation of past simple regular endings at this point using examples from the text: *walked* /t/; *died* /d/; *emigrated* /ɪd/. Encourage students to pronounce each regular past simple correctly and drill the pronunciation if they are still having problems.

c) Ask students to read through answers 1 to 6. Go through the example and remind them of the question form, if necessary. Remind them that *Because* answers usually have a *Why* question and that they can look at the verb in the answer if necessary to help them work out the question. Students complete the exercise. Check answers, making sure students are clear about question forms. They can refer back to the text on page 8 as necessary.

Answers
2 did they go
3 did they go
4 did it take
5 Why did people walk
6 How many people died

d) This exercise can be set for homework.

First, students read through the gapped text. Tell them to ignore the gaps. Then go through the example, and ask them why the verb is left (*because it is the irregular past simple of* leave).

Stronger classes: Students complete the exercise. Remind them that they need to look carefully at the verb in brackets and decide first if it is regular or irregular and then they need to look at the form they need to use it in.

Weaker classes: Elicit the past simple forms of the verbs from the text and put them on the board (this could be done in jumbled order). Students then use the elicited past simple forms from the board and also from the chart in Exercise 6b, to complete the text.

Students can compare answers in pairs before a whole class check.

Answers
1 hoped   2 made   3 didn't find   4 decided
5 was   6 travelled   7 used   8 didn't have
9 walked   10 carried   11 didn't have   12 went
13 died   14 caught   15 had

Grammar notebook
Encourage students to note down all the verbs and the past simple forms from Exercise 6 and to learn them.

┌─ OPTIONAL ACTIVITIES ─────────
Stronger classes
Books closed. Use paragraph 1 of the text in Exercise 6d for this. Read each sentence in the paragraph out slowly and when you come to a gap in the text say 'beep'. Students must decide which verb goes in the gap and use it in the correct form. Once you have read each sentence out for students to fill in the gaps, read the whole gapped text out again. Students can compare answers in pairs. Check answers.

Answers See above.

7 Pronunciation
Linking sounds in the past simple

a 🔊 Students turn to page 120 and read through sentences 1 to 6. Ask students what the difference is between sentences 1–3 and sentences 4–6 (in 1–3 the d in the past simple verb is followed by a vowel, in 4–6 it's followed by another consonant). Ask them what the difference in pronunciation might be. Play the first one and ask students to think about how the underlined part was pronounced. Write the linked part only on the board to show students how the /d/ sound at the end of *happened* is pronounced. Then Play the rest of the recording for students to listen.

TAPESCRIPT
1 It happened in 1850.
2 Many people died on the way.
3 They wanted a lot of people.
4 It happened last night.
5 He died ten years ago.
6 We wanted to go home.

b 🔊 Play the recording again, pausing for students to repeat each sentence.

8 Speak

Divide the class into pairs. Students read through the topics in the box and the prompt questions. Choose a stronger pair and ask them to demonstrate the example dialogue to the rest of the class.

Stronger classes: They can choose from the topics in the box or add more of their own.

Weaker classes: They may prefer to choose only one or two topics from the box.

Give students a few minutes to ask and answer in pairs. Monitor and help as necessary, checking that students are using the correct tenses and the correct question and answer forms. Note down any repeated errors to discuss as a class after the exercise. Ask pairs to feedback to the class.

--- OPTIONAL ACTIVITY ---
What did you do last weekend?
Whole class or small groups. Students must talk for one minute and use as many past simple forms as they can to describe what they did last weekend.

If a student makes a mistake, the others can make a buzzer sound to show they are out. You can use a large clock or timer for this and the student who can talk for one minute or as near to one minute without making a mistake is the winner!

Weaker classes
You may want to put some base forms on the board to help them with this.

9 Read and listen

It may be useful to introduce the characters for the story; some students may remember some of them from Student's Book 1.

Dave: Was in Student's Book 1 and was one of Amy's friends. They had plans to form a band.

Joanne: She is new in this level.

Saturday jobs: Dave works in a CD shop at the weekends. This is a common way for teenagers to earn extra money. Teenagers must be 16 years old to work in a shop.

Warm up

Ask students if they remember Dave from Student's Book 1 and what they can remember about him. If they can't remember or haven't used Student's Book 1, ask them to look at the photos and predict what they think he might be like. Discuss this as a class, in L1 if appropriate.

a 🔊 Ask students to read through the questions and to look at the photos. Play the recording while students read and listen. Students can compare answers in pairs. Check answers, playing and pausing the recording again as necessary.

TAPESCRIPT
See the story on page 10 of the Student's Book.

b Students read through sentences 1 to 7. Go through the first one as an example, if necessary. Remind students quickly how to deal with true/false exercises: they must locate the relevant point in the text and find the key words and then check the facts. Students complete the exercise. Students can correct the false answers. Students can compare answers in pairs. Check answers as a class.

Answers
1 T
2 F (She says she lives just a few streets away from the shop.)
3 F (He only works there on Saturdays.)
4 T
5 F (It will be in four weeks' time.)
6 F (The band who gets first prize gets the chance to make a CD with a record company. This may or may not lead to a recording contract.)
7 T

10 Everyday English

(a) Read through the expressions from the story as a class. Go through the first one with them as an example, if necessary. Students complete the exercise. Check answers.

Stronger classes: They can do this without looking back at the story.

Answers

1 Joanne   2 Dave   3 Joanne   4 Dave

(b) Look at sentence 4 in Exercise 10a with students and elicit translations of the word 'actually'. Are there any similarities with the English?

(c) Students read through expressions 1 to 3 and definitions a to c. Check any problems. Go through the first item as an example, if necessary. Students complete the exercise. Check answers.

Answers

1 c   2 b   3 a

> **Language note**
> *Bloke* is a colloquial word used to describe a teenage boy or a man.

(d) Students read through dialogues 1 to 3. Go through the first one with them as an example. Students complete the exercise with the expressions from Exercise 10a.

Students can compare answers in pairs, ask some pairs to read out their dialogues and check answers as a class.

Answers

1 round here   2 bloke   3 Actually   4 Too right

OPTIONAL ACTIVITIES

These optional activities can be used after every Everyday English exercise in the Student's Book.

Stronger classes

They can write their own short dialogues using the expressions. They can then act them out in front of the class. Make sure they are saying them with the correct intonation and expression and in the right context.

Weaker classes

They can act out the dialogues. Make sure they are saying them with the correct intonation and expression and in the right context.

Vocabulary notebook

Encourage students to start a section called *Everyday English* and to note down the expressions from Exercise 10. They may find it useful to note down a translation for each expression too.

11 Write

Warm up

Ask students if they have filled in any forms recently. If so, what for and what type of information did they have to give. If not, ask them what kind of information they might need to think about when filling in a form. Elicit some examples and put them on the board.

(a) Ask students to read through questions 1 to 5 and words a to e. Go through the example with them, pointing out the connection between *family name* and *surname*. Students now match the other items. Check answers.

Answers

2 c   3 e   4 a   5 b

(b) Ask students to read through the form. Complete the first part of the form as an example with your own information and write it on the board. Students then complete the form about themselves. Students can compare forms in pairs. Ask a few students to tell the class what they filled in.

② That's an idea!

Unit overview

TOPIC: Inventions
Stories in the past

TEXTS
Reading and listening: a magazine article about famous inventions
Listening: a ghost story
Reading: a story about a young inventor
Reading: an article about the history of jeans
Writing: a text about an inventor and his/her invention

SPEAKING AND FUNCTIONS
Describing past activities
Discussing jeans

LANGUAGE
Past continuous
Past continuous vs. past simple; *when* and *while*
Vocabulary: phrases with *get*
Pronunciation: *was* and *were*

1 Read and listen

Warm up

Ask students (in L1 if appropriate) what they think people did before these inventions, e.g. the telephone, TV, computer, fridge, etc. Ask them if they know when these things were invented and who they think invented them. Check they know the meaning of *invent* and *invention*.

(a) Ask students to read through the words in the box. Check any problems with meaning or pronunciation. Go through the first item as an example, explaining that they must write the relevant number in the boxes. Students complete the exercise. Check answers.

Answers
1 b   2 d   3 c   4 g   5 e   6 a   7 f   8 h

(b) Students read the texts, trying to guess any unknown vocabulary from context. If students are having problems, check the meaning of any unknown vocabulary using the pictures to help, e.g. *fried potatoes*, *the cook*, *thick*. Students complete the exercise.

Do not check answers at this point, this will be done in Exercise 1c.

(c) 🔊 Play the recording while students listen and check their answers. Play the recording again, pausing as necessary to clarify any problems.

TAPESCRIPT

It was 1933 and Percy Shaw, from England, was driving home at night along a dark road. He was worried because it was raining and he couldn't see very well. Then he saw something in the middle of the road. There was a cat and in the lights of his car he could see very clearly its shining yellow eyes. 'That's an idea!' he thought. And in 1934 Percy Shaw invented something which we can see on many roads in the world: cat's eyes.

In 1853, in a restaurant in New York, people were having dinner. A man was eating fried potatoes, but he didn't like them. He called for the cook and told him that the potatoes were too thick. The cook, George Crum, got angry. He went back to the kitchen and cut some potatoes very, very thinly. Then he cooked them and gave them to the customers in the restaurant. Mr Crum got a surprise. The customers loved them and wanted more and more. Mr Crum became famous as the inventor of crisps.

In the 1920s in Scotland, John Logie Baird and a friend were talking on the phone. Baird thought the telephone was an amazing invention. While he was listening to his friend, he began to think "I'd really like to invent a machine like this – but for the eye, not for the ear." He worked for many years to make a machine that could show pictures and in 1925 he produced the first television picture.

In 1907, a French chemist called Eugene Schueller was talking to a woman in his shop. She was getting older, and her hair was going grey. She was very unhappy because she didn't want to use a wig, but in those days hair dyes were not very good for people's hair. A few years later, the French chemist started to produce a new hair dye which was safe to use.

In 1935, in a newspaper office in Budapest, a young Hungarian reporter was writing an article for the next day. He was unhappy with his pen because while he was writing he had to stop many times to fill it with ink. And so he started to think. The man's name was Lazlo Biro and he invented a new kind of pen. In 1938, he and his brother went to Argentina and started the production of their invention there. It was named after them – the biro.

Answers
Text 1: cat's eyes
Text 2: crisps
Text 3: TV
Text 4: hair dye
Text 5: biro™

d 🔊 Ask students to read through questions 1 to 4. Check any problems. If necessary, go through the first item as an example, pausing the recording after text 1. Play the recording again while students complete the exercise. Remind students to listen for the key words they think they will need to answer each question. Students can compare answers in pairs before a whole class check.

Answers
1 a cat
2 Because the customers loved the crisps.
3 Because she was getting older and her hair was turning grey.
4 Biro

⌐ OPTIONAL ACTIVITY ══════════════
As a lead in to the study of the past continuous in the next exercise, ask students if they can remember …
1 … what Percy Shaw was doing when he saw the cat in the road. (**He was driving.**)
2 … where George Crum, the cook, was working when he invented crisps. (**He was working in a New York restaurant.**)
3 … what John Logie Baird was doing when he thought about inventing the TV. (**He was talking on the telephone.**)
4 … what Biro was doing when he invented the ballpoint pen. (**He was writing.**)
5 … who the chemist was talking to in Paris, 1907, which led to the invention of hair dye. (**He was talking to a woman whose hair was going grey.**)

2 Grammar
Past continuous

a Students read through the example sentences. Ask them to tell you how the past continuous tense is formed (*was/were* + *-ing* form of main verb).

b Read the instructions with the class. Go through the first text with them as an example and underline the first past continuous verb they come across. Give them a few minutes to re-read the texts and find further examples of the past continuous. Students can compare answers in pairs before a whole class check.

Answers
Text 1: was driving; it was raining
Text 2: people were having dinner; a man was eating …
Text 3: he was listening
Text 4: she was getting older
Text 5: … was writing

Students now complete the table with the correct form of the past continuous. Do the first item with them as an example. Check answers and then read through the rule as a class. Check students understand when to use the past continuous. It may be useful to remind them when we use the present continuous.

Answers
Positive: was; were
Negative: wasn't
Question: was; were
Short answer: was; wasn't; were; weren't
To check understanding of the form at this point, call out a few verbs in the present continuous and students can put them into the past continuous.

┌───┐
Language notes
1 Remind students that we use *was* in the first and third persons singular and *were* for all other persons with this tense.
2 Remind them of the spelling rules for *-ing* verb forms if necessary.
└───┘

c Read the instructions and the verbs in the box with students and go through the example as a class, focusing on the picture. Check students can explain why *was* is used. Students complete the exercise. Remind them to look at the picture and each sentence carefully and to think about the spelling rules for *-ing* forms. Students can compare answers in pairs before a whole class check.

Answers
2 were dancing   3 was sitting   4 were drinking
5 was talking

d This exercise can be set for homework. Students read through dialogues 1 to 5. Go through the example, eliciting the verbs for B's part. Remind students of the question form. Students complete the exercise. In pairs, students compare answers. Ask a few pairs to read out their dialogues to the class to check answers.

Answers
1 B: was running; was waiting
2 A: were you doing
    B: was watching
3 A: Were your parents living
    B: were living; was working
4 A: Was your sister dancing
    B: were dancing
5 A: were you playing
    B: was playing

Grammar notebook
Encourage students to note down the completed table and the rule from Exercise 2b.

3 Pronunciation
was and *were*

a 🔊 Students turn to page 120 and read through items 1 to 5. Write the first item on the board. Play the recording, pausing it after the first item to do as an example. Ask a student to come out and underline or circle as appropriate. Remind students that they are circling when the form is weak and underlining when the form is stressed. Play the recording for students to complete the exercise. Check answers.

1 What was he doing?
2 He was making a phone call.
3 He wasn't watching TV.
4 Was it raining?
5 Yes, it was.

b 🔊 Play the recording again, pausing for students to repeat.

c 🔊 Write the first sentence on the board and say it yourself as an example and ask them if *were* is stressed or unstressed (unstressed). Circle *were*.

Play the recording for students to listen and circle or underline *were/weren't*. Students can compare answers in pairs. Play the recording again for students to check or change their answers.

TAPESCRIPT/ANSWERS
1 What were they doing?
2 They were sitting down.
3 They weren't having dinner.
4 Were they listening to music?
5 No, they weren't.

d 🔊 Play the recording again, pausing for students to repeat each sentence.

4 Speak

a Divide the class into pairs. Read the example dialogue as a class or ask a stronger pair to read it out. Encourage students to use the wrong verbs in places in order to produce negative short answers.

Students complete the activity. Monitor them as they do this, to make sure they are using the weak forms correctly.

Ask a few pairs to model some of their questions and answers for the rest of the class.

b Read through the example dialogue as a class. In pairs, students ask and answer about themselves using the past continuous. Give students a few minutes to do this. Then ask for some pairs to feedback to the rest of the class.

5 Listen

Warm up

Ask students to look at the picture and to predict what happened.

a Ask students to read the question and the beginning of the story to check their *Warm up* predictions and the answer to the question.

Stronger classes: You can ask a confident reader to read it aloud.

Weaker classes: Read it aloud yourself, with students following in their books.

Ask for some ideas about what happened next. Do not give answers at this point.

b 🔊 Play the recording while students listen to see if any of their ideas from Exercise 5a were correct. Check answers.

TAPESCRIPT
I took the little boy along the road back to the town. While we were walking, he started to cry again. I said: "My name's Samantha. What's yours?" But the little boy didn't say anything.

We were getting close to the town when suddenly the little boy stopped. "My dog!" he said. "Where's my dog?" And then he started to run, back up the road towards the forest and the cave.

I shouted: "Come back!" but he didn't stop. I ran after him and I saw him run into the cave.

I went back into the cave. The little boy wasn't there but a small white dog was sitting on the ground. It was looking at me. And then it ran out of the cave and into the forest.

I didn't see the boy or the dog again. It was getting dark, so I walked back to the town and went home. I told my mother about the boy and the dog.

My mother said: "That's strange! Twenty years ago, a little boy and a dog disappeared in that forest!"

c Discuss this as a class.

6 Grammar

Past continuous vs. past simple

a Write the sentence on the board and ask a stronger student to come out and underline the past continuous and circle the past simple verb in it. Leave it on the board as it will be needed in Exercise 6b.

b Copy the diagram onto the board above the example sentence you wrote in Exercise 6a. Explain how the first action is going on when the other action interrupts it. Ask them the questions and elicit the answers (*past continuous tells us background action and past simple happened at one moment*). Students now complete the rule box. Check answers.

Answers
past continuous
past simple

c 🔊 Students read through sentences 1 to 3. Go through the first item as an example, if necessary. Students complete the exercise. At this point, you could play the recording in Exercise 5b again for students to listen and check their answers. Check answers as a class.

Answers
1 were walking/started
2 were getting/stopped
3 wasn't/was sitting

when/while

d Ask students to read through the two examples. Ask them which action is the background action (walking through the trees) and which action interrupts the background action at one particular moment (found a cave). Now ask them to read through the rule box and complete it using the examples to help them. Check answers.

Answers
simple; continuous

> **Language note**
> Students may find it useful to translate the example sentences into their own language and think about how these tenses are used.

(**e**) Ask students to read through sentences 1 to 5. Check any problems. Go through the example with students and ask them to explain why each tense is used. Students complete the exercise. Students can compare answers in pairs before a whole class check.

Answers
2 was running; fell
3 were playing; arrived
4 was having; had
5 was talking; went

(**f**) This exercise can be set for homework. Read through the two examples as a class and ask students if they can remember with which tense to use *while* (past continuous) and *when* (past simple). Students now join the sentences in Exercise 6e in both ways. Check answers.

Answers
2 Harry was running to school when he fell and hurt his leg. / While Harry was running to school, he fell and hurt his leg.
3 Alex and Sue were playing tennis when Lucy arrived. / While Alex and Sue were paying tennis, Lucy arrived.
4 Antonio was having breakfast when he got a great idea. / While he was having breakfast, Antonio got a great idea.
5 Carlo was talking on the phone when his father went out. / While Carlo was talking on the phone, his father went out.

Grammar notebook
Encourage students to note down the rules from Exercise 6 and some example sentences. They may find it useful to translate some of the sentences.

┌─ OPTIONAL ACTIVITY ─────────────────
To check students have understood the difference in the two tenses, give them the following sentences and ask them to explain what they mean. Remind them to think about which action happened first. Is the meaning the same or different?
1a When my brother arrived, we cooked a meal.
 (**They cooked a meal after he arrived.**)
 b When my brother arrived I was cooking a meal.
 (**I was in the middle of cooking a meal when he arrived.**)

2a While I was eating dinner, the phone rang.
 b I was eating dinner when the phone rang.
 (**2a and b mean the same. I was in the middle of eating dinner when the phone rang.**)
3a When he saw her, she ran away.
 b When he saw her, she was running away.
 (**He saw her and then she ran away because of seeing him.**)

7 Read

(**a**) Students look at the pictures and give their ideas. Ask students to read the first two paragraphs of the text quickly and check their answers. Remind them that they should only be looking for the information to answer their question and they don't need to understand every word in the text.

Answer
Camoculars (binoculars with a camera inside)

(**b**) Students read items 1 to 6 and a to f. Check any problems. Students read the text silently, or read it aloud to the class yourself. Go through the example, making sure students know what to do.

Students complete the exercise. They can compare answers in pairs before a whole class check.

Answers
2 a 3 f 4 b 5 c 6 d

(**c**) Students discuss the question as a whole class or in small groups. Ask for groups to feedback. Find out if anyone has an idea for an invention of their own.

8 Vocabulary

get

(**a**) Read the instructions with the class. Go through the example, making sure students understand why *became* is the answer. Students write the meaning of *get* in the sentences. Check answers.

Answers
2 arriving 3 becoming 4 arrived 5 received
6 receive

(**b**) This exercise can be set for homework. Students read through the phrases in the box. Make sure they understand them all. Go through the example, eliciting why this is the only possibility.

Students complete the exercise. Remind them to look carefully at the tenses they need to use and to choose the past simple or the past continuous. Check answers.

Answers
2 got to school
3 was getting wet
4 got an idea
5 got angry
6 got a surprise

Vocabulary notebook
Encourage students to note down the various meanings of *get* from Exercise 8 and to write some example sentences of their own.

Culture in mind

9 Read

If you set the background information as a homework research task, ask students to tell the class what they found out.

BACKGROUND INFORMATION

Levi Strauss: In 1850, Levi Strauss was a 20-year-old German immigrant in the USA. He arrived in San Francisco in 1853 with a supply of rough canvas usually used for tents and wagon covers. Instead of using it for tents and wagon covers he made trousers out of it. They were worn a lot by miners at this time but they were modified because the miners complained they rubbed their skin too much. Strauss then used a softer fabric, called 'serge de Nîmes', to make the next trousers. It was this material which became known as denim.

California Gold Rush: See Unit 1, Exercise 5.

Warm up

Ask students if they wear jeans a lot, if they know who invented them and if they think they are fashionable.

(a) Students look at the pictures. See if they can describe the styles of the jeans in the pictures. At this point, you could pre-teach *metal buttons*, *decorated*, *patterns* and *sequins*. Students look at the questions. Students read the text quickly to answer the questions and check their answers from the *Warm up*. Remind them they don't need to understand every word.

Answers
1 Levi Strauss   2 In the 1960s

(b) Read through titles 1 to 3 with students. In pairs, students decide which title they think is most appropriate. Ask for feedback, does the class agree?

Answer
1 From workwear to fashion

(c) Ask students to read through questions 1 to 6. Check any problems. If necessary, go through the first item as an example, locating the point in the text. Students complete the exercise. Students can compare answers in pairs before a whole class check.

Answers
1 Germany, 1829
2 For work
3 Men during the gold rush
4 From the part of France called Nimes, 'de Nimes'
5 Why they're called jeans.

Discussion box
Stronger classes: In pairs or small groups, students go though the questions in the box and discuss them.
Weaker classes: They can choose one question only to discuss. If necessary, elicit a few prompts for the question they have chosen to help them with their discussion.

Monitor and help as necessary, encouraging students to express themselves in English.

Ask pairs or groups to feedback to the class and discuss any interesting points further.

10 Write

The preparation for this can be done in class and the story written for homework.

(a) Ask students to read through questions 1 to 3. Check any problems. Pre-teach any vocabulary (*burrs, tape*). Go through the first item as an example, if necessary. Students then read through the story and answer the questions. Check answers.

Answers
1 Velcro™, George de Mestral
2 Because it helps fasten clothes, shoes, etc. and it's quick and easy to use.
3 When he was walking in the woods and he got lots of burrs stuck on his clothes which were difficult to get off.

(b) Students now match the questions with the paragraphs in the text. If necessary, do the first one with them as an example. Check answers.

Answers
1 A   2 C   3 B

(c) Students now choose an invention from this unit or they could think of one of their own. If they can't think of a real invention, they can make one up. Remind students of the structure of Alex's story in Exercise 10b. Encourage students to make notes and swap them with a partner to correct. They can then write up their notes into full sentences and produce a final version.

Students can illustrate their stories and add pictures and photos. Students can read out their stories to the class and the class can vote on the best invention.

3 She jumped well

Unit overview

TOPIC: Record-breaking sports stars
Sporting events

TEXTS
Listening: information about record-breaking sports stars
Reading: a story about the Extreme Games
Reading and listening: Story: *Was she pretty?*
Writing: a magazine report of a sports event

SPEAKING AND FUNCTIONS
Making comparisons
Describing a sports event
Comparing yourself with others

LANGUAGE
Comparative and superlative adjectives
Intensifiers with comparatives
as ... as comparatives
Adverbs, comparative adverbs
Vocabulary: Antonyms
Pronunciation: *than* and *as*
Everyday English: *had a go at me*; *Stop it!*; *Hold on!*;
I'm off

1 Listen

If you set the background information as a homework research task, ask students to tell the class what they found out.

BACKGROUND INFORMATION

Nadia Comaneci: Was born in Romania. She became a star during the 1976 Olympics when, at the age of 14, she won two gold medals for her gymnastic performances. She was the first gymnast ever to win a perfect score of 10.

Raymond Clarence Ewry (Ray): Was an American track and field athlete who won more Olympic gold medals than any athlete in history. This was all the more amazing an achievement because Ewry was severely disabled by polio as a child. At the 1900, 1904 and 1908 Olympic games he won 10 medals.

Pipin and Audrey Ferreras: Were a husband and wife free diving team. Free diving means diving as far as a person can without an oxygen tank, using only one breath.

Francisco Pipin Ferreras was born in 1962 in Cuba. His professional career began in 1987 when he won his first world record by diving

to a depth of 67 metres. In 2000, he set a new world record of diving to a depth of 162 metres.

Audrey Mestre-Ferreras was born in France in 1974. She learned to dive from a very young age with her spearfisher grandfather and mother. In 2001, she set a world record of diving to 130 metres. However, in 2002 she died while attempting to dive to a depth of 171 metres to break her husband's record.

Warm up

Ask students if they have any sporting heroes/ heroines. If so, in what sports? Ask them to give reasons why they like these people. Ask them to look at the photos and see if anyone has ever done any of the sports in the photos. Discuss this as a class, in L1 if appropriate.

Alternatively, you can ask students if they do sports regularly and if so which sports they do, how often they do them and if they are team or individual sports.

(a) Ask students to read through the sports in the box and look at the photos. Do the first item with them as an example, if necessary. Students complete the exercise. Check answers.

Answers
1 a   2 b   3 d   4 c

(b) 📢 **Stronger classes:** Divide the class into pairs. Ask students to read the questions and the profiles of the athletes. Check any problems. Give students a few minutes to predict the type of missing information (e.g., score will need a number, some sentences may need a comparative or superlative. As them which sports they think each person does and feedback to the class. Do not give answers at this point. Explain that they will now hear a recording which will give them the answers to the predictions. Play the recording. Check answers, playing and pausing the recording again as necessary.

Weaker classes: First of all refer students to the missing information next to *sports* on the profiles. Give students a few minutes to predict what the sports are (for Pipin and Audrey Ferreras the picture gives the answer away). Remind them that they should only be looking at the first gap in the profiles to complete the names of the sports and that they do not need to understand every word. It may be better to play each profile and then pause the tape to check answers. Then follow the procedure as for stronger classes. Pause and play the recording again as necessary.

TAPESCRIPT

In gymnastics, the "perfect score" – the highest number of points that an athlete can get – is 10 points. In the Olympic games in Montreal in 1976, Nadia Comaneci from Romania achieved seven perfect scores and won three gold medals and the all-round title in gymnastics. Nadia was only 14 at the time, younger than most of the other athletes in gymnastics. But she wasn't the youngest athlete in the 1976 games. Robin Consiglia won a silver medal with the US swimming team. She was only 13.

Who was the most successful Olympic athlete ever? An American called Raymond Ewry. Between the 1900 Paris Olympics and the 1908 Olympics in London Ewry won 10 gold medals. This makes him the most successful athlete in Olympic history – no other athlete has as many gold medals as Ewry. Of course today's athletes jump much higher and further than he did. Ewry's records were one point six five metres in the high jump – he did this in Paris in 1900 – and in 1908 in London he did three point four seven metres in the long jump.

One of the most extreme sports is free diving, going down under the water without oxygen, "on one breath only". Pipin Ferreras, the world's best free diver, holds the record: 162 metres. He achieved this amazing record on 18th January 2000, on his 38th birthday. But he believes that he can go deeper – maybe as far as 200 metres! In May 2001, after practising hard for two years, Pipin's wife Audrey set the world record for free diving among women – 130 metres. Sadly, Audrey died on October 12th 2002 while she was trying to beat her husband's record.

Answers

Nadia Comaneci:
- gymnastics
- 10
- 7; 3
- 14; younger; youngest; 13

Raymond Ewry:
- high jump and long jump
- 10
- most
- many
- jump; higher; further
- high jump; 3.47; long jump

Pipin and Audrey Ferreras:
- free diving
- 162
- deeper; far
- 130

(c) In pairs or small groups, students discuss the questions and give reasons for their answers. Ask some pairs or a spokesperson from each group to give their views to the rest of the class. Does everyone agree? If there are any interesting opinions, encourage students to talk about them further and see what the rest of the class think.

OPTIONAL ACTIVITIES

Stronger classes

Ask students to research a sporting record breaker from their own country. Students could make a profile card similar to the ones in Exercise 1b. Students can research this for homework and bring the information into class the next lesson and present it.

Weaker classes

Divide students into small groups of four or five. Choose one student who must think of a sporting hero/heroine. The other students have 20 questions to guess who the person is thinking about. The person who has thought of the sporting person can only answer Yes or No. The person who guesses before the 20 questions can think of their hero/heroine next and if no one guesses after 20 questions the person can tell them the answer and choose again. For example:
S2: Are you a footballer?
S1: No, I'm not.
S3: Are you a man?
S1: Yes, I am. etc.

2 Grammar
Comparative and superlative adjectives

(a) **Stronger classes:** Students read through the example. Ask them if the words in bold are a comparative or superlative. Elicit *superlative*. Ask them how they know this and elicit because it has *the* in front of the adjective and *-est* on the end of the adjective. Elicit the comparative form to check they remember from Student's Book 1 (*younger than*). Students now go through the profiles of the athletes on page 18 and underline other examples of comparatives and superlatives.

Weaker classes: Books closed. Write the following examples (or some of your own) on the board: *I am younger than my brother* or *I am the youngest in my family*. Ask students to identify the comparative and superlative form and elicit or explain how to form comparatives and superlatives.

Ask a student to come out and underline each form on the board. Students now open their books at page 19 and look at the superlative example from the text. Do the first item in the Nadia Comaneci profile with them as an example. Students complete the exercise.

Check answers, asking students to tell you which are the comparatives and which the superlatives.

Answers

Nadia Comaneci text: younger than most athletes; the youngest athlete
Raymond Ewry text: the most successful athlete; much higher and further than ...
Pipin and Audrey Ferreras: can go deeper ...

(b) Ask students to read through the adjectives in the box and the table. Go through the examples with them making sure they remember which are comparatives and which are superlatives. Students complete the exercise. Check answers.

It may be helpful to copy the table onto the board and to ask students to come out and complete it with their answers.

Answers
-er/-est: fat; fast; quiet; high; deep; new
-ier/-iest: tidy
more/most: interesting
Irregular comparatives: bad

> **Language notes**
> 1 Students may produce incorrect comparatives, e.g. *more interesting that*. Remind them we use *more ... than* in English.
> 2 It may be useful to remind students of the spelling rules for comparatives and superlatives at this point:
> • one syllable adjectives: add -er/-est, e.g. *fast – faster – fastest*
> • one syllable adjectives which end consonant + vowel + consonant: double the final consonant + -er/-est: *big – bigger – biggest*
> • two syllable adjectives ending in consonant + -y, delete the -y and add -ier/-iest: *tidy – tidier – tidiest*
> • two or more syllable adjectives: add more/most in front of the adjective: *more/most successful*
> • irregular adjectives: learn them! *far – further – furthest*

Intensifiers with comparative adjectives

Stronger classes: Students look at the pictures and the example sentences. Ask them to identify the comparative adjectives in each sentence and then elicit or explain what difference the words *much/far/a lot* make (*much* is used with comparative adjectives to show a big difference; *a bit/a little* is used with comparative adjectives to show a small difference). To check understanding at this point, ask students to give you an example of their own for one or both of the intensifiers.

Weaker classes: Books closed. Write two example sentences of your own on the board (e.g. I'm much younger than my brother./I'm a bit older than you.). Ask students to identify the comparative adjectives (younger/older). Ask them to look at the words before each adjective and explain the purpose of each (*much* is used with comparative adjectives to show a big difference; *a bit* or *a little* is used with comparative adjectives to show a small difference). Students now open their books at page 19 and look at the picture and example sentences.

(c) Students read through prompts 1 to 6. Go through the example and then ask students to produce another example sentence using *easy*. Students complete the exercise. Remind them they must use the correct comparative forms and to start each sentence with *I think ...* . Monitor and check students are using the forms correctly noting down any repeated errors for further discussion. Students can compare answers in pairs before a whole class check.

Possible answers
1 I think watching TV is much/far easier than reading a book. / I think reading a book is a bit / a little more interesting than watching TV.
2 I think a computer is much more expensive than a mobile phone. / I think a mobile phone is much more useful than a computer. / I think a mobile phone is a bit / a little more useful than a computer.
3 I think boys are much more intelligent than girls. / I think girls are much tidier than boys. / I think girls are a little / a bit more intelligent than boys.
4 I think English is much more difficult than History. / I think History is a bit / a little easier than English.
5 My father is far/much younger than my mother. / My mother is a bit / a little older than my father. / My mother is a little / a bit taller than my father.
6 The Pacific ocean is a lot / far deeper than the Atlantic ocean. / The Pacific ocean is much/far bigger than the Atlantic ocean. / The Pacific ocean is a bit / a little deeper than the Atlantic ocean.

Grammar notebook
Students should note down the table and rules from Exercise 2 and write some examples and translations of their own.

> ─ OPTIONAL ACTIVITY ───────────
> Divide the class into pairs. Students think of four (or more) cities from their own country (or countries in the world) and make sentences about them using *much/far / a lot / a bit / a little* and comparative adjectives. Students then discuss their sentences with their partner. Ask pairs to feedback to the class.

3 Vocabulary and grammar
Antonyms

(a) Ask students to read through adjectives 1 to 12 and check understanding. Go through the example with them. Students complete the exercise. Check answers.

Students now read the second part of the instruction. Go through the first item with them as an example, eliciting the first comparative as an example. Students complete the exercise. Students can compare answers in pairs before a whole class check.

Answers

1 unsuccessful – successful;
   successful – more successful – most successful,
   unsuccessful – more unsuccessful – most
   unsuccessful
2 slim – fat;
   fat – fatter – fattest, slim – slimmer – slimmest
3 boring – interesting;
   interesting – more interesting – most interesting,
   boring – more boring – most boring
4 shallow – deep;
   deep – deeper – deepest, shallow – shallower
   – shallowest
5 low – high;
   high – higher – highest, low – lower – lowest
6 slow – fast;
   fast – faster – fastest, slow – slower – slowest
7 noisy – quiet;
   quiet – quieter – quietest, noisy – noisier –
   noisiest
8 messy – tidy;
   tidy – tidier – tidiest, messy – messier – messiest
9 difficult – easy;
   easy – easier – easiest, difficult – more difficult
   – most difficult
10 near – far;
   far – further – furthest, near – nearer – nearest
11 good – bad;
   bad – worse – worst, good – better – best
12 old – young; old – new;
   young – younger – youngest, new – newer –
   newest, old – older – oldest

> **Language note**
> Remind students that some adjectives can have
> more than one opposite, e.g. *old/young*; *old/new*;
> *tidy/messy*; *tidy/untidy*, etc.

as ... as comparatives

b **Stronger classes:** Ask students to read through the
two examples. Explain to them that we use *as ... as*
when we compare two things. Elicit what is being
compared in the first example sentence (*my sister
and I*) and in the second (*Tom's feet and his father's
feet*). Students now go back through the text on
page 18 and find more examples.

Weaker classes: Books closed. Illustrate the two
example sentences on the board. Label picture 1:
me/my sister and label picture 2: Tom's feet/Tom's
dad's feet. With example sentence 1, ask students:
Who is taller? And elicit that 'me' is taller. Do the
same with picture 2 and elicit that their feet are the
same size. Students now open their books at page 19
and read through the example sentences.. Explain to
students that we use *as ... as* to say two nouns are
the same and not *as ... as* to say that the first noun is
less than the second. Students now go back through
the text on page 18 and find further examples; do
the first one with them as an example, if necessary.

Students complete the exercise. Check answers.

Answers
Raymond Ewry: ... as many gold medals as ...
Pipin and Audrey Ferreras: ... as far as ...

c Ask students to read through sentences 1 to 6.
Go through the example, asking students to explain
why *as ... as* is used. Students complete the exercise.
Remind them to use adjectives they have seen already
in this unit and to think about how the two sentences
will mean the same using the construction (not) *as ...
as*. Check answers.

Answers
2 as tidy as   3 as slow as   4 as quiet as
5 as difficult as   6 isn't as interesting as

> **Language notes**
> 1 Students may produce statements like ... *(not) as
>   quiet than*. Remind them in English we use *as ...
>   as* in positive sentences when two things are the
>   same and *more ... than* in comparative sentences.
> 2 Explain to students that we use *as ... as* to say
>   two nouns are the same and not *as ... as* to say
>   that the first noun is less than the second.

4 # Pronunciation

than and *as*

a 🔊 Students turn to page 120 and read through
sentences 1 to 5. Play the recording, pausing it after
the first item and go through the example. Play the
recording again for students to listen and underline
the stressed syllables. Play the recording again, pausing
as necessary for students to check or change their
answers.

TAPESCRIPT/ANSWERS
1 Sarah's brother isn't as old as she is.
2 Peter's messier than his sister.
3 Peter isn't as tidy as his sister.
4 Travelling by train is often faster than
   travelling by bus.
5 Travelling by train isn't as slow as
   travelling by bus.

b 🔊 Play the recording, pausing for students
to listen to the pronunciation of *as* and *than*.
Play the recording again, pausing for students
to repeat each sentence.

5 Read

If you set the background information as a homework research task, ask students to tell the class what they found out.

BACKGROUND INFORMATION

X Games: These are the Extreme Games, which are held every winter and summer in various locations across the globe. Competitors take part in daring and death defying feats on skateboards, snowboards, motocross and BMX bikes, freestyle skiing and surfing.

Tara Dakides: Was one of the stars of the 2000 X Games.

Vermont: Is one of the states of the USA.

Mammoth Mountain, California: Is a ski resort on the edge of the Sierra Nevada mountains.

Warm up

Ask students to look at the photos and the sports depicted. Ask if any of them have ever done/seen any sports like this. What are the most daring sports students have done?

Discuss this as a class, in L1 if appropriate.

(a) Students look at the pictures again and the text title and read the questions. Elicit some ideas. Students then read the text quickly to check their ideas. Remind them that they don't need to understand every word at this stage. Check answers.

Answers
Snowboarding
Yes, she did.

(b) Students read through sentences 1 to 5. Check any problems. Go through the first one as an example, showing students how to locate the answer in the text. Students complete the exercise. Check answers and then ask students to correct the false statements.

Weaker classes: You may want to pre-teach the following words before students begin the exercise: *dramatic; regular; competition; position; round; scores; board; winner.*

Answers
1 F (Para 2, lines 1–3: ... with Tara in tenth position.)
2 T   3 T   4 T   5 F (Para 5, lines 1–2: ... party a little over the weekend ...)

6 Grammar

Adverbs, comparative adverbs

(a) **Stronger classes:** Students read through the two examples. Elicit the formation of regular adverbs (adjective + *-ly*).

Students now go through the text on page 20 and underline other examples of adverbs. If necessary, find the first one as a class. Check answers.

Weaker classes: Books closed. Write the following sentences on the board:
1 I am very nervous before exams.
2 I waited nervously before the exam results arrived.

Ask students which sentence contains an adjective (1) and which an adverb (2). Elicit the formation of regular adverbs (adjective + *-ly*). Students open their books at page 21 and look at the example sentences. Students now go through the text on page 20 and underline other examples of adverbs. Tell them there are nine in total. If necessary, find the first one as a class. Check answers.

Answers
Para 2: nervously; well; brilliantly; quickly
Para 3: badly; well
Para 4: regularly; fast; quickly; easily
Para 5: easily

(b) **Stronger classes:** Ask students to read through the questions and then elicit the form of each type of adverb.

Weaker classes: It may be useful to put an example of each type on the board for them and then elicit the formation rules (e.g. *quick; easy; fast*).

Answers
- Regular adverbs: add *-ly* to the adjective, e.g. *quick – quickly*
- Adjectives ending in *-y*: change the *-y* to *-i* and add *-ly*, e.g. *easy – easily*
- Irregular adverbs: learn them! e.g. *fast; good; hard*

To check understanding at this point, call out several adjectives of your choice (e.g. *nervous; bad; easy; slow; hard*) and ask students to give you the adverbs.

(c) Ask students to read through the diary entry. Go through the example with them, making sure they are clear that they have to circle the correct option. Students complete the exercise. They can then compare answers in pairs before a whole class check.

Answers
1 quickly   2 terrible   3 fluently   4 badly
5 easy   6 quickly   7 good   8 happily

(d) **Stronger classes:** Students read through the example sentences. Explain that comparative adverbs are used when two actions are compared. Ask students to tell you what the two actions are in the example sentences (Sentence 1: going down the hill; Sentence 2: winning). Students then read and complete the rule box.

Weaker classes: Books closed. Put two examples of your own on the board (e.g. *I can speak L1 more quickly than English. / I understand French more easily than Spanish.*). Ask a student to come out and underline the comparative adverbs. Point out that we use *more ... than* with adverbs as well as adjectives for comparison and explain that comparative adverbs are used when two actions are compared. Students open their book at page 21 and read the example sentences and complete the rule box.

Answer
more

(e) **Stronger classes:** Ask students to read through the examples in the box. Go through the example with them. Students complete the exercise. Check answers.

Weaker classes: Write the headings: *Regular/ Adjectives ending in -y/Irregular* on the board. Ask a student to come out and write *soon/sooner* under the correct column (*Regular*). Do the same with all the other examples in the box asking a student to come out each time and write the correct comparative under the correct column heading.

Answers
Regular: soon – sooner; fast – faster; hard – harder
Adjectives ending in -y: early – earlier
Irregular: good – better; bad – worse; far – further

(f) This exercise can be set for homework. Students read through sentences 1 to 8. Check any problems. Go through the example with them, if necessary. Students complete the exercise. Remind them to look carefully at each adjective and decide if it is regular or irregular. Check answers.

Answers
2 more fluently   3 more clearly than
4 faster than   5 harder   6 more easily
7 better   8 further

Grammar notebook
Remind students to note down the examples and rules for comparative adjectives and adverbs from this exercise.

7 Speak

Divide the class into pairs. Students read through the verbs in the box. Check any problems. Ask a stronger pair to read out the example to the rest of the class. Students now take turns to compare themselves with family members and friends. Monitor and check students are using the forms correctly and note down any repeated errors to go through as a class after the exercise. Ask for some feedback and follow up any interesting comparisons as a class.

OPTIONAL ACTIVITY

Small groups or whole class. Students choose an adverb and they must mime an action using that adverb. The other students have to guess what the action is and how the student is doing it. Set a time limit of e.g. 15 seconds for each group/class to guess the action and adverb. Use the following prompts if necessary:

• waiting nervously before an exam
• smiling happily at someone you like
• running quickly to catch a bus/train
• speaking English fluently

Was she pretty?
8 Read and listen

Warm up

Ask students if they can remember the characters from the last story episode (*Dave and Joanne*) and what happened (*Joanne met Dave in the shop where he works and offered him her phone number. She was keen to join their band.*).

(a) 🔊 Read through the questions as a class and ask students to predict the answers. Play the recording while students read and listen to check their predictions. Check answers. Play the recording again, pausing as necessary for students to clarify any problems.

Answers
1 Dave and Amy
2 Walking on a bridge (in Cambridge)
3 The band they want to form and who might be in it.

TAPESCRIPT
See the story on page 22 of the Student's Book.

(b) **Stronger classes:** Students read through the questions and answer them without playing the recording again.

Weaker classes: Students read through the questions. Play the recording for them, pausing it after the first question and go through it as an example. Play the recording again for students to listen and complete the exercise.

Check answers, playing and pausing the recording again as necessary to clarify any problems.

Answers
1 Because Mr Dobson had a go at him (told him off).
2 Because he doesn't want her to get jealous.
3 Because she's the singer.
4 He put an advert in the paper.
5 Because she is annoyed with Dave and she is worried about Joanne joining the band as a singer.

9 Everyday English

(a) Ask students to read through expressions 1 to 4 and to locate them in the story on page 22 and decide who says them.

Weaker classes: Check answers at this stage.

Students then match the expressions with the definitions. Go through the first item with them as an example, if necessary. Check answers.

Answers
1 b Dave   2 c Dave   3 d Amy   4 a Amy

(b) Ask students to read through dialogues 1 to 4. Check any problems. Go through the first dialogue with them as an example, if necessary. Students complete the other dialogues with the expressions from Exercise 9a. Check answers.

Answers
1 I'm off   2 stop it   3 had a go at me
4 Hold on

┌─ OPTIONAL ACTIVITIES ━━━━━━━━━

See Unit 1, Exercise 10 Everyday English, Optional Activities.

10 Speak and write

(a) Ask students to read through the instructions and then questions 1 to 6. Check any problems. If necessary, go through the first item as an example. Students read through the report and answer the questions. Check answers.

Answers
1 A football match.
2 Last Saturday afternoon in London.
3 Rooney played brilliantly.
4 Rooney scored for England.
5 England won 2 – 1.
6 Yes, he did. It was exciting and his team played brilliantly.

(b) Students read through topics 1 to 3. Students read the report again, this time matching each paragraph with a topic. Check answers.

Answers
1 B   2 C   3 A

(c) In pairs, students think of a sports event they have seen. If they have not seen a live sports event they can think of one they watched on television. Students take turns to ask and answer the questions from Exercise 1a about the event. Monitor and check students are taking turns to ask and answer. Ask for some pairs to feedback to the class about the events they talked about.

(d) This exercise can be set for homework. Students now use the information from Exercise 10c and the questions in Exercise 10a and write up their own reports. Encourage them to follow the report on page 23 as a model and to use as many adverbs and adjectives as they can to describe how they felt and what the atmosphere was like. Collect in the reports to correct or students can swap reports with a partner.

4) Our world

TOPIC: The environment

TEXTS
Reading and listening: a text about the future of the planet
Listening: a radio interview about renewable forms of energy
Writing: an article for a school website about your town/environment

SPEAKING
Discussing environmental problems
Predicting future events
Discussing renewable forms of energy

LANGUAGE
Vocabulary: the environment and forms of renewable energy
will/won't and *may / might (not)* for prediction
First conditional
unless in first conditional sentences
Pronunciation: /əʊ/ *won't*

1 Read and listen

Warm up

As a class or in small groups, students discuss problems with the environment. Ask them what problems we are facing. You could elicit some of the vocabulary in the unit, e.g. global warming, pollution, climate change, etc. Ask them what sort of things they can do to help. Ask for some groups to feedback to the rest of the class and discuss any interesting ideas further. This can be discussed in L1 if appropriate.

(a) Students read through the question. Elicit some ideas. Students then read the text quickly to check their ideas. Remind them they don't have to understand every word in the text at this stage. Check answers as a class.

Answer
There are more tornadoes, thunderstorms and hurricanes now than there were in the past and there are more floods and much less rain.

(b) 🔊 Ask students to read through items 1 to 4 and a to d.

Stronger classes: They can read the text and match the two parts of the sentence. Then play the recording for them to listen and check only.

Weaker classes: Play the recording, pausing it after the first item and ask them to match this as an

example. Then play the rest of the recording while students read and listen and match the other sentences. Remind students that they will not hear the exact sentence in the text but they must listen for some key words which will have the same meaning as the sentences they are matching. Check answers. Play the recording again, pausing as necessary to clarify any problems.

TAPESCRIPT
See the reading text on page 24 of the Student's Book.

Answers
1 c   2 d   3 b   4 a

OPTIONAL ACTIVITIES

Stronger classes
In small groups, students discuss if they have noticed any of these weather types in their own country. Ask for feedback and discuss any interesting points further.

Weaker classes
Students may find it useful to do the following short comprehension exercise on the text at this point.
1   What is another name for a tornado? (**Twister.**)
2   How many tornadoes are there in the USA each year? (**1,000.**)
3   How many tornadoes are there in Britain every year? (**More than 50.**)
4   Are the climate changes natural? (**No, they aren't / they're not.**)
5   What do scientists think is the problem? (**Human activity: cutting down trees and burning too much oil.**)

2 Vocabulary

The environment

(a) Ask students to read through phrases 1 to 6. Go through the first item as an example.

Stronger classes: Students work through the other expressions and work out their meaning. Remind them to try and work out the meaning from context by looking at the other sentences.

Weaker classes: You can ask them the following concept questions to help them with the meaning of each expression:
1   Is the number of thunderstorms going up or down?
2   Are these temperatures happening all over the world? Are they going up or down?
3   What is the part of the world called which has a north and south part where you can find polar bears and penguins and lots of snow and ice? What is the verb we use in English when ice becomes water?
4   Will the islands still be there or not?

5 What do we call a lot of water which comes from the sea and covers the land? If a town is near the sea it is said to be on the ..... .

6 What is it called when the temperature is rising and there are problems with the planet?

Check answers as a class or if students prefer they can check answers in a dictionary.

Answers
1 going up/getting bigger
2 going up
3 the two points at the top and bottom of the Earth (North and South); when a solid becomes a liquid
4 vanish
5 a large amount of water from a river or the sea which has spread on to an area of land; situated on or near the sea
6 the increase in temperature of the world's climate

(b) 🔊 Ask students to read through words 1 to 8 in the box and to look at the pictures.

Stronger classes: Elicit the words students know already and ask them to match them. Students then match the other words.

Weaker classes: Go through the first item as an example. Students then match the other words.

Students compare answers in pairs. Play the recording for students to listen and check or change their answers. Play the recording again, pausing for students to repeat each word.

TAPESCRIPT/ANSWERS
a 6 the atmosphere   b 2 litter   c 4 factory fumes
d 3 pollution   e 5 rainforests   f 7 rubbish
g 8 a power station   h 1 recycling

(c) Students read through the verbs in the box. Check any problems. Go through the example, if necessary. Students complete the exercise. Check answers.

Answers
1 pick it up   2 recycle   3 waste   4 clean up
5 pollute   6 cut down

Vocabulary notebook
Students should start a section called *The environment* and note down all the new words from Exercise 2.

3 Speak

(a) Divide the class into pairs. Read through the example sentences and explain to students that they must think of more problems in the environment and make a list. Give students a few minutes to complete the exercise. Remind them to think about what they discussed in the *Warm up* in Exercise 1 and to use the pictures in Exercise 2 to help them. Ask for feedback and put a selection of ideas on the board.

(b) Students now rank the problems in order of seriousness. If necessary, rank one of the items on the board with them as an example. Give students a few minutes to continue to rank the other items in their lists. Then put each pair with a new pair to make groups of four and pairs compare lists. Ask for feedback and ask students to come out and rank the items on the board. Are there any interesting results? Does the whole class agree? Encourage students to discuss with the rest of the class why they feel certain problems are more/less important than others.

(c) In the same or different pairs, students now make a list of things ordinary people can do to help the environment. Put the examples on the board and elicit a few more. Give students a few minutes to discuss this. Ask for feedback and write down their ideas on the board or ask some students to come out and write their ideas up.

(d) In small groups, students discuss which of the things from Exercise 3c they do to help the environment. Ask for feedback.

┌─ OPTIONAL ACTIVITY ─────────────────────
Environmentally friendly classrooms
In small groups, students decide how they could be more environmentally friendly in the classroom. They can use the ideas from Exercise 3 or think of some new ideas for the classroom, e.g. always recycle paper, switch the lights off when they are not needed, share paper for making notes in an exercise, bring in plants, etc.

Students can then make posters illustrating what they aim to do to help improve their classrooms and the posters can be displayed on the walls.

4 Grammar

will/won't and *might / may (not)* for prediction

(a) **Stronger classes:** Read through the examples with students, pointing out the use of *will* and *might*. Ask students if it is definite that the weather will get worse and elicit *Yes*. Ask them if it is definite that some islands will disappear and elicit *No, it is only possible*. To check understanding at this point, ask a few students to give you an example of their own for each verb. Students now go back through the text on page 24 and underline other examples of *will/won't* and *may / might (not)*.

Weaker classes: Books closed. Write a few examples of your own on the board (e.g. *I will/might be at school tomorrow. / It will/might rain tomorrow. / (Juventus) will/might win the league this year.*). Ask students how likely each of these things is to happen. Elicit that it is very likely that you will come to school tomorrow and circle *will* in the example on the board. Ask a student to come out and choose the correct answer in the next example and another for a third example if you have used one. At this point, elicit or explain the difference between *will/won't* and *may / might (not)* and when we use *them* (*will/won't* for certainty and *may / might (not)* if there is an element of doubt). To check understanding at this point, ask a few students to give you an example of their own for each verb. Students now open their book at page 26 and read through the examples from the text. Then they go back through the text on page 24 and underline other examples of *will/won't* and *may /might (not)*.

Check answers.

Answers
Para 2: ... the weather will get worse ...; ... climate change won't go away ...
Para 4: the ice at the poles will melt; sea levels will rise; some islands might disappear; there may be many other ...

Students now read the rule box and complete it. Check answers.

Answers
will; might

> **Language note**
> Remind students that the negative form of *will* is *won't* and that it is the same for all persons.

(b) Students read through sentences 1 to 5. Check any problems. Go through the example as a class, if necessary. Students complete the exercise. Check answers.

Answers
2 will travel   3 will/arrive   4 'll buy   5 won't take

(c) Students read through sentences 1 to 7. Go through the example, if necessary. Students complete the exercise. Check answers.

Answers
2 might be   3 might like   4 might break
5 might not pass   6 might live   7 might have

(d) This exercise can be set for homework. Students read through sentences 1 to 7. Check any problems. Go through the example, if necessary, making sure students understand why *might* is the correct answer. Students complete the exercise. Remind them to think about the degree of possibility before they choose their verb. Check answers.

Answers
2 won't   3 might   4 will   5 might   6 A: will
B: might   7 won't

Grammar notebook
Remind students to note down the rules for the use of *will/won't* and *may / might (not)* from this unit and some example sentences of their own.

Pronunciation
/əʊ/ *won't*

Students turn to page 120 and read through sentences 1 to 4. Play the recording, pausing after each sentence for students to repeat. If students are still having problems, play the recording again and drill the sound a few more times.

TAPESCRIPT
1 I won't open it.
2 He won't answer the question.
3 She won't tell me.
4 They won't come.
5 We won't be late.

6

Speak

Divide the class into pairs. Students read through the topics in the box. Ask a stronger pair to read out the example exchange to the class. Draw students' attention to the use of *will* and *might* in the exchange. Give students a few minutes to discuss the topics in the box. Remind them to use *will/won't* and *might/may not* wherever possible. Monitor and check these are being used correctly and note down any errors or pronunciation problems to go through as a class later.

Weaker students: They could choose three topics only from the box.

Ask for pairs to feedback to the class. If there are any interesting points, discuss these further as a class.

7

Grammar and speaking
First conditional

(a) **Stronger classes:** Read through the example sentences with students and ask them to offer suggestions to complete the gaps. Students then turn to the text on page 24 again and check or change their answers. Remind students how to form the first conditional by asking them which verb goes in each half of the sentences. Students read through the rule box and complete it using the examples to help them.

Weaker classes: Books closed. Write a few examples of your own on the board (e.g. *If I study hard for my exam, ... /If it doesn't rain tomorrow, I ... /If I save up enough money I ...*). Ask students to offer suggestions to complete each sentence. Ask students what they notice about the verbs in each half of the sentence. Elicit that the first one is present simple and the second one is *will/won't*. Students now open their books at page 27 and read through the example sentences. Students look back at the text on page 24 and complete the sentences. Students read through the rule box and complete it using the examples to help them.

Check answers.

Answers

Sentence 1: ... the ice at the poles will melt.
Sentence 2: ... sea levels will rise.

Answer

present simple/will/won't

To check understanding of the first conditional at this point, ask students to produce an example sentence each about themselves.

(b) Students read through sentences 1 to 6. Go through the example, if necessary. Students complete the exercise. Check answers.

Answers

2 are / will be
3 see/will/give
4 increases / will die
5 won't tell / don't come
6 will be / see

Language notes

1 Remind students that the *If* phrase can come first or second in the sentence but the present simple tense always goes with the *If* phrase.
2 Remind students to use the contracted form in conditional sentences. It is more natural in English to say *If the weather is good tomorrow, I'll go to the beach* than ... *I will go to the beach*.
3 Students may produce sentences like *If I will go..., I will ...* . Ask them to think about how these sentences work in their own language and to translate them if necessary.

(c) This exercise can be set for homework. Students read through questions 1 to 6. Go through the example, if necessary, pointing out the word order in questions. Students complete the exercise. Remind them to use the correct question forms and to look for the *If* phrase carefully since it may not always be at the start of each question. Check answers.

Answers

2 will/go/go
3 will/buy/go
4 don't go / will/do
5 doesn't give / will/do
6 phone/will / talk about

(d) Divide the class into pairs. Ask a stronger pair to read out the example exchange and draw students' attention to the use of the first conditional in the question and *might* in the answer. Remind students that *might* is used if we are unsure of something. Give students a few minutes to ask and answer the questions. Monitor and check that students are taking turns to ask and answer. Note down any problems they are having with the question and answer formation or pronunciation to go through later as a class. Ask for feedback from pairs on what each person answered.

(e) Divide the class into pairs (or keep the same pairs as Exercise 7d). Students look at the pictures. Go through the example sentence as a class, drawing students' attention to the use of the first conditional structure. Give students time to complete the exercise. Ask a few pairs to read out their sentences to the class.

Weaker classes: They may need more support with vocabulary here. Offer them the following prompts (or others of your own choice) for each picture:
2 police / arrest
3 study / do well
4 turn the music down / father get angry
5 watch television / not pass exams
6 stop reading / walk into the ladder

Possible answers

2 If the police see him, they'll arrest him.
3 If he doesn't study for his exams, he won't do well.
4 If she doesn't turn the music down, her father will be very angry.
5 If you watch television, you won't pass your exams.
6 If she doesn't stop reading the book, she'll walk into the ladder.

Grammar notebook

Students should note down the rules for the first conditional from this unit and some example sentences of their own.

OPTIONAL ACTIVITY

Write the following prompts on the board:
• more cars on the road / more pollution
• pollution increase / plants and animals die
• ice melt / sea levels rise
• more people recycle / save the planet

Divide the class into small groups of four or five. Each group chooses a prompt and must make as many first conditional sentences from it to form a chain. For example:

S1: *If there are more cars on the road, there will be more pollution.*
S2: *If there is more pollution, there will be more illness.*
S3: *If there is more illness, there will be more work for doctors.*
S4: *If there is more work for doctors, they will be busy.* etc.

Ask some groups to read out their chain sentences to the rest of the class.

---

unless in first conditional sentences

(f) Stronger classes: Students read through the example sentences from the text. Ask them what they notice about the verb following *unless* in each sentence and elicit that it is positive. Students complete the rule.

Weaker classes: Books closed. Write two examples on the board (e.g. *Unless you study hard, you won't* *pass your exams. / If you study hard, you'll pass your exams.*). Ask students to identify the first conditional sentence (sentence 2) and then ask them what they notice about the *unless* sentence. Elicit or explain that the verb following *unless* is positive but the second verb is negative. Students now open their books at page 27 and look at the examples from the text. Students then complete the rule. Draw students' attention to the meaning of *unless*.

Check answers.

Answer
don't do

To check students have understood the meaning of *unless* at this point, ask them to produce a sentence with *unless* about themselves.

> **Language notes**
> 1 Remind students that *unless* means *if not*.
> 2 Students may produce statements like **Unless I don't work, I will ….* Remind them that *unless* is always followed by a positive verb.
> 3 Students may find it useful to think about how this phrase works in their own language and translate some of the example sentences.

(g) Students read through items 1 to 5 and a to e. Go through the example, if necessary. Students complete the exercise. Check answers.

Answers
1 d   2 e   3 a   4 b   5 c

Grammar notebook
Encourage students to note down the rules for *unless* and an example sentence or two of their own.

Culture in mind

8 Listen

Warm up

Ask students what types of energy are used in the classroom and elicit a few examples and put them on the board. Then ask them what type of energy they use at home and what they use it for. Elicit a few more examples and add them to the list on the board.

(a) 🔊 Students read through items 1 to 7 and look at the pictures. Go through the first item as an example and see if they can match any more items if their suggestions from the *Warm up* are included. Students complete the exercise. Play the recording for students to check answers. Play the recording again, pausing after each item for students to repeat.

TAPESCRIPT/ANSWERS
a 6 oil
c 7 hydro-electric dam
d 2 wind energy
e 1 solar energy
f 3 nuclear energy
g 4 waves

(b) **Stronger classes:** Ask students if they can explain the phrase *renewable/non-renewable energy*.

Weaker classes: Discuss *renewable/non-renewable energy* in L1 if appropriate.

Refer students to the pictures and ask them to identify the different types of energy. Check answers.

Answers
Renewable: solar; hydro-electric; wind; wind; waves
Non-renewable: oil; coal; nuclear

(c) 🔊 Before they listen, ask students what problems they think there are with non-renewable sources of energy such as coal, oil and nuclear energy. Do this in L1 if necessary, translating/eliciting new vocabulary in English as students explain. **Weaker classes:** You could write the new vocabulary on the board first. Students copy these and listen and tick the words as they hear them mentioned on the recording.

TAPESCRIPT

Woman   On today's programme, we're talking to Dr Anthony Gregg, about different forms of renewable energy around the world. Good afternoon, Doctor Gregg.

Man   Good afternoon.

Woman   Now, a lot of places around the world use coal to produce energy, don't they?

Man   That's right. Since the nineteenth century, the most popular way to produce energy has been coal. But of course there are problems with this.

Woman   Like what, for example?

Man   Well, when you burn coal, there are a lot of fumes that pollute the atmosphere. Of course the same is true for oil. Another problem is that oil and coal are non-renewable and will eventually disappear, we can't continue to use them forever. This is also true of gas, of course.

Woman   So, many places now use nuclear energy, don't they?

Man   Yes, indeed. But of course, many people feel nuclear energy is dangerous for many reasons. The explosion in Chernobyl in Russia in 1986, for example, killed a lot of people because of radiation. There's also the problem of what to do with the nuclear waste.

Woman   But there are alternatives, aren't there, to these forms of energy?

Man   Oh, lots of alternatives! These days, people are looking more and more for different forms of energy – things that we'll be able to use again and again in the future and that won't pollute the environment.

Woman Can you give us some examples?

Man Certainly. One way is to use solar energy – using the sun.

Woman Uh huh.

Man And then of course there's hydro-electric energy; you can see hydro-electric dams in many countries around the world.

Woman That's using water, right?

Man Yes, that's right. And another way is to use waves – waves in the sea, or waves in rivers. Unfortunately, very few countries are using this at the moment.

Woman And wind energy?

Man Yes, wind energy is an excellent way to get renewable energy.

Woman OK. So there are lots of different possibilities. Which countries are using …

Answers

Coal/Oil: they produce lots of fumes which pollute the atmosphere.

Nuclear power: there are fears about radiation and there is a problem with disposing of nuclear waste.

(d) 🔊 Students read through the table. Check they know the countries in the table and how to pronounce them correctly. Play the recording, pausing it after the example item, making sure students understand what they have to do. Play the recording for students to listen and complete the exercise. Students can compare answers in pairs before a whole class check. Play the recording again pausing as necessary to clarify any problems.

TAPESCRIPT

Woman OK. So there are lots of different possibilities. Which countries are using renewable energy, and what kinds of renewable energy are they using?

Man Erm, well, there are many countries that use renewable energy – I can't possibly talk about them all on this programme. But let's start with the United States, the USA. They're using solar energy and wind energy. Erm … in California, for example, there's a solar power station called Solar One, which opened in 1982, and California also has a lot of wind farms too.

Woman And what about in Europe? Which countries use the most renewable energy?

Man Well, one of the most advanced countries in Europe for renewable energy is Sweden. They use a lot of wind energy, and now they are starting to use wave energy too. And if you look at a country like Austria, it now has 25% of its energy from renewable sources … er … Austria uses a lot of hydro-electric and solar energy.

Woman You said Sweden is using wave power now. Are there any other countries using it?

Man Well, France has a big power station on the River Rance, which uses waves from the river. But still, around the world, hydro-electric energy is more popular. For example, countries like Brazil rely a lot on hydro-electric energy. The USA has a lot of hydro-electric energy too, of course.

Woman And the future? Will we see more renewable energy being used?

Man Oh, yes, there's no doubt about that. Erm, in my opinion, in a few years' time, there'll be more and more …

Answers

	Austria	Brazil	France	Sweden	USA
Wind energy				✓	✓
Solar energy	✓				✓
Wave energy			✓	✓	
Hydro-electric energy	✓	✓			✓

Vocabulary notebook

Students should start a section called *Energy* and note down the different energy types from this unit. They should separate them under Renewable and Non-renewable.

9 Speak

Divide the class into small groups. Ask students to read through the questions and then go through the information in the box at the bottom of page 28. Give students time to find the answers to the questions. Ask groups to report back to the class.

Answers

Most renewable energy: Sweden (25.4%)

Least renewable energy: Germany (2.4%), Ireland (2.0%), UK (about 1%)

Discussion box

Stronger classes: In pairs or small groups, students go through the questions in the box and discuss them.

Weaker classes: They can choose one question only to discuss. If necessary, elicit a few prompts for the question they have chosen to help them with their discussion.

Monitor and help as necessary, encouraging students to express themselves in English.

Ask pairs or groups to feedback to the class and discuss any interesting points further.

10 Write

(a) Ask students to read through the instructions and the questions. Students then read through the web article quickly to find the answers. Check answers.

Answers
Four (Para 1: more cycle lanes; Para 2: more clubs for teenagers; Para 3: more places for teenagers to play sports; Para 4: stop people dropping litter)

(b) Elicit any words/phrases students know to introduce ideas and to give opinions. Write them on the board under the headings *Introducing ideas/Giving opinions*. Ask students to read through the instructions. Go through the example in the web article as a class, making sure students understand which words are for opinions and which are for introducing the article. Refer them back to their ideas on the board if necessary. Students complete the exercise. Check answers by asking students to come out and write their phrases under the relevant heading on the board.

Answers
Introducing ideas: Para 3: Also; Para 4: In addition; Para 5: Finally
Giving opinions: Para 2: I think that ... ; Para 3: I believe that ... ; In my opinion ... ; Para 5: I'm sure that ...

(c)
(d) This can be set for homework with the preparation done in class. Read through the bullet points as a class and the three-point plan in Exercise 10d. Give students time to plan their articles in class, answering any questions and helping them with the structure as necessary. Students then complete the exercise for homework.

Weaker classes: Students make notes for each of the three points. They then expand their notes into full sentences. Students can then swap sentences with a partner to check. Students can then write a final version.

Vocabulary notebook
Encourage students to note down the expressions from Exercise 10 and to use them whenever possible in their writing and speaking.

Module 1 Check your progress

1 Grammar

(a) 1 saw   2 was looking   3 started   4 was crossing
5 heard   6 was coming   7 stopped   8 didn't hit

(b) 1 best   2 easier/easiest   3 more exciting/most exciting   4 worse/worst

(c) 2 nervously   3 fluently   4 badly   5 easily
6 well

(d) 2 more easily   3 faster   4 earlier   5 better
6 further

(e) 2 'll go   3 won't come   4 'll try   5 won't tell
6 'll know

(f) 2 might be   3 might go   4 might give
5 might see

(g) 2 work/will give   3 'll phone/doesn't arrive
4 speak/won't understand   5 phones/will/tell
6 won't know/don't tell

2 Vocabulary

(a) 2 slow   3 shallow   4 slim   5 messy   6 noisy
7 difficult

(b) 2 getting/old   3 got a surprise   4 get home
5 gets good ideas   6 get the answer

(c) 1 drop   2 poles   3 global   4 recycle (x2)
5 rubbish   6 waste   7 pick   8 forest   9 clean
Mystery word: pollution

3 Everyday English

2 too right   3 Actually   4 Stop it   5 Hold on
6 I'm off

How did you do?
Students work out their scores. Check how they have done and follow up any problem areas with revision work for students.

Module 2
Different lives

YOU WILL LEARN ABOUT ...

Ask students to look at the pictures on the page. Ask students to read through the topics in the box and check they understand each item. You can ask them the following questions, in L1 if appropriate: *Which countries do the two flags belong to in picture 5? What is the woman wearing in picture 2? How old do you have to be in (students' own country) to drive? What do you think the clown is doing? What is the stunt woman doing in picture 7? Who are these Hollywood stars?*

In small groups, students discuss which topic area they think each picture matches.

Check answers.

Answers
1 Hollywood film starts and their lifestyles
2 A Japanese ceremony
3 Minimum age limits around the world
4 Clown doctors
5 Canada and the USA
6 A coming of age ceremony on a Pacific island
7 A stuntwoman

YOU WILL LEARN HOW TO ...

See Introduction.

Use grammar
Students read through the grammar points and the examples. Go through the first item with students as an example. In pairs, students now match the grammar items in their book. Check answers.

Answers
Question tags: You live round here, don't you?
Present perfect + *just*: I've just finished my exams.
Present perfect + *already/yet*: Have you done the washing up yet?
Present simple passive: Thousands of trees are cut down every day.
let/be allowed to: My parents let me stay up late.
Present perfect + *for/since*: I've lived here since I was 10.
Verbs + *ing* or infinitive: I enjoy cycling, so I've decided to buy a new bike.

Use vocabulary
Write the headings on the board. Go through the items in the Student's Book and check understanding. Now ask students if they can think of one more item for the *British/American English* heading; can they think of any words from films or songs? Elicit some responses and add them to the list on the board. Students now do the same for the other headings. Some possibilities are:

British/American English: *sweets/candy; garden/yard; lift/elevator; trousers/pants*

Describing age: *teenage; middle-aged; retired; baby; toddler; child*

Verb/noun pairs: *get an idea; do the washing up; have a shower/bath*

Film: *western; science fiction; horror; musical; producer*

Unit overview

TOPIC: Canada and the USA

TEXTS

Reading and listening: a quiz about Canada and the USA
Reading: a text about a young poet from Vancouver
Reading: a poem: *Whale Song*
Listening: a dialogue about recently completed holiday activities
Reading and listening: Story: *You said 6.30, didn't you?*
Writing: an email about a holiday

SPEAKING AND FUNCTIONS

Checking information
Talking about recently completed holiday activities

LANGUAGE

Question tags
Present perfect with *already* and *yet*
Present perfect with *just*
Pronunciation: Intonation in question tags
Vocabulary: British English vs. North American English
Everyday English: *Sure*; *off we go*; *Nice one!*; *Wicked!*

1 Read and listen

If you set the background information as a homework research task ask students to tell the class what they found out.

BACKGROUND INFORMATION

Canada: Is the second largest country in the world and is situated in the north part of the continent of America. It has 10 provinces and two federal territories, and the capital is Ottawa. Both French and English are spoken in Canada. Famous tourist attractions include Niagara Falls, the Rocky Mountains, and the Great Lakes.

The USA: Is the world's fourth largest country in terms of population and area. It consists of 50 states and the capital is Washington, DC. The largest state is Alaska (which borders Canada) and the smallest is Rhode Island. Chicago is the city with the highest population and the cities of New York, Los Angeles and Chicago are the largest cities.

Warm up

Ask students to look at the pictures and ask them what the capital of Canada is (*Ottawa*) and the capital of the USA (*Washington, DC*). Ask them what else they know about Canada and the USA. If you've time, small groups or pairs could brainstorm ideas together, before feeding back to the whole class.

(a) Students then read the quiz and select their answers. If you have done the *Warm up* exercise students will be able to answer questions 1 and 2 correctly. Remind them to read all the answer options carefully before making their decision. Do not give answers at this point.

At this point, students could compare ideas in pairs. Encourage them to use the phrases for giving opinions they learned in Unit 4. E.g. *I think number one is …*

(b) 🔊 Ask students to read through the instruction. Play the recording once for students to check or change their answers. Play the recording again, pausing as necessary to clarify any problems.

TAPESCRIPT

Tony You're from Canada, aren't you, Laura?
Laura Yes, I am. I'm from Toronto.
Tony But you live in the USA, don't you?
Laura Yes. My family moved to New York six years ago.
Tony Oh, right. So, you can tell me about the USA and Canada, can't you?
Laura Well, I can try!
Tony So, you live in New York. That's the capital of the USA, isn't it?
Laura No, silly! Washington, DC's the capital.
Tony Yeah, right. So, you're from Toronto. But Toronto isn't the capital of Canada, is it? Montreal's the capital, isn't it?
Laura No. Toronto's the biggest city, but Ottawa's the capital. You don't know much about Canada, do you?!
Tony No, I don't. I'd love to go there. It's a really big country, isn't it?
Laura Yeah. In fact it's the second biggest country in the world. Only Russia is bigger.
Tony Yes, but the USA's big too – there are 50 states, aren't there?
Laura Yeah, there are.
Tony But the USA's got a much higher population than Canada, hasn't it?
Laura Yes, it has. In fact, Canada's population is very small, only about 30 million people live there. That's much lower than some European countries. For example, Italy's population is over 57 million, nearly double the population of Canada, and Italy is much smaller.

Tony Wow! That's amazing. Most people in Canada speak English as their first language, don't they?

Laura Yeah. But a lot of people speak French as their first language, about 30 per cent of the population, and a lot of people learn both English and French. But where I live, you can hear a lot of people speaking Chinese too – it's the third most spoken language in Canada now. In fact, Vancouver has the biggest population of Chinese people outside China.

Tony Really? That's amazing! What about the States – a lot of people speak Spanish as well as English there, don't they?

Laura Yeah. There are a lot of immigrants from Mexico and South America, so more and more people speak Spanish now. In fact about 28 million people speak Spanish as their first language, and a lot more speak it as a second language.

Tony Maybe I should learn Spanish! So, tell me more about Canada. People really like ice hockey there, don't they?

Laura Yes, ice hockey's probably the most popular sport, but of course people love the outdoors in Canada. Skiing is very popular too, so is mountain climbing and things like that.

Tony What about the USA? People play a lot of baseball there, don't they?

Laura Yes, they do, and American football's really popular too. That's a very different game to the football you play in England and basketball's very popular too, but baseball's probably the most popular sport, yes, baseball definitely.

Tony Really? Have you ever been to a baseball match?

Answers

1 b   2 c   3 a   4 b   5 a   6 b   7 c   8 b
9 b   10 b

OPTIONAL ACTIVITIES

Stronger classes

Students write their own quizzes about their own countries using the quiz in Exercise 1 as a model. Once the quizzes are written students swap them with a partner to answer the questions. Encourage students to research the facts and to find some more interesting ones!

Weaker classes

They can do further research on Canada and the USA and find out some more facts to report back to the rest of the class.

2 Grammar

Question tags

a **Stronger classes**

🔊 Ask students to read through the gapped sentences. Go through the example and ask students why they think the tag is negative and elicit because

the expected answer is *Yes*. Students complete the exercise. Remind them to look carefully at the verb used before they decide which tag is required. Students can compare answers in pairs. Play the recording for students to listen and check or change their answers. At this point, ask students what they notice about the verbs in each sentence and the tags at the end. Elicit that where there is a positive verb there is a negative tag and where there is a negative verb there is a positive tag. Explain to students that we use a positive verb and a negative tag when we are checking information and we expect the answer to be *Yes*. Elicit from students that we use a negative verb and a positive tag when we expect the answer to be *No*.

Weaker classes: Books closed. Ask a few questions with question tags of your own (e.g. *It isn't raining today, is it?/ You aren't (Chiara), are you?/ You saw the aeroplane outside, didn't you?* etc.) but do not explain the use of tags at the moment. Students open their books at page 35 and follow the procedure above for stronger classes. When students have finished the exercise focus again on your own examples and elicit the information from students.

TAPESCRIPT
See above.

Answers

2 don't   3 can't   4 isn't   5 is   6 do

b Ask students to read through the instructions and then complete the rule. Remind them of the tags used in Exercise 2a and refer them back to their completed answers if necessary.

Answers

negative/positive; do/did

To check understanding at this point, ask students to ask and answer a few questions of their own across the class.

> **Language note**
> Students may find this concept a little difficult because of the way their own language works. They may produce statements like: **He's Carlos, is he? *It's raining, is it?*
>
> Remind them that in English the tag is always the opposite of the verb in the main part of the sentence.

c Ask students to read through items 1 to 10 and the list of question tags. Go through the example with students. If students are still having problems, refer them back to the rules in Exercise 2b. Students complete the exercise. Check answers.

Answers

2 does she?   3 can't she?   4 are they?   5 aren't they?   6 isn't it?   7 will she?   8 do you?
9 haven't you?   10 have you?

(d) This exercise can be set for homework. Ask students to read through items 1 to 8. Go through the example, asking students to explain why the tag is *didn't he (because the verb is in the past simple and we use the auxiliary did/didn't in past simple questions)*. Students complete the exercise. Students can compare answers in pairs before a whole class check.

Answers
2 do they   3 doesn't she   4 were you   5 didn't they   6 doesn't she   7 did they   8 didn't she

Grammar notebook
Encourage students to note down the rules for question tags and a few examples of their own.

3 Pronunciation
Intonation in question tags

(a) 🔊 Students turn to page 120. Read through the explanation as a class and give students an example of your own for each type of intonation. Ask students to say if your voice goes up or down at the end of each question. Students now read through questions 1 to 6. Play the recording, pausing it after question 1 and go through this as a class. Make sure students understand that they only have to write U or D. Play the recording again for students to listen and complete the exercise. Check answers as a class, playing and pausing the recording as necessary for students to clarify any problems.

TAPESCRIPT/ANSWERS
1 You're from Canada, aren't you? D
2 New York's the capital, isn't it? U
3 You don't know much about Canada, do you? D
4 There are 50 states, aren't there? U
5 The USA's got a higher population than Canada, hasn't it? D
6 People like ice hockey there, don't they? U

(b) 🔊 Play the recording again, pausing after each question for students to repeat.

4 Speak

(a) Divide the class into groups of four. Ask students to read through the six questions. Explain that they must ask each person in their group the questions and try to remember their answers without writing them down. Monitor and check students are taking turns in asking and answering. Make sure they are not writing answers down, and note any repeated errors to discuss later as a class.

(b) Go through the example, if necessary, pointing out the use of the question tag to check information. Remind them their intonation should go down at the end of a question if they are checking information and are sure of the answer and up if they are not sure of the answer.

Weaker classes: Students now report back their findings from Exercise 4a to the rest of their group.

Stronger classes: Encourage some students to report their findings back to the whole class.

Monitor and check students are using the correct question tags and the correct intonation.

If students are still having problems with intonation at this stage, drill a few more examples as a class.

(c) Divide the class into pairs. Students read through the prompts on the page and then ask a student the example question, making sure your intonation goes up to show you are not sure of the answer. Students ask and answer the question in their pairs, using question tags. Monitor and check students are using the correct tags and intonation and note down any problems for further discussion. Ask a few stronger pairs to read out their questions and answers to the rest of the class.

5 Read

If you set the background information as a homework research task, ask students to tell the class what they found out.

BACKGROUND INFORMATION
Vancouver: Is a city in the west of Canada situated in the south west of the province of British Columbia. It is Canada's largest city in the west and is set against the backdrop of the beautiful Coast Range mountains.

British Columbia: Is one of Canada's western provinces. The province is almost entirely mountainous, with the Rocky Mountains in the east and the Coast Range mountains in the west.

Warm up
Ask students to look at the photo and the title of the text and to predict how old they think the girl is (16) and how much money she won as her prize ($1,000).

(a) Ask students to read through the questions. Encourage them to read the text quickly to check their answers. Remind them they don't need to understand every word. Students can compare answers in pairs before a whole class check.

Answers
1 It is a poetry competition.
2 When she came out of an elevator and saw a painting of a whale on a wall.
3 She wants to work in something to do with the sea.

You can do the following short comprehension exercise on the text.

1 Where is Linda from? (**Richmond, Vancouver.**)
2 What is her poem called? (**Whale Song.**)
3 How many poems has she written already? (**30.**)
4 Did she expect to win? (**No, she didn't. It was a big surprise.**)
5 What does she want to study at university? (**Marine biology.**)

b 🔊 Students read through the instructions and questions. You may need to explain the meaning of *bucks* (*dollars*) to students before they listen. Play the recording. Students listen and note their answers. Students can compare answers in pairs. Encourage students to report back their opinions to the rest of the class.

TAPESCRIPT

See the poem on page 36 of the Student's Book.

Stronger classes

Students can write their own short poems using the model in the Student's Book. Remind them to think of a topic they would like to write about and then to think of some rhyming words to help them express their ideas.

6 Vocabulary
British vs. North American English

🔊 Ask students if they know any words which mean the same but are different in North American English and British English. Students may remember some from the Module opener page and if possible elicit a few more. Put any suggestions on the board. Read through the pairs of words in the box as a class and ask students to focus on the pictures. Go through the first item as an example, eliciting the word to match the first picture in English. Students complete the exercise. Play the recording for students to check or change their answers. Play it again if necessary, pausing to clarify any problems.

TAPESCRIPT

Tony You have different words for lots of things, don't you?
Laura Yeah, that's right. We Canadians use a lot of the same words as the Americans, words that you don't use.
Tony Can you give me some examples?
Laura Sure. There are loads. For example, you say pavement, but we say sidewalk.
Tony Oh yes, I knew that one. Also you say elevator for lift, don't you?
Laura Yeah. And in American English, pants are what you call trousers. We also say subway ... but you say underground, don't you?

Tony Oh yeah. I know another one. The American word for flat is apartment, isn't it?
Laura That's right. Oh, and we say garbage, but you say rubbish ...

Answers
a pavement (BE) – sidewalk (AE)
b lift (BE) – elevator (AE)
c pants (AE) – trousers (BE)
d underground (BE) – subway (AE)
e flat (BE) – apartment (AE)
f garbage (AE) – rubbish (BE)

Vocabulary notebook

Encourage students to start a section called *British/ North American English* and to note down the words from Exercise 6.

7 Grammar
Present perfect with *already* and *just*

a **Stronger classes:** Elicit how to form the present perfect tense (*has/have* + past participle). Ask students to read through the examples and ask them what they notice about the position of *already* and *yet* (*already* goes between *has* and the past participle, *yet* goes at the end). Ask them if Linda has decided what to do with her prize money and elicit the answer *Yes*. Ask them if she has decided what to do for a career and elicit the answer *No*. Explain that *already* means that something has happened before the time of speaking and that *yet* means something has not happened up to the point of speaking but is likely/expected to happen. Ask students to practise a few questions and answers of their own across the class to check they have understood.

Weaker classes: Books closed. Write a few examples of your own on the board (e.g. *I've already had my (breakfast)./I haven't had my (lunch) yet.*). Ask them: *Have I had my (breakfast)?* and elicit the answer *Yes*. Then ask: *Have I had my (lunch)?* Elicit the answer *No*. Explain the meaning of *already* (something has happened before the time of speaking) and *yet* (something has not happened up to the point of speaking but is likely/expected to happen). Ask students to practise a few questions and answers of their own across the class to check they have understood. Students now open their books at page 37 and look at the examples. Follow the procedure for stronger classes if students are still unsure about this structure.

Students now go through the text on page 36 and find other examples of the present perfect, then complete the rule. Check answers.

Answers
Para 1: has won
Para 2: has already written; has never entered
Para 4: has already decided; has just done; haven't decided ... yet
Para 5: I've won ...

Answers

have/past participle; negative; past participle/yet

> **Language note**
> Students may produce statements like: *Already I've finished my homework. *Has she yet done the shopping?* because of L1 differences. Encourage them, where possible, to think carefully about the position of *already* and *yet* in English.

(b) Ask students to read through dialogues 1 to 4. Check any problems. Go through the example, reminding them of the rules from Exercise 7a. Students complete the exercise. Students can compare answers in pairs before a whole class check. Ask a few stronger pairs to read out their completed dialogues to the rest of the class.

Answers

1 B: I've already finished the Maths but I haven't started the History yet.
2 A: ... I haven't bought their new CD yet.
   B: I've already bought it for you.
3 A: Has Maria done the shopping yet?
   B: ... she's already bought everything for the party.
4 A: Have Sam and Tom seen the film yet?
   B: ... they've already read the book, too.

Grammar notebook

Encourage students to note down what the rules for this are and a few examples of their own.

8 Listen and speak

(a) 🔊 Ask students to read through the instructions and prompts 1 to 6. Check any problems. Play the recording, pausing after the first prompt if necessary and elicit the correct answer. Explain that students should use a tick if he has already done it or a cross if he has not done it yet. Play the recording while students complete the exercise. Do not check answers at this point.

TAPESCRIPT

Girl Hello?
Boy Gill? Hi, it's me, Steve!
Girl Steve? You're in New York, aren't you?
Boy That's right. I'm on holiday here!
Girl Great! Are you having a good time?
Boy Brilliant, thanks! I've already seen lots of things, it's great!
Girl So, tell me – have you seen the Empire State Building yet?
Boy Yes, I have. It was wonderful.
Girl And have you had a ride in a yellow cab yet?
Boy No, not yet. We're going to do that tomorrow! But I've already travelled on the underground several times.
Girl You mean the subway?

Boy Yeah, the subway! Sorry.
Girl What else have you seen?
Boy Well, I've already been to the Hard Rock Café, and that was great.
Girl And what about baseball? Have you seen a baseball match yet?
Boy No, not yet. I think we're going at the weekend. And Gill – something else, but you won't believe me!
Girl What?
Boy I haven't eaten an American hamburger yet!
Girl What? Steve, I don't believe it! But you love hamburgers, don't you?
Boy Yeah, well, I'm here for another four days so ...

(b) 🔊 In pairs, students ask and answer questions from Exercise 8a to check their answers. Remind students to use *yet* in their questions. Monitor and check students are forming the questions correctly and are taking turns to ask and answer. Ask a few pairs to report back to the class. Play the recording again, pausing it as necessary to clarify any problems.

Answers

1 ✓ 2 ✗ 3 ✓ 4 ✓ 5 ✗ 6 ✗

9 Grammar
Present perfect with *just*

(a) **Stronger classes:** Students look at the example. Ask them what they notice about the position of *just* and elicit that it goes between *has/have* and the past participle. Ask them if they can explain what the example sentence means. Ask them a few questions to help them if necessary: *Did Linda do her exam a long time ago? (No) Has she done her exams recently? (Yes)* and explain that *just* means a short time ago.

Weaker classes: Books closed. Give students a few examples of your own and put them on the board (e.g. *We've just started Exercise 9. We've just finished Exercise 8.*). Ask them what they notice about the position of *just* and elicit that it goes between *has/have* and the past participle. Ask students: *When did we start Exercise 9? When did we finish Exercise 8?* and elicit that you finished it a few minutes ago. Explain that using *just* with the present perfect shows that something happened a short time ago. Students open their books at page 37 and look at the example sentence. If necessary, follow the procedure for stronger classes with the example sentence to make sure students have understood the concept correctly.

Students complete the rule. Check answers.

Answer

just

To check understanding at this point, ask students to think of a few questions of their own and to ask and answer them across the class.

b Ask students to look at pictures 1 to 6 and read the prompts. Go through the example, if necessary. Remind students where *just* and *yet* go in their sentences. Students complete the exercise. Check answers.

Answers

2 He's just done the shopping, but he hasn't done the cooking yet.

3 She's just gone to bed, but she hasn't switched off the light yet.

4 She's just made breakfast, but she hasn't eaten it yet.

5 She's just bought a new DVD, but she hasn't watched it yet.

6 They've just scored a goal, but they haven't won the match yet.

Grammar notebook

Encourage students to note down the rules and some examples from Exercise 9. They may find it useful to translate the examples into their own language.

┌─ OPTIONAL ACTIVITY ─────────────

Write the following prompts out on cards or pieces of paper:

- win/lottery
- buy/new car
- wash/hair
- cook/a meal
- buy/bunch of flowers
- wake up

Do this as a whole class activity. Mime the first prompt yourself and students try and guess what you have just done. You can only nod or shake your head if they are right or wrong. Students must answer correctly producing statements like: *You've just won the lottery*, etc. The student who guesses correctly comes out and chooses a prompt for the rest of the class to guess.

You said 6.30, didn't you?

10 Read and listen

Warm up

Ask students what they remember about the previous episode and what happened (*We were introduced to Joanne and Amy was not happy and walked away*

from Dave.). Ask students to look at the photos and predict what they think will happen in this episode (*Amy arrives late and Joanne has already started singing.*).

a 🔊 Ask students to read through the questions. Play the recording while students listen for the answers and check their *Warm up* predictions. Check answers, giving students the opportunity to discuss question 4 as a class. Play the recording again, pausing as necessary to clarify any problems.

TAPESCRIPT
See the story on page 38 of the Student's Book.

Answers

1 Dave, Matt and Joanne

2 Amy

3 Surprised and annoyed

4 Students' own answers

b 🔊 Ask students to read through sentences 1 to 6. Check any problems. Go through the first item as an example, reminding them of how to locate the answer in the text before making their decision. Students complete the exercise. Check answers and ask students to correct the false statements. Play the recording again if necessary, to clarify any problems.

Answers

1 F (What's her name?) 2 F (... can start without her ...) 3 T 4 T 5 T 6 F (She replies 'Hi'.)

11 Everyday English

a Ask students to read through expressions 1 to 4 and to locate them in the story on page 22 and decide who says them.

Weaker classes: Check answers at this stage.

Students then match the expressions with the definitions. Go through the first item with them as an example, if necessary. Check answers.

Answers

1 c Matt 2 a Joanne 3 d Matt 4 b Dave

b Ask students to read through dialogues 1 to 4. Check any problems. Go through the first dialogue as an example, if necessary. Students complete the other dialogues with the expressions from Exercise 9a. Check answers.

Answers

1 wicked

2 off we go

3 Sure

4 Nice one

See Unit 1, Exercise 10 Everyday English, Optional Activities.

12 Write

If you set the background information as a homework research task, ask students to tell the class what they found out.

BACKGROUND INFORMATION

San Francisco: Is in western California and sits on a peninsula between the Pacific Ocean and San Francisco Bay, known as the Golden Gate. Many people came to California during the Gold Rush and the city still has a cosmopolitan feel to it. The earthquake and fire of 1906 devastated the city but it was rebuilt following these events. It is a city full of hills and cable cars carry people up and down them every day.

See Unit 9, Exercise 1.

Alcatraz prison: Is situated on Alcatraz Island, in San Francisco Bay in west California. The prison is sometimes called The Rock and is a maximum security jail.

Golden Gate bridge: Is one of the world's largest suspension bridges. Built 1934–1937, it spans the entrance to San Francisco Bay. It is approximately 2,824 metres long.

San Francisco Giants: Are a famous American baseball team.

Warm up

Ask students what they know about California and San Francisco and elicit as much as they know.

The preparation for this can be done in class and students can write the email for homework.

a Ask students to read through questions 1 to 5. Check any problems.

Stronger classes: Students read through the email and answer the questions.

Weaker classes: Read through the email as a class. In pairs, students then answer the questions.

Check answers.

Answers
1 San Diego and Los Angeles
2 Alcatraz prison. She liked it.
3 No, but she's seen it.
4 Yes.
5 A San Francisco Giants baseball cap.

b Ask students to read through questions 1 to 3. Check any problems.

Stronger classes: They may not need to read the email again to answer these questions. If they can do this from memory they can read it only to check answers.

Weaker classes: Look at the first question with them and ask them to read the start of the email and find the answer. Do this with each question.

Check answers.

Answers
1 Hi Mark!   2 Love, Sarah   3 PS

Language note
PS in English means *post script*, literally 'after writing'. Ask students how they make these additions to letters or emails in their language and what the abbreviation stands for.

Weaker classes
You may find it useful to do this before students write their emails in Exercise 12c.
Ask students to match the following topics to each paragraph to help them think a bit more about the structure of the email before they write their own emails.
1 what Sarah and her family have already done/not done yet in San Francisco
2 the family's plans for tonight
3 where she is now and what shes doing
4 places they've already visited on their holiday

Answers
1 Paragraph 2   2 Paragraph 4   3 Paragraph 1
4 Paragraph 3

c Students may need time to do some research for this.

Stronger classes: Students read through the cities in the box and choose one, or they can choose and research a city of their own if they prefer. Remind them to follow the model in Exercise 12a and write their own email. They can then send their email to a partner to read and check and then correct any mistakes.

Weaker classes: Students read through the cities in the box. If they don't want to choose one of them, help them decide on a different city. Remind them of the structure of Sarah's email and ask them to plan their email first by making some notes for each paragraph about the city they have chosen. Check the notes and provide help as necessary. Then ask them to write a draft version of their email, expanding their notes into full sentences and forming paragraphs correctly. They can then send their email to a partner to read and check. Students then write a final version based on their checked drafts.

Encourage students to read out their emails to the rest of the class.

6 Growing up

Unit overview

TOPIC: Growing up in different parts of the world

TEXTS
Reading and listening: a text about a coming of age ceremony on Pentecost Island
Listening: the origins of the coming of age ceremony
Reading and listening: a quiz about age limits
Writing: about a special day in your country

SPEAKING AND FUNCTIONS
Describing a ceremony
Retelling a story
Talking about permission
Discussing age limits

LANGUAGE
Present simple passive
let / be allowed to
Vocabulary: describing someone's age
Pronunciation: /aʊ/ allowed

1 Read and listen

If you set the background information as a homework research task, ask students to tell the class what they found out.

BACKGROUND INFORMATION

Pentecost Island: Is one of the islands which makes up the republic of Vanuatu.

Vanuatu: Is a chain of islands to the east of Australia in the south west Pacific. It is an independent republic and was 'discovered' in 1606 by the Portuguese. It used to be called the New Hebrides. The capital is Vila and it is situated on the island of Efate. The national language is a form of pidgin English and the population is mainly Melanesian.

Warm up

Ask students at what age someone is classified as an adult in their country, and if they celebrate certain birthdays in special ways because of the age a person is. If so, how do they celebrate and what ages are special? Discuss this as a class, in L1 if appropriate.

(a) Ask students to look at the pictures and find lianas and a tower. Read through the two questions and ask them for their suggestions before they read the text. Students then read the text quickly to answer the

questions. Remind them they don't need to understand every word in the text at this stage. Check answers.

Answers
1 Pentecost Island in the Pacific.
2 They are holding a coming of age ceremony.

(b) 🔊 Ask students to read through questions 1 to 4. Check any problems. Play the recording, pausing it after the second paragraph and ask students to give you the answer to question 1. Play the recording while students read and listen to answer the questions. Check answers. Play the recording again, pausing as necessary to clarify any problems. You may want to pre-teach the following vocabulary: *ceremony*; *bamboo*; *tower*; *platform*; *liana*; *problems*.

TAPESCRIPT
See the reading text on page 40 of the Student's Book.

Answers
1 25 metres
2 To find lianas.
3 They tie them to their foot and the tower.
4 They got the idea for the sport of bungee jumping.

(c) Divide the class into small groups.

Stronger classes: Ask students to read through the question and discuss it in their groups.

Weaker classes: Ask students to read through the question and then put the heading *N'gol/Bungee jumping* on the board. Elicit as many of the dangers and other aspects of each sport from students as possible, using L1 if appropriate. Write them under the appropriate heading or ask students to come out and put them on the board. Students then use the ideas from the board to discuss the question.

Ask groups to feedback to the rest of the class and see if the class can agree.

┌─ **OPTIONAL ACTIVITY** ─────────────
Give students the following true/false questions on the text:
1 Pentecost Island is in the Atlantic Ocean. **(False: the Pacific)**
2 The ceremony is held in August. **(False: April and May)**
3 Bamboo trees are used to build the tower. **(True)**
4 The tower is about 5 metres high. **(False: about 25 metres high)**
5 Boys tie lianas to the tower and their feet. **(True)**
6 The N'gol ceremony gave British people the idea for bungee jumping. **(True)**

2 Grammar

Present simple passive

a Ask students to read through the instruction and the examples. Ask them to identify the verb *be* in each sentence and elicit why *are* is used in the first example (because bamboo trees is plural) and *is* in the second (because bamboo tower is singular). Then ask them to point out the past participles.

b Students go back through the text on page 40 and find other examples of the present simple passive. Check answers.

Students then read through the rule box. Go through the first example in the table as a class, asking them why *is* is used (*because liana is singular*). Check answers.

Answers
Para 1: ... is held
Para 2: ... are cut down; ... is built; ... is made
Para 4: ... is watched by tourists

Table
Positive: are
Negative: isn't/aren't
Question: Is/Are
Short answers: is/aren't

To check understanding at this point, ask students to think of one example sentence in the present simple passive about their own country.

Language notes
Students may have a different verb in their own language for this structure and they may have problems using this structure correctly. Monitor them carefully when they use it, making sure they are using the correct form.

c Students read through sentences 1 to 6. Check any problems. Go through the example, if necessary. Students complete the exercise. Remind them that they can use the irregular verb list on page 123 if necessary. Check answers.

Answers
2 are written   3 is sold   4 isn't grown/is grown
5 Are/sent   6 are made

d This exercise can be set for homework. Students read through sentences 1 to 7. Check any problems. Go through the example, pointing out the changes from the active sentence to the passive sentence. Students complete the exercise. Check answers.

Answers
2 ... is picked up every morning.
3 ... of trees are cut down every year.
4 ... water is wasted.
5 ... of letters are delivered by postal workers.
6 ... successful films made in Hollywood?
7 ... coffee grown in Kenya?

e This exercise can be set for homework. Students look at the pictures and read through prompts 1 to 4. Do the first prompt with them as an example, eliciting a passive sentence. Students complete the exercise, making passive sentences for the other pictures. Check answers.

Answers
1 A torch is taken to the Olympic city.
2 A flag is carried into the stadium.
3 A flame is lit with the torch.
4 The Games are opened with a speech.

Grammar notebook
Encourage students to note down the rules and some examples of the passive. They may want to translate some examples if their own language uses a different construction to express this.

3 Listen and speak

a Divide the class into pairs. Read the instructions as a class. Students then look at the pictures and try and put them in order. Do the first one with them as an example, if necessary. Elicit some possibilities from the class and put them on the board but do not check answers at this point.

b 🔊 Play the recording for students to listen and check or change their answers. Play the recording again, pausing as necessary to clarify any problems.

TAPESCRIPT
Where does this ceremony come from? Are there any reasons why the men do this? Well, people on the island of Pentecost tell a story about a king and queen of the village hundreds of years ago.

The king was not a very nice man, and one day the queen ran away from where they lived. She ran into the forest, and the angry king ran after her. When the queen saw her husband coming, she was frightened and climbed a tree.

The king saw her in the tree, and asked her to come down because he was sorry. She said no. Then the king got very angry and he climbed the tree to get her. When he got to the top, the queen jumped. When the king saw this, he jumped after her. But he did not know that she had some lianas tied to her feet. The king died, but the queen of course did not.

When the queen came back to the village, the women in the village were very happy and they laughed at the men. The men of course were very angry. They wanted to show that men could do the same thing as the queen. So they built a tower and invented the ceremony that we can still see today.

Answers
3 b   4 h   5 a   6 d   7 f   8 c

Students may find it useful to have a prompt for each picture before retelling the story. Elicit a prompt for each, replaying the recording as necessary.

Write the prompts on the board, if necessary. Students then retell the story with their partner.

Note down any errors to go through later. Encourage some pairs to retell the story to the rest of the class.

4 Vocabulary
Describing a person's age

a 🔊 Books closed. Draw a line on the board with 0 years at one end and 65 years at the other end. Elicit as many words as possible from students for different ages and write them on the line at various points. Students read through the words in the box and look at the pictures. Check the pronunciation of each item. Do the first item as an example, if necessary. Students complete the exercise. Play the recording for students to check or change their answers. Play the recording again, pausing after each word for students to repeat.

TAPESCRIPT/ANSWERS
a 4 a baby   b 5 a toddler   c 2 a child
d 3 a teenager   e 1 a young adult
f 6 a pensioner

b Students read through sentences 1 to 6. Check any problems. Go through the first item as an example, if necessary. Students complete the exercise. Remind them to use the time line from the board to help them if you used this in Exercise 4a. Students can compare answers with a partner before a whole class check.

Possible answers
1 two   2 two or three and a half   3 12   4 13/19
5 18   6 65

c Divide the class into small groups. Students read through the questions and discuss them in their groups. Ask for groups to feedback to the class and see if everyone agrees. Are there any similarities in the students' own language?

Vocabulary notebook
Encourage students to start a section called *Describing a person's age* and to note down the words from this exercise. They may find it useful to note down translations of the words too.

5 Grammar
let / be allowed to

a 🔊 Students read through the gapped dialogue and questions 1 to 5. Check any problems. Go through the first question as an example, if necessary. Play the recording for students to listen and read. Give students a few minutes to answer the questions. Students can compare answers in pairs. Play the recording again for students to check or change their answers, pausing as necessary to clarify any problems.

TAPESCRIPT
See the dialogue on page 43 of the Student's Book.

Answers
1   To a music festival in Leeds.
2   Because his parents say he is too young.
3   Because her dad didn't let her.
4   They let him stay out until midnight at weekends.
5   Stay up late and watch TV.

b Students read through the examples. Elicit or explain that the first example means permission was not given and in the second example permission was given, but that *let/be allowed* mean the same thing, as do *don't/didn't let/not allowed*. Students then underline other examples of *let/be allowed* in the dialogue in Exercise 5a and complete the rules. Check answers.

Answers
I'm not allowed …
… didn't let me go …
… usually let me …
I'm allowed to say out …
… we're allowed breathe
… never lets me do …
… let you stay up late …

Students can now complete the rule.
Weaker classes: Do the first example as a class.

Answers
be allowed to
let

To check understanding at this point, elicit a few more examples from the class of things they are allowed / not allowed to do.

> **Language note**
> Students may produce statements like *My dad let me to stay out late*. Remind them that in English we don't use *to* after the expression *let someone do something*. Students may produce statements like *I'm allowed stay out late*. The expression *allow someone to do something* is always followed by the infinitive with *to*.

c This exercise can be set for homework. Students read through the instructions and sentences 1 to 6. Check any problems. Go through the example as a class, if necessary. Students complete the exercise. Remind them to use short forms where possible. Check answers.

Answers
2 're not allowed to   3 're not allowed to
4 're allowed to   5 isn't allowed to   6 allowed to

d This exercise can be set for homework. Students read through the instructions and sentences 1 to 6. Go through the example as a class, if necessary. Students complete the exercise. Remind them to use short forms where possible. Check answers.

Answers

2 My parents let me watch the late-night movie on Fridays.
3 I don't let my brother use my computer.
4 The teachers don't let us run in the corridors.
5 The principal doesn't let us wear trainers to school.
6 My dad lets me drive our car sometimes.

(e) Read through the instructions as a class. Individually, students note down things they are allowed / not allowed to do. Then divide the class into pairs. Students read through the instructions. Ask a stronger pair to demonstrate the example exchange. Students then ask and answer to exchange information. Monitor and check students are using the structures correctly and note down any repeated errors to go through as a class later. Ask pairs to feedback to the class.

Grammar notebook

Remind students to note down the rules and explanations for this structure and to write a few examples of their own.

┌─ OPTIONAL ACTIVITY ═══════════════
Write the following prompts on the board and elicit a few more from students:
• using a mobile phone
• doing homework
• using the computer
• wearing trainers to school

Students use the prompts to write questions using *be allowed to* for a survey. They go round the class asking their questions and note down the answers from as many students as possible. Then in small groups of four or five students put their information together. Ask for groups to feedback to the rest of the class.

6 Pronunciation
/aʊ/ allowed

(a) 🔊 Students turn to page 120 and read through words 1 to 6. Play the recording, pausing after the first word for students to repeat. Make sure students are pronouncing them correctly. Continue playing the recording, pausing after each word for students to repeat.

TAPESCRIPT

1 now   2 how   3 out   4 shout   5 loud
6 allowed

(b) 🔊 Students read through items 1 to 4 and underline the /aʊ/ sound. Go through the first one with them as an example, if necessary. Play the recording for students to listen and check or change their answers. Play the recording again, pausing after each item for students to repeat.

TAPESCRIPT/ANSWERS

1 How are you now?
2 I'm allowed to go out.
3 We're allowed to play loud music.
4 You aren't allowed to shout.

7 Culture in mind
Read
Warm up

Ask students to discuss how old they think the people are in each picture. What are the people doing in the pictures? You may want to pre-teach *vote* at this point. Do they know anyone who has got married very young? What do they think of this? Do they know anyone who has just passed their driving test? Discuss this as a class, in L1 if appropriate.

Ask students to read through the quiz and check any problems. Students then answer the questions individually. Divide the class into pairs and students compare answers with a partner. Ask pairs to feedback to the class but do not give answers at this stage.

8 Listen

🔊 Play the recording for students to listen and check their answers to the quiz in Exercise 7.

TAPESCRIPT

Girl Hey Alex. What are you doing?
Boy I'm doing a quiz in this magazine. It's about minimum age limits around the world: it's called 'Call yourself an adult?'!
Girl That sounds interesting. Can I try?
Boy Sure. OK, number one's easy. 'In Britain, you're allowed to drive a car from the age of ...'
Girl Yeah, easy. It's B – when you're seventeen.
Boy Yes, that's right. OK, number two. 'In Britain, you're allowed to get married when you are ...'
Girl Erm ... sixteen, I think. Answer A.
Boy Right again! But you have to have your parents' permission. Now for question 3. 'You can't vote until you are ...'
Girl That's easy too! 18 of course!
Boy Yes. It's crazy, really, you can get married when you're 16, but you aren't allowed to vote until you're 18! Anyway, now the questions get harder, OK?!'
Girl OK!
Boy Right, number four. 'In the USA, you're allowed to vote from the age of ...
Girl Oh! Erm ... 18?
Boy Yes, that's right! Did you know?
Girl No, I guessed! Let's try the next one – number five.
Boy OK. 'In most American states, you're allowed to drive a car ...'
Girl Actually, I do know this one. It's A – sixteen.

Boy Absolutely right! Five out of five so far. Let's try number six. 'In New York, you're allowed to get married from the age of ...'

Girl In New York? Not the USA?

Boy No, just New York!

Girl OK. Erm – eighteen?

Boy No, the answer's A – sixteen. And here's question seven: 'But in California, you can only get married from the age of ...'

Girl OK, another guess. Eighteen.

Boy Yes, that's right.

Girl That's strange – different laws in different states.

Boy Yeah, but that's what the USA is like! Now – let's go to China! Number eight: 'In China, women can get married from the age of ..., and men from ...'

Girl Wow! No idea! Different ages for men and women! Oh – erm – answer A.

Boy Yes that's right again! Brilliant! Girls can get married when they're 20 and men when they're 22.

Girl Hmmm. What's the next question?

Boy It's about Japan – getting married again! 'In Japan, you're allowed to get married from the age of ... if you're a girl, and ... if you're a boy!'

Girl OK, another guess – answer B, sixteen and eighteen.

Boy Wow, you're really lucky! Right again – answer B. And the last question, Japan again. 'How old do you think you have to be before you can vote?'

Girl Is it 18?

Boy No, wrong! It's 20.

Girl Really? That's older than a lot of countries, isn't it ...

Answers
1 b   2 a   3 b   4 c   5 a   6 a   7 c   8 a
9 b   10 b

Discussion box

Stronger classes: In pairs or small groups, students go through the questions in the box and discuss them.

Weaker classes: They can choose one question only to discuss. If necessary, elicit a few prompts for the question they have chosen to help them with their discussion.

Monitor and help as necessary, encouraging students to express themselves in English.

Ask pairs or groups to feedback to the class and discuss any interesting points further.

---

9 Write

If you set the background information as a homework research task, ask students to tell the class what they found out.

BACKGROUND INFORMATION

Japan: Is situated off the coast of Asia and consists of four main islands: Hokkaido, Honshu, Shikoku and Kyushu.

Seijin No Hi ceremony: This is a coming of age ceremony in Japan for 20-year-olds. It is celebrated on the second Monday in January every year and young women dress up in traditional Japanese clothes (the kimono). Men can also wear the kimono for the ceremony but often they will opt for a more traditional suit. Young men and women will visit a shrine and the day is a national holiday. Twenty is the legal age in Japan for voting, drinking and smoking.

Kimono: This is a traditional Japanese costume for men and women, dating back to the Edo period (1603–1867), which is made from one single piece of cloth. There are various different types of kimono: young women wear a kimono with long sleeves and an Obi (a wide silk sash about 12 feet long and 12 inches wide). The Obi is tied round her waist to cover the ribs and then tied at the back with a special fastening. Men can also wear kimonos and they tend to wear dark blue, brown, back or grey ones.

Warm up

Ask students to look at the pictures and predict how old they think this girl is (20) and what the name is for the type of clothes she is wearing (kimono).

The preparation for this can be done in class and the writing set as a homework exercise.

(a) Students read through the question and then read the text quickly to find the answers to this and their *Warm up* predictions. Remind them they don't need to understand every word in the text. Check answers.

Answer
It is a coming of age ceremony.

(b) Students read through questions 1 to 3 and then match them with the paragraphs in the text. Do the first one with them as an example, if necessary. Check answers.

Answers
1 A   2 C   3 B

(c) Elicit some special days which students celebrate (or if you did the *Warm up* in Exercise 1 in this unit remind them of their suggestions from there) and write them on the board.

7 Have a laugh!

Unit overview

TOPIC: What makes people laugh

TEXTS

Reading and listening: an interview with a clown doctor
Reading: a questionnaire
Listening: completing the words of a song
Writing: an email reply to a penfriend
Reading and listening: Photo story: *Who's going to sing?*

SPEAKING AND FUNCTIONS

Talking about unfinished situations
Asking and answering a questionnaire
Talking about having fun

LANGUAGE

Present perfect simple
Pronunciation: *have, has, for*
Vocabulary: Verb and noun pairs (*have/tell*)
Everyday English: *I see; What do you reckon?; To be honest ...; Let's get a move on*

1 Read and listen

If you set the background information as a homework research task, ask students to tell the class what they found out.

BACKGROUND INFORMATION

Clown doctors: Are part of the Humour Foundation. This was set up in Australia in 1997 as a charity by the performer J.P. Bell and the general practitioner Doctor Peter Spitzer. The clown doctors bring support, fun and laughter to hospital patients. They use a variety of clowning skills to do this, to try and help children in hospital overcome their feeling of fear, anxiety, loneliness and boredom. Great Ormond Street Children's Hospital in London uses clown doctors and they are very popular with the patients.

Warm up

Refer students to the photos. Ask them where the child in the photo is (*hospital*); who else they can see in the photo (*a person dressed as a clown wearing a doctor's white coat*).

Ask students if they have ever been in hospital, and how they felt or if they can imagine how they might feel. Discuss this as a class, in L1 if appropriate.

a Students read through the instructions and the question. Elicit students' predictions. Students then read the text quickly (ignoring the gaps) to check their answers. Remind them that they do not need to know every word in a text to understand it. Check answers.

Answer
To make the children in hospital laugh and smile.

b Students read through the list of questions. Check any problems. Remind them that the text is an interview with a clown doctor (the man in the photo). Students read the text again and try and put the interviewer's questions into the gaps. Play the recording for students to listen and check or change their answers. Play it again if necessary, pausing after each question to help weaker students.

TAPESCRIPT
See the reading text on page 46 of the Student's Book.

Answers
Gap a: Question 5
Gap b: Question 3
Gap c: Question 4
Gap d: Question 1
Gap e: Question 2

c Students read questions 1 to 3 and then read the text again in detail and answer the questions. Students can compare answers in pairs before a whole class check.

Answers
1 No, they don't. They think laughter is the best medicine.
2 He makes funny faces.
3 He enjoys working with children.

d Write 'Laughter is the best medicine' on the board. Ask students why Fran says this, referring them back to the text if necessary (*Because it's important for sick children to laugh, smile and enjoy themselves.*). Divide the class into small groups. Students discuss whether they agree with what Fran says or not. Ask some students to tell the rest of the class what their group thinks.

OPTIONAL ACTIVITIES

Stronger classes
They can write and act out their own interview in pairs (one is the clown doctor, one is the radio interviewer, changing the questions and answers and adding some new questions of their own.

Weaker classes
They can act out the interview from the Student's Book in pairs (one is the clown doctor, one is the radio interviewer).

Ask some pairs to act out their dialogues in front of the class.

Grammar

Present perfect simple

(a) **Stronger classes:** Students read the example. Elicit the answer to the questions and then students complete the rule. Check answers. Ask students how this tense is formed and elicit *has/have* + past participle.

Weaker classes: Books closed. Write the following example sentence (or some of your own) on the board: *I've been an English teacher for ten years.* Ask students the following questions: Am I still an English teacher now? (*Yes*) and elicit or explain that this action started in the past (*10 years ago*) and is still continuing now. Then ask students how this tense is formed and elicit *has/have* + past participle.

Students now open their books at page 46 and read the example from the interview and the following question. If necessary, refer them back to the interview where they can see the two sentences in context. Students answer the question and try to complete the rule. Check answers.

Answers
Yes, she is.
Present perfect simple

(b) Students go back through the interview and underline more examples of the present perfect. Check answers.

Answers
How long have you been a clown doctor?
I've been a clown doctor for three years.
And how long have you worked here in London?
I've worked here since last year.

At this point, ask some students to give you an example of their own for each tense to check they have understood the form and meaning correctly.

> **Language note**
> Ask students to translate the examples into their own language and compare the tense they use. If students use the present tense in their own language for this structure, point out that this can't be done in English.

(c) Students read through sentences 1 to 8. Check any problems. Go through the example sentence with them and ask if they can explain why the present perfect has been used (*Because he/she still has his/her bicycle now*). Refer them to the rule they have just completed in Exercise 2a, if necessary. Students complete the exercise. Check answers.

Answers
2 has worked   3 Has ... lived   4 have ... been
5 hasn't studied   6 have been   7 haven't had
8 Has ... seen

for and *since*

(d) **Stronger classes:** Students look at the questions and answers from the interview with the clown doctor (refer them back to the text if necessary). Write the questions and answers on the board. Explain to students (using this year as a time marker) that Fran has been a clown doctor for three years and is still one now. Students now try to answer the question.

Weaker classes: Write the following sentences on the board (or some of your own): *I've been an English teacher for 3 years./I've been an English teacher since 1999.* Elicit or explain the difference between *for* and *since* in each sentence. Students now try to answer the question in their books.

Answers
We use *for* to show a period of time; we use *since* to show a point in time.

Students read through the words in the box. Go through the examples with the whole class (*for a week*; *since yesterday*). Remind them of the rule for *for* and *since*, if necessary. Students complete the exercise. Check answers as a class.

Answers
For: a week; two years; an hour; a month; a long time; days
Since: yesterday; Christmas; 1999; Saturday; I was 11; last weekend

Call out a few more time expressions at this point to check students have understood when to use *for* and when to use *since*. For example: *December*; *ten years*; *half an hour*; *last week*.

(e) Look at the table as a class and do the first item as an example (*I've studied English since I was 11 years old. / since 2001. / since yesterday. / for ages.*). In pairs, students now make as many sentences as they can. Set a time limit of e.g. three minutes. Remind them that there can be more than one possibility for each sentence. Check answers as a class.

Possible answers
I've studied English since I was 11 years old. / since 2001. / since yesterday./for ages.

They've been married since I was 11 years old. / for 20 years. / since last Christmas. / for two weeks./ since 2001. / for ages. / since yesterday.

John has had his bicycle since I was 11 years old. / for 20 years. / since last Christmas. / for two weeks. / since 2001. / for ages. / since yesterday.

I haven't seen Mark since I was 11 years old. / for 20 years. / since last Christmas. / for two weeks. / since 2001./for ages./since yesterday.

We've lived here since I was 11 years old./for 20 years./since last Christmas./for two weeks./since 2001./for ages./since yesterday.

Maria hasn't spoken to John since I was 11 years old./for 20 years./since last Christmas./for two weeks./since 2001./for ages./since yesterday.

(f) This exercise can be set for homework. Students read through sentences 1 to 6. Check any problems. Go through the example and point out the time marker (*I was ten*). Students complete the exercise. Remind them to look for the time marker in each sentence to help them decide whether *for/since* is necessary. Remind them too that they will have to change the verb in each sentence. Check answers as a class.

Answers
2 've had / for
3 's studied / for
4 haven't seen / since
5 haven't been / for
6 hasn't written / since

> **Language note**
> Students may produce statements like: **I am working here since two years ago*. Remind them that in English we only use *ago* with the past simple in English.

Grammar notebook
Encourage students to note down the rules for the present perfect and expressions which follow *for/since* in their grammar notebooks.

3 Pronunciation
have, *has* and *for*

(a) 🔊 Students turn to page 120 and read through sentences 1 and 2. Play the recording, pausing it after the first item and go through this as an example, making sure students understand which words are stressed. Play the recording again for students to listen and underline the stressed words in the other items. Check answers.

TAPESCRIPT/ANSWERS

Woman <u>How long</u> have you been a <u>clown doctor</u>?

Man 1 For <u>three years</u>.

Woman <u>How long</u> has she <u>worked</u> in <u>London</u>?

Man 2 For a <u>year</u>.

(b) 🔊 Discuss the pronunciation of *has/have* and *for* as a class, making sure students are clear about how to pronounce them. Play the recording again, pausing for students to repeat each question and answer.

4 Speak and read
Warm up

Books closed. Ask students if they enjoy doing questionnaires. Do they do them often? Students now open their books on page 48 and look at the questionnaire and the title. Elicit what they think the questionnaire will be about.

(a) Divide the class into pairs. Students read through the question prompts. Ask a stronger pair to read out the example exchange, drawing students' attention to the question and the use of *for/since* in the answers. Students ask and answer the questions in their pairs. Monitor and check students are taking turns to ask and answer and using the correct question forms and answering using *for* and *since*. Make a note of any repeated errors to go through later as a class.

Weaker classes: Elicit the past participles of the verbs in each prompt before they begin and put them on the board. This will help them form the questions correctly.

(b) Students read through the questionnaire. Check any problems and pre-teach any vocabulary and expressions (*to feel hurt*; *to make fun of*; *big deal*) or ask students to look up the words in a dictionary. In the same pairs from Exercise 4a, students now ask and answer the questions in the questionnaire, then swap roles. Once both students have checked their scores and read the results on page 122, they compare results. Put pairs into groups to compare and discuss results. Ask for class feedback and put the results on the board to see if there is a personality type which dominates.

5 Vocabulary
Verb and noun pairs

(a) Ask students if they can remember what Fran, the clown doctor does, accept all true answers but elicit *She made sick children in hospital laugh./She made funny faces*. Write the verbs *have/make* on the board. Ask students to read through the list of words in the box and go through the example (*have a good laugh*). Students complete the exercise. Remind them to look back at the reading texts on pages 47 and 48 to help them find these expressions. Check answers, explaining that some expressions use *have* and some *make*.

Answers
Have: fun; a good time; a drink
Make: funny faces; fun of someone; a fool of yourself; a mistake; someone laugh/smile

(b) This exercise can be set for homework. Students read through sentences 1 to 6. Check any problems. Go through the example, if necessary. Students complete the exercise. Students can compare answers in pairs before a whole class check.

Answers
1 make   2 have   3 made; made   4 having; have
5 make   6 had

Vocabulary notebook
Encourage students to start a section called *Verb and noun pairs* and to note down any new vocabulary in their notebooks.

6 Listen

If you set the background information as a homework research task, ask students to tell the class what they found out.

BACKGROUND INFORMATION

Don't Worry, Be Happy: This song was recorded by the American artist Bobby McFerrin in 1988. Bobby McFerrin is a ten-time Grammy winner and, although best known for his vocals, is also an accomplished classical conductor.

He was born to opera singer parents in New York in 1950 and moved to Hollywood in 1958. His father was the first African-American male soloist at the famous Metropolitan Opera.

Bobby McFerrin formed various bands before going solo, starting at high school with the Bobby Mack Quartet. The album *Simple Pleasures,* on which *Don't Worry, Be Happy* features, was released in 1988 and soon became record of the year, while the song itself was song of the year.

Warm up

Ask students to look at the title of the song and ask them the following questions: Do they know this song? Have they heard it before? What do they think it is about? Ask them what makes them worry and how they make themselves or other people happy when they are worried. Discuss this as a class, in L1 if appropriate.

(a) Students read the instructions and then translate 'Don't worry' into their own language.

(b) Pre-teach the vocabulary in the box by giving examples of the words in sentences or students can look up the words in a dictionary. In pairs, students check they know the words.

(c) Students read through the words in the two columns. Check any problems. Explain that the words in column 1 all rhyme with words in column 2. Do the first one with them as an example (*smile – style*). Students then complete the matching part of the exercise. Check answers. Check students' pronunciation of each word; if they have made mistakes it could be because they are unsure of how a word is pronounced. Drill the words as necessary.

Students now read through the whole song (remind them to ignore the gaps) and in pairs, complete the gaps.

Answers
1 c 2 a 3 e 4 b 5 d

(d) Play the first verse and pause the recording for students to check or change their answer to the first gap. Continue in this way until students have checked their answers.

Answers
1 wrote 2 trouble 3 bed 4 smile 5 down

(e) Divide the class into pairs. Students read the questions and discuss them. Ask for class feedback. Do they all agree?

Vocabulary notebook
Remind students to note down any new vocabulary from the song.

OPTIONAL ACTIVITIES

Stronger classes
In small groups, students write the next verse of the song. Ask for class feedback. The class votes for the verse they prefer.

Weaker classes
Students find more rhyming words to continue Exercise 6c. This can be done as a chain round the class or students can discuss this in small groups and feedback as a class. Put all the rhyming words from the song on the board. For example:
smile; style; dial; file, etc.
trouble; double; bubble, etc.
frown; down; clown, etc.
wrote; note; goat; boat, etc.
bed; head; red; read; said, etc.

Students can note these down in their vocabulary books.

Who's going to sing?

7 Read and listen

Warm up

Ask students what happened in the last episode of the story. Ask someone if they can summarise the story so far. Ask them: Who is in the picture? Can they remember anything about their relationship? Where are they? How do they know? What are they talking about?

(a) ◁))) Students read the questions. Elicit suggestions. Play the recording for students to listen and check answers. Play the recording again, pausing as necessary to clarify any problems.

Answers
1 They are in the cinema entrance.
2 They are talking about the band.

(b) Students read questions 1 to 5. Check any problems.

Stronger classes: They can answer the questions and listen and read to check their answers. Remind them to back up their answers with information from the text.

Weaker classes: They may find it helpful to read and listen again before answering the questions. Check answers.

Answers
1   They are going to see a film.
2   They think she is a good singer.
3   He wants Amy and Joanne to sing; Amy will play the keyboards while Joanne sings.
4   Amy feels nervous about the contest because she hasn't sung in front of a big crowd before.
5   They are going by bus next Saturday.

┌─ OPTIONAL ACTIVITY ─────────
In pairs, students can act out the dialogue from the story.

8 Everyday English

(**a**) Ask students to read through expressions 1 to 4 and to locate them in the story on page 50 and decide who says them. Check answers. Then students match each expression with a definition. Go through the first one as an example, if necessary. Check answers.

Answers
1 c Amy   2 d Dave   3 a Amy   4 b Amy

(**b**) Ask students to read through dialogues 1 to 4. Check any problems. Go through the first dialogue as an example, if necessary. Students complete the other dialogues with the expressions from Exercise 8a. Check answers.

Answers
1 to be honest   2 reckon   3 get a move on   4 see

Vocabulary notebook
Students should note down the expressions and any translations from this exercise in their *Everyday English* section.

┌─ OPTIONAL ACTIVITIES ─────────
See Unit 1, Exercise 10 Everyday English, Optional Activities.

9 Speak and write

The preparation for this exercise can be done in class and the writing task done for homework with the replies collected in and marked.

Warm up

Ask students if they send or receive emails. How often do they send/receive them? Who do they email? What do they talk about in their emails? Discuss this as a class, in L1 if appropriate.

(**a**) Students read the question then read the email silently or you could ask a stronger student to read it aloud. Remind students that they should only read the email to look for the answers to the questions, it doesn't

matter at this stage if they don't understand everything. Check answers.

Answers
Brad wants you to tell him what makes you laugh, what you do to have a good time, how often you do those things, how long you've done them for and why you think having fun is important.

He wants to know this information because he is doing a project at school on how different teenagers round the world have fun.

(**b**) Divide the class into pairs. Students look at the questions in the email. Go through the example first, or ask a stronger pair to read out the example exchange. Students take turns to ask and answer the questions. Remind them to use the expressions from Exercise 5 where possible. Monitor and check students are taking turns and that they are asking and answering correctly. Note down any repeated errors to go through as a class later. Then put pairs into small groups where they can compare answers. Ask for some answers round the class. If there are any interesting or unusual answers, you could discuss these in more detail as a class.

(**c**) Students now write a reply to Brad's email. Before they start, remind them that emails are informal ways of communicating and they don't have to include all the information they would on a letter (e.g. address, date, Dear, etc.). Quickly brainstorm and write on the board some words and expressions which may be useful when writing an email (*Hi/Hello there; Thanks / Sorry / Must go / Be in touch soon / Let me know how the project goes*, etc.).

Remind them of their answers in Exercise 9b and go through the example email opening (*Sorry I haven't written sooner, I've been very busy at school / I've been ill / etc.; Anyway, you want to know how we have fun in England, well, let me tell you! … *)

Students write their replies and then send their emails to another student to read and check. Ask some students to read out their emails to the class.

8 A great film!

1 Read and listen

Warm up

Ask students to look at the photos. Ask them if they have seen actions like this in films they have seen. Which films were they? Which films have they seen recently? Ask them if they know what activities like this are called in films (*stunts*). Ask them if they know what the job is called of a person who does activities like this in films (*stuntman/woman*). Discuss these questions as a class, in L1 if appropriate.

a Students read the questions and look at the photo. They then read the text quickly to find the answers. Remind them they don't have to understand every word in the text at this point. Explain that the text is about a woman and her name is Alex /ælɪks/.

Answers
1 She is a stuntwoman.
2 She has to jump out of exploding cars or burning buildings, stand on the wings on a plane.

b 🔊 Students read through questions 1 to 3. Check any problems. while students read and listen and answer the questions. Check answers.

Weaker classes: You may want to pre-teach the following vocabulary: *stuntwoman; movies; nine-to-five; exploding; thriller; wing; to end up; film set; pit; can't stand.*

TAPESCRIPT
See the reading text on page 52 of the Student's Book.

Answers
1 She thinks it is very exciting and she likes doing stunts.
2 She didn't go into the hole full of snakes, (because she hates snakes)
3 She isn't worried about the danger because there are lots of people who check the stunts before she does them and the director doesn't want her to die.

c Students read through the definitions. Check any problems. Go through the first item as an example. In pairs, students complete the exercise. Remind them to think carefully about what type of word they are looking for in each case. Check answers.

Answers
1 nine-to-five job (para 1)
2 terrifying (para 2)
3 safe (para 3)
4 can't stand something (para 4)
5 earn money (para 5)

> **Language notes**
> *movies:* this is more commonly used in American English to refer to films; British English would usually refer to films.
>
> *nine-to-five job:* this timetable refers to the traditional working hours in Britain. Usually when people work in an office or for a company they are usually said to be working from nine o'clock in the morning until five o'clock in the afternoon. However, nowadays this is changing and people don't always work a nine-to-five timetable.

d Divide the class into small groups. Write the words *For* and *Against* on the board. Ask the class for one reason why they would like to be a stuntman/woman and one reason why not. Write the reasons under the headings on the board. Explain that they must now discuss and come up with five good reasons why they would/would not like to be a stuntman/woman. Monitor and check students are discussing this in English; encourage them to express their ideas in English as best they can. Ask one student from each group to feedback to the class. What is the general view?

Grammar
Verbs + -ing / verbs + infinitive

> **Language note**
> Some verbs in English can be followed by both the -ing form and the infinitive and it is difficult to give set rules for these areas. However, in this exercise students will only deal with the -ing form following these verbs. It may be useful to ask students to note down the verb categories in this activity in their vocabulary notebooks/grammar notebooks and learn a few each week.

(a) Students read through the list of verbs. Go through the example, explaining that *hate* is followed by -ing. Students go through the other verbs, locate them in the text on page 52 and note down the verbs which follow them. Check answers.

Answers
1 hated working (para 1)
2 decided to become (para 1)
3 prefer doing (para 1)
4 like doing (para 1)
5 don't mind being (para 3)
6 don't want to die (para 3)
7 refused to go in (para 4)
8 can't stand looking at (para 4)
9 enjoy doing (para 5)
10 hope to continue (para 5)
11 imagine doing (para 5)

(b) Write the following headings on the board: Verb + -ing; Verb + infinitive. Do the first two items from Exercise 2a as examples, writing one under each heading. Remind students that they should write the base form of the verb in the columns not the tense seen in the text. Quickly check students know the infinitives of the verbs they will be classifying (e.g. *to not mind*; *to not be able to stand*). Students complete the exercise. Check answers. If there is time, ask some students to come out and write the verbs under the correct column on the board. Then ask students to classify the other five verbs.

Answers

Verb + -ing	Verbs + infinitive
hate	decide
prefer	want
like	refuse
not mind	hope
not be able to stand	learn
enjoy	offer
imagine	promise
agree	
love	

(c) Students read through sentences 1 to 5. Check any problems. Go through the example, explaining tha they will have to read each sentence carefully and work out which verb will be correct with the

meaning. Remind them to check their lists of verbs from Exercise 2b if they are not sure. Students complete the exercise. They can compare answers in pairs before a whole class check.

Answers
2 don't like   3 prefer   4 don't mind
5 can't stand

Look
Explain to students that we use *prefer* when we are comparing two things and it is followed by the -ing form + *to*.

(d) This exercise can be set for homework. Students read through sentences 1 to 7. Check any problems. Go through the example, making sure students remember that *want* is followed by the infinitive. Again, remind them of the columns they completed in Exercise 2b which they should check if they are unsure which verbs are followed by the -ing form and which by the infinitive. Students complete the exercise. They can compare answers in pairs before a whole class check.

Answers
2 promise to bring
3 hope / am hoping to go
4 learn to drive
5 offered to help
6 decided to leave
7 refused to give

(e) This exercise can be set for homework. Students read through sentences 1 to 6. Check any problems. Go through the example, pointing out that in this exercise students have to choose the most appropriate verb from the box as well as choose the correct form. Again, remind them of the columns they completed in Exercise 2b which they should check if they are unsure which verbs are followed by the -ing form and which by the infinitive. Students complete the exercise. They can compare answers in pairs before a whole class check.

Answers
1 listening/watching   2 eating / to cook
3 getting up   4 to go / to let   5 doing / to help
6 dancing / to be

Grammar notebook
Remind students to note down the list of verbs from Exercise 2b.

┌─ **OPTIONAL ACTIVITY** ─────────
│ Call out a student's name and a verb from the list of
│ verbs in Exercise 2a. The student must call out an -ing
│ form or infinitive form after the verb as appropriate.
│ For example:
│ *T: Maria – offer*
│ *Maria: to bring / to help / to give, etc.*

3 Speak

a) Divide the class into pairs. Ask students which things they like/love/can't stand doing and elicit a few replies. Now ask a stronger pair to read out the example exchange in their books. Students now choose as many items as they can from the box and exchange information. Remind them to think about the verbs they are using and which verbs follow it. Monitor and check they are taking turns to exchange information and that they are using the correct verb forms. Note down any repeated errors to go through as a class later. Ask some pairs to tell the class the information they have found out about their partner.

b) Divide the class into pairs (or keep the same pairs from Exercise 3a). Ask a stronger pair to read out the example exchange, drawing students' attention to the use of *prefer + -ing*. Give students a few minutes to exchange information about their preferences. Monitor and check they are taking turns to do this and are using the correct verb forms. Note down any repeated errors to go through as a class later. Ask some pairs to feedback to the class.

c) Students read through the list of activities. Check any problems. Ask a stronger pair to read out the example exchange, drawing students' attention to the verbs used. Students now exchange information about things they did/didn't do. Ask some pairs to feedback to the class.

4 Vocabulary

Films

Warm up

Ask students to look at the photos on the page. Do they know any of these films? Have they seen any of them? Which one(s) do they like best/prefer? Now ask them about films which they remember because of the music. Elicit a few titles. Ask them if they associate particular types of music with particular types of film, elicit a few examples. Discuss this as a class and in L1 if appropriate.

a) 🔊 Explain that students will hear music from eight different types of films. They must look at the photos of the films and try and match the soundtrack to the film depicted. Play the first soundtrack as an example. Explain that they must write the numbers in the boxes next to the pictures as they listen. Continue playing the recording for students to match the other pictures. Check answers as a class.

Answers

Track 1: thriller	Track 5: horror
Track 2: comedy	Track 6: western
Track 3: science fiction	Track 7: romance
Track 4: action	Track 8: drama

b) 🔊 Students read through the words in the box. Check they understand what each type of film is.

Students look at the stills again and decide which type of film they are. Go through the first one with them as an example, if necessary. Play the recording for students to check or change their answers. Play it again, pausing after each answer for students to repeat.

TAPESCRIPT/ANSWERS

1 thriller   2 comedy   3 science fiction   4 action
5 horror   6 western   7 romance   8 drama

c) Divide the class into pairs. Elicit or give an example of a recent thriller film on release or one which you have seen recently. Ask the class if they can think of any other recent thriller films. Elicit answers. Students now find examples for the different types of films. Ask for class feedback. Are there some films which have occurred more often than others? Discuss the different types of films they have chosen.

d) Students read through words 1 to 7 and definitions a to g. Check any problems. They should remember *director* and *film set* which appear in the reading text on page 52. Go through the example, if necessary. Students match the rest of the words with their definitions. Check answers.

Answers

2 g   3 f   4 b   5 c   6 a   7 d

e) Students read through sentences 1 to 7. Go through the example, if necessary. Students complete the exercise. Remind them they must use words from Exercise 4d. Check answers.

Answers

2 storyline   3 script   4 director   5 soundtrack
6 special effects   7 film set

Vocabulary notebook

Remind students to start a section called *Films* and to note down any new vocabulary in their notebooks.

5 Speak

Divide the class into pairs or small groups. Students read through the list of questions. Check any vocabulary problems. Choose a student and do the first question and answer exchange as an example.
T: Juan, how often do you go to the cinema?
Juan: I go to the cinema every weekend.

Students ask and answer the questions. Monitor and check students are taking turns to exchange information. Note down any repeated errors to go through as a class later. Ask pairs/groups to feedback to the class. Discuss any interesting answers as a class.

OPTIONAL ACTIVITY

Students choose a scene from their favourite film and describe it to a partner without telling them the title of the film. The partner must guess which film it comes from.

6 Pronunciation
Consonant clusters

a 🔊 Students turn to page 120 and read the list of words. Do the first one with them as an example. Play the recording for students to listen to the pronunciation of the underlined letters. Play the recording again, pausing after each word for students to repeat.

TAPESCRIPT

1 space travel 2 science fiction 3 script 4 drama
5 stuntwoman 6 frightening 7 thriller

b 🔊 Play the recording again, pausing after each sentence for students to repeat.

TAPESCRIPT

1 Alex does frightening stunts in thrillers.
2 Stuntwomen don't learn scripts.
3 I like science fiction films about space travel.

7 Read

Warm up

Ask students to look at the photos of the people. Elicit which type of film they think each person might like to go and see.

Students then read through the information about the people in the photos and the film reviews. Check any vocabulary (scenery; in love; pioneers). Students decide which film would be most appropriate for each person. Remind them that there are more films than people so they will have some films which they can't match with a person. Students can compare answers in pairs before a whole class check. Remind students to give reasons for their choices. At this point, you can also see if their *Warm up* predictions were correct.

Answers
Carolina: Yesterday
Kasia: Busters
Serkan: High School Days
Sandra: Freddy
Hugo: Rangers

8 Listen

a 🔊 Tell students that they will hear two people talking about one of the films in Exercise 7. Students must listen and decide which film is being talked about. Play the recording for students to listen and answer the question. Check answers, asking students to give reasons for their choices. Play the recording again if necessary, stopping it at points where students are given information about the film.

TAPESCRIPT

Karen What did you do last night?
James Oh, not much. I stayed home and watched a film – a video I got from the new store in town.
Karen Oh yeah? So what did you see?
James A science fiction film. It's set in the future.
Karen Oh yeah, I think I've seen it. It stars Peter Arnold, doesn't it ...?
James Uh huh.
Karen ... and it's about a man who wants to change the world and it's the year 3000.
James Yes, that's right. I thought it was great. The special effects were amazing. It's set in Mexico City, I think. ... Did you like it?
Karen Well, not really. I mean, some of it was good – but I didn't like the acting at all, and I thought the ending was stupid.

Answer
Rangers

b 🔊 Students read through sentences 1 to 4 and the words in the box.

Stronger classes: They can complete the sentences and listen and check only.

Weaker classes: Go through the first sentence as an example, playing and pausing the recording. Play the recording again and then give students a few minutes to complete the exercise. Check answers.

Answers
1 It's set in 2 It stars 3 It's about 4 acting/ending

Vocabulary notebook
Remind students at this point to make a note of any new vocabulary from this section.

9 Speak

Divide the class into pairs. Remind students of the phrases in the box in Exercise 8b. In pairs, students now discuss a recent film they have seen.

Weaker classes: Remind them they must talk about the following points:
- who's in it
- who the director is
- where it's set
- what it's about
- what they liked about it
- what they didn't like about it
- why they would recommend it to a friend

Give students a few minutes to discuss this and then ask some pairs to feedback to the rest of the class. Is there a favourite film in the class?

Culture in mind

Read

If you set the background information as a homework research task, ask students to tell the class what they found out.

BACKGROUND INFORMATION

Macaulay Culkin: Was born in 1980 in New York. He made his name in 1990 in the film *Home Alone* when he was just 10 years old. His relationship with his manager-father has troubled him over the years.

Marilyn Monroe: The famous Hollywood actress had a troubled life and had been married and divorced three times before she died in 1962 to aircraft factory worker called James Dougherty, then the baseball star Joe DiMaggio, and then the playwright Arthur Miller.

River Phoenix: Was born in 1970 and became a successful young actor. Some of the better-known films he starred in include *Stand By Me*, and *Indiana Jones* and the *Last Crusade*. He was at the height of his career when he died outside a nightclub in 1993 from a drug overdose.

Richard Gere: The Hollywood actor has made a lot of films but is probably best-known for his role in *Pretty Woman* (1990). He was married to the supermodel Cindy Crawford in 1991 but they divorced in 1995.

Tom Cruise: The famous American actor has starred in many films over the years. Some of the more famous ones include *Top Gun* (1988), *Mission Impossible* (1996) and *Vanilla Sky* (2000). He was married to the actress Mimi Rogers, and then to the actress Nicole Kidman. Both marriages ended in divorce.

Nicole Kidman: See Tom Cruise above. The Australian-born actress is famous for her film roles in films such as *Moulin Rouge* and *The Hours*, and recent theatre roles.

Kate Winslet and Jim Threapleton: The British born actress and star of *Titanic*, married Threapleton in 1998. They divorced in December 2001. Kate Winslet is now married to the film director Sam Mendes.

Warm up

Ask students if they know any films the people in the photos have starred in? Do they know the nationalities of the people? (They are all American except Nicole Kidman, who is Australian, and Kate Winslet and Jim Threapleton, who are British.) What do they think these people have in common? Elicit suggestions.

a Ask students to name the people in the photos (Marilyn Monroe; Kate Winslet and former husband Jim Threapleton; Nicole Kidman and former husband Tom Cruise; River Phoenix)

b Students read through the three possible titles. Remind students that the article on the page is for a school web magazine. Ask them who they think may want to read such an article and what information it may have in it. Students now read the article quickly and choose one of the three titles for it. Remind them not to worry if they don't know all the words in the text. Ask for feedback and ask students to justify their answers.

Answer
2

c Students read through the questions. Check any problems. Students read the text in detail and answer the questions. Check answers.

Weaker classes: You may want to pre-teach the following vocabulary: *dream*; *successful*; *luxury*; *goldfish bowl*; *paparazzi*; *drugs*; *marriage*; *cosmetic surgery*. Students can also check new words in a dictionary.

Answers
1 She says the good things are earning millions of dollars, buying almost anything they want, living in fantastic houses, wearing expensive designer clothes and driving the best cars in the world, travelling to wonderful places, staying in luxury hotels, sailing in private yachts, going to parties, seeing their photos on magazine covers.
2 The three main problems are: the paparazzi, problems in their private lives and the pressure to spend money on cosmetic surgery.

d Students read through words 1 to 5. Go through the first expression as an example, if necessary. Students now go back through the text and find these expressions. Check answers.

Answers
1 clothes designed by famous names in the fashion industry (e.g. Gucci, Calvin Klein, etc.)
2 hotels which offer the best of everything in the rooms and facilities
3 literally, a container for fish. Here when everyone can see what the rich and famous do in their lives through magazines and newspapers
4 journalists and photographers from magazines and newspapers who follow the rich and famous around hoping to find a good story or some interesting photographs
5 operations performed in order to improve one's face or body

Vocabulary notebook
Remind students at this point to make a note of any new vocabulary from the reading text.

11 Listen

Warm up

🔊 Ask students if they recognise the actor in the photo (Macaulay Culkin) and ask if they know which films he has starred in (Home Alone). Students quickly read through the text and check their predictions.

Play the recording, pausing it after the first gap and go through this as an example. Remind students to think carefully about the context of each. Students listen and complete the text. Check answers, playing and pausing the recording again as necessary to clarify any problems.

TAPESCRIPT

Mike   Hey Amy – I liked your article on the website!

Amy   Thanks, Mike.

Mike   I was interested in the bit about Macaulay Culkin, because I watched that film *Home Alone* on video the other day.

Amy   Oh, right! Well, I just love Macaulay Culkin.

Mike   Tell me more about him.

Amy   Well, he was born in 1980, in New York – he's a real New Yorker, he still lives there. And do you know, he was only four years old when he worked in the theatre for the first time!

Mike   Four? Really?

Amy   Yeah, and he made his first film in 1987 – when he was only seven. I can't remember what the film was, but *Home Alone* was the one that made him famous – he got a *Best Young Actor* award for the film, er, in 1991.

Mike   So he was very successful when he was very young?

Amy   He certainly was! After *Home Alone*, he became the highest-paid child actor of all time.

Mike   Amazing! But you said in your article that he wasn't very happy.

Amy   No, not very. He didn't have an easy home life and he stopped acting when he was fourteen, he didn't enjoy it any more.

Mike   So, is he still not acting?

Amy   No, he started again when he was twenty.

Mike   Is he married?

Amy   Well, he was married – he got married when he was only seventeen, to a girl called Rachel Miner. They were friends together at school, she was only seventeen too. But they split up in 2000.

Mike   So he's a good example of how being a film star isn't always easy.

Amy   That's right, he is. I think he's a great actor, though!

Answers
1 New York   2 4 years old   3 1987   4 1991
5 highest   6 14   7 20   8 17   9 2000

Discussion box

Stronger classes: In pairs or small groups, students go through the questions in the box and discuss them.

Weaker classes: They can choose one question only to discuss. If necessary, elicit a few prompts for the question they have chosen to help them with their discussion.

Monitor and help as necessary, encouraging students to express themselves in English.

Ask pairs or groups to feedback to the class and discuss any interesting points further.

12 Write

(a) Students read the heading and the film review quickly. Check any problems. If necessary, do the first one with them as an example. Students then match the headings with each paragraph of the review. Check answers.

Answers
1 C   2 B   3 A

(b) Students now write their own review of a film for their school magazine. Remind them of the following things:

* to choose a film they like
* to plan their review before writing it (tell them to look at the structure of Dave's review in Exercise a)
* to use some of the language they have seen in the grammar in this unit (verbs followed by *-ing* and verbs followed by the infinitive). Ask them to look at Dave's review for this and pick out examples of these verbs (*want to marry*; *doesn't want to leave*; *promises to look after*; *don't usually like watching ...*; *decided to watch*)

Students can read out their reviews to the rest of the class. The class can vote for the best review.

Module 2 **Check your progress**

1 **Grammar**

(a) 2 doesn't she   3 isn't he   4 aren't we   5 are they
6 has she   7 can he   8 will you   9 did they
10 didn't you

(b) 2 are produced   3 are held   4 isn't written
5 are sold   6 are bought   7 is/held

(c) 2 've already had   3 Have/bought   4 've already
finished   5 Has/seen   6 have just come   7 've
not arrived/they haven't arrived

(d) 2 're not allowed to   3 don't let   4 're allowed to
5 lets   6 're allowed to

(e) 2 's been/for   3 have lived/for   4 haven't seen/
since   5 haven't listened/for   6 has phoned/since
7 haven't eaten/since

(f) 2 to give   3 listening   4 to study/to go
5 putting   6 to help

2 **Vocabulary**

(a) 2 lift   3 trousers   4 garbage   5 pavement
6 subway

(b) 1 adult   2 young   3 child   4 middle
5 elderly   6 pensioner   7 teenager
Mystery word: toddler

(c) People: director, actress
Kinds of films: thriller, science fiction, western
Other words about film: script, storyline, soundtrack

3 **Everyday English**

2 get a move on   3 to be honest   4 I see
5 I reckon   6 Nice one

How did you do?
Students work out their scores. Check how they
have done and follow up any problem areas with
revision work for students.

Module 3
Weird and wonderful

YOU WILL LEARN ABOUT ...

Ask students to look at the pictures on the page. Ask students to read through the topics in the box and check they understand each item. You can ask them the following questions, in L1 if appropriate: *Is the disaster in picture 7 natural or unnatural? What do you call a group of people who live together? How do you remember important things? Do you know the names of any brilliant musicians? Do you know where pop music came from/how it started?*

In small groups, students discuss which topic area they think each picture matches.

Check answers.

Answers
1   The history of popular music
2   Intelligence and memory
3   Why tsunami waves happen
4   A brilliant young musician
5   A tribe in Borneo
6   Life in Australia
7   Some natural disasters

YOU WILL LEARN HOW TO ...

See Introduction.

Use grammar
Student read through the grammar points and examples. Go through the first item as an example. In pairs, students now match the grammar items in their book. Check answers.

Answers
Present simple passive: The city was destroyed by the earthquake.
Definite and indefinite articles: There's a basin in the bedroom.
too much/too many/not enough: There were too many people and not enough chairs.
will vs. *going to*: We're going to visit the USA this summer.
Determiners (*everyone/no one* etc.): Someone did it, but no one knows who it was.
mustn't vs. *don't have to*: You don't have to listen, but you mustn't make any noise.
Present perfect continuous: I've been working all morning.

Use vocabulary
Write the headings on the board. Go through the items in the Student's Book and check understanding. Now ask students if they can think of one more item for the *Disasters* heading. Elicit some responses and add them to the list on the board. Students now do the same for the other headings. Some possibilities are:
Disasters: *forest fire*; *earthquake*
Homes: *semi-detached*; *detached*; *terraced*
Remembering/forgetting: *forget*; *memorise*; *remind*
Music: *folk*; *keyboard*; *drums*; *country* and *western*

9 Disaster!

Unit overview

TOPIC: Natural disasters

TEXTS

Listening: a radio broadcast about a famous earthquake
Reading: a magazine article about a tidal wave
Reading and listening: Story: *Let's talk about it later*
Writing: a newspaper article about a forest fire

SPEAKING AND FUNCTIONS
Talking about news events
Talking about and describing dreams

LANGUAGE
Past simple passive
a / an / the
Pronunciation: silent letters
Vocabulary: disasters
Everyday English: *What's up with …?*; *get rid of*; *got a point*; *sort of*

1 Vocabulary and listening

Warm up

Ask students if they can name any natural disasters. Elicit what they know and write them on the board. Have they ever experienced a natural disaster? If they have, encourage them to give details about their experience. If not, can they imagine what it must be like? Discuss this as a class, in L1 if appropriate.

a 🔊 Students read through words 1 to 5 in the box and look at the photos. Go through the first item as an example, if necessary. Give students a few minutes to match as many words as they can using any items they suggested in the *Warm up* exercise. Students can compare answers in pairs. Play the recording for students to listen and check or change their answers. Play the recording again, pausing after each word for students to repeat.

TAPESCRIPT
a 5 a volcano   b 1 an earthquake   c 3 a tsunami
d 4 a nuclear bomb   e 2 an avalanche

b Students read through the questions. Elicit the reason why: It is an unnatural/man-made disaster.

Vocabulary notebook
Students should start a section called *Disasters* and note down words from this exercise. Encourage them to use translations and illustrations if it will help them remember each word better.

c If you set the background information as a homework research task, ask students to tell the class what they found out.

BACKGROUND INFORMATION

San Francisco: See Unit 5, Exercise 12

San Francisco earthquake: And subsequent fires occurred on 18 April 1906 and caused a huge amount of damage to the city. The earthquake shock was felt from Oregon to Los Angeles and as far east as central Nevada. More than 3000 people died in the quake and the fires.

Richter scale: Is a scale used to measure the size and strength of earthquakes all over the world. It was named after Charles Richter, a professor of seismology in California. It uses logarithms to calculate the strength of the earthquake, so a 7 on the Richter scale is 10 times stronger than an earthquake measuring a 6 and produces 30 times more energy.

🔊 Students look at the photo and read the question and in pairs or small groups discuss where they think it happened. Do not give answers at this point but accept a few suggestions and write them on the board. Play the recording for students to listen and check their predictions. Play the recording again, pausing as necessary to clarify any problems.

TAPESCRIPT

Interviewer   to talk to us about the effects of earthquakes and what can be done about them, here is Doctor Susan Harris. Good afternoon, Dr Harris.

Dr Harris   Good afternoon.

Interviewer   I know you've done a lot of research into one particular earthquake.

Dr Harris   Yes. One of the most famous earthquakes on record happened in 1906, in San Francisco, California. I also look into what the city of San Francisco is doing these days, to prepare for any more earthquakes …

Answer
1906, in San Francisco.

d Students read through the words in the box. Make sure they understand them all. Ask students to read through the summary, ignoring the gaps. Go through the example, if necessary. Students now complete the exercise. Students can compare answers in pairs but do not give answers at this point.

e 🔊 Play the second part of the recording for students to listen and check their answers. Play the recording again, pausing as necessary to clarify any problems.

TAPESCRIPT

Interviewer Can you tell us about the earthquake of 1906?

Dr Harris Well, it happened very early in the morning of April the eighteenth, 1906. The earthquake hit the city of San Francisco at about 5 o'clock in the morning, while most people were still sleeping.

Interviewer And how long did it last?

Dr Harris Only about one minute – but it was very strong, about 8.3 on the Richter scale, we think – erm, in 1906 people didn't have the same kind of equipment we have now – and, er, so, one minute of an earthquake that's as strong as that can do – you know, really an awful lot of damage.

Interviewer Yes indeed – and just how much damage did it do?

Dr Harris Well, three thousand people were killed – people sleeping in their beds and the buildings just fell down around and on top of them. And many, many other people were injured – it's hard to know exactly how many, but we believe that around 225,000 people were injured, one way or another.

Interviewer And what about the buildings – houses, blocks of flats, shops, things like that?

Dr Harris Well, I can't tell you exactly how many buildings, but almost five hundred buildings were destroyed – some by the earthquake itself, and some by the terrible fire that started because of the earthquake. The damage to the city meant that about 400 million dollars was lost – but that's dollars in 1906, not dollars today. So, you can see, it was a really terrible event ...

Answers
1 3,000   2 killed   3 injured   4 buildings
5 destroyed   6 money   7 lost

2 Grammar
Past simple passive

a **Stronger classes:** Read the examples and the explanations with the class, and elicit the difference between the past and present simple passive which they saw in Unit 8 (the verb *be* is in the past tense in these examples). Students then go back through the summary in Exercise 1d and find more examples of the past simple passive.

Weaker classes: Books closed. Write the following prompts and dates (in jumbled order) on the board:
• last football World Cup/held/2002/Japan and South Korea
• Sistine Chapel/built/1473 (or another famous example from students' own country)

Elicit the past passive questions from students: Where and when was the last football World Cup held?/When was the Sistine Chapel built? Then ask students to match each prompt with the correct date. Ask them if they can remember how to form the present simple passive from Unit 8. Elicit the form and then ask them what they notice about the verb in each question: it is the past tense of the verb *be* and the past participle. Students open their books at page 63 and read through the examples. Students go back through the summary in Exercise 1d and find more examples of the past passive.

Check answers.

Explain to students that this construction is usually used when we are more interested in the action and not the person who did it and we do not usually use '*by* + person' with it.

Answers
... were killed ...; ... were injured; ... were destroyed; ... was lost ...

Students now complete the rule. Check answers.

Answer
to be/past participle

> **Language note**
> If students make errors with *was/were* in the past passive construction, remind them that *was* is only used with first and third persons singular.

b Students read through sentences 1 to 5. Go through the example as a class, if necessary. Ask students why it is *was* and not *were* and elicit that it is because *photo* is singular. Students complete the sentences. Remind them to check the subject first to see if they need to use a singular or plural form of the verb *be*. Check answers.

Answers
2 was stolen   3 were built   4 was written
5 weren't used

c This exercise can be set for homework. Students read through sentences 1 to 5. Check any problems. Go through the example as a class, highlighting how the active sentence changes when it becomes a passive sentence. Elicit the differences (the active object becomes the passive subject 'the house'; we do not need to know who found the dead man so we do not use *by* + person). Students complete the sentences. Remind them that we don't need to know who carried out the action and that they need to think carefully about all the changes that need to happen from active to passive. Check answers.

Answers
2 The house was robbed at midnight.
3 A film was made about the San Francisco earthquake.
4 The Empire State Building was completed / was built in 1932.
5 The classroom window was broken (last night).

Grammar notebook
Remind students to note down the rule and some examples of their own for the past passive.

3 Pronunciation
Silent letters

a 🔊 Students turn to page 121. Read through the instructions as a class and elicit some examples of words with silent letters (students may be able to remember some from Student's Book 1, Unit 14. Students read through words 1 to 5. Go through the example as a class, then students underline the silent letters in the other words. Students can compare answers in pairs. Play the recording for students to check or change their answers. Play the recording again, pausing after each word for students to repeat.

TAPESCRIPT/ANSWERS
1 li<u>s</u>ten   2 bom<u>b</u>   3 <u>w</u>rite   4 b<u>ui</u>ld   5 <u>k</u>nocked

b 🔊 Students read through words 1 to 5. Go through the first word with them as an example. Students then underline the silent letters in the other words. Students can compare answers in pairs. Play the recording for students to check or change their answers. Play it again, pausing after each word for students to repeat.

TAPESCRIPT/ANSWERS
1 ans<u>w</u>er   2 <u>w</u>rong   3 clim<u>b</u>   4 high
5 mount<u>ai</u>n

c 🔊 Students read through sentences 1 to 4. Drill each one as a class. Play the recording, pausing after each sentence for students to repeat.

TAPESCRIPT
1   Listen and write.
2   It's the wrong answer.
3   He climbed a high mountain.
4   They're building a big bomb.

4 Speak

a Divide the class into Student A and B pairs. Tell Student As to read through the questions and answers on page 63 and Student Bs to turn to page 122 and look at their questions and answers. Go through Student A's example with all the As and then do the same for Student Bs. Make sure students understand that they have to make past passive questions and then they must choose the correct answer. Students should note down their partner's answers. Give students a few minutes to complete the exercise.

Monitor and check students are using the correct past passive question forms and make a note of any repeated errors to go over as a class later.

b Ask a few pairs to read out their answers to the class and then give them the correct answers. Students work out how many they got correct and then compare with other pairs. If you prefer, you can allocate a score for each correct answer, e.g. 5 points. The winner is the pair with the most points. Is there a class winner?

Answers
Student A:
1   1989   2   J.R.R. Tolkein   3   The Beatles   4   In Paris
5   1963
Student B:
1   Arizona   2   1925   3   John Lennon   4   Adidas
5   1997

5 Read

If you set the background information as a homework research task, ask students to tell the rest of the class what they have found out.

BACKGROUND INFORMATION

Richter scale: See Exercise 1c.

Hawaii: Is a state of the USA and is made up of eight major islands and various smaller islands. It is situated in the Pacific Ocean to the south west of San Francisco. The capital is Honolulu and the islands are of volcanic origin and have many coral reefs. Hawaii was struck by 13 significant tsunamis in the 20th century.

Hilo: (Pronounced hee-low) Is on the east coast of the island of Hawaii, 200 miles from Honolulu. Hilo has suffered from many tsunamis, and is sometimes referred to as the tsunami capital of the USA.

Warm up

Ask students if they have ever experienced any severe weather conditions. If so, what? Discuss this as a class and in L1 if appropriate.

a Students read through questions 1 to 3. Check any problems. Do the first question with students as an example, if necessary. Students complete the exercise. Remind them they don't need to understand every word in the text at this stage. Check answers.

Weaker classes: You may want to pre-teach the following vocabulary: *damage*; *destruction*; *harbour*; *coast*; *ocean floor*; *hit*; *warn*; *protect*.

Answers
1   The name comes from a Japanese word meaning 'harbour wave'.
2   30 metres high.
3   An earthquake at the bottom of the sea.

(b) Students read through topics 1 to 4. Students now match the topics with the paragraphs in the text. Check answers. Ask students to explain their choices.

Answers
1 B   2 D   3 A   4 C

(c) Students read through the instructions and look at the four pictures. **Stronger classes:** Students order the pictures. Check answers. **Weaker classes:** Read the second and third lines in paragraph 2 again. Elicit which picture best represents those sentences (pictures c and d). Students then read the rest of the paragraph and order the other two pictures. Check answers.

Answers
b 3   c 4   d 1   a 2

(d) Students read through the definitions. Check any problems. In pairs, students find the words in the text to match the definitions. Set a time limit if you want to add a competitive element to this activity. Check answers. The pair that has the most correct answers is the winner.

Answers
1 huge   2 coast   3 ocean floor   4 protect

Vocabulary notebook
Students may find it useful to note down any new vocabulary from the reading text in their notebooks.

OPTIONAL ACTIVITY

Stronger classes
Divide the class into pairs. Each pair provides (looking up words in a dictionary, if necessary) definitions of five more words in the text. Then they exchange definitions with another pair. Each pair has to find the matching words in the text (as in the exercise above).

---

6 Grammar

a/an or *the*

(a) Elicit the definition of 'an article' (*a*, *an* or *the*). Go through the example as a class. Read the instruction and the text aloud, pausing to point out the example. Students then underline the articles and the nouns they qualify while you read the rest of the text. Explain to students that *a/an* are used when we refer to something for the first time and *the* is used when we are referring to something we have already mentioned. Check answers.

Answers
Line 3: a volcanic eruption
Line 4: The earthquake
Line 5/6: the strongest earthquake
Line 7: the volcano
Line 8/9: a Roman town

(b) Students read through the rule box and complete the rule. Check answers.

Answers
a / an
the

Refer to the underlined text again and check the validity of the rule: The first time the earthquake and the volcano are mentioned, the article *a* is used with the noun. After that, the article *the* is used, as the reader knows which earthquake and volcano are being referred to.

(c) Students read through the sentences. Check any problems. Go through the example as a class, if necessary. Students complete the text. Check answers.

Answers
1 a, a, the, the
2 a, a, The, the, the
3 an, a, a, the, the

Grammar notebook
Remind students to note down the rules for this area and to make a note of a few examples of their own if necessary.

OPTIONAL ACTIVITY

Read out the following text and make a beep sound every time you come to *a/an* or *the*. Students must write down the word they think goes in each gap. Students can compare answers in pairs before a whole class check.

It was **a** dark night in 1989. I was walking along the beach when I saw **a** boat. It was a very rough sea. The lighthouse was not working. I was sure **the** boat was going to hit **the** rocks. I had **a** white towel with me so I ran down to **the** shore and waved and waved **the** towel. Suddenly, **the** lighthouse light came on again and **the** boat turned and ...

Stronger classes
They can then write their own ending for the story.

---

7 Speak

(a) Ask students to read through the gapped dialogue. Check any problems. Go through the example as a class. Students complete the dialogue using *a/an/the*. Students can compare answers in pairs before a whole class check.

Answers
1 a   2 the   3 a   4 The   5 a   6 The   7 the
8 a   9 a   10 the   11 a   12 The   13 an   14 an

(b) Divide the class into pairs. Read through the instructions as a class and make sure that students understand they must now make up their own dreams and use *a/an/the* in each sentence. Remind them of the model in Exercise 8a they have just completed.
Weaker classes: You could give them a first sentence to get them started.

Monitor and check that students are taking turns to say a sentence and are using *a/an/the* in each sentence.

Ask pairs to read out their dreams to the rest of the class.

Let's talk about it later

8 Read and listen

Warm up

Ask students what they remember about the previous episode and what happened. (Dave suggested that both Amy and Joanne sing in the concert; Amy felt nervous about the concert.)

a Students read through the questions. Play the recording while students listen and read. Check answers. Play the recording again, pausing as necessary to clarify any problems.

TAPESCRIPT
See the story on page 66 of the Student's Book.

Answers
1 London   2 Unhappy   3 Students' own answers

b Ask students to read through items 1 to 7 and items a to g. Check any problems. Go through the example, if necessary. Students complete the exercise. Play the recording again if necessary to clarify any problems.

Answers
2 e   3 f   4 a   5 g   6 d   7 c

OPTIONAL ACTIVITY

In groups of four, students can act out the dialogue from the story.

9 Everyday English

a Ask students to read through expressions 1 to 4 and to locate them in the story on page 66 and decide who says them. Check answers. Then ask students to offer translations for each expression.

Answers
1 Joanne   2 Amy   3 Dave   4 Dave

b Ask students to read through dialogues 1 to 4. Check any problems. Go through the first dialogue as an example, if necessary. Students complete the other dialogues with the expressions from Exercise 9a. Check answers.

Answers
1 What's up with   2 got a point   3 sort of
4 get rid of

Vocabulary notebook
Students should note down the expressions and translations from this exercise in their *Everyday English* section.

OPTIONAL ACTIVITIES

See Unit 1, Exercise 10 Everyday English, Optional Activities.

10 Write

a Students read the article silently. Ask them the two questions.

Answers
1 A man was blown off a cliff, into the sea.
2 It happened because the wind was very strong.

b Divide the class into pairs. Ask students to read through the phrases in the box. Check any problems. Ask a stronger student to describe picture 1 using phrases from the box. Students continue describing the pictures. Remind them to use the past simple passive where possible. Monitor and check students are using the construction properly and note down any repeated errors to go through as a class later. Ask a few pairs to feedback to the class.

Possible answers
1 The weather was very hot. Someone in the forest dropped a cigarette end.
2 The dry leaves caught fire.
3 There were some very strong winds which made the fire worse. The fire was spread because of strong winds.
4 The fire fighters could not control the fire and it spread to houses nearby.

c Students can do the preparation in class, and complete the writing at home.

They should organise their work so that each paragraph answers one of the three questions. Remind students to refer back to the model text in Exercise 10a if necessary. They should use the words and phrases from Exercise 10b, and write their text as if it was a newspaper article, using the passive, where possible. When they have finished, ask them to read their article to the class or to a partner.

10 A place to stay

Unit overview

TOPIC: Homes around the world

TEXTS
Reading and listening: a text and email about adventure holidays in Borneo
Listening: people describing their homes
Reading: a text about life in Australia
Writing: an email about holiday plans

SPEAKING AND FUNCTIONS
Describing quantity
Talking about your home
Discussing stereotypes

LANGUAGE
too much / many + not enough
will vs. *be going to*
Pronunciation: sound and spelling: *-ough*
Vocabulary: homes

1 Read and listen

If you set the background information as a homework research task, ask students to tell the class what they found out.

BACKGROUND INFORMATION

Kuching: (or Kucing) Is a city on the north coast of the island of Borneo in the Malaysian state of Sarawak.

Borneo: Is the world's third largest island. It is divided into different parts. Indonesia holds about 70% of the island, an area called Kalimantan. The other parts of the island are Brunei and the Malaysian states of Sarawak and Sabah Darussalam. The island is covered with jungles and forests and one of its highest mountains is Mount Kinabalu (4101 metres).

Iban people: Are native people of Borneo, famous for their hospitality and family spirit.

Iban longhouses: is where most Iban people choose to live and a longhouse can house an entire village under the one roof. The houses are built on stilts and often the animals live underneath the living areas.

Warm up

Ask students where they usually go on holiday and where they stay. What is the most exciting holiday they have been on? Discuss this as a class, in L1 if appropriate.

a Ask students to read the questions and look at the pictures. Students then read the text quickly to answer them. Encourage them to use the visual clues to help them. Remind them they don't have to understand every word at this stage. Check answers.

Answers
1 An adventure holiday   2 Borneo

b Students read through items 1 to 3. Encourage them to read the text again quickly to find the answers. Go through the first item with them as an example, if necessary. Students can compare answers in pairs before a whole class check.

Weaker classes: You may want to pre-teach the following vocabulary: *trip*; *amazing*; *separate*; *roof*; *poles*; *stay*; *friendly*; *village*; *lifestyle*; *traditional*; *trek*; *orang-utans*.

Answers
1 Iban
2 In longhouses
3 They join the traditional dances, visit the farms where the Iban work, go on a trek into the jungle and see orang-utans and crocodiles.

OPTIONAL ACTIVITY
Ask students the following true/false questions about the reading text and ask students to correct the false statements:
1 The first stop after London is Kuching. **(False; Jakarta)**
2 A longhouse is a house on its own. **(False; It's separate apartments all under one roof)**
3 30 families can live in one longhouse. **(True)**
4 The poles are 5 meters high. **(False; 3 metres)**
5 Orang-utans and crocodiles live in the jungle. **(True)**

c Students read through the instructions and the questions. Check any problems. Play the recording while students read and listen for the answers.

Weaker classes: Pause the recording after the answer to the first question and go through this as an example. Continue playing the recording for students to answer the second question.

Check answers.

TAPESCRIPT
See the reading text on page 68 of the Student's Book.

1 She thought the village was fascinating and she liked the longhouses. She liked the Iban food and enjoyed the jungle trek.
2 They had to travel to the village in a bus because there were too many people for the longboat. There weren't enough rooms in the longhouse so they had to sleep in a tent. She ate too much and felt ill. There wasn't enough food for everyone the second day and there wasn't enough time to see everything on the jungle trek.

2 Grammar

too much / many + not enough

(a) Remind students of countable and uncountable nouns by eliciting a few examples of each. Make sure students remember what the differences are, ask them: *Can we count water? (No) Can we count chairs? (Yes)*. Refer students to the examples and ask them to underline the countable and uncountable nouns in each.

(b) Students go back through the email on page 68 and underline more examples of expressions with *too much/many/not enough*.

Answers
... I don't think we spent enough time there.
... too many people ...
... weren't enough rooms ...
... too much delicious food ...
... wasn't enough food ...
... not enough time ...

(c) Ask students to look at pictures 1 to 4 and the sentences below each. Ask them to give you the countable and uncountable nouns in each sentence and then ask them what they notice about the words used before the nouns. Elicit that *too many* is used with countable nouns and *too much* is used with uncountable nouns. Make sure students understand that *too + much/many + adjective* has a negative meaning (more than desirable) and compare it with *a lot of*. To make sure students understand give them the following sentences (students covered these areas in SB1: *much/many* in Unit 4 and *too + adjective* in Unit 12) and ask them to compare them and explain the difference in meaning: *My computer is very old now. My computer is too old now*.

(d) Students read through the rule box and complete it using the information from Exercise 2c. Check answers.

Answers
many; much; uncountable

To check understanding at this point call out a few nouns, making sure you include a variety of countable and uncountable ones. Students have to say *too much/many* with the noun you call out. For example: *T: Nicolo, chairs*.

S1: Too many chairs.
T: Francesco, milk.
S2: Too much milk. etc.

> **Language note**
> Students may produce statements like: **They are too much old*. Remind them that we use *too + adjective* and *too much / many + noun*.

(e) Ask students to look at the four pictures and to read through the gapped sentences. Check any problems. Students complete the exercise. Remind them to look carefully at the noun before they choose *too much/ many*.

Weaker classes: Ask students to underline the nouns and to identify them as countable or uncountable before they fill in the missing words.

Check answers.

Answers
1 too much   2 too many   3 too much
4 too many

(f) Students read through the examples from the email on page 68. Ask students to look carefully at the nouns and the verbs in each example and ask them if they are countable or uncountable (*rooms* is countable and the verb is plural; *food* is uncountable and the verb is singular). Then ask them what they notice about the word *enough* and elicit that it doesn't change whether the noun is countable, uncountable, singular or plural. Students then read through the rule and complete it. Check answers.

Answers
countable; uncountable

> **Language notes**
> 1 Students may produce statements like: **There wasn't enoughs rooms*. Remind them that *enough* always stays the same regardless of the noun being singular or plural in English.
> 2 Check students are pronouncing *enough* /ɪˈnʌf/ correctly.

(g) This exercise can be set for homework. Students read though the gapped text. Check any problems. Go through the example, asking them to explain why it is *too many*. Students complete the exercise. They can compare answers in pairs before a whole class check. Make sure students can explain their answer choices.

Weaker classes: Ask students to go through the text and underline all the nouns first. They can then identify if they are countable or uncountable and then decide which phrase goes in each gap.

Answers
1 too many   2 too much   3 enough
4 too many   5 aren't enough

h Divide the class into pairs. Students read through the items in the box. Ask a stronger pair to demonstrate the example and point out the use of *not enough* and *too much*. Students make true statements about themselves using the items in the box and exchange information with their partner. Monitor and check that students are taking turns to give information and make sure that they are using *too much / many / not enough* statements correctly. If there are repeated errors, note them down to go through later as a class. Ask for some pairs to feedback to the class and if there are any interesting statements ask students to give more details.

Grammar notebook

Encourage students to note down the completed rules from this unit and some example sentences of their own. Students may find it useful to translate some of the examples.

┌─── OPTIONAL ACTIVITIES ─────────────

Stronger classes

Divide the class into pairs. Student must think about the town/city where they live and discuss what they like/dislike about it. Students must use *too much / many / (not) enough* in their conversations. Remind them to think about the buildings, the people, the places you can go, the places tourists can visit, the transport. Monitor and check students are exchanging information and using the phrases from the grammar section correctly. Ask pairs to feedback to the class and see if they all agree.

Weaker classes

They can write five (or more) sentences about their own town/city using *too much / many / (not) enough*.

3 Pronunciation

Sound and spelling: -ough

a 🔊 Ask students to turn to page 121 and read the words. Play the recording, pausing after each word for students to repeat. If they are still having problems, play the recording again or drill the problem words as a class.

TAPESCRIPT

1 enough   2 cough   3 through   4 tough

b 🔊 Students read through sentences 1 to 5. Drill each sentence as a class. Play the recording for students to listen and check they are pronouncing them correctly. Play the recording again, pausing after each sentence for students to repeat.

TAPESCRIPT

1 I walked through the park.
2 I've got a very bad cough.
3 I can't eat this meat, it's too tough.
4 There aren't enough chairs.

┌─── OPTIONAL ACTIVITY ─────────────

In pairs, students make one sentence using as many of the *-ough* words as they can in it. Ask pairs to read out their sentences to the rest of the class. The class can vote on the best sentence.

4 Vocabulary

Homes

a 🔊 Books closed. Elicit the names of different types of houses students know in English and write them on the board. Ask students to explain, in L1 if appropriate, what kind of house each one they mention is. Students now open their books at page 70 and read through the words in the box and look at the pictures. Students match as many of the words as they can then compare answers in pairs. Play the recording for students to check or change their answers. Play the recording again, pausing for students to repeat each word.

TAPESCRIPT/ANSWERS

a a block of flats
b a caravan
c a bungalow
d a detached house
e a cottage
f terraced houses
g a semi-detached house
h a housing estate

b Students read through the words in the box. Check any problems. Go through the first item as an example, if necessary. Students complete the exercise and compare answers in pairs. Check answers as a class.

Answers

Picture b: a TV aerial
Picture c: a gate; a chimney; a TV aerial
Picture d: a TV aerial; a (small front) garden; a garage (just visible)
Picture e: a chimney; a garden
Picture g: a gate, a chimney (just visible); a (small, front) garden

c Students read through questions 1 to 3. Check any problems. In pairs, students discuss the questions. Ask for some pairs to feedback to the rest of the class.

Answers

1 In: a semi-detached house (picture g); a detached house (picture d); a block of flats (picture a); a cottage (picture e).
2 In a block of flats (picture a).
3 A bungalow (picture c); a caravan (picture b).

Vocabulary notebook

Remind students to start a section called *Homes* and to note down the new vocabulary from this exercise, with translations if necessary.

5 Listen

🔊 Explain that students are going to hear six people talking about where they live. Students must listen and write the number of the speaker in the boxes in the photos in Exercise 4a. Elicit the kind of words students think they might hear and write them on the board. Play the recording, pausing after the first type of home is mentioned and go through this as an example, if necessary. Play the recording again for students to listen and complete the exercise. Students can compare answers in pairs before a whole class check. Play the recording again, pausing as necessary to clarify any problems.

TAPESCRIPT

1 **Girl** Our new house is smaller than our old one but it's really nice. Erm ... it hasn't got a garage. Er, it's joined to another house, but our neighbours are nice, they don't make much noise ... It's got a garden at the front.

2 **Boy** I live with my parents and my two brothers. We're on the tenth floor, so we've got a great view over the city. From my bedroom window I can see the river! But it's not so good when the lift is out of order. Then we have to climb up hundreds of stairs!

3 **Woman** My house is small and I don't have a garage, but the garden is big and I love gardening. My grandchildren like coming to see me and climbing the trees but they complain because I don't have a computer! Luckily the house is all on one floor – so there are no stairs to worry about.

4 **Man** Our house has three floors. The kitchen and the living room are on the ground floor, then there are two bedrooms and a bathroom upstairs. You go upstairs again to get to the spare bedroom. We've got neighbours on both sides, but noise is not a problem. They probably hear us more than we hear them!

5 **Woman** My husband and I always wanted to live in the countryside, and now we don't have to go to work any more, we do! We've got a lovely little place with a thatched roof and a really pretty garden. It's very quiet at night and sometimes I miss the sound of the traffic ...

6 **Boy** We're lucky because our house is quite big. We've got 4 bedrooms and mine is the biggest because I'm the oldest. We've also got a big garden and we can play football in it. And we haven't got any neighbours so I can play my music really loudly and there's no one next door to complain!

Answers

1	g (semi-detached)	4	f (terraced house)
2	a (block of flats)	5	e (cottage)
3	c (bungalow)	6	d (detached)

6 Speak

Divide the class into pairs. Students read through the example. Remind them to think about the following things: the type of house/flat they live in; the number of rooms it has; who sleeps in which room; how many other rooms it has; if it has a garden; what the neighbours are like; if they like it. Give students a few minutes to discuss their homes. Monitor and check students are taking turns to discuss this and that they are able to express themselves clearly. Ask for a few pairs to feedback to the class.

7 Grammar

will vs. *going to*

If you set the background information as a homework research task ask students to tell the class what they found out.

BACKGROUND INFORMATION

China: Is officially known as The People's Republic of China and is situated in East Asia. It is the world's third largest country and the world's most highly populated country. The capital, and second largest city, is Beijing and other major cities include Shanghai, the largest city, and Tianjin.

Qinghai: Or Tsinghai province in western China. The capital of this province is Xining (Sining).

Tibet: Is an autonomous region in south west China. The capital is Lhasa. Tibet is surrounded by mountains, including the Himalayas.

Hong Kong: Is in south east China. It is made up of Hong Kong island, the Kowloon peninsula and the New Territories.

a 🔊 Students read through the question and the dialogue. Check any problems. Play the recording for students to read and listen for the answer. Check answers.

Weaker classes: You may want to pre-teach the following vocabulary: *stay*; *tents*; *pack*; *jumper*; *comfortable*; *boots*.

TAPESCRIPT
See the dialogue on page 71 of the Student's Book.

Answer
He's going to stay in a tent with some Tibetan people.

b **Stronger classes:** Students read through the examples from the dialogue in Exercise 7a. Ask them if Jake decided to go to China before he spoke to his Gran (*Yes*) and if he decided to send her a postcard before he spoke to her (*No*). Elicit that we use *going to* for future decisions made before the moment of speaking and *will* for decisions made at the moment of speaking. Students then read through the rule box and complete it.

Weaker classes: Books closed. Write the following examples on the board (or use some of your own): *I'm going to England for my holidays this summer. Here are my tickets. / My mobile phone's ringing. I'll answer it.*

Ask students which sentence shows something that has been planned already (example 1) and which sentence shows something that you decide to do at the moment of speaking (example 2). Students now open their books at page 71 and read the two examples from the dialogue. Follow the procedure for stronger classes from here.

Check answers.

Answers
going to   will/won't

To check students have understood the difference clearly, ask them to provide an example of their own for *will / going to*.

Look
Students read through the examples. Make sure they understand that we don't usually use *going to + go to*.

Language notes
1   Students may produce statements like: **I will go to Brazil on holiday*. Remind them that if something is already arranged we use *going to*.
2   Students may find it useful to translate some of the examples in Exercise 7 into their own language to compare them.

(c) This exercise can be set for homework. Students read through dialogues 1 to 7. Go through the example as a class. Ask students to explain why *I'll carry them* is the correct answer. Students complete the exercise. Remind them to look carefully at each situation before deciding which verb is appropriate. Check answers, making sure students can explain why they made their choices.

Answers
2 he's going   3 I'll open   4 we're going to see
5 she's going to take   6 I'll lend   7 I'll have

Grammar notebook
Remind students to note down the rules for *will / going to* and some examples of their own.

8 Culture in mind

Read

If you set the background information as a homework research task, ask students to tell the class what they found out.

Warm up
Ask students if anyone has ever been to Australia. If so, where did they go and what did they do? Encourage them to discuss this with the rest of the class. If not, encourage students to think about what life in Australia might be like and elicit some suggestions. Discuss this as a class or in L1 if appropriate.

(a) Students read the question and the title of the text and look at the photos. In pairs or small groups, students discuss what they know about Australia and add to any suggestions from the *Warm up*. Ask for some pairs/groups to feedback.

(b) **Stronger classes:** Divide the class into pairs. Give them a few minutes to discuss the question and ask them for suggestions. Students then read the text quickly and check their answers.

Weaker classes: Write the headings *Australia/ Britain* on the board. Elicit what students think the differences are between life in the two countries. Encourage them to think about the suggestions from Exercise 8a and to add more suggestions of their own. Write the suggestions under each heading or ask students to volunteer to come out and write them up. Students then read the text quickly and check their answers. How many of their predictions were in the text?

Possible answers
Australia: live more of an outdoor life; weather is good; have lots of barbecues; houses have swimming pools; houses are bigger; most people live in bungalows; lots of insects
Britain: life is spent indoors more; weather not always good; many different styles of houses; not many houses have swimming pools; insects not a big problem

(c) Students read through questions 1 to 5. Check any problems. Go through the first item as an example, if necessary. They then read the text again and answer the questions. Students can compare answers in pairs before a whole class check.

Weaker classes: You may want to pre-teach the following vocabulary: *hit*; *relaxed*; *good-humoured*; *suntanned*; *stereotype*; *average*; *mosquitoes*; *screen*

Answers
1 They think they all live by the beach and swim and surf all day.
2 They often have barbecues.
3 They like the pool and the bigger houses; they don't like the insects.
4 They do the same sorts of things.
5 They are really friendly.

Discussion box

In pairs or small groups, students go through the questions in the box and discuss them.

Weaker classes: They can choose one question only to discuss. If necessary, elicit a few prompts for the question they have chosen to help them with their discussion.

Monitor and help as necessary, encouraging students to express themselves in English.

Ask pairs or groups to feedback to the class and discuss any interesting points further.

---

9 Write

The preparation for this can be done in class and the writing can be done for homework.

(a) Students read through questions 1 to 3. Check any problems. Students then read through the two adverts and answer the questions. Check answers.

Weaker classes: You may want to pre-teach the following vocabulary: *converted barn*; *guests*; *healthy*; *meal*; *chance*.

Answers
1 A: four days; B: ten days
2 They are both in Britain; they are both staying in a home, with a family.
3 A: You learn how a farm works. B: You learn about life in Britain and improve your English.

(b) Students read through the questions and then quickly read the email to find the answers. Check answers.

Answers
1 Her older brother and her friend Anna from school.
2 To write to her when she gets back.

(c) Students read through the instructions and then re-read advert B. Students then plan their email using the model in their book. Remind them of the structure and format of emails and encourage them to plan their email before writing a final version.

Weaker classes: Go through the model with them encouraging them to look at the content of each paragraph carefully:
• Opening greeting
• Para 1: Introduction
• Para 2: Gives information about the type of holiday she's going on and what she is going to do.
• Para 3: What she will do now and what she intends to do when she gets back.
• Sign off

Once students have written their emails they can send them to a partner.

11 Your mind

Unit overview

TOPIC: Memory

TEXTS

Reading and listening: a text about how to improve your memory
Listening: an interview about 'multiple intelligences'
Reading and listening: Story: *The winners are …*
Writing: a competition entry

SPEAKING AND FUNCTIONS
Discussing intelligence
Discussing memory

LANGUAGE
Determiners (*everyone, no one, someone* etc.)
must/mustn't vs. *don't have to*
Vocabulary: Remembering and forgetting
Pronunciation: *must*
Everyday English: *Come on; Never mind; mates; I wonder*

1 Read and listen

If you set the background information as a homework research task, ask students to tell the class what they found out.

BACKGROUND INFORMATION

Mozart: Born Wolfgang Amadeus Mozart in 1756 in Salzburg, died in Vienna 1791. He started composing at the age of five and throughout his life he wrote many operas and musical compositions.

Warm up

Ask students if they are good at remembering things. What kinds of things do they remember (e.g. birthdays, football scores, phone numbers, etc.). Discuss if there are things some students remember better than others, and if so why this might be. Discuss this as a class, in L1 if appropriate.

a Explain to students that they are going to do a memory test. Students turn to page 122 and look at the picture for Unit 11. Explain that they have thirty seconds to look at the picture. After thirty seconds, tell students to close their books and give them a few minutes to write down all the things they saw in the picture. Ask for feedback and then tell students they can open their books and check their answers. How many students remembered everything?

Explain that students are going to hear some numbers and that they must listen to them all before writing anything down. Once the recording has finished they can write the numbers down. Play the recording, making sure students' pens are on their desks. Students then note down the numbers. Students compare answers again before a whole class check. Has anyone remembered all the numbers and in the correct order?

TAPESCRIPT

20   30   12   32   44   16

b Students read the question and look at the title of the text. Elicit suggestions on ways to improve memory and then students read the text quickly to check their predictions.

Answers
Use new information immediately; break big things down into smaller chunks to remember; review information; relax.

c Students read through sentences 1 to 6. Check any problems. Play the recording while students listen and read. Give them a few minutes to answer the true/false questions.

Weaker classes: You may want to pre-teach the following vocabulary: *powerful; weigh; tips; helpful; sections; review; relax; stressed.*

Check answers. Encourage students to correct the false answers. Play the recording again if necessary, pausing to clarify any problems.

TAPESCRIPT
See the reading text on page 74 of the Student's Book.

Answers
1 F (Lines 2/3: … it can hold much more information than most computers.)   2 F (Lines 4/5: Computers don't forget information they are given.)   3 T
4 T   5 F (Lines 37/38: … always do something to help improve your memory …)   6 T

2 Grammar
Determiners (*everyone, no one, someone* etc.)

a Read through the examples as a class. Ask students what they notice about the words in bold and elicit or explain the meaning of the determiners in each sentence, asking students if they are used in this case to refer to people, places or things.

Explain that these words are called determiners in English. Then give students a few minutes to go back through the text on page 74 and find more. Elicit or explain that *none* is always followed by *of*.

Check answers.

Answers
Text 1: … *No one … everything*
Text 2: … *Everyone can … ; All of them … none of them … ; … meet someone … ; … something … ; … nothing is easy … ; … do something … ; … everyone's memory …*

(b) Students read through the table while you copy it onto the board.

Stronger classes: They can complete the table using the words they found in Exercise 2a.

Weaker classes: Encourage students to look for connections between the words in each column and, if necessary, go through each gap as a class eliciting the correct determiner. Explain that *all/some/none of them* refer back to something mentioned previously.

Answers
Column 1: everything; all of them
Column 2: someone
Column 3: nothing; no one; none of them

Language notes
1 Explain that words ending in -*thing* refer to things, words ending in -*one* refer to people and words ending in -*where* refer to places. Explain that no*body*, some*body*, etc. can be used instead of no *one*, etc. with no difference in meaning.
2 *some-* and *every-* words are used in positive statements and *no-* words are used in negative statements with positive verbs. A typical mistake for students of many nationalities is to use double negatives (e.g. **I don't know nothing* – something which isn't correct in English (for more details on this see Look box below).
3 Students may find it useful to translate the words in the table into their own language and compare them.

(c) This exercise can be set for homework. Students read through the words in the box and sentences 1 to 7. Check any problems. Go through the example as a class asking students to explain why the correct answer is *someone*. Students complete the exercise. Remind them to look carefully at each sentence and decide if the missing words are a person, place or thing before they make their choices. Students can compare answers in pairs before a whole class check.

Answers
2 no one   3 everyone   4 none of them
5 everything   6 everywhere   7 all of them

Look
Students read through the examples in the box. Make sure they understand that when we use a *no-* word we must use a positive verb in English and an *any-* word uses a negative verb. It may be helpful for

students to translate these examples into their own language to see how they work.

Grammar notebook
Encourage students to note down the completed table and some examples of determiners from this exercise.

3 Vocabulary
Remembering and forgetting
Warm up
Ask students which words they know to do with remembering and forgetting. Elicit examples and write them on the board.

(a) Draw students' attention to the cartoon and ask a stronger student to explain it to the rest of the class. Students now read through the list of words; check pronunciation.

Discuss what these are in students' own language. Are there any similarities?

┌─ **OPTIONAL ACTIVITY** ─────────
│ Students can put each word in Exercise 3a into a sentence of their own.

(b) This exercise can be set for homework. Students read through sentences 1 to 5. Check any problems. Go through the first item as an example, if necessary. Students complete the exercise. Remind them to read each sentence carefully and to try and work out the meaning and the part of speech they need before they choose their words. Students can compare answers in pairs before a whole class check.

Answers
1 forget; memorable
2 forget
3 A: forget
   B: remind; remember
4 memory; remind
5 memorised

(c) Divide the class into pairs. Students read through questions 1 to 3. Check any problems. Give students a few minutes to discuss the questions. Ask pairs to feedback to the class and if there are any interesting points discuss these further as a class. Encourage students to contribute their ideas for question 3.

Vocabulary notebook
Students should start a section called *Remembering and forgetting* in their notebooks and note down all the new words and expressions from this exercise. Encourage them to try and use some of the ideas from Exercise 3c, question 3 the next time they have to learn vocabulary.

Students may also find it helpful to draw a mind map for the verbs and words in the exercise. They can put *remember* and *forget* in the centre and all the connected words around them.

4 Listen

If you set the background information as a homework research task, ask students to tell the class what they found out.

a Divide the class into pairs. Ask students to read the question and look at the pictures on the page. Give them a few minutes to discuss the question. Ask for feedback. Play the recording for students to listen and check their answers. Were any of them correct?

TAPESCRIPT

Interviewer   Good morning, and welcome to the programme. Today, we are discussing memory and intelligence, and with us in the studio is Dr Jane Cairns, a psychologist. Dr Cairns, you have said that Albert Einstein and Tom Cruise have similarities, can you explain what you meant by that?

Dr Cairns   Well, obviously, there are lots of differences between Albert Einstein and Tom Cruise. Einstein was a great scientist, and Tom Cruise is a famous actor. Einstein was German, Cruise is American – and so on. But they have something in common: they weren't very good at school!
Albert Einstein didn't speak until he was four years old, and he couldn't read until he was seven. His teacher said he was very slow, and he was always daydreaming. And Tom Cruise didn't get good marks at school, because it took him a long time to learn to read.

Interviewer   But actors have to remember their lines, you know, the words they have to say in a film. How can Tom Cruise learn his lines if he can't read?

Dr Cairns   Well, he can read now of course, but they say that he learns his lines by listening to them on a tape. He's much better at memorising something that he has heard than something that he sees on a page. And then of course there are other things he can do extremely well. He's an excellent actor, isn't he?

Interviewer   And what about Albert Einstein? What was he not good at?

Dr Cairns   Well, that's a really interesting story. When Einstein was at school, he never listened. He was always daydreaming so he got very bad marks, that's why his teachers thought that he wasn't a very intelligent person.

Interviewer   Oh, really? Einstein? Not an intelligent person? It's hard to believe.

Dr Cairns   Yes, and there's this story, you know, when Einstein was a famous scientist, somebody asked him, "Professor Einstein, when did you first get your ideas about space and time?" And Einstein answered, "When I was 12." The man was very surprised because he knew that Einstein was very bad at school. So Einstein told the man that when he was twelve, back at school, he daydreamed all the time. And in his daydreams, he imagined that he wasn't sitting in his classroom, but that he was travelling in space, out in space, with the stars and the planets! And this is how he got his ideas, while his teachers thought he was just stupid.

Interviewer   That's certainly a fascinating story. So what can we …

Answer
Neither man was very good at school.

b Students read through questions 1 to 4. Check any problems. Play the recording again for students to answer the questions. Check answers. Play the recording again, pausing as necessary to clarify any problems.

Weaker classes: You may want to stop the recording after the answer to question 1 and go through this as an example.

TAPESCRIPT   See above.

Answers
1 Speak: 4 (years old); Read: 7 (years old).
2 By listening to them on tape. Because he's much better at memorising something he's heard than something he's seen on a page.
3 No, they didn't because he was always daydreaming.
4 In his daydreams, he imagined that he wasn't sitting in his classroom, but that he was travelling in outer space with the stars and planets.

This new outlook on intelligence differs greatly from the traditional view, which usually recognises only two intelligences, verbal and computational.

Due to the complex nature of the topic, we have simplified the language used in Gardner's theory in the Student's Book and only included one of the personal intelligences – that which he has labelled 'interpersonal intelligence'.

c 🔊 Students look at the phrases in the box and sentences 1 to 6. As a class, discuss what students think each type of intelligence is. Go through the first sentence as an example. Students complete the exercise. Students can compare answers in pairs. Do not give the answers at this point. Play the recording, pausing as necessary to clarify any problems.

TAPESCRIPT

Interviewer So, Dr Cairns, both of these men weren't very good at school, but became very successful later on in life. How do you explain this?

Dr Cairns Well, they probably had intelligences that other people, their teachers, or even their parents, didn't see in them.

Interviewer "Intelligences"? What do you mean by "intelligences"?

Dr Cairns Well, people can be intelligent in many, many different ways. Usually we call someone intelligent if they're good at one of two intelligences: the logical-mathematical one, and/or the verbal intelligence. Logical-mathematical intelligence means someone is good at things like mathematics, good at thinking logically and solving problems. And verbal intelligence means that someone is good with words – good at speaking, reading, writing, all things to do with words.

But there are many other intelligences. Someone might be very poor at the logical-mathematical intelligence, for example, and be very bad at school, but then later, this person becomes a famous opera singer or a great guitar player, because he or she has a lot of musical intelligence.

Interviewer I see. Can you give any more examples?

Dr Cairns Yes, ... someone perhaps doesn't have much verbal intelligence, you know, isn't very good with words, but he or she becomes a famous painter, or an architect, because they have a lot of visual intelligence.

Interviewer You've mentioned logical-mathematical, verbal, musical and visual intelligences. Are there others?

Dr Cairns Oh yes! There's body intelligence. Just think of an excellent dancer, or a good sports player, for example. They need a lot of body intelligence.

Interviewer Right.

Dr Cairns And then there's also interpersonal intelligence. This is very important – and many successful people in business have a lot of this! Your interpersonal intelligence is linked to how well you can work with and understand other people, and it's an important intelligence to have!

Interviewer Dr Cairns, thank you very much – that's all we have time for today ...

Answers
2 body intelligence
3 visual intelligence
4 interpersonal intelligence
5 musical intelligence
6 verbal intelligence

┌─ **OPTIONAL ACTIVITY** ═══════════════
Elicit, or write on the board, five different professions and ask students what kind of intelligence they think are needed for each one. Students can do this in pairs or small groups. For example, architect (strong visual intelligence); athlete or dancer (strong body intelligence); interpreter (strong verbal intelligence); nurse or teacher (strong interpersonal intelligence) etc. Alternatively, groups could come up with their own professions and intelligences, and present their ideas to the class, justifying why they think certain intelligences are needed for certain professions.

5 Speak
What's your strongest intelligence?
Warm up

In small groups, students discuss the question. Ask for feedback.

a Explain that you will give students three short memory tests to see what kind of intelligences they have (i.e. more strongly visual, verbal, or body). Divide the class into Student A and B pairs and keep those pairs for all three tasks.

Test 1: Tell students to write ten numbers from 1 to 50 on a piece of paper. Tell Student As to show Bs their numbers for ten seconds. Student Bs have to memorise the numbers and then write the numbers down after ten seconds. Student Bs then show student As their numbers and Student As write them down after 10 seconds. Pairs then compare numbers to see how many numbers each person remembered.

Test 2: Students A and B write ten new numbers between 1 and 50 on a piece of paper. Student As then read out those numbers to Student Bs who must listen and write them down after hearing them. Student As must not show Student Bs the numbers. Student Bs then read out their numbers and Student As do the same. Monitor and make sure students are not writing down the numbers until all ten have been read out.

Students compare the numbers they wrote down and see how many they remembered correctly.

Test 3: Students A and B write ten new numbers between 1 and 50 on a piece of paper. Remind students they must be different from the ones used in tests 1 and 2. Student B then closes his/her eyes while Student A traces the numbers out on his/her hand. Student B keeps his/her eyes closed until all the numbers have been traced onto their hand and then they must open their eyes and try and write down all the numbers. Student B then follows the same procedure with Student A writing the numbers. Monitor and check students are keeping their eyes closed throughout the tracing part. Students compare lists and see how many numbers they remembered.

(b) Ask for a show of hands for each test result and write the results on the board. Students with higher scores for test 1 are more likely to remember things best after seeing them first. Students with higher scores for test 2 are more likely to remember things best after hearing them, and students with higher scores for test 3 are more likely to remember things best after doing, or 'feeling' them. Go through the results as a class to see what different types of memory people have, more strongly visual, verbal, or body (kinaesthetic). Discuss why certain people remember certain things in a certain way but stress that this test is only for fun, and most people remember things best when the information is repeated and they have a chance to both see, and hear or discuss what they've learned.

┌─ OPTIONAL ACTIVITY ══════════════
Students can draw up the results of the memory game on a class bar chart.

6 Grammar
must/mustn't vs. don't have to

(a) Read through the question as a class. Students then read the letters and decide which answers they prefer. Students compare answers in pairs before feeding back. Ask students to give reasons for their choice of answer.

Weaker classes: You may want to pre-teach the following vocabulary: *grades*; *lazy*; *fair*; *waste time*.

(b) Students read through the examples from the letters and then underline more examples of *must/mustn't / don't have to* in the letters. Elicit or explain the difference in meanings between *must/mustn't* and *don't / doesn't have to*. Students then complete the rule.

Answers
Letter
... must try ... I have to work; ... doesn't have to; ... mustn't waste your time; ... must work ...

Reply A
... mustn't think; ... must listen to
Reply B
... don't have to do; ... mustn't worry; ... don't have to be

Answer
must/mustn't; have to
don't / doesn't have to

┌─────────────────────────────────────┐
Language notes
1 Students may produce statements like: **I mustn't to forget to do my homework.* Remind them that in English *mustn't* is followed by an infinitive without *to*.
2 Check students' pronunciation of *mustn't* /ˈmʌsᵊnt/ and *have to* /ˈhæftə/.
3 Students may find it useful to translate some of the sentences from this exercise into their own language and compare them.
└─────────────────────────────────────┘

(c) Students look at pictures 1 to 4 and read through the sentences. Check any problems. Go through the first one as an example. Students complete the exercise. Remind them to look carefully at each situation before they choose the verb. Check answers, asking students to explain their choice of verb.

Answers
1 mustn't   2 don't have to   3 don't have to
4 mustn't

(d) This exercise can be set for homework. Students read through sentences 1 to 6. Go through the example, if necessary. Students complete the exercise. Remind them to think carefully about each situation before they choose the verb. Check answers, asking students to explain their choice of verb.

Answers
2 must   3 don't have to   4 must
5 doesn't have to   6 mustn't

Grammar notebook
Remind students to make a note of the rules for this grammar point and to note down some examples of their own and translations, if necessary.

7 Pronunciation
must

(a) 🔊 Students turn to page 121. Read out the first sentence and ask students if *must* is stressed or unstressed (*unstressed*).

Students read through the instructions. Make sure they remember to circle *must* if it is weak and underline *must* if it is stressed. Play the recording for students to circle and underline *must* as appropriate.

Check answers, playing and pausing the recording again as necessary.

1 I (must) go now, it's late.
2 You must see that film, it's great!
3 You must remember to do your homework!
4 I (must) phone my friend tonight.
5 I (must) start doing some exercise!

b 🔊 Students read through the questions. Elicit the answers, saying the sentences yourself for students to hear them again, if necessary. Play the recording again, pausing for students to repeat each sentence.

Answers
1 Sentences 2 and 3. Sentence 2 is a strong recommendation and sentence 3 is a strong obligation. The 't' on *must* isn't pronounced when *must* is weak.

The winners are ...

8 Read and listen

Warm up

Ask students what they can remember about the last episode of the story (Joanne suggested that she, Dave and Matt form a new three-person band without Amy. Amy was very upset about this when Dave told her.).

a 🔊 Students read through the questions. Check any problems and give students a few minutes to think about their answers. Play the recording while students read and listen to check their answers. Check answers as a class. How many students were correct?

TAPESCRIPT
See the story on page 78 of the Student's Book.

Answers
1 They are backstage at the concert.
2 Because she knows she didn't sing very well.
3 The winning band.

b Students read through sentences 1 to 7. Check any problems. Go through the example as a class, if necessary. Remind them that they may not always find enough information in the story for an answer. Students complete the exercise. Students can compare answers in pairs and correct the false answers before a whole class check.

Answers
2 T
3 Not enough information
4 F (Picture 3: They don't know good singing ...)
5 Not enough information
6 T
7 F (Picture 4: ... I wonder why they're talking to Amy?)

OPTIONAL ACTIVITY
In groups of four, students can act out the dialogue from the story.

9 Everyday English

a Ask students to read through expressions 1 to 4 and to locate them in the story on page 78 and decide who says them. Check answers. Then ask students to match each expression with definitions a to d. Go through the first one as an example, if necessary. Check answers.

Answers
1 c Joanne   2 d Dave   3 b Joanne   4 a Dave

b Ask students to read through dialogues 1 to 4. Check any problems. Go through the first dialogue as an example, if necessary. Students complete the other dialogues with the expressions from Exercise 9a. Check answers.

Answers
1 Never mind   2 mates   3 wonder   4 Come on

Vocabulary notebook
Students should note down the expressions and translations from this exercise in their *Everyday English* section.

OPTIONAL ACTIVITIES
See Unit 1, Exercise 10 Everyday English, Optional Activities.

10 Write

The preparation for this can be done in class and the writing task can be completed for homework.

a Students read the advertisement. Check any problems. Ask students what they have to do to enter the competition.

Answers
Write a composition in English on one of the topics.

b Students read through the entry and find Frances' answers to the questions.

Answers
1 Swimming, dancing, Maths, Art.
2 Languages.
3 Swimming and dancing: good body intelligence; Maths and Art: good visual and logical intelligence.
4 Architect, because she's good at Maths and likes drawing things and she doesn't have to speak a foreign language.

c Students now write their own competition entry using the model on page 79 to help them. Remind them to think about the different types of intelligences they talked about earlier in the unit and encourage them to use *must / don't have to* structures where possible.

Encourage students to read out their entries to the rest of the class.

Unit overview

TOPIC: Music

TEXTS

Reading and listening: a text about a young musician
Listening: people talking about music and musical instruments
Reading: about a history of pop music in Britain and the USA
Writing: a letter about your favourite type of music

SPEAKING AND FUNCTIONS

Describing recently completed and unfinished actions
Talking about music and musical instruments
Discussing pop music and fashion

LANGUAGE

Present perfect continuous
Present perfect continuous and present perfect simple
Vocabulary: music
Pronunciation: sentence stress: rhythm

1 Read and listen

If you set the background information as a homework research task, ask students to tell the class what they found out.

BACKGROUND INFORMATION

Young Musician of the Year competition: Is regarded as Britain's leading classical musical event for young people and was started in 1978. The standard of musicianship is extremely high, and many of the winners of the competition go on to successful classical music careers. Competitors can enter in any one of five musical categories: percussion, keyboard, strings, brass and woodwind.

Jennifer Pike: Is a very gifted young violinist and at 12 years old she was the youngest ever winner of the prestigious Young Musician of the Year competition in 2002. There were over 500 contestants at the start of the competition. She attends a well-known specialist music school in Manchester.

Robbie Williams: Was born in 1975, in Stoke-on-Trent, England. His early show business experiences were with local theatre companies and in local musicals. At the age of 16, in 1991, he saw an advert for a band who were looking for a fifth member, and he joined *Take That*.

After five years with the band he left it. His solo career had a slow start but he had a hit single *Angels* and continues to be a very successful solo artist.

Warm up

Ask students if they play a musical instrument. If so, which one do they play? If not, would they like to play one? Discuss this as a class, in L1 if appropriate.

(a) Students read the questions and look at the picture and the title of the text. Elicit suggestions for the first question. Students then read the text quickly to check their predictions. Remind them that they don't have to understand every word in the text at this point. Check answers.

Answers
1 12. 2 Because she is only 12 years old and won the Young Musician of the Year competition.

(b) Students read through questions 1 to 5. Check any problems. Do the first sentence as an example, if necessary, reading through the text as a class or playing the first part of the recording. Students complete the exercise. Students can compare answers in pairs before a whole class check.

Weaker classes: You may want to pre-teach the following vocabulary: *sensational*; *immediately*; *amazing*; *dream*; *non-stop*; *concert*.

TAPESCRIPT
See the reading text on page 80 of the Student's Book.

Answers
1 He's a music teacher.
2 When she was five years old.
3 Yes, she was.
4 To invite her to play in concerts.
5 Pop music, playing tennis, swimming, text messaging

(c) In pairs or small groups students discuss this question. Monitor and check students are discussing this in English as far as possible. After a few minutes, ask for feedback. Does everyone agree?

OPTIONAL ACTIVITY

Give students the following True/False questions on the text to check their understanding. Students can correct the false statements. Check answers.
1 Jennifer won the competition in 2000. **(False: 2002)**
2 She is from Cheshire. **(True)**
3 Jennifer's sister is three years older than her. **(True)**
4 She plays a lot of basketball. **(False: She'd like to but can't because she might hurt her hands.)**

2 Grammar
Present perfect continuous

(a) **Stronger classes:** Students read through the examples. Ask them what they notice about how this tense is formed and elicit that it is *have/has* + *been* + *-ing* verb. To check students understand the meaning of the tense, ask them the following questions:

Sentence 1: Is her father still teaching? (Yes)
Sentence 2: Do you still play tennis? (Yes)

Elicit or explain that this tense is used to show that something started in the past and continues into the present. Ask students to give you an example of their own to check they have understood correctly.

Weaker classes: Books closed. Write the following examples (or some of your own) on the board: *I have been teaching English for x years. / She has been waiting for half an hour.* Ask them what they notice about how this tense is formed and elicit that it is *have/has* + *been* + *-ing* verb. To check students understand the meaning of the tense, ask them the following questions:

Sentence 1: Do I still teach English (Yes)
Sentence 2: Is she still waiting? (Yes)

Elicit or explain that this tense is used to show that something started in the past and continues into the present. Students now open their books at page 81 and read the two examples on the page. If you feel students need a bit more work on the meaning of the tense, ask them the concept questions from the stronger classes procedure.

(b) Students go back through the text on page 80 and underline other examples of the tense. Check answers.

Answers
Para 1: ... has been teaching
Para 2: ... has been playing; ... I've been teaching ...
Para 3: ... I've been dreaming ...
Para 4: ... has been ringing ...
Para 5: ... I've been playing ...

Students then read through the table and complete it. Check answers.

Answers
Positive: 's (has) been
Negative: haven't been
Question: Has/been
Short answer: have/haven't/hasn't/hasn't

Students then complete the rule box.

Answer
past

Language notes
1 Students may find it useful to translate some of the example sentences into their own language and compare them.

2 Remind students that we don't need to repeat the main verb in short answers with this tense.
3 Remind them that *it's* in *it's been working* = *it has been working* not *It is been working*.

(c) Students look at the pictures and read through prompts 1 to 6. Check any problems. Go through the example as a class, if necessary. Students complete the exercise. Check answers.

Answers
2 He's been cooking all morning.
3 I haven't been feeling well.
4 You haven't been practising enough!
5 They haven't been playing football.
6 We've been watching too much TV!

(d) This exercise can be set for homework. Students read through sentences 1 to 8. Check any problems. Go through the example as a class, if necessary. Students complete the exercise. Check answers.

Answers
2 I've been waiting a long time for you!
3 He hasn't been sleeping enough.
4 What have you been doing this morning?
5 I haven't been learning English very long.
6 How long have you been eating?
7 They've been doing their homework for three hours.
8 How long have we been walking?

Grammar notebook
Remind students to note down the form and rules for this tense and any translations they may find helpful.

OPTIONAL ACTIVITY
Divide the class into small groups. Students choose an activity of their choice and mime it to the group. After the student has stopped miming and sat down, students have to guess what that person has been doing. Make sure students realise they must give some indication of the action they have been doing (e.g. holding a phone in their hand; closing a book, etc.).

3 Pronunciation
Sentence stress: rhythm

(a) 🔊 Students turn to page 121 and read through sentences 1 to 5. Go through the example as a class, either reading it out yourself or playing and pausing the recording. Students underline the stressed syllables in the other sentences. Students can compare answers in pairs. Play the recording, pausing after each sentence for students to check or change their answers. Play the recording again if necessary to clarify any problems.

1 Her <u>fa</u>ther's been <u>tea</u>ching music for <u>ma</u>ny <u>years</u>.
2 The <u>phone</u>'s been <u>ring</u>ing all <u>week</u>.
3 <u>She</u>'s been <u>doing</u> <u>well</u> at <u>school</u>.
4 How <u>long</u> has she been <u>play</u>ing the violin?

(b) 🔊 Play the recording again, pausing after each sentence for students to repeat.

4 Grammar

Present perfect continuous and present perfect simple

(a) Write the following examples on the board (or some of your own): *I've been teaching since X o'clock this morning. / I've drunk two cups of coffee this morning.*

Ask: Am I still teaching now? (Yes) and Am I drinking coffee this morning? (No). Elicit or explain that the present perfect continuous often shows that an action started in the past and is still continuing in the present, and the present perfect simple is used when an action started in the past but has now finished. Tell them that this action may have a result in the present, or the time span may not have finished and the action may be continued later. (e.g. *I've drunk two cups of coffee this morning.* This morning hasn't finished yet and I may drink more coffee.) It may be helpful to compare the use of the past simple (e.g. *Charles Dickens **wrote** a lot of books. / J.K. Rowling **has written** a lot of books.* Dickens is dead and won't write any more; Rowling is alive and may write more.) The present perfect continuous is often used when we want to stress the activity and the duration of the activity more than the result of the activity, whereas the present perfect simple is often used when we want to stress the completed result of the activity. (e.g. *I'm tired because I've been working hard all day.* vs. *I've written ten emails today.*) Students open their books at page 82 and read the example sentences.

Students read through the examples. Ask: Does Jennifer still play the violin? (Yes) and Is she playing in a concert now? (No). Elicit or explain the difference in the two tenses used: This first example shows that something started in the past and continues to the present while the second example shows several shorter, completed actions which started in the past and have now finished (but may continue in the future as the year described in the text is not finished yet).

Students then read through the rule box and complete the rules. Check answers.

Answers

present perfect simple; present perfect continuous
present perfect simple; present perfect continuous

To check understanding at this point, ask students to give you an example of their own for each tense to make sure they are using the tenses correctly.

Language note

Students may produce statements like: **I am studying English for two years.* Ask them to translate some of the examples from this exercise or examples of their own to compare how this structure works in English and their own language.

Look

Students read through the Look! box information. Give them some more examples of other verbs which are not normally used in continuous tenses in English: *see, hear, smell, taste* etc. *want, prefer, like, love, hate, think, feel, forget, remember.*

(b) Students read through sentences 1 to 7. Check any problems. Go through the example, if necessary, making sure students are clear why the present perfect simple is used. Students complete the exercise. Remind them to check the context of each sentence carefully before they choose the tense. Check answers, asking students to explain their choice of verb.

Answers

2 read   3 had   4 cut   5 been cutting   6 won
7 has known

(c) This exercise can be set for homework. Students read through sentences 1 to 7. Check any problems. Go through the example if necessary, asking students to explain why the present perfect continuous is used. Students complete the exercise. Check answers.

Answers

2 Have/finished   3 has/been doing   4 Has/made
5 haven't started   6 's cleaned   7 's been raining

Grammar notebook

Remind students to copy down the rules and some examples for this grammar point. They may also find it useful to translate some of the examples.

5 Speak

If you set the background information as a homework research task, ask students to tell the class what they found out.

BACKGROUND INFORMATION

David Bowie: Was born in 1947 in London. His real name is David Robert Hayward-Jones. He changed his name in 1966 since there was another singer called David Jones at that time. His first hit was with *Space Oddity* in 1969, a song based on the Stanley Kubrick film *2001: A Space Odyssey*. Throughout the 1970s David Bowie had many more musical successes and was also well-known for his extreme costumes and outfits on stage. He has also acted in films, e.g. *The Man Who Fell to Earth* (1976). He continues to have hit singles today.

Warm up

Books closed. Ask students if they have heard of David Bowie. If so, ask them what they know about him. Elicit information from the class and write it on the board.

a Students open their books at page 82. Ask students to read the short text and to find out what David Bowie's wife's name is (*Iman*).

b Divide the class into Student A and B pairs. Tell Student As to read through the question prompts and their information on page 82, Student Bs to turn to page 123 and look at their question prompts and information there. Ask a stronger pair to demonstrate the example question and answer. Make sure students understand that they have to make questions, and answer their partner using the information they have on their page and the present perfect continuous and simple tenses. Give students a few minutes to complete the exercise. Monitor and check students are using the correct present perfect question and answer forms and make a note of any repeated errors to go over as a class later.

Answers

Student A
He's been singing for more than 30 years.
He's been making / He's made records for more than 25 years.
He's been married to Iman for more than ten years.
Student B
He's been playing / He's played the saxophone for more than 40 years.
He's made more than five films.

6 Vocabulary

Music

If you set the background information as a homework research task, ask students to tell the class what they found out.

BACKGROUND INFORMATION

Country: Often referred to as country and western music, this type of music is based on a type of traditional music from the west and south of the USA. The songs usually have a guitar as the main instrument.

Reggae: A type of popular music from Jamaica with a strong second and fourth beat.

Jazz: Is music which originates from African-Americans. Jazz has a strong rhythm and usually true jazz artists improvise.

Folk: Is traditional music, or modern music which can be attributed to traditional origins.

Heavy metal: Is a type of rock music which is played with highly-amplified electrical instruments and has a strong beat.

Classical: Music is said to be of lasting value. It tends to be associated with the music of famous composers such as Mozart, Beethoven and Brahms.

Warm up

Books closed. Ask students what type of music they like listening to and elicit a few answers. Now ask them what types of music they know and elicit the names and write them on the board.

a 🔊 Students open their books at page 83. Ask them to read through the types of music in the box and explain any they haven't heard of before. If there is time, ask students to give you an example of a group/singer for each type of music. Explain that they are going to hear examples of these types of music and that they must match the music they hear with the words in the box. Play the recording, pausing after the first piece of music and elicit the answer. Play the rest of the recording while students listen and complete the exercise. Students can compare answers in pairs before listening again to check or change their answers. Play the recording again, pausing for students to repeat each word.

Answers
1 Folk   2 Jazz   3 Classical   4 Reggae
5 Heavy metal   6 Country

b 🔊 Elicit as many words from students as they know for musical instruments and write them on the board. Students then read through the words in the box and match as many of the words as they can with the pictures. Play the recording for students to listen and check or change their answers. Play the recording again, pausing after each word for students to repeat.

TAPESCRIPT/ANSWERS

a a trumpet   b an electric guitar   c a piano
d keyboards   e a violin   f a saxophone   g a flute
h a clarinet   i a synthesiser   j drums

c Divide the class into pairs. Students read through the questions and discuss them. Set a time limit for this and then ask for pairs to feedback. Does everyone agree?

Weaker classes: They may find it helpful to use a dictionary for this.

Answers
1 live music: music that is seen or heard while it is happening;
   recorded music: music that is put onto magnetic tape or CDs using electronic equipment in a studio
2 an album: a CD or a record that has several pieces of music/songs on it;
   a single: a CD or a record that has one main piece of music/song on it.

3 a hi-fi: /ˈhaɪfaɪ/ a set of electronic equipment which is used to play recorded music;
a personal stereo: a small electronic machine that plays music and which has headphones so that you can listen to music while you are doing other things and without other people hearing

Vocabulary notebook

Remind students to start a section called *Music* and to note down all the new items from this unit. Students may find it helpful to illustrate or translate the new items.

7 Listen

🔊 Students read through the table; make sure they know how to pronounce the names. Play the first part of the recording pausing after Tom mentions the instrument he plays and go through the example as a class.

Stronger classes: Play the rest of the recording right through for students to listen and note down their answers. Remind them to think about the key words they should be listening for in each part of the table.

Weaker classes: Play the recording, pausing after each speaker to give students time to note down their answers. Remind them to think carefully about the kind of words they might hear in each part.

Check answers, playing and pausing the recording again as necessary.

TAPESCRIPT

Boy Hi, my name's Tom ... erm ... I'm a big music fan. I play the saxophone, erm ... in a jazz band, I'm the saxophone player in a jazz band, and er ... I've been playing the saxophone now for about five years, I think ... and I'm not bad! Well, as you can guess, jazz is my favourite kind of music, I often go to a jazz club near here, I've been going there for about two years now, there are some good musicians. I think that's the best way to listen to music – live music, it's just wonderful, especially when it's jazz. I mean, I listen to music in the car and at home, of course – but live music in a club, that's my favourite.

Girl My name's Alice, and, er ... music is something very important in my life. I just love music! I play an instrument – erm, I'm learning to play the piano ... I'm not really very good at it yet, because ... er ... I mean, I've only been learning for about six months. I have lessons every Friday, my teacher's really good, it's great. My favourite types of music are ... erm ... well, I love classical music, my favourite composer is Schubert ... and I really like country music too. I really like listening to music on headphones, you know, or on a personal stereo – it's really good because you can hear everything! It's definitely my favourite way of listening.

Boy Hello there, my name's Phil and I'm seventeen. Er ... I'm a drummer, I play the drums, erm ... in

a group here in town. I started playing the drums when I was ten – my parents gave me a drum set for my birthday! – so I guess I've been playing for about seven years now. One day I want to be a really good drummer, you know, like Ginger Baker or somebody like that! Erm ... well, I play drums in a rock group, and rock's my favourite kind of music, erm ... well, rock music and reggae, I love reggae too, I'm a big Bob Marley fan. Er ... I really like going to concerts, I go to rock concerts whenever I can, but I think my favourite way of listening to music is in the car! I've got a car now, an old one, and I put a CD player in it, so I can drive and listen to rock music at the same time – brilliant!

Girl Hi, I'm Vanessa, Vanessa Green. Erm ... I'm sixteen, and music's something I really like, I spend lots of money on CDs and things. Erm ... musical instruments, well I play the violin a little, erm ... I started violin lessons about three years ago, I've been learning for about three years, yes. Why did I start the violin? Well, it's because my favourite music is folk music, traditional English folk music, and there's a lot of violin playing in that ... erm, well, actually the instrument is called a fiddle, but it's basically the same thing! ... so I want to play violin in a folk group if I can, one day. I listen to music a lot – mostly folk music, of course – and I think the best way to do that, my favourite way, is listening to live music, there's a good folk club in this town and I go there every weekend. I play there too sometimes, a little!

Answers

	Musical instrument	Time spent playing/ learning	Favourite type(s) of music	Favourite way of listening to music
1 Tom	saxophone	5 years	jazz	live in a club
2 Alice	piano	6 months	classical and country	on a personal stereo
3 Phil	drums	7 years	rock	in the car
4 Vanessa	violin	3 years	folk	going to a folk club/ live music

8 Speak

Divide the class into pairs. Students read through the questions.

Stronger classes: Give students a few minutes to discuss the questions. Put pairs with another pair to form small groups to compare answers before class feedback.

Weaker classes: Students can choose one or two questions only to discuss.

Ask for feedback. If there are any interesting points, encourage students to give more information to the rest of the class.

Culture in mind

9 Read

If you set the background information as a homework research task, ask students to tell the class what they found out.

BACKGROUND INFORMATION

As many artists are named in the article, it isn't possible to give background details for them. Instead, these notes provide some more information about each decade, and also refer to some of the other major artists not referred to in the text who may be of interest to students.

1950s: Rock 'n' roll originated in the 1950s as a popular form of dance music. It had a heavy beat, but songs were usually simple melodies. The stars of rock 'n' roll were a mixture of white performers such as Elvis Presley and Bill Haley, and black ones such as Chuck Berry and Little Richard. Its origins were in black music forms such as rhythm and blues ('R & B'), jazz and gospel.

1960s: Music became louder during the 1960s with the increased use of electronic amplification and sound effects. Black American music developed into 'soul', a tuneful and emotional form of music sung by the likes of Aretha Franklin and Marvin Gaye.

1970s: 'Glam rock' became popular with theatrical performers such as David Bowie and Queen. Reggae music from Jamaica became globally famous in the 1970s, with Bob Marley being its greatest star.

1980s: Fashion was as important as music for the British 'new romantic' bands such as Duran Duran. A more down to earth type of rock was played by one of the most successful American performers at this time, the singer-songwriter Bruce Springsteen.

1990s: One of the most influential American bands of the early 1990s was Nirvana, who played a type of rock called 'grunge'.

The early 2000s: A loud form of rap-influenced rock music is played by 'nu metal' bands such as Linkin Park. The most successful rap artist is the American Eminem.

Warm up

Write the decades from the text on the board and ask students what kind of music or which singers and groups they associate with each decade. Write their suggestions on the board or ask students to come out and write them up.

(a) Students look at the decades and the pictures. Do the first one as an example, if necessary. Students complete the exercise. Students then read the text quickly to check their answers and they can also check if any of their predictions from the *Warm up* appear in the text.

Answers
1950s b;   1960s a;   1970s e;   1980s c;   1990s d

(b) Students read through questions 1 to 5. Check any problems. Go through the first one as an example, if necessary. Students read the text again and answer the questions. Students can compare answers in pairs before a whole class check.

Answers
1   The USA.
2   The 1960s.
3   It was the first time it was 100% electronically produced.
4   Because it was played on synthesisers.
5   DJs in the USA.

Discussion box
Stronger classes: In pairs or small groups, students go through the questions in the box and discuss them.

Weaker classes: They can choose one question only to discuss. If necessary, elicit a few prompts for the question they have chosen to help them with their discussion.

Monitor and help as necessary, encouraging students to express themselves in English.

Ask pairs or groups to feedback to the class and discuss any interesting points further.

10 Write

The preparation for this can be done in class and the writing task set for homework.

(a) Students read the letter and answer the question. Check answers.

Answer
She wants to know about what music Sandy likes.

(b) Students read through the letter and match the paragraphs to the questions in Exercise 10a. **Weaker classes:** you may want to do the first two examples with the class first.

Answers

She likes country music. She's been a fan for two years. She loves Shania Twain and she also likes Garth Brooks, Brian Landrie, Meredith Edwards and Jessica Andrews. She likes country music because the singers have great voices and the lyrics are good. She listens to country music nearly all the time and she usually listens to music on headphones alone, but sometimes her friends come round to her house and they listen together.

(c) Students now write their own letters, replying to Jenny's questions using their own answers.

Weaker classes: They may find it useful to answer the questions first and then to expand their answers into a letter. They can draft their letter and then swap letters with a partner for them to check. They can then write a final version.

Module 3 Check your progress

1 Grammar

(a) 2 were killed   3 was invited   4 were beaten
5 was heard   6 wasn't injured   7 were damaged/weren't destroyed

(b) a; a; a; a; The; the; the

(c) 2 n't enough   3 n't enough   4 too many   5 too much   6 too many   7 n't enough

(d) 2 'm going to wash   3 are/going to meet
4 'll pay   5 's going to visit   6 'll buy   7 's going to give   8 'll carry

(e) 2 nothing   3 someone   4 everything
5 somewhere   6 none of them   7 no one

(f) 2 don't have to   3 mustn't   4 mustn't   5 doesn't have to   6 mustn't

(g) 2 sent   3 been talking   4 been playing
5 visited   6 been reading/finished

2 Vocabulary

(a)

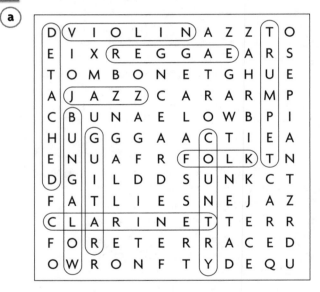

(b) 2 memory   3 garage   4 bomb   5 keyboards
6 guitar   7 semi-detached

(c) 2 memorable   3 forget   4 remember   5 remind
6 memorise

3 Everyday English

1 mates   2 sort of   3 get rid of   4 got a point
5 never mind

How did you do?
Students work out their scores. Check how they have done and follow up any problem areas with revision work for students.

Module 4
Dreams and reality

YOU WILL LEARN ABOUT ...

Ask students to look at the pictures on the page and to read through the topics in the box. Check they understand each item. You can ask them the following questions, in L1 if appropriate: *What do you think the person in picture 4 is doing? What do you think the girl in picture 7 did? Do you know who is the youngest person to have designed a website? What kind of problems do you think computers can cause? Where were the Incas from? Where are the statues in picture 1? Who do you think the boy in picture 2 is? Do you have any superstitions? What do you think the things in picture 6 mean?*

In small groups, students discuss which topic area they think each picture matches.

Check answers.

Answers
1 An ancient terracota army in China
2 A shoeshine boy who became a film star
3 Some of the problems computers can cause
4 Medicine in the past
5 The discovery of an ancient Inca city
6 The history of some superstitions

YOU WILL LEARN HOW TO ...

See Introduction.

Use grammar

Students read through the grammar points and the examples. Go through the first item with students as an example. In pairs, students now match the grammar items in their book. Check answers.

Answers
Defining relative clauses: That's the shop where I bought this shirt.
used to: When I was young, I used to cry a lot.
Second conditional: If I knew, I'd tell you.
Past perfect: My bike wasn't there – someone had stolen it.
Reported statements: He told me he would write to me.
Reported questions: My father asked me why I was late.
Third conditional: I would have invited her if I'd seen her.

Use vocabulary

Write the headings on the board. Go through the items in the Student's Book and check understanding. Now ask students if they can think of one more item for the *Medicine* heading. Elicit some responses and add them to the list on the board. Students now do the same for the other headings. Some possibilities are:

Medicine: *hospital, ambulance, tablets, injection, nurse, surgeon*

Computer technology: *virus, crash, disk, hard disk, laptop, keyboard*

Noun suffixes *-r, -er, -or* and *-ist*: *teacher, actor, builder, scientist*

Noun suffixes *-ation* and *-ment*: *demonstration, communication, government, entertainment*

13 Doctor's orders

Unit overview

TOPIC: Medicine

TEXTS
Reading and listening: a text about medicine in the past
Listening: a dialogue at the doctor's
Listening: a dialogue about Dr. Joseph Lister
Reading and listening: Story: *I used to like Joanne*
Writing: a magazine article about a famous scientist

SPEAKING AND FUNCTIONS
Expressing past habits

LANGUAGE
Defining relative clauses
Used to
Pronunciation: /z/ or /s/ in *used*
Vocabulary: medicine
Everyday English: *You're kidding! Congratulations; ended up with; hang on to*

1 Read and listen

If you set the background information as a homework research task, ask students to tell the class what they found out.

BACKGROUND INFORMATION

Ancient Egypt: The Egyptian civilisation is one of the world's oldest civilisations, dating back 5000 years.

Middle Ages: The period in western European history between approximately the 11th and the 16th centuries, when the power of kings and people of high rank was strong.

Native Americans: See Unit 1, Exercise 5.

Warm up

Ask students what they do if they have a headache and elicit a few suggestions.

Weaker classes: Give them a few possible answer options to choose from (e.g. lie down, take some medicine, have a drink of water, phone a doctor, call an ambulance).

(a) Students look at the pictures and read the captions and the questions. Check any problems. Elicit suggestions and write them on the board. Students now read the text to check their ideas. Remind them they don't have to understand every word at this

point. Were any of their ideas correct? Were they surprised at the correct ideas?

(b) 🔊 Students read through sentences 1 to 5. Check any problems. Play the recording while students read and listen and decide if the statements are true or false. If necessary, pause the recording after the first statement and go through this as an example.

Weaker classes: You may want to pre-teach the following vocabulary: *headache; herbs; chemical; aspirin; developed world; tablet; ceramic; afford; leech; suck; pain; painful; strange; toothache.*

Check answers and then ask students to correct the false statements.

TAPESCRIPT
See the reading text on page 90 of the Student's Book.

Answers
1 N
2 F (Para 2: *... let the headache out ...*)
3 T
4 N
5 F (Para 4: *... on the neck.*)

(c) Divide the class into pairs or small groups. Students read through the question. Give them a few minutes to discuss it. Monitor and check students are discussing this in English and encourage them to express themselves as best they can. Ask pairs or groups to feedback and if there are any interesting points discuss these further as a class.

If you are short of time, do this as a class discussion and elicit ideas from the class.

2 Grammar
Defining relative clauses

(a) **Stronger classes:** Students read through the example sentences. Ask them:

Sentence 1: Which people could afford to go to doctors? (Rich people) Explain or elicit that *who* refers to the people who can afford to go to the doctor.

Sentence 2: Which plant do Native Americans use? (the plant which contains chemicals) Explain or elicit that *which* in this sentence refers to the plant. Students go through the text and find more examples of defining clauses. Check answers.

Weaker classes: Books closed. Write the following examples (or some of your own) on the board:
Mr Brown is the teacher who teaches in class 2./ Those are the books which we use to learn English.
Ask students:

Sentence 1: Which teacher teaches in class 2? (Mr Brown) Explain or elicit that *who* refers to the teacher *who* teaches in class 2.

Sentence 2: Which books do we use to learn English? (those books) Explain or elicit that *which* in this sentence refers to the books. Students open their books at page 91 and read through the example sentences. Follow the Stronger classes procedure above from this point.

Answers

Para 1: ... *common health problem that people have*; ... *use plants which contain* ...
Para 4: ... *people who were rich* ... *where the pain was.*
Para 5: ... *people that had toothache.*

Students now read through and complete the rule box. Check answers.

Answers

who/that   which/that   where

To check understanding at this point, ask students to give you an example sentence of their own using a defining relative clause.

> **Language notes**
> 1 Students may produce statements like: *She is the woman which works in the library*. Remind them we can only use *who/that* for people.
> 2 Students may find it useful to translate the example sentences into their own language and compare the two.

(b) This exercise can be set for homework. Students read through sentences 1 to 7. Go through the example, if necessary. Ask students to explain why *that* is the correct answer. Students complete the exercise. Remind them to look carefully at the subject of each sentence before they decide which word to choose. Check answers, asking students to explain their choice.

Answers

2 who   3 where   4 who   5 who   6 that
7 where

Grammar notebook

Remind students to note down the rules for defining relative clauses and a few examples of their own.

3 Vocabulary

Medicine

(a) Students read through sentences 1 to 6. Check any problems. Go through the example, if necessary. Students complete the exercise. Remind students to think carefully about the subject of the first half and to look for some key words which relate to that subject in the second half. Play the recording. Students check answers.

TAPESCRIPT/ANSWERS

1 A doctor is someone who tries to make sick people better.
2 A hospital is a place where doctors and nurses work.

3 A patient is someone who has a health problem.
4 A dentist is someone that you visit if you have a problem with your teeth.
5 A tablet is something which you take with water to make you feel better.
6 An ambulance is a vehicle that takes people to hospital.

(b) Books closed. Elicit all the illnesses, aches and pains that students know in English. Write them on the board. Students open their books at page 91. Ask them to look at the pictures and read through sentences a to h. Check any problems. Go through the first item as an example, if necessary. Students complete the exercise. Students can compare answers in pairs. Play the recording for students to listen and check or change their answers. Play the recording again, pausing for students to repeat.

TAPESCRIPT/ANSWERS

1 c My eyes hurt
2 d I've got a temperature
3 g I've got a cold
4 a I've got a toothache
5 e I've got a sore throat
6 b I've got stomach ache
7 h I've got a pain in my chest
8 f My ankle hurts

> **Language notes**
> 1 Students may produce statements like *My head it is hurting me*. Remind them that in English we say either *My ..... hurts* or *I've got a sore ..... .*
> 2 Students may find it useful to translate some of the sentences in Exercise 3b into their own language and compare the two.

(c) Students read through the instructions. Make sure they understand that they must choose from the illnesses in Exercise 3b. Play the recording, pausing after the first patient, and ask students what the answer is. Continue playing the recording for students to complete the exercise. Students can compare answers in pairs. Play the recording again for students to check or change their answers. Play it again as necessary to clarify any problems.

TAPESCRIPT

1 **Doctor** OK, I see. And how long has it been like this?
   Boy Since last Saturday. I was playing football in the park and I fell over.
   Doctor Does it still hurt a lot?
   Boy Yes, it does.
   Doctor OK, take your shoe off, please, and your sock and let me have a look at it. Hmm, yes, that looks bad – does it hurt if ...
2 **Doctor** And you've been like this since last week.
   Woman That's right, doctor.
   Doctor Do you smoke, Mrs Jones?

Woman   Me? No doctor, I don't smoke.

Doctor   OK, well let me have a look, please. Open your mouth – that's right. Now, say "Aaaah".

Woman   "Aaaah."

3 **Doctor**   And tell me, what did you have to eat last night?

Girl   Nothing very much. Just some fish, erm … with chips of course.

Doctor   Fried fish?

Girl   Yes.

Doctor   Hmmm. And do you feel sick?

Girl   Yes, I do – it really hurts!

Doctor   OK, don't worry. It might be something you ate, but I can give you ……

4 **Doctor**   And how long have you been like this?

Man   About a week, doctor. I stayed in bed yesterday and the day before.

Doctor   Have you taken any tablets?

Man   No, I haven't.

Doctor   Do your eyes hurt? Have you got a cough?

Man   Yes, and I'm sneezing a lot too!

Doctor   Yes, well, nothing much to worry about, I think – it's just an ordinary cold …

Answers
1   His ankle hurts.
2   She's got a sore throat.
3   She's got stomach ache.
4   He's got a cold.

4 Grammar

used to

(a) **Stronger classes:** Students read through the examples. Ask the following questions:

Is the action still going on? (No) Did it happen once in the past or lots of times? (Lots of times.) Elicit or explain that we use *used to* when we are talking about a repeated action in the past but which is finished now.

Weaker classes: Books closed. Write the following examples (or some of your own) on the board: *I used to work in Greece./My brother used to like heavy metal music.*

Ask students the following questions:

Sentence 1: Do I work there now? (No) Did I work there in the past? (Yes) Did I work there once or for a period of time in the past? (For a period of time)

Sentence 2: Does he like heavy metal music now? (No) Did he like it once or over a period of time in the past? (Over a period of time). Elicit or explain that we use *used to* when we are talking about a repeated action in the past but which is finished now. Students now open their books at page 92 and read the two examples. Follow the procedure for Stronger

classes above if you need to check students have understood the concept correctly.

(b) Students look at the two pictures and the sentences.

Stronger classes: Elicit the difference in meaning. Remind students of the explanations for the example sentences in Exercise 4a.

Weaker classes: Ask them the following questions about each picture:

Picture 1: Does she still listen to Abba now? (No) Did she listen to Abba in the past? (Yes) Did she listen once or over a period of time? (Over a period of time)

Picture 2: Did she listen to Mariah Carey this morning? (Yes) Is she listening to Mariah Carey now? (No) Did the action happen once or over a period of time in the past? (Once)

Elicit or explain that we use *used to* when we are talking about a repeated action in the past but which is finished now but we use the past simple to show a completed action in the past.

To check understanding at this point, ask students to give you a sentence of their own using *used to*.

(c) **Stronger classes:** Students read through the rule and the table and complete them.

Weaker classes: Encourage students to look back at the examples they have seen in the exercise so far to help them work out the form for *used to*. If they are having problems, give them a few more examples of your own to elicit the form. Check answers.

Answers
Positive: used to
Question: did/use to
Short answer: did/didn't
Rule: past/now

> **Language notes**
> 1   Students may produce questions like: **Did he used to like punk music?* Remind them that the question form is *did + use to*.
> 2   They may also produce statements like: **Did she used to going to university?* Remind that we use *used to + infinitive* without *to*.
> 3   Students may find it helpful to translate some examples into their own language and compare the two.

(d) This exercise can be set for homework. Students read through sentences 1 to 5 and a to e. Check any problems. Go through the first sentence as an example, if necessary. Ask students to explain their choice of answer. Students complete the exercise. Remind them to look for some key words in the second sentence which will link it with the first. Check answers, asking students to explain their choice of answer.

Answers

1 d 2 a 3 e 4 b 5 c

(e) This exercise can be set for homework. Students read through sentences 1 to 8. Check any problems. Go through the example, if necessary, focusing students' attention on the use of the present simple in the second part. Students complete the exercise. Remind them to read each one carefully and to think about which verb should be in the present simple. Check answers.

Answers

2 used to be / say
3 used to live / don't live
4 doesn't smoke / used to smoke
5 isn't / used to be
6 didn't use to listen / love
7 Did you use to like / love
8 Did your father use to play / is

Grammar notebook

Remind students to copy down the rules and the completed table from this exercise. They may also find it useful to write a few examples and some translations.

┌─ OPTIONAL ACTIVITY ──────────────
│ In small groups, students think about their own town or city and how it has changed over the years. They must produce a sentence using *used to* to describe how their city has changed. For example:
│
│ *S1: There used to be a vegetable shop on the corner of the square. There's a big supermarket there now.*
│
│ Ask groups to feedback to the rest of the class.

5 Pronunciation

/z/ or /s/ in *used*

(a) 🔊 Students turn to page 121 and read through the instructions and sentences 1 to 5. Check any problems. Explain that the sentences focus on the verb *used to* and *used*. Write the first sentence on the board. Play the recording, pausing it after the first sentence and go through this as an example, if necessary. Ask a student to come out and circle or underline the /s/ sound in *used*. Make sure students understand the difference in the sound of each verb at this point. Play the recording again while students listen and complete the exercise.

(b) Play the recording, pausing it as necessary for students to check their answers. Play it again, pausing after each sentence for students to repeat. If students are still having problems with the pronunciation, drill a few more times as a class. The 'd' in *used* is silent in these examples because the following word starts with a consonant (the 'd' in *used* is pronounced if the following word starts with a vowel – as in *I used a lot of water*).

TAPESCRIPT/ANSWERS

1 I used the dictionary.
2 I used to watch a lot of videos.
3 Who used the computer?
4 John used to live in London.

6 Speak

(a) Divide the class into Student A and B pairs. Tell Student As to read through the information on page 93 and Student Bs to turn to page 123 and look at their information.

Give students a few minutes to tick the information that is true for them.

(b) Ask a stronger pair to demonstrate the example question and answer, with Student A starting first. Make sure students understand that they have to use *used to* in the statements they make. Give students a few minutes to ask and answer and tick their box about their partner. Monitor and check students are taking turns to ask and answer and that they are using the correct forms of *used to*. Make a note of any repeated errors to go over as a class later. Ask pairs to feedback to the rest of the class. If there are any interesting points, encourage students to discuss these further.

7 Listen

If you set the background information as a homework research task, ask students to tell the class what they found out.

BACKGROUND INFORMATION

Joseph Lister: 1827–1912, was an English surgeon who introduced the principle of antiseptics to the medical world. He worked in Scotland and was the first doctor to carry out the first modern surgical operation, in 1865. He used an acid called carbolic acid for cleaning and encouraged the sterilization of surgical instruments, thus reducing the number of deaths following operations.

Antiseptics: Destroy or inhibit the growth of bacteria, thus preventing infection. They are used before surgical procedures to clean the skin.

Warm up

Ask students if they have ever been in hospital? If so, what were they in for? What kind of experience did they have? If they haven't been in hospital, perhaps they can think about someone they know who has. Discuss this as a class, in L1 if appropriate.

(a) Students read through the question. Discuss this as a class and elicit suggestions.

b 🔊 Students read the question. Play the recording for student to listen and find the answer. Check answers.

TAPESCRIPT

Boy Hi Vicky.

Girl Hi Andy. Hey, did you see that programme on telly last night?

Boy Which programme?

Girl The documentary about Joseph Lister.

Boy Lister? Who was he?

Girl He was a doctor, from England – and he was the first doctor who used antiseptics in hospitals.

Boy Oh yeah?

Girl Yeah. He lived in the nineteenth century. Do you know – in those days, hospitals used to be really dirty.

Boy Did they?

Girl Yeah, and a lot of patients used to die because everything was so dirty. You know, even the doctors didn't use to wash their hands before they touched patients, or before they operated on them.

Boy Eugh!

Girl Yeah – just imagine. Anyway, Lister used to work in a hospital, in a city in Scotland, and he saw all these people dying, and he started to think: 'Perhaps we just need to keep everything clean.' So he told the nurses to wash their hands and everything – but still, about 50% of patients died!

Boy 50%!

Girl Yeah! Anyway, then he started to use antiseptics to wash the medical instruments and things – and after that, only 15% of the patients died.

Boy Oh right, so was he a hero after that?

Girl Well, sort of. Do you know, when he tried to tell other doctors about antiseptics, a lot of the doctors used to laugh at him!

Boy But in the end they saw he was right, did they?

Girl Yeah, it was an interesting programme, you know – Lister was a really important man.

Boy Yeah, it sounds like it …

Answer

Because no one washed their hands before treating a patient or before operating on one.

c 🔊 Students read through the summary. Check any problems.

Stronger classes: Go through the first item as an example, if necessary. Encourage students to guess the meaning from context and encourage them to think about what kind of word is missing (e.g. noun, verb, etc.). Students complete the exercise. Play the recording for students to listen and check or change their answers. Play it again, pausing as necessary to clarify any problems. Check answers.

Weaker classes: Put the following words on the board in jumbled order:

Scotland; *nineteenth*; *hospitals*; *dirty*; *die*; *wash*; *dying*; *nurses*; *50*; *antiseptic*; *right*

Students choose the words they think go in each gap and then they listen and check or change their answers.

Answers

1 England   2 19th   3 hospitals   4 dirty
5 die   6 wash   7 dying   8 nurses   9 50
10 antiseptic   11 15   12 right

I used to like Joanne

8 Read and listen

Warm up

Ask students to tell you what happened in the last story episode (the group didn't win the competition, but Amy was approached by the winning band and was talking to them at the end of the last episode).

a Students read the questions. Elicit suggestions but do not give answers at this point.

b 🔊 Play the recording while students read and listen and check their predictions from Exercise 8a. How many were correct? Encourage students to discuss their predictions to the second question in more detail at this point.

TAPESCRIPT

See the story on page 94 of the Student's Book.

Answers

1 Amy was talking to the band who won the concert.
2 Students' own answers

c Students read through questions 1 to 7. Check any problems. Go through the first one as an example, if necessary. Students complete the exercise. They can compare answers in pairs before a whole class check.

Answers

1 Dave
2 Joanne
3 To be their lead singer.
4 She said she'd think about it.
5 They're very pleased for her.
6 She isn't very happy.
7 He doesn't like her as much as he used to.

┌─ **OPTIONAL ACTIVITY** ─────────────

In groups of four, students can act out the dialogue from the story.

9 Everyday English

a Ask students to read through expressions 1 to 4 and to locate them in the story on page 94 and decide who says them. Check answers. Then students match each expression with a definition. Go through the first one as an example, if necessary. Check answers.

Answers

1 b Joanne   2 c Dave   3 d Joanne   4 a Matt

b Ask students to read through dialogues 1 to 4. Check any problems. Go through the first dialogue as an example, if necessary. Students complete the other dialogues with the expressions from Exercise 9a. Check answers.

Answers

1 Congratulations
2 You're kidding
3 hang on to
4 ended up with

Vocabulary notebook

Students should note down the expressions and translations from this exercise under their *Everyday English* section.

┌─ OPTIONAL ACTIVITIES ────────
See Unit 1, Exercise 10 Everyday English, Optional Activities.
└

10 Write

If you set the background information as a homework research task, ask students to tell the class what they found out.

BACKGROUND INFORMATION

Marie Skłodowska-Curie: 1867–1934, was Polish and married into the Curie family, a family of French scientists. She is best known for her work on radioactivity and radium and, with her husband Pierre, shared the 1903 Nobel Prize for Physics.

Christiaan Barnard: 1922–2001, born in South Africa. He performed the first heart transplant on a human in Cape Town in December 1967. Unfortunately the patient died after only 18 days but the operation was heralded as a success and was a major triumph in terms of transplant surgery.

Alexander Fleming: 1881–1955, was a Scottish bacteriologist who discovered penicillin in 1928. He shared the 1945 Nobel Prize for Physiology and Medicine for his work on penicillin.

a Students read the question.

Stronger classes: Ask students if they know the answer and elicit their suggestions. Give them a few minutes to read the notes and the article to check their predictions.

Weaker classes: Give them a few minutes to read the notes and the article to find the answer.

Check answers.

Answer

Because she discovered radium.

b The preparation for this can be done in class and the task set for homework. Students read through the notes about Christiaan Barnard and Alexander Fleming. Check any problems. Students choose either of these people or someone of their own choice (if students did the optional activity for Exercise 7 then they may want to use the person they researched for that).

Stronger classes: Students expand their notes, using Dave's article as a model and write up their article.

Weaker classes: Go through the model article as a class and look at how it is structured. Compare it with the notes where possible to show students how the information has been expanded. Students write out the notes for the person they have chosen into full sentences. They can swap these with a partner to check. Then they write their final version.

If students complete the task for homework, encourage them to add a picture of the person they have chosen and any more information they can find.

14 If I had ...

1 Read and listen

Warm up

Ask students how many of them have computers at home. If they don't have a computer at home, do they have access to a computer? If so, where? Elicit answers and discuss them as a class or in L1 if appropriate.

(a) Students read through the questions. Elicit answers and discuss this as a class. Are there any interesting results? If so, encourage students to discuss these further as a class.

(b) Write the names of the people in the text on the board and make sure students know how to pronounce them correctly (/'dʒerəmi/, /'mændi/, /'eɪdriən/). Students read through the three bullet points and then read the text quickly to find the answers. Remind them they don't have to understand every word in the text at this point. Check answers.

Answers
good fun: Adrian
important for everything: Mandy
not as good as books: Jeremy

(c) 🔊 Students read through sentences 1 to 6. If necessary, play the recording, pausing after the answer to the first sentence and go through this as a class. Play the recording while students listen and read and complete the exercise. Students can compare answers

in pairs. Play the recording again for students to check or change their answers and clarify any problems. Ask students to correct the false statements.

TAPESCRIPT
See the reading text on page 96 of the Student's Book.

Answers
1 F (He thinks it's boring and not as much fun as using books.)   2 F (He doesn't.)   3 T   4 T
5 T   6 T

┌─ **OPTIONAL ACTIVITIES** ─────────────
│ Students must imagine they cannot use a computer for a whole day. They must work out a timetable for that day which includes all the things they would do instead of using a computer.
│
│ **Weaker classes:** Elicit or give them some ideas of things they could do instead (e.g. go out with friends, phone friends, write letters, watch TV, read a book, do their homework, etc.).

2 Grammar

Second conditional

(a) **Stronger classes:** Students read through the questions and the example sentences. Elicit the answer (*imagined*). Explain that this is the second conditional and that we use it when we talk about imaginary situations.

Weaker classes: Books closed. Write the following example (or some of your own) on the board: *If I had lots of money, I'd buy a new car.*

Ask them: Do I have lots of money? (No) Is the situation real or imagined? (Imagined) Explain that this is the second conditional and that we use it when we talk about imaginary situations. Students open their books at page 97 and read through the example sentences. If necessary, follow the procedure for stronger classes from this point to check they have understood the concept.

(b) **Stronger classes:** Students go through the text on page 97 and find more examples of the second conditional and then complete the rule. Check answers.

Weaker classes: After students have gone through the text check the examples they have found and ask them what they notice about how this tense is formed. Elicit or give *If* + past simple + *would* + verb. Students can then complete the rule. Check answers.

Answers
Para 1: *How would our lives be different, if we didn't have them?*
Jeremy: *...we would need more books ... if we didn't have computers; ... if I had one, I'd only use it for emails.*

Mandy: *If I had enough money, I'd buy ...* ; *If we didn't have one*; *...what I would do.*
Adrian: *If I had the time, I'd start ...* ; *If I had my own site, I'd put ...*

Answers
past; would

At this point students may find it useful to compare the form of the first conditional with a second conditional sentence. You can put a first conditional sentence on the board and ask students to give you an example of a second conditional sentence, e.g.

If I win the lottery, I'll buy a new car.

If I had lots of money, I'd buy a new car.

Language notes

1 Students may produce statements like: *If I would be rich, I would buy a new car*. Remind them that we can't use *would* in the *If* clause in the second conditional.

2 Explain to students that after *If I* in the second conditional we can use *was* or *were*, e.g. *If I were you, I'd ...* or *If I was you, I'd ...* Explain too that *were* can also be used with third person singulars in the second conditional.

3 Remind them that the *If* clause can go at the beginning or at the end of the conditional sentence.

Look
Students read through the information in the box; explain any problems.

(c) This exercise can be set for homework. Students read through sentences 1 to 6. Check any problems. Go through the example, if necessary. Students complete the exercise. Remind them to look carefully at the verbs and to see where the *If* clause is before they make their choice. Check answers.

Answers
2 would pass / worked
3 lived / wouldn't have
4 would come / asked
5 was / would go
6 would give / knew

(d) This exercise can be set for homework. Students read through sentences 1 to 6. Check any problems. Go through the example, if necessary. Students complete the exercise. Remind them to look carefully at the sentences and to see where the *If* clause is before they choose which verb form to use. Check answers.

Answers
2 would you do / ran
3 would talk / were
4 would do / had
5 didn't have / wouldn't buy
6 would you invite / won

Grammar notebook
Remind students to copy down the rule for the second conditional from this exercise and to note down a few examples of their own and any translations if necessary.

3 Pronunciation
'd

(a) 🔊 Students turn to page 121 and read through sentences 1 to 4. Play the recording, pausing after the first sentence and go through this as an example. Play the recording again for students to listen and complete the exercise. Remind them that they should circle the word they hear. Check answers, playing and pausing the recording again as necessary.

TAPESCRIPT/ANSWERS
1 I read a book.
2 I'd go for a walk.
3 I'd close the window.
4 I talk to the teacher.

(b) 🔊 Students read through sentences 1 to 4. Play the recording, pausing after each sentence for students to repeat.

TAPESCRIPT
1 I'd go to the doctor.
2 I'd study more.
3 I'd search the Internet.
4 I'd go to the library.

4 Speak

(a) Divide the class into pairs. Remind students of the second conditional and elicit a few examples to check they remember how to form it correctly. Students then read through situations 1 to 6. Check any problems. Ask a stronger pair to read out the example exchange. Students then continue asking and answering each situation. Monitor and check students are taking turns to ask and give advice and that they are forming the second conditional correctly. Make a note of any repeated errors to go through as a class later.

Weaker classes: They may need more support with the advice they want to give. Elicit or give examples of advice they could give. For example:

1 get a job; do more jobs round the house; ask for more pocket money; sell some of your CDs
2 talk to them more; ask your brother/sister what to do; think about how you could change your behaviour
3 do you want him/her back, if so you should call them / leave a text message / arrange to meet them and talk about the problem
4 take a tablet; see a doctor; lie down; stop using the computer; get your eyes tested
5 have a drink of water; lie down; wear your glasses more; don't eat so much; see a doctor

6 don't work so hard; get out more; go to bed earlier, etc.

Ask some pairs to feedback to the class.

(b) Reorganise the pairs from Exercise 4a or let students work in the same pairs. Students read through questions 1 to 7. Check any problems. Ask a stronger pair to read out the example dialogue, drawing students' attention to the use of the second conditional in the question. Students complete the questions. Check answers. Students then ask and answer the questions. Monitor and check students are asking and answering the questions correctly and that they are forming the second conditional correctly. Note down any repeated errors to discuss later as a class. Ask a few pairs to feedback to the rest of the class.

Answers
2 Where would you live if you had to live in a different town?
3 What would you buy if you won 10,000 euros in the lottery?
4 If you could marry any famous person you wanted, who would you marry?
5 If you could meet a famous person, who would you meet?
6 What would you do if you were invisible for a day?
7 If you could have one wish, what would you wish for?

5 Read

If you set the background information as a homework research task, ask students to tell the rest of the class what they found out.

BACKGROUND INFORMATION

Goosehead: Is the name of a website and book created by Ashley Power. The name *Goosehead* came from a story in her childhood when she accidentally knocked the head off a garden goose ornament. Please note that Ashley's website, Goosehead.com, no longer exists.

Warm up

Ask students if they have ever designed a website. If so, what was it for? If not, would they like to and what would they design one for? Or do they know anyone who has? Discuss this as a class, in L1 if appropriate.

(a) Students read through the questions. Elicit suggestions. Students then read the text quickly and check their predictions. Remind them they don't need to understand every word of the text at this point. Check answers.

Answers
1 She is Ashley Power.
2 She launched her own website when she was 16.

(b) Students read through questions 1 to 5. Check any problems. Go through the first item as an example, if necessary. Students complete the exercise. Check answers.

Weaker classes: You may want to pre-teach the following vocabulary: *success*; *design*; *crazy*; *stressed*; *friendship*; *independent*.

Answers
1 When she was eight.
2 Because she couldn't find any websites for teenagers to meet and talk.
3 16.
4 How to design a website and run a business. It also gives general advice to teenagers, based on Ashley's experiences.
5 It's important to love them but not rely on them.

(c) Students read through the expressions from the text. Go through the first one as an example, encouraging students to guess the meaning from context. Students complete the exercise.

Weaker classes: Put the following meanings on the board in jumbled order: *using*; *begin something new*; *the result of a search on the Internet*; *to need someone*; *give someone new ideas*. Students then match the expressions in their book with the definitions on the board.

Students can check answers in a dictionary before a whole class check.

Answers
1 using the Internet
2 begin a new website
3 'visits' to a particular website
4 to need or depend on someone
5 give someone new ideas

Vocabulary notebook
Encourage students to note down the expressions from Exercise 5c and to provide some translations if necessary.

6 Vocabulary
Information technology and computers

(a) 🔊 Books closed. Elicit as many words to do with computers as students know and write them on the board. Students open their books at page 99, look at the picture and read through the words in the box. Students complete the exercise. Play the recording for students to listen and check or change their answers. Play the recording again, pausing after each word for students to repeat.

1 CD drive   2 screen   3 keyboard   4 mouse
5 mouse pad   6 printer   7 disk drive

b Students read through the words in the box and the text, remind them to ignore the gaps for the moment. Check any problems. Go through the example as a class, making sure students understand why *starts up* is the correct answer. Students complete the exercise. Students can compare answers in pairs. Play the recording for students to check or change their answers. Play the recording again, pausing for students to repeat each word.

TAPESCRIPT/ANSWERS
When my grandmother was a little girl, the only person in her village with a telephone was the doctor and Logie Baird was just inventing the television! But now she has a computer that she uses every day! She gets emails from all the family, so she **starts up** her computer in the morning and **logs on** to the Internet. She **surfs** the net for information. She says it's better than walking to the library because it saves her old legs! She likes to **download** all sorts of things for free, and then **print** them out in full colour. She gets angry if the computer **crashes** and she has to start it up again. Once she lost some files so now she always **saves** everything on the hard disk. She even bought a CD writer the other day so now she can **burn** all her files on a CD.

The language of the Internet

c Students read through words 1 to 5 and definitions a to e. Check any problems. Go through the first item as an example, if necessary. Students complete the exercise. Students can compare answers in pairs before a whole class check.

Answers
1 c   2 d   3 e   4 a   5 b

Vocabulary notebook
Encourage students to start a section called *Information technology and computers* in their notebooks and to note down all the new words and expressions from this exercise. They can add illustrations and translations as necessary.

┌─ OPTIONAL ACTIVITY ═══════════════
Students discuss their favourite websites. Divide the class into pairs. Students think about a website they like and they explain to their partner what the website is and why they like it. Monitor and check students are taking turns to ask and answer and provide help and encouragement as necessary. Ask pairs to feedback.

7 Speak

Divide the class into pairs. Students read through the questions and then discuss them.

Weaker classes: They can choose one question only and discuss it.

Monitor and check students are taking turns to ask and answer. Help and encourage students to express themselves in English as far as possible. Ask pairs to feedback to the class.

Culture in mind

8 Read

Warm up

Ask students to read the title of the text and ask them for their opinions on how great they think computers are. Elicit a few suggestions.

a Divide the class into pairs. Students read the question. Give them a few minutes to write their lists and then ask pairs to feedback. Write some of their suggestions on the board.

b Students now read the text quickly to check their predictions and to note down any other problems the text mentions. Ask for feedback. Students can come out and tick the items on the board from Exercise 8a. How many students predicted the problem the text mentions?

Answers
problems with eyesight; hand and arm injuries; less time exercising; more overweight people; stress; addiction; loneliness and depression.

c Divide the class into pairs or use the same pairs from Exercise 8a. Students read through questions 1 to 3. Check any problems. Give students a few minutes to find the answers. Ask for feedback. As a class, discuss if students agree with the problems the text mentions and if they know anyone who has suffered from any of these.

Answers
1 Problems with their eyesight; arm and hand injuries (repetitive strain injury); and more people become overweight because they are sitting down more and exercising less.
2 Stress, pressure and addiction. People get stressed because computers and the internet have made our lives much faster, and there is more pressure to do things quickly.
3 They need to know when to log off and go and do something different.

9 Listen

a 🔊 Students look at pictures 1 to 3.

Stronger classes: They can look at the pictures and predict what they think the problems are. Then they listen and check their predictions.

Weaker classes: Play the recording while students match each speaker to a problem. Remind students of the problems the text in Exercise 8 mentioned and remind them to listen for key words to do with computer problems.

Check answers.

TAPESCRIPT

1 **Boy** I use a computer a lot – you know, for my emails, to play games and to search for information on the Internet. I do a lot of homework on my computer, too. I guess I spend about three hours a day on the computer – maybe more at the weekend. And it's making my eyes bad, I think. I already wear glasses, but very soon I'm going to need some new ones! My eyes get very tired, and sometimes I get headaches too. I try to make sure that I stop looking at the screen every ten minutes or so – but sometimes I forget!

2 **Girl** I don't have any problems from using a computer – but my father does! He works at home – he's a writer, you know, he writes articles for magazines and things. And, er ... he doesn't really type very well, he isn't a typist, so now he has problems in his wrist and fingers. It's because he's typing on the keyboard and using the mouse all the time. Now he has to wear a special kind of glove on his hand, and he's bought a better keyboard, one that supports his hands – but his hands and arms still hurt at the end of the day!

3 **Boy** Yeah, I've got a problem with computers – I'm addicted to the Internet! I spend hours every day on the net, just surfing and going to chat rooms – I love it! You know, some people are addicted to chocolate and things like that, they have to eat it all the time – well, I have to surf the Internet all the time. Some of my friends think I'm crazy, but for me it's the best way to relax. My mother thinks I'm crazy though – sometimes she has to pull me away from my computer!

Answers
a 3   b 1   c 2

b 🔊 Students read through questions 1 to 5. Check any problems.

Stronger classes: Students answer the questions first and then listen to check.

Weaker classes: Play the recording while students listen and answer the questions. Play the recording again for students to check or change their answers, pausing as necessary.

Answers
1 About three.
2 He wears glasses and he tries to stop looking at the screen every ten minutes.
3 He's a writer.
4 He wears a special kind of glove.
5 They think he's crazy.

Discussion box
Stronger classes: In pairs or small groups, students go through the questions in the box and discuss them.

Weaker classes: They can choose one question only to discuss. If necessary, elicit a few prompts for the question they have chosen to help them with their discussion.

Monitor and help as necessary, encouraging students to express themselves in English.

Ask pairs or groups to feedback to the class and discuss any interesting points further.

10 Write

The preparation for this can be done in class and the writing task set for homework.

a Students read the question. Students then read the advertisement and the article to find the answer. Check answers.

Answer
Topic 1

b Students decide if they are going to write about topic 2 or 3.

Stronger classes: Give them a few minutes to make notes for their topic. Go through Sam's article with them and ask them to think about the structure of the article and the topic of each paragraph. Students then expand their notes into full sentences and put them into paragraphs. Remind students to refer back to Sam's article if they have problems.

Weaker classes: Elicit some ideas from them and help them with their note-taking. Encourage students to expand their notes into full sentences. Students can swap their sentences with a partner for their partner to check. Once their partner has checked them, students write out a final version putting their sentences into paragraphs.

15 Lost worlds

Unit overview

TOPIC: Acts of bravery; Taking risks

TEXTS

Reading and listening: a text about the discovery of Machu Picchu

Listening: a radio programme about the army of Xian

Reading and listening: Story: *I don't think so*

Writing: a short story

SPEAKING AND FUNCTIONS

Describing events in the past and earlier past

Telling a picture story

LANGUAGE

Past perfect

Pronunciation: *had* and *'d*

Vocabulary: noun suffixes: *-r, -er, -or, -ist*

Everyday English: *stuff; though; give it a go; Good luck!*

1 Read and listen

If you set the background information as a homework research task, ask students to tell the rest of the class what they found out.

BACKGROUND INFORMATION

The Incas: Were a pre-Columbian Indian people with an empire in western South America. Their language was Quechua and when the empire was at its peak it stretched from Cuzco in Peru through the entire Andean region. The Incas were famous for their incredible feats of construction, including the city of Machu Picchu.

Machu Picchu: Was the fortress city of the Incas. It was situated between two peaks to the north west of Cuzco in Peru. What remains is a series of terraced stonework, approximately $13 km^2$, linked by more than 3,000 steps.

Hiram Bingham: 1874–1956. He found the ancient Inca city of Machu Picchu in 1911 and he was also the first person to climb Mount Coropuma.

Peru: Is in the western part of South America. The capital city is Lima and the official languages are Spanish and Quechua.

Cuzco: Is a city in the south of Peru. It is said to have been founded by Manco Capac and was the capital of the Inca empire. It was destroyed by an earthquake in 1950, but most of its historic buildings have since been restored.

The Andes: Is the mountain range which extends from the north of South America, in Venezuela, to the south at Cape Horn. The mountain range is approximately 7,200 kilometres in length. The highest peak is Aconcagua (6,960 metres) in Argentina. The Peruvian Andes were the centre of the Inca civilisation.

Warm up

Ask students if they know where the Incas came from and elicit suggestions. Students look at the photos. Ask them if anyone has ever visited Machu Picchu and how old they think it is. Discuss this as a class or in L1 if appropriate.

(a) Students read the questions and then read the text quickly to find the answers. Remind them that they don't need to understand every word at this point. Check answers.

Answers
1 In the Andes mountains of Peru
2 The Incas

(b) 🔊 Students read through questions 1 to 4. Check any problems. Play the recording while students listen and read and answer the questions. Check answers, playing and pausing the recording again as necessary.

TAPESCRIPT

See the reading text on page 102 of the Student's Book.

Answers
1 In a small hotel in Peru because he wanted to find a lost Inca city.
2 1800 metres
3 A ten-year-old boy
4 Machu Picchu, Inca houses, temples and a square

2 Grammar
Past perfect

(a) **Stronger classes:** Students read through the information in the box and sentences 1 to 6. Check any problems. If you think it will help students draw a line on the board and mark two points above it, for example:

- before 24-7-1911   • on 24-7-1911

_____

Then go through the first sentence as an example marking on the line in this way:

- before 24-7-1911   • on 24-7-1911

_____✗_____

Explorers had looked for the lost city ...

Students work out when the other sentences happened using the line on the board to help them. Check answers, asking students to come out and write the sentence on the line on the board where it happened (on or before 24-7-1911).

Weaker classes: Books closed. Write the following sentence (or an example of your own) on the board: *I had finished my homework when the telephone rang.*

Ask students what happened first (*I finished my homework*). Students now open their books at page 103 and read through the information in Exercise 2a. Follow the procedure for stronger classes from this point.

Answers
1 B 2 B 3 B 4 A 5 A 6 B

(b) Ask students what they notice about the verb in all the sentences which happened before 24-7-1911 and elicit or explain that they use *had* + past participle. Explain that this tense is called the past perfect and is used when we want to make clear that one action happened before another in the past.

Stronger classes: Students now go through the text on page 103 and complete the rule box and the table.

Weaker classes: Students go through the text on page 102. Check answers. Then read through the rule as a class and elicit the missing words. Students read through the table and complete it. Check answers.

Answers
Para 1: *Other explorers had looked for …*
Para 2: *Bingham had always been fascinated … ; … and had studied … ; … and some scientists had travelled … ; … had gone up … ; … they had travelled higher up. ; … they had spent the night …*

Answers
Rule: before
Negative: hadn't
Question: Had
Short answer: had/hadn't

To check understanding at this point, ask students to give you a few examples of their own using the past perfect.

Language notes
1 Students may confuse the past perfect with the present perfect and produce statements like: **I have finished my homework when the phone rang.* Remind them of the use of the past perfect in English.
2 Students may find it useful to translate a few examples into their own language and compare the two.
3 Remind them that we don't repeat the main verb in short answers. We don't say: **Yes, I had played.*

(c) This exercise can be set for homework. Students read through sentences 1 to 7. Check any problems. Go

through the example as a class, making sure students understand the form correctly. Students complete the exercise. Remind them to think carefully about the past participle they need to use and if they need a regular or an irregular past participle. Check answers.

Answers
2 had lost ('d lost)   3 hadn't made   4 hadn't bought   5 had changed ('d changed)   6 had/left
7 had/gone

(d) This exercise can be set for homework.

If you set the background information as a homework research task, ask students to tell the rest of the class what they found out.

BACKGROUND INFORMATION

Francisco Pizarro: 1476–1541, a Spaniard who led an expedition to Peru in 1530, with his partner Almagro, in search of the Inca empire. He captured and murdered the Inca leader Atahualpa in 1533. After conquering Peru he captured Cuzco. He is said to have founded Lima in 1535.

Thor Heyerdahl: 1914–2002, was a Norwegian explorer and anthropologist. He sailed across the Pacific in 1947, the Atlantic in 1970 and the Persian Gulf in 1977 in replicas of ancient sailing vessels. He wrote books describing his voyages, the most famous of which is the *Kon-Tiki Expedition,* written after his voyage across the Pacific.

Students read through the texts. Check any problems. Go through the example as a class, asking students to explain why the past simple is the correct answer. Students complete the exercise. Check answers, asking students to explain their choice of verb.

Answers
1 b had built   c had lived
2 a was   b had built   c had sailed   d went on

(e) This exercise can be set for homework. Students read through sentences 1 to 5. Check any problems. Go through the example as a class. Students complete the exercise. Check answers, asking students to explain their choice of verb.

Answers
2 lost / had to / left   3 hadn't seen
4 found/went   5 didn't enjoy / had seen

Grammar notebook
Remind students to note down the rules for the past perfect and the completed table from Exercise 2b. They may also find it useful to note down some examples and translations of their own.

3 Pronunciation
had

a 🔊 Students turn to page 121 and read through the instructions. Play the recording, pausing it after the first sentence and go through this as an example. Make sure students know they must circle the weak forms and underline the strong forms. Play the rest of the recording while students listen and complete the exercise.

Weaker classes: Students may find it useful to listen once for the weak forms and then listen a second time for the stressed forms.

Do not give answers at this point.

TAPESCRIPT/ANSWERS
1   I <u>had</u> a strange dream last night.
2   It was like a dream that (had) come true.
3   My dad <u>had</u> no time to help me.
4   Other explorers (had) looked for the city, but they <u>had</u>n't found it.

b 🔊 Students read the question. Elicit the answer (when *had* is used as the main verb, not an auxiliary verb, it is stressed). Play the recording again for students to listen and check their answers. Play the recording again, pausing after each sentence for students to repeat.

c 🔊 Students read through sentences 1 to 4. Play the recording pausing after each sentence for students to repeat. Make sure students are saying the stressed and unstressed forms correctly. Drill some examples as a class if there are still problems.

TAPESCRIPT
1   There was no chocolate left – I'd eaten it all!
2   When the test finished, she'd only answered three questions!
3   We didn't go to the cinema because we'd seen the film before.
4   He didn't laugh at the joke because he'd heard it before.

4 Speak

a Divide the class into pairs. Students read through the table. Check any problems. Ask a stronger pair to read the example to the rest of the class. Give students a few minutes to make as many sentences as they can. Monitor and check they are using the correct verb forms and note down any repeated errors to go through as a class later. Ask some pairs to read out some of their sentences to the rest of the class.

Possible answers
My parents were angry because I'd come home late.
My friend was unhappy because she hadn't passed the test.
We were tired because we'd come home late.
You were surprised because you'd passed the test.
The teacher was angry because they hadn't passed the test.

b In pairs, students read through the words in the box and look at pictures a to f. Go through the first word as an example, asking students to find a ladder in one of the pictures. Students complete the exercise. Check answers.

Answers
a ladder: all of them
a kitten: all except picture a
a window cleaner: all of them
a small boy crying: picture a
a garage roof: pictures a and f

c Ask pairs which picture they think is the first one in the story and elicit the answer. Students then work out the order of the pictures to tell the story. Remind them to think carefully about the order of events and which things happened before others. Check answers.

Answers
2 c   3 f   4 e   5 a   6 d

d **e**

Students read the instructions. Ask a stronger pair to read out the example sentences to the rest of the class. Draw students' attention to the use of the past continuous and past perfect tenses. Students continue to retell the story in their pairs. Monitor and check students are taking turns to do this and make sure they are using the correct verb forms. Note down any repeated errors to go through later as a class.

Weaker classes: Elicit or give some prompts for each picture before students begin to retell the story. For example:
Picture a: girl/sees boy crying/runs after window cleaner
Picture b: boy/play/kitten/garden
Picture c: window cleaner/ladder/garage roof
Picture d: window cleaner/ladder/rescue boy and kitten/mother
Picture e: window cleaner move ladder/walk away/boy playing on roof
Picture f: woman/pay window cleaner/boy climb ladder

Do this round the class, encouraging pairs to add as much information as they can.

f Students work in the same or different pairs. They read though the instructions then ask a stronger pair to read out the example dialogue. Draw students' attention to the use of the past perfect in the example and remind them to use this in their own situations. Give students a few minutes to discuss their situation. Monitor and check that they are taking turns to ask and answer and that they are using the past perfect correctly. Ask pairs to feedback and if there are any interesting stories encourage students to give more information to the rest of the class.

Listen

The army of Xi'an

If you set the background information as a homework research task, ask students to tell the rest of the class what they found out.

BACKGROUND INFORMATION

China: See Unit 10, Exercise 7.

Xi'an: (pronounced 'shee – an') Is the capital of the Shaanxi province in North central China. The tomb of Qin Shi Huang (see below), the Qin emperor who, ruled China from 259 – 210 BC, was discovered there in 1974. His tomb was filled with the terracotta army of life-size figures of people and horses and is now one of China's most important archaeological sites. Each figure was made to represent an actual person living at the time of the emperor's death and is made with individual features and dressed in clothing or armour. All segments of Qin society are represented and there are over 6,000 figures altogether.

Qin Shi Huang: The Chinese emperor who unified China and set up a centralised imperial system. Construction of the Great Wall of China began under his leadership as well as many roads and canals. Writing was standardised under his leadership too. Before he died he had the terracotta army made and ordered for it to be put in his tomb with him to protect him.

Warm up

Ask students to look at the pictures. Do they know where the statues come from? Has anyone heard of them? If so, what can they tell the class about them? Discuss this as a class or in L1 if appropriate.

(a) 🔊 Students read the instructions and look at the pictures.

Stronger classes: Go through the first item as an example. Give students a few minutes to complete the exercise.

Weaker classes: Elicit the order of the pictures from students and write it on the board. If you have time, ask students to come out and write the order up on the board.

Play the recording while students listen and check their order and their *Warm up* predictions. Check answers.

TAPESCRIPT

Man   Good morning. On today's programme, we're talking about the army of terracotta figures that was found in China some years ago. Here to tell us about it is archaeologist Dr Jean McRae. Good morning, Dr McRae.

Woman   Good morning.

Man   So tell us – this army in China – how was it found?

Woman   Well, it was in 1974, and one day, a man, a Chinese man, was in a field near a city called Xi'an – he was actually digging a hole, he was looking for water. And while he was digging, he found some little pieces of terracotta – and he also saw part of a head, and part of a face, made out of terracotta! He was very surprised, so he ran to tell his friends, the other men in the field, about what he had found. And of course they told the Chinese authorities, and soon there were scientists there, and they did some digging too, and they found more soldiers and even some horses, all made out of terracotta, and all buried in the ground. And a few years later, they opened a museum there in Xi'an – and the man who found the first pieces, the man who was digging and looking for water, he became quite famous, and the tourists at the museum asked him for his autograph! There he was, a farmer, writing his name for the tourists!

Man   I see. And Dr McRae, can you tell us ...

Answers

2 e   3 a   4 f   5 d   6 b

(b) 🔊 Students read through questions 1 to 6. Check any problems. If necessary, play the recording and stop it after the answer to the first question and go through this as an example. Play the recording for students to listen and answer the questions. Remind them to listen for key words from the questions in the recording to help them find the answers. Check answers, playing and pausing the recording again to clarify any problems.

TAPESCRIPT

Man   ... And Dr McRae, can you tell us more about what they found near Xi'an?

Woman   Yes. Well, it was amazing. They found a complete army of figures – soldiers, horses and everything. They found more than six thousand figures altogether.

Man   Six thousand? That's incredible.

Woman   Yes, it is. And even more amazing – every figure is different – even the horses aren't the same – and each figure looks like a real person. They all have different expressions on their faces and were dressed in clothes which were painted in different colours. They even have different hairstyles! They aren't small either, most of them are 1.8 metres tall.

Man   That's amazing! How old are they, and why were they under the ground?

Woman   Well there was a famous Chinese emperor, called Qin Shi Huang, and he wanted an army to protect him, even when he was dead. So he ordered people to put this army of life-like terracotta figures in the ground beside him! When the Chinese man found them, they'd been in the ground for more than two thousand years! We think that it took about thirty years to make all the figures.

Man Goodness! And can people see the figures?

Answers
1 More than six thousand.
2 They all have different expressions on their faces, different hairstyles and their clothes are painted in different colours.
3 A famous Chinese emperor wanted an army built to protect him even when he was dead.
4 More than two thousand years.
5 About thirty years.

6 Vocabulary

Noun suffixes: -r, -er, -or and -ist

(a) Write the suffixes on the board and elicit as many jobs as students know for each suffix. Leave these on the board as you will need them again in Exercise 6b.

Stronger classes: Students then read through the definitions. Go through the first item as an example, eliciting the job from students. Students then complete the exercise, referring back to the text on page 102.

Weaker classes: Write the following jobs in jumbled order on the board: *professor*; *explorer*; *owner*; *scientist*; *archaeologist*. Ask students to read through the definitions. Go through the first item with them as an example. Students then match the other jobs or the words with the definitions. They then check their answers in the text on page 102.

Answers
1 archaeologist   2 explorer   3 professor
4 scientist   5 owner

> **Language note**
> Explain to students that the stress on words often changes when we make a new noun, e.g. 'photograph – pho'tographer.

(b) Students read through the list of words. Check any problems. Go through the example, if necessary. Students complete the exercise.

Weaker classes: Ask students to come out and write the correct noun under the suffixes you put on the board in Exercise 6a.

Students can check their answers in a dictionary before a whole class check.

Answers
2 artist   3 footballer   4 photographer
5 tourist   6 journalist   7 farmer   8 cyclist
9 driver   10 receptionist

(c) Students read through sentences 1 to 6. Check any problems. Go through the example, if necessary. Students complete the sentences. Remind them to

think carefully about the context of each sentence before choosing which noun they need from Exercise 6b. Students can check answers in pairs before a whole class check.

Answers
1 artist   2 photographer   3 painter
4 receptionist   5 farmer   6 journalist

Ask students to give you any more jobs they know with these suffixes, at this point.

Vocabulary notebook
Remind students to start a section for each suffix from this unit and to note down any new words from this exercise under the relevant suffix.

I don't think so

7 Read and listen

Warm up

Ask students to tell you what happened in the last story episode (*Amy was going to practise with the band who won the competition. Dave and Matt decided they didn't like Joanne as much as they thought they had at first.*).

(a) 🔊 Students read the questions; elicit suggestions. Play the recording while students read and listen and check their predictions.

TAPESCRIPT
See the story on page 106 of the Student's Book.

Answers
1 At the bus station.
2 Students' own answers.

(b) 🔊 Students read through sentences 1 to 7. Check any problems. Go through the first item as an example, if necessary. Students complete the exercise. Play the recording again for students to check or change their answers. Encourage students to correct the false statements.

Answers
1 F (*Are you sure you aren't coming back ...?*)   2 T
3 F (*It's OK, Dave.*)   4 N   5 F (*I know I'm not the world's greatest singer ...*)   6 T   7 N

┌─ OPTIONAL ACTIVITIES ─────────

Stronger classes
Divide the class into groups of three or four. Students think about how they think the story will end and write their own dialogues. Encourage groups to read them out to the rest of the class. The class can vote for the best ending.

Weaker classes
In groups of four, students can act out the dialogue from the story.

8 Everyday English

(a) Ask students to read through expressions 1 to 4 and to locate them in the story on page 66 and decide who says them. Check answers. Then students translate them into their own language.

Answers
1 Dave   2 Dave   3 Amy   4 Dave

(b) Ask students to read through dialogues 1 to 3. Check any problems. Go through the first dialogue as an example, if necessary. Students complete the other dialogues with the expressions from Exercise 8a. Check answers.

Answers
1 give it a go/good luck   2 stuff   3 though

Vocabulary notebook
Students should note down the expressions and translations from this exercise in their *Everyday English* section.

┌─── OPTIONAL ACTIVITIES ──────────────
│ See Unit 1, Exercise 10 Everyday English, Optional
  Activities.

9 Write

A short story

The preparation for this can be done in class and the writing task set for homework.

(a) Students look at pictures 1 to 3 and read through the text. Check answers, asking students to explain their choice. **Weaker classes:** You may want to pre-teach the following vocabulary: *alone*; *warm*; *relax*; *dig*; *reddish-brown*; *bomb*; *fortunately*; *blow up*; *dangerous*.

Answer
Picture 2

(b) Students read through topics 1 to 4. Check any problems. Go through the first item as an example, if necessary. Students complete the exercise. Check answers.

Answers
1 B   2 D   3 A   4 C

(c) Students read the two questions. Draw their attention to the underlined expressions in the text and elicit the answers.

Answers
1 about a month ago; when (I looked at it); fifteen minutes later
2 first; then; the next day

Discuss the third question as a class and elicit the answers (suddenly; immediately; fortunately).

(d) Students read the instructions. Give them time to decide if they are going to choose one of the other pictures in Exercise 9 or something of their own choice.

Stronger classes: Encourage them to make notes about the sequence of events, using the model in Exercise 9 to help them. Students then expand their notes into full sentences and put them into paragraphs. Remind students to refer back to the short story on page 107 if they have problems.

Weaker classes: Encourage them to choose one of the other pictures in Exercise 9a. Elicit or give some prompts for each picture and help them make some notes about the sequence of events and the content of their story. Refer them back to Exercise 9b to think about the order of events. Encourage students to expand their notes into full sentences. Students can swap their sentences with a partner for their partner to check. Once their partner has checked them, students write out a final version putting their sentences into paragraphs. Remind them to use the model on page 107 if they have any problems.

16 Good or bad luck?

Unit overview

TOPIC: Good and bad luck/Superstitions

TEXTS

Reading and listening: a text about a young Brazilian film star
Listening: a dialogue about an unlucky day
Listening: a description of superstitions in Britain
Reading and listening: a text about where superstitions come from
Writing: an email to apologise for something

SPEAKING AND FUNCTIONS
Reporting statements and questions
Discussing superstitions

LANGUAGE
Reported statements and questions
Third conditional
Pronunciation: *would've/wouldn't have*
Vocabulary: Noun suffixes: *-ation* and *-ment*

1 Read and listen

If you set the background information as a homework research task, ask students to tell the rest of the class what they found out.

BACKGROUND INFORMATION

Rio de Janeiro: Is a major city in Brazil and is situated on the south west shore of Guanabara Bay. It has many tourist attractions, including Sugar Loaf Mountain, Corcovado Peak with its statue of Christ and the famous Copacabana beach.

Brazil: Is the largest country in South America. Its capital city is Brasilia and the national language is Portuguese. Other major cities include Rio de Janeiro and São Paulo.

Central Station: Is the title of the 1998 Brazilian film directed by Walter Salles (see below), which starred Vinícius de Oliveira. The Brazilian actress Fernanda Montenegro, said to be one of Brazil's greatest actresses, plays the character Dora.

Walter Salles: Is the director of the above film and also a documentary maker. The main themes of much of his work are exile and the search for identity.

Warm up

Ask students to translate the unit title into their own language. Ask them if they have had any good or bad luck recently. If so, encourage them to explain to the rest of the class what happened. Discuss this as a class, in L1 if appropriate.

(a) Students read the question and look at the pictures. Elicit suggestions. Students then read the text quickly to check their predictions. Remind students they don't have to understand every word at this point. Were any of them correct?

(b) 🔊 Students read through questions 1 to 7. Check any problems. Play the recording, pausing after the answer to the first question and go through this as an example. Play the recording while students listen and read and answer the other questions. Students can compare answers in pairs before a whole class check. Play the recording again as necessary, pausing to clarify any problems.

Weaker classes: You may want to pre-teach the following vocabulary: *a lucky break*; *shoeshine boy*; *businessmen*; *film test*; *entertainment*; *performance*.

TAPESCRIPT
See the reading text on page 108 of the Student's Book.

Answers
1 Eleven
2 Because he was wearing trainers.
3 Because he was poor.
4 Because he said he couldn't act and he had never see a film before.
5 When Salles agreed to let the other shoeshine boys do the film test.
6 1,500
7 Because if Walter Salles hadn't been wearing trainers he would never have had the conversation with Vinícius.

2 Grammar
Reported statements

(a) Students read through statements 1 to 5. Go through the example, if necessary. Students then go back through the text on page 108 and find who said each one.

Stronger classes: They can try and do this from memory and can refer back to the text to check answers only.

Check answers.

Answers
2 Vinícius   3 Vinícius   4 Vinícius   5 Salles

(b) Students look at number 1. Give them a few minutes to find the reported speech in the text: *... he said he wanted Vinícius to do a film test*. (Paragraph 4). Elicit or explain that the verb changes from present simple to past simple. Ask them if they notice any other changes in the two sentences and elicit or explain that the pronoun changes from *you* to *him*. Students complete the exercise. Remind them to look carefully at the tenses in the statements in Exercise 2 and to look for tense changes within the text.

Check answers.

Answers
2 ... told Salles he couldn't act.
3 ... said he'd never seen a film.
4 ... said he'd do the test.
5 ... said he was very happy with his performance.

(c) Students read through the table. Elicit the first item as an example. Explain to students that each tense in direct speech moves back a tense in reported speech. Students complete the exercise. Remind them to think carefully about how each tense will move back a tense before they write their answer. Check answers.

Answers
Present simple → Past simple
Present perfect → Past perfect
can/can't → *could/couldn't*
will/won't → *would/wouldn't*

To check understanding at this point, give students a few example sentences of your own and ask them to put them into reported speech.

> **Language notes**
> 1 Students may not change the tenses in reported speech and produce statements like: *He said they want to leave at 8 o'clock*. Tell them that this is only correct if the fact is still true or hasn't happened yet. For example, in the above sentence the student may be talking about the future, in which case it is correct and the past simple would also be correct. However, if the student is referring to what has already happened he/she will need to use the past simple.
> 2 Remind students that pronouns may also need changing in reported speech and some time words, e.g. *this – that*; *here – there*, etc.
> 3 Students may find it useful to translate some direct speech into reported speech in their own language and notice if the same changes take place.

(d) Students read through sentences 1 to 6. Go through the example, drawing students' attention to the verb and pronoun changes. Students complete the exercise. Remind them to look carefully at the verbs and pronouns in the reported speech before they decide how it will be said in direct speech. They can also refer back to the completed table in Exercise 2c to help them. Check answers.

Answers
2 'I live in Rio,'
3 'I'm going to make another film,'
4 'The other boys can come,'
5 'You'll earn a lot of money,'
6 'I haven't seen a better young actor,'

(e) This exercise can be set for homework. Students read through sentences 1 to 6. Go through the example, drawing students' attention to the changes in tense and pronouns. Students complete the exercise. Remind them to look carefully at the verbs and pronouns in each sentence before they make their decisions about the tense changes. Check answers.

Answers
2 was going   3 had worked   4 would do his homework   5 could phone   6 had never had

Grammar notebook
Remind students to note down the completed table from Exercise 2c and some examples of their own.

┌─ **OPTIONAL ACTIVITY** ─────────
Divide the class into small groups of four or five. One student thinks of a sentence about themselves in direct speech. They whisper it to the next person in the group who must then report the first student's sentence to the next person and add a new sentence in direct speech about themselves. This continues until the last person in the group can report back all the sentences. Continue like this until everyone has had a turn at reporting back all the sentences. For example:
S1 to S2: I'm going to the cinema tonight.
S2 to S3: Marco said he was going to the cinema tonight. I'm studying for a test tonight.
S3 to S4: Marco said he was going to the cinema tonight, Magda said she was studying for a test tonight. I'm ... etc.

3 Vocabulary

Noun suffixes: *-ation* and *-ment*

Write the endings *-ation* and *-ment* on the board. Elicit as many nouns with these endings as students know and write them up under the relevant suffix. If there is time, you can ask students to come out and write up the nouns themselves. Students now read through sentences 1 to 7. Check any problems. Go through the example, drawing students' attention to the connection between the noun and the verb it comes from. Students complete the exercise. Remind them to think carefully about each verb before they decide whether to add *-ment* or *-tion*. Check answers.

Answers
2 improvement   3 communication   4 equipment
5 information   6 calculation   7 management

Vocabulary notebook

Encourage students to note down the noun suffixes and the new nouns from this exercise. They may find it useful to add some translations.

OPTIONAL ACTIVITY

Give students the following verbs and ask them to work out the *-ment* and *-ation* nouns from them. Check answers.

1 enjoy   2 advertise   3 present   4 motivate
5 inform   6 pay

Answers

1 enjoyment   2 advertisement   3 presentation
4 motivation   5 information   6 payment

4 Grammar

Reported questions

a Remind students of the reported statements they saw earlier in this unit and ask one or two stronger students to tell the class what changes from direct to reported speech (the tenses, pronouns and time references). Students now read through questions 1 to 4 and reported questions a to d. Go through the first item as an example, drawing students' attention to the change in tenses, word order and the pronoun changes. Then ask students if they can remember who asked the question and elicit *Vinícius*. Students complete the exercise. Remind them to look for tense changes in a to d and to refer back to the text on page 108 to check who asked them, if necessary. Check answers.

Answers

1 b Vinícius   2 c Salles   3 d Vinícius   4 a Salles

b Students read the questions. Elicit or give the answers. Students then go back through the text on page 108 and find further examples. Remind them to look for the question word *ask* to help them. Students then read through the table and complete the rule. Check answers.

Weaker classes: Check answers after students have found examples in the text. Students then read through the table and complete the rule.

Answers

Questions 1 and 3
Questions 2 and 4
Examples from text:
Para 3: *... he asked a man if he wanted him to ...*
Para 4: *... he asked the man if he had any money ...*

Para 4: *... the man asked him what his name was ...*
Para 4: *... he asked Vinícius where he lived, how old he was ...*
Para 5: *... Vinícius asked if the other boys could ...*
Para 6: *... Salles asked him if he would take the part ...*
Para 6: *... and asked Salles when he could start ...*

Answer

do/does;   if

To check understanding at this point, give students a few example direct questions of your own and ask students to make them reported questions.

c Students read through sentences 1 to 6 and the introductory text. Check any problems. Go through the first item as an example, drawing students' attention to the word order. Students complete the sentences. Check answers.

Answers

2 They asked me why I was late.
3 I asked them if they were angry.
4 They asked me where I'd been.
5 I asked them if I could go out again on Saturday.
6 They asked me where I wanted to go.

OPTIONAL ACTIVITY

In pairs, students continue the reported conversation from Exercise 4c and make their own endings. Ask pairs to read out the conversation to the rest of the class. The class can vote for the best ending.

d Students read the instructions and the example. Play the recording for students to write down the questions.

Weaker classes: You can pause the recording after each question to give them time to write them down.

Check answers, playing and pausing the recording again to clarify any problems.

TAPESCRIPT/ANSWERS

Aunt   How old are you, Joe?
Joe   I'll be sixteen next birthday.
Aunt   Do you like your school?
Joe   It's OK. I like some subjects.
Aunt   What's your favourite subject?
Joe   I like Computer Science and sports.
Aunt   Have you got a computer?
Joe   Yes, I have.
Aunt   What do you want to do when you leave school?
Joe   I'm not sure, I haven't decided yet.

(e) Go through the example, drawing students' attention again to the differences between the direct and reported questions. Students complete the exercise. Remind them of the rules for reported questions if necessary. Check answers.

Answers

2 Do you like your school? – She asked him if he liked his school.
3 What's your favourite subject? – She asked him what his favourite subject was.
4 Have you got a computer? – She asked him if he had a computer.
5 What do you want to do when you leave school? – She asked him what he wanted to do when he left school.

If students are still having problems, refer them back to the table in Exercise 4b and remind them of the rules.

(f) 🔊 Play the recording again for students to note down Joe's answers. Go through the first answer as an example, asking a stronger student to give the answer in reported speech. Students complete the exercise. Check answers, playing and pausing the recording again to clarify any problems.

Weaker classes: You can pause the recording after each answer to give them time to write them down.

Answers

1 I'll be sixteen next birthday. – He said he would be sixteen next birthday.
2 It's OK. I like some subjects. – He said it was OK and he liked some subjects.
3 I like computer science and sports. – He said he liked Computer Science and sports.
4 Yes, I have. – He said he had a computer.
5 I'm not sure, I haven't decided yet. – He said he wasn't sure. He hadn't decided yet.

Grammar notebook

Remind students to note down the table and the rules from Exercise 4b. They may find it useful to note down a few examples and translations of their own.

5 Speak

Divide the class into Student A and B pairs. Tell Student As to read through the information on page 110 and Student Bs to turn to page 123 and look at their information.

Give students a few minutes to read through their questions. Encourage stronger pairs to think of some more questions of their own to ask.

Ask a stronger pair to demonstrate the example question and answer, with Student A starting first. Give students a few minutes to ask and answer. Monitor and check students are taking turns to ask and answer and that they are not writing down their partner's answers. After a few minutes, swap pairs and students report the information about their first

partner. Ask pairs to feedback to the rest of the class. Monitor and check students are using the reported statements and questions correctly. Make a note of any repeated errors to go over as a class later. If there are any interesting points, encourage students to discuss these further.

6 Listen

(a) 🔊 Students read the questions. Play the recording for students to listen for the answers. Remind them that they will be listening for a place in question 1 and a time in question 2. Students can compare answers in pairs before a whole class check.

TAPESCRIPT

Girl   Hello?
Boy   Hi. Can I speak to Sarah please?
Girl   Speaking.
Boy   Oh, hi Sarah. It's Jack here.
Girl   Hi Jack – how are you?
Boy   Fine. Listen, Sarah, I was thinking – would you like to go to the cinema tonight? With me?
Girl   The cinema? Well, yes sure. That would be nice. What's on?
Boy   Oh, there's a new comedy on, I think. It starts at seven forty-five.
Girl   Great.
Boy   OK – so, I'll meet you at the cinema, OK? At half past seven?
Girl   Sounds good. See you there, Jack.
Boy   Yes, see you Sarah. Bye.

Answers

1 To the cinema.
2 At half past seven.

(b) 🔊 Divide the class into pairs (or if students checked their answers in pairs for Exercise 6a use the same pairs). Students look at the pictures. Go through the first picture as an example. Students complete the exercise. Ask students for their answers and put them on the board. Do not give the answers at this point. Play the recording for students to check or change their answers. Play the recording again, pausing as necessary to clarify any problems.

TAPESCRIPT

Girl   I hear you missed your date with Sarah last night, Jack.
Boy   Yeah, it was terrible! If I'd looked at my watch before, I'd have been OK.
Girl   What do you mean?
Boy   Well, I left the house late and I ran. If I hadn't run, my glasses wouldn't have fallen off.
Girl   Your glasses?
Boy   Yeah, they fell off and broke on the ground. So I had to go home and get my other ones. Then I decided to catch the bus, but it was late! If the bus had arrived on time, I wouldn't have been late!

Girl And if you hadn't been late, you'd have seen the film with Sarah! Oh no, how embarrassing!

Answers

1 c   2 e   3 a   4 d   5 b

c 🔊 Students read through the dialogue. Check any problems. Go through the example, if necessary.

Stronger classes: Students can complete the dialogue and listen and check answers only.

Weaker classes: Play the recording again for students to complete the gaps. Check answers, playing and pausing the recording as necessary to clarify any problems.

Answers

1 run   2 fallen off   3 had   4 wouldn't
5 hadn't

7 Grammar

Third conditional

a **Stronger classes:** Students read through the examples. Ask them the following questions and elicit the answers:

Sentence 1: Did he look at his watch? (No) Is the situation real or imagined? (Imagined) Is the situation in the past or the present? (Past) Now ask them to look at the verbs used and elicit the form of the third conditional.

Sentence 2: Did he run? (Yes) Did his glasses fall off? (Yes) Would his glasses have fallen off if he hadn't run? (No) Elicit or explain that the sentence is showing the person imagining how things might have been different in the past.

Students then read and complete the rule. Check answers.

Weaker classes: Books closed. Write the following example (or some of your own) on the board: *If I had studied more, I would have done better in the exam.*

Now ask the following questions: Did he study hard? (No) Did he do well in the exam? (No) Is the situation in the present or the past? (Past) Is it real or imagined? (Imagined)

Students open their books at page 11 and read the examples. Follow the procedure for stronger classes from this point, if necessary.

Answers

past perfect/have

b Refer students back to the dialogue in Exercise 6c. Go through the first example of a third conditional as a class. Students then underline other examples. Check answers.

Answers

If I'd looked at my watch, I'd have been OK.
If I hadn't run, my glasses wouldn't have fallen off.
If the bus had arrived on time, I wouldn't have been late.

> **Language notes**
> 1 Students may produce statements like *If I looked at my watch, I'd have been OK*. Remind them of the form of the third conditional if necessary.
> 2 Remind them (as in all conditional sentences) that the *If* clause can go at the beginning or the end.

c This exercise can be set for homework. Students read through sentences 1 to 6. Check any problems. Go through the example, if necessary. Students complete the exercise. Remind them of the form of the third conditional before they begin. Check answers.

Answers

2 had studied/would have passed
3 wouldn't have won/hadn't played
4 wouldn't have bought/hadn't had
5 would have gone/had looked
6 wouldn't have got wet/had taken

8 Pronunciation

would ('d) have / wouldn't have

a 🔊 Students turn to page 121 and read through sentences 1 to 3. Play the recording, pausing it after the first sentence for students to hear the pronunciation of the underlined part clearly. Play the recording for students to listen to each sentence. Elicit the answer to the question (*have* is shortened to /əv/ in third conditional sentences because it is a weak form).

TAPESCRIPT

1 I'd have been OK.
2 My glasses wouldn't have broken.
3 I wouldn't have been late.
4 You'd have seen the film.

b 🔊 Play the recording again, pausing after each sentence for students to repeat. Make sure students are using the same rhythm. If students are still having problems, drill the sentences as a class.

Culture in mind

9 Read and listen

Warm up

Ask students if they are superstitious at all and discuss this as a class. Ask them if they have any lucky charms or anything in particular they will/won't do at certain events or do they know anyone who does (e.g. certain footballers always touch the end of the tunnel before they come out onto the pitch). Discuss this as a class, in L1 if appropriate.

a 🔊 Divide the class into pairs. Students read the instructions and look at the list of superstitions. Ask them which of the items they can see in the pictures. Students then discuss each item and decide if they think it brings good or bad luck. Elicit answers and write them on the board but do not give answers at this point. Play the recording for students to check their answers.

TAPESCRIPT

Girl 1   Look! A black cat. Great!

Girl 2   Why?!

Girl 1   Well, don't you know – black cats bring good luck.

Girl 2   Really? In my country they're bad luck! Anyway, you're not superstitious, are you? You really believe in all that?

Girl 1   Well, you know, not *really*. It's just a British superstition, I suppose.

Girl 2   Are there any other strange British superstitions?

Girl 1   Oh, yes – lots!

Girl 2   What, for example?

Girl 1   Well, a lot of people think that walking under a ladder is bad luck, of course.

Girl 2   Uh huh.

Girl 1   And then ... erm ... oh yes, some people put a horseshoe over their door.

Girl 2   A horseshoe?

Girl 1   That's right. It's supposed to bring good luck to the house.

Girl 2   I see. And I think I heard something about broken mirrors?

Girl 1   Oh, yes, absolutely. If you break a mirror, you get seven years' bad luck.

Girl 2   Seven years! That's a lot.

Girl 1   Well, if you believe it! Oh, and another thing – a lot of people say 'touch wood' and actually try to touch something made of wood if they want good luck.

Girl 2   Really?

Girl 1   Yes, for example, you might say: "It isn't going to rain tomorrow – touch wood".

Girl 2   That's interesting.

Girl 1   Oh, that reminds me, one more – it's supposed to be bad luck if you open an umbrella inside a house.

Girl 2   Bad luck?

Girl 1   That's right – but I don't know why!

Answers

1 G   2 B   3 G   4 B   5 G   6 B

(b) Students read questions 1 to 5. Check any problems. Students then read the text and answer the questions. Check answers, encouraging students to explain their answers with evidence from the text.

Weaker classes: You may want to pre-teach the following vocabulary: *evil spirits*; *witches*; *devil*; *pet*; *nearby*; *spill*.

Answers

1 No. (Para 1: ... *hard to know where, when and how superstitions started.*)

2 Evil spirits. (Para 1: *Evil spirits lived in trees ...*)

3 The moon. (Para 2: ... *it is shaped like a moon ...*)

4 To prevent accidents at sea (Para 3: ... *to prevent an accident at sea ...*)

5 Because it is thought the Devil might be waiting there and the salt will go in his eye. (Para 4: ... *the Devil is always waiting ...*)

Discussion box

Stronger classes: In pairs or small groups, students go through the questions in the box and discuss them.

Weaker classes: They can choose one question only to discuss. If necessary, elicit a few prompts for the question they have chosen to help them with their discussion.

Monitor and help as necessary, encouraging students to express themselves in English.

Ask pairs or groups to feedback to the class and discuss any interesting points further.

10 Write

The preparation for this can be done in class and the writing task set for homework.

Warm up

Remind students of Jack and Sarah from Exercise 6 and ask students to tell you what happened. (Jack was late for their date at the cinema because his glasses broke; he had to go home and change them and then the bus was late and crowded.)

(a) Divide the class into pairs. Students read the instructions and then the email and find the three false facts. Check answers.

Answers

1 He said his watch was broken but really he left the house late / forgot to look at it. (His glasses were broken, not his watch.)

2 He didn't miss the first bus.

3 He didn't fall over a cat and get his trousers dirty.

(b) Students read the questions and then read the email again to find the answers. Check answers. You can elicit words they know for apologising and inviting before they do this exercise. They can then use these words to help them find Jack's words.

Answers

1 I want to apologise; I'm really sorry

2 Can we go out ...?; Would you like to come with me ...?

c Students read the instructions. Give them a few minutes to discuss some reasons in pairs. Ask for their suggestions and write them on the board.

d **Stronger classes:** Students now plan their email using Jack's one as a model. Encourage students to think about how the email is structured and to think carefully about what they must put in each paragraph. Students complete the exercise. They can then send their emails to a partner to read.

Weaker classes: Go through Jack's email in more detail before students begin. Ask them to say what information is given in each paragraph:
Para 1: Reason for writing
Para 2: What happened
Para 3: A new invitation
Para 4: Signing off

Students then make notes for each paragraph of their own email using the information above. They can then expand their notes into full sentences and swap with a partner to check. After their draft is checked they can write their final version and send them to a new partner to read.

Module 4 Check your progress

1 Grammar

a 2 where   3 who   4 who/that   5 that/which
6 who/that

b 2 live/used to live   3 enjoy/used to hate
4 used to eat/doesn't like   5 didn't use to use/use
6 Did/use to have/don't have

c 2 knew/'d tell   3 Would/surf/had
4 got/would/be   5 would go/asked
6 was or were/wouldn't buy

d 2 felt/hadn't slept   3 had/hadn't been
4 was/had forgotten   5 Had/lived/moved
6 Had they known/got married

e 2 ... he wanted to go home.
3 ... he hadn't done his homework.
4 Luis said he would pay for the meal.
5 My aunt told me my brother couldn't come.
6 He said he'd never been to the USA.

f 2 ... if I liked the music.
3 ... where she lived.
4 Sally asked me if I had bought this/that shirt in London.
5 I asked her where she was going.
6 He asked me if I had ever been to Italy.

g 2 wouldn't have bought/had known
3 had known/would have told
4 would've phoned/hadn't forgotten
5 would you have done/had found

2 Vocabulary

a 2 ambulance   3 pain   4 tablet   5 temperature
6 hurt   7 patient

b Parts of a computer: disk drive, mouse, CD drive
The Internet: log on, offline, chat room
Using a computer: start up, crash, burn

c 2 owner   3 scientist   4 improvements
5 equipment   6 information   7 receptionist

3 Everyday English

2 though   3 you're kidding   4 give it a go
5 stuff   6 end up with

How did you do?
Students work out their scores. Check how they have done and follow up any problem areas with revision work for students.

Project 1
A group presentation

Divide the class into groups of three or four. Read through the instructions with the class.

Exercise 1c could be set as a homework research task, giving students more time to research their invention.

1 Do your research

(a) Students read the instructions and look at the pictures. Give them a few minutes to choose their invention or encourage stronger classes to think of their own idea.

(b) Students read through the instructions and the model on the page. Each group should appoint someone to take notes at this stage.

Elicit the reasons from each group and write them on the board; alternatively ask one person from each group to come out and write a reason on the board.

(c) Read the instructions. They should brainstorm ideas for resources: names of magazines, newspapers, books they have heard of, website addresses, or people that could recommend these resources.

If you set this as a homework research task, ask students to share their information and visuals with the rest of the group. Alternatively, give students time to search the Internet or look up the invention in an encyclopaedia and to find some pictures.

2 Prepare the presentation

(a) Students work on this in class. They will need to go through all the information they have collected, and decide which of it they are going to use, and how. It is important to tell them that the presentation should be a minimum of two minutes and a maximum of ten minutes.

If students want to (and if you have time) a presentation can take the form of a large poster, with handwritten or printed text, pictures, photos, drawings, real objects (if the project is about an invention, for example). Students can then use the poster as a background for the oral presentation.

(b) Group members decide who is going to talk and what they are going to talk about. Monitor and check that everyone has a speaking role, no matter how small.

(c) Give groups time to decide on a way to present their information. They will need to practise the presentation. They can do this in their groups in class, or, if this is too noisy, you could ask certain groups to work outside the classroom, in a corridor (if possible) or another space inside the school. Monitor and check students are using the correct language and pronunciation and support them as necessary.

(d) Students should do their presentations in the next lesson. Students can vote for the best presentation.

Project 2
A class survey: how we have fun

1 Do the survey

You may find it useful to take in some magazine questionnaires with you for this lesson.

You may find it useful to make copies of the questionnaires before students do Exercise 1b.

(a) Read through the instructions with the class. Go through the example with them, drawing their attention to the different types of questions. In small groups (of three or four) students look at the pictures and decide on six questions they can ask in their survey. Remind them to use the pictures to help them think about topics and questions they may want to include. Remind them to use different forms of questions to make their survey more interesting.

(b) Students read through the model questionnaire (or show them some examples from magazines if you have brought them in). Students then prepare their own questions. Remind them to think about various possibilities for the answers to their questions.

Monitor and check that each member of the group is noting down the questions, since they will all need to ask the questions in Exercise 1c.

(c) Students ask the other students in their group the questions and note down their answers. Then students circulate round the class asking as many students as they can, noting down their answers. Monitor and check students are using the correct question forms and intonation and pronunciation. Note down any problems to discuss at the end of the lesson.

2 Write up the results

(a) Students regroup in their original questionnaire group (from Exercise 1) and discuss their answers. They can work out how many people they interviewed and what percentage answered in the same way. Monitor and help as necessary.

(b) Read through the example with the class and show how it relates to the example question in Exercise 1b. Using their own information from Exercise 2a, students now write sentences to describe their results. Make sure each student in the groups completes this task. Monitor and help as necessary. Ask students to feedback to the rest of the class. Were there any interesting results? If so, discuss these further as a class.

Students can transfer all their sentences onto a poster and add illustrations and more details if they want.

Project 3

A poster: homes around the world

Divide the class into groups of three or four.

1 Do your research

(a) Read through the instructions as a class and look at the photos. Write two headings on the board: *My country/Other countries*. Elicit the types of houses in students' own country and then elicit the names and types of houses in the photos. Write the names under the relevant heading on the board. Each group decides which type of house they are going to write about.

(b) Students read through the instructions and think about the questions they may want to answer. They should brainstorm ideas for resources: names of magazines, newspapers, books, website addresses, etc. Give students time to search the Internet or look up the invention in an encyclopaedia.

(c) Students read through the instructions. They choose four or five different types of home. In their groups, they think about why they want to compare and contrast those types of home. Encourage groups to think about the information they want to include and why they find it interesting. They should now make notes on the different types of houses they have chosen.

2 Make the poster

(a) This part of the project can be set for homework. As a class, brainstorm ideas for finding visuals, e.g. in website addresses, magazines, comics, etc., that students can bring to the next class.

(b) Students look at the pictures the groups have collected and select a few to illustrate their poster. In their groups, students write short texts about the houses they are going to include on their poster. This should be done in their notebooks or on rough paper. When students are satisfied that their short texts are written correctly they can transfer them to the poster.

(c) Give each group a large sheet of paper and sticky tape or glue. They should write the title at the top of the paper, leaving space for writing at the bottom.

(d) Students now write their personal opinions of the houses they chose on their posters. Students can check their texts in their groups before deciding on final versions and sticking them on to their poster.

(e) Each group should prepare a short presentation to explain their poster to the class. Encourage other groups to ask questions about posters. Display the posters around the class. Students can vote for the best poster and presentation.

Project 4

Designing a website

Divide the class into groups of three or four.

1 Prepare your website

(a) Students read through the instructions and questions. They then look at the pictures and read the web page and answer the questions. Check answers.

Answers
1 Four students.
2 The name of the school, number of students, subjects, sports activities, clubs and teachers.

(b) **Stronger classes:** Using the web page as a model, give students time to think about their school and the information they want to include on their website.

Weaker classes: Write these question prompts on the board:
Name of school?
How many pupils?
Which subjects?
Sports?
Clubs?
Teachers?

Students note down information for each prompt in their groups.

(c) Students read the instructions and the web page again to find out the links. They can decide which links they want for their site and make notes on each link, or substitute the links from the model with notes about their own school.

(d) Students think about the kind of photos they would like to include. Encourage them to think about how the pictures will link with the texts.

2 Make your website

(a) **Stronger classes:** Using the model on page 119 students write a rough version of their own home page with the information they discussed in Exercise 1b. Encourage them to think about the unique qualities of their school. Remind them to write the copy for their link pages, using the notes they made in Exercise 1c.

Weaker classes: Students can expand the notes they made from the prompts on the board in Exercise 1b and then include their information on the link pages from Exercise 1c.

Once students are happy with their draft versions, they can transfer the information onto their large sheets of paper.

(b) Display the web pages around the class. Students can vote for the best website.

Workbook key

1 Explorers

1 **a** 2 noun   3 preposition   4 verb
5 adverb   6 adjective

b 2 live   3 explore   4 settlement   5 remains

2 **a** 2 likes   3 plays   4 spends   5 isn't spending
6 is saving   7 has   8 wants   9 knows
10 is training

b 2 Does Mark usually spend all his money on books?
3 When does Mark play football?
4 Is Mark spending a lot of money at the moment?
5 What is Mark's great ambition?
6 Why is Mark training hard at the moment?

c 2 No. He usually spends all his money on CDs.
3 He plays football most evenings.
4 No. (He's saving up.)
5 He wants to climb Mount Everest next July.
6 Because he knows it will be difficult.

d 2 Do, want   3 is washing   4 A: Do, listen to
B: don't   5 don't watch, don't have   6 am doing
7 is sleeping

3 **a** drink drank
eat ate
find found
make made
put put
run ran
sing sang
sink sank
speak spoke
write wrote
be was

b 2 travelled   3 believed   4 was   5 was
6 were, didn't have   7 died

c 2 F   3 T   4 F   5 T   6 T   7 T

d 2 What did you do there? f
3 How did you travel through the jungle? d
4 Did you go to Bangkok? a
5 What was the weather like? b
6 Did you like the food in Thailand? c

e 2 wanted   3 stayed   4 took   5 didn't like
6 looked   7 didn't find   8 arrived   9 phoned
10 drove   11 saw   12 knew   13 didn't want

f 2 Why did John move to London?
3 How long did he look for Rex?
4 Did John find Rex?
5 When did he arrive at Mandy's home?
6 What did Mandy do when Rex arrived?
7 Did John ever return to London?

g 1 drives, had, had to
2 likes, is learning, started
3 don't think, said
4 don't (usually) like, am reading, started

4 **a** TAPESCRIPT/ANSWERS
1 He play<u>ed in</u> the school football team. /ˈpleɪdɪn/
2 She wait<u>ed at</u> home. /ˈweɪtɪd ət/
3 They want<u>ed to</u> leave. /ˈwɒntɪ tə/
4 I need<u>ed to</u> buy it. /ˈniːdɪd tə/

b 1 They walk<u>ed out</u> of the room.
2 She work<u>ed in</u> a bank.
3 She listen<u>ed to</u> the radio.
4 They ask<u>ed the</u> teacher.

5 2 round here   3 too right!   4 actually

6 **b** 1 She *failed* her driving test and so <u>she had to
take it again</u>.
Verb
didn't pass/didn't reach a high enough standard.

2 Look, <u>you've got tomato sauce all over your shirt</u>!
Why don't you <u>wear</u> an *apron* when you <u>cook</u>?
Noun
a piece of clothing which is tied behind the neck
and round the waist to protect your clothes.

3 This plane is really *cramped* – there's <u>no space to
move my legs</u>!
Adjective
small – there's not enough room, the seats are
too close together.

7 2 a   3 b   4 b

TAPESCRIPT

Sheila OK, if I could just have everyone's attention please.
Excuse me, excuse me …

Voices sh … quiet … sh …

Sheila OK, thank you. Well, I hope you all enjoyed your
meal and if I could just have a few words, I'd like to
tell you about tomorrow's trip. The bad news is you all
have to be ready to leave the hotel by 6am. That's 6am.
So I suggest an early night for everyone.
But the good news is we're going to spend the whole
day in the Amazon jungle. We're going to take a bus
to the port, then a boat for about three hours and then
we're going to walk for another two hours before we
start heading back. It will be hard, but lots of fun.
Now are there any questions? Yes, Julia.

Julia Yes, is it a good idea to take my video camera?

Sheila If you don't mind the extra weight, then yes.
There are lots of good things to film there. Paul?

Paul Isn't it a bit dangerous? I mean, with all the snakes
and crocodiles?

Sheila Don't worry, Paul. We'll have a local guide to make
sure we don't meet any dangerous snakes. We probably
won't see any, anyway. But there will be lots of

crocodiles. They're usually more scared of us than we are of them. OK, any more questions? Tim?

Tim What birds will we see?

Sheila It's impossible to say what we'll see exactly, but we will get parrots and toucans for sure. OK, so let's ... yes, Paul?

Paul What about mosquitoes? I heard they can be dangerous?

Sheila Yes, there will be mosquitoes, so wear insect repellent. You might get some bites, but they certainly won't kill you. Of course, Paul, if you're really worried, you can stay at the hotel if you like.

8 **(a)** Rio de Janeiro, Ouro Preto, Foz do Iguaçu, Campo Grande, the Pantanal, Manaus

(b) 1 3, 4, 5, 8
2 1, 4, 5, 8, 10
3 5, 6, 7, 10
4 4, 5, 6, 7, 9

Unit check

1 2 shipwrecks 3 remains 4 discovered
5 bottom 6 cities 7 explore 8 wants to
9 works on 10 is making plans

2 2 a 3 c 4 c 5 a 6 b 7 a 8 b 9 c

3 2 I live in Green Street and my friend *lives* there too.
3 I *don't know* why George is angry.
4 Yesterday my friends *did not phone* me.
5 Jane *is watching* TV in her room.
6 Kate speaks French, but she *does not speak* Spanish.
7 At the moment, Dr Ballard *is working* on a new project.
8 Where *did you go* for a holiday last year?
9 *Do you live* round here?

2 That's an idea!

1 **(a)** 2 was dancing 3 were sitting
4 was drawing 5 were laughing
6 were kissing 7 was trying

(b) 2 weren't cooking 3 wasn't reading
4 wasn't having a shower 5 wasn't sleeping
6 weren't eating

(c) 2 Was Jenny reading a book? No, she wasn't. She was eating a sandwich.
3 Was Mike looking out of the window? Yes, he was.
4 Were my parents cooking dinner? No, they weren't. They were talking.
5 Was I watching TV? Yes, I was.
6 Were my grandparents eating dinner? No, they weren't. They were asleep/sleeping.

(d) 2 were you playing 3 were they going
4 were you talking 5 was he holding
6 was she waiting 7 was she eating

2 **(a)** traffic lights – driving – cat's eyes
typewriter – writing – biros
potatoes – eating – crisps
wig – hair – hair dye

(b) 2 the TV 3 the biro 4 traffic lights 5 crisps

(c) *Get* + noun
to school an idea a surprise an illness
home homework

Get + adjective
dry angry confused tired cold
close wet

(d) 2 get angry 3 got (very) confused
4 got (very) wet 5 got home
6 get dry 7 got a surprise

3 **(a)** 2 was having, rang 3 was watching, ate
4 stole, was swimming 5 fell, was playing
6 was sunbathing, jumped

(b) 2 While we were listening to music, the lights went off.
The lights went off when we were listening to music.
3 I lost my keys when I was running on the beach.
While I was running on the beach, I lost my keys.
4 Somebody stole my bag when I was talking to my friend.
While I was talking to my friend, somebody stole my bag.
5 Danny called when you were taking the dog for a walk.
While you were taking the dog for a walk, Danny called.
6 While I was getting ready for the beach, it started to rain.
It started to rain when I was getting ready for the beach.

(c) 2 When I came into the classroom today, the boys were having a fight.
3 While I was eating dinner last night, I talked to my parents.
4 While I was cleaning my teeth last night, the lights went out.
5 While I was doing my homework last night, I listened to some music.
6 When I left the house this morning, the sun was shining.

4 TAPESCRIPT/ANSWERS
1 **A:** I was <u>waiting</u> for you.
B: No, you weren't! You were <u>going</u> <u>without</u> me.
2 **A:** You <u>weren't</u> <u>crying</u>.
B: Yes, I <u>was</u>!
3 **A:** She was <u>sleeping</u>.
B: No, she <u>wasn't</u>! She was <u>reading</u>.
4 **A:** They were <u>kissing</u>.
B: No, they <u>weren't</u>! They were <u>dancing</u>.

5 A: We were <u>doing</u> our homework.
　B: No, you <u>weren't</u>! You were <u>playing games</u>.
6 A: I <u>wasn't writing</u> a letter.
　B: Yes, you <u>were</u>!

5 2 trousers　3 fabric　4 buttons　5 wear　6 casual
7 fashionable　8 styles　9 flared　10 patterns

6 <u>types</u>
jacket　shorts　trousers

<u>styles</u>
baggy

<u>parts of clothes</u>
zip　pockets

<u>material</u>
leather　lycra

7 (**b**) 4 F　5 F　6 T　7 F　8 N

8 2 a　3 c　4 a

TAPESCRIPT

1 **Boy** So the Menches brothers …
Girl What, the people who say they invented the hamburger?
Boy Yes. Well, they also say that once they were working at a fair, selling ice cream and at that time people ate ice cream from dishes. Anyway, it was so busy that they didn't have any more dishes, so Charles, one of the brothers, noticed a man who was selling this kind of sweet pastry. Menches tasted it, then got the idea of rolling it into the shape of a cone! He bought everything the man had.
Girl So that's how they invented the ice cream cone!

2 **Girl** I read another story on the Internet about 'Old Dave', another guy who said he invented the hamburger.
Boy So what was that about?
Girl Well, he said that he was selling chips with his hamburgers, except they didn't have a name for them then.
Boy Americans call them French fries, don't they?
Girl Well, yes, that's the point. A journalist asked Dave where he got the idea for his potatoes from, and he said 'Paris', meaning Paris, Texas. That's where he was from, you see.
Boy And the journalist thought he meant Paris, France?
Girl Exactly. So people started calling them French fries.
Boy That can't be true! No way!

3 **Girl** It's interesting, isn't it, how food got invented?
Boy Yes – and what about this one? In about 1750 – you know, hundreds of years ago – an important man in England was really very busy, so busy that he didn't have time for lunch, and he asked his cook just to put some meat between two pieces of bread! And so we got …
Girl Sandwiches?
Boy That's right.
Girl But why that name?

Boy Because the man in England was the Earl in a town called Sandwich.
Girl You're joking!
Boy No, I'm not – it's true!

4 **Girl** And did you ever hear about Thomas Adams?
Boy No. What about him?
Girl Well, he had some stuff called 'chicle' – a bit like rubber, you know? From trees in Mexico. And he tried to make car tyres with it, and he tried to make rubber shoes with it, but nothing worked.
Boy What has this got to do with food?
Girl Well, one day, he was thinking, and he put a piece of this 'chicle' in his mouth – and he started chewing it, and he liked it!
Boy Oh, no! Don't tell me! Chewing gum?
Girl That's right. He invented chewing gum! He started selling it in 1871.

Unit check

1 2 didn't hear　3 get　4 got to school
5 got a horrible surprise　6 got nervous　7 didn't get
8 was shining　9 was getting　10 got wet

2 2 b　3 c　4 a　5 c　6 a　7 a　8 a　9 c

3 2 While I was talking to Steve, it *started* to rain.
3 I think I *wrote* ten emails yesterday.
4 My father *was living* in Paris when he met my mother.
5 I was watching TV when my parents *got* home.
6 What *were* you doing when the phone rang?
7 I was cooking spaghetti when they *arrived*.
8 I was sitting in my room when I *heard* the phone.
9 Tom was getting hot, so he *took off* his jacket.

(3) She jumped well

1 (**a**) 2 the worst　3 the oldest　4 much tidier
　　5 older　6 the cleverest

(**b**) 2 fatter than　3 the happiest　4 the tallest
　　5 better than　6 further than
　　7 more boring than　8 the most successful

(**c**) 2 It's a bit/little colder today than it was yesterday.
　　3 A Ferrari is much/far/a lot faster than a Fiat.
　　4 Mr James is much/far/a lot older than Mrs James.
　　5 Steve is a bit/a little lighter than Harry.

2 (**a**) 2 quiet　3 fast　4 fat　5 boring　6 cold
　　7 beautiful　8 brilliant　9 tidy
　　Mystery word: difficult

(**b**) easy

3 (**a**) 2 e　3 a　4 b　5 f　6 c

(**b**) 2 John isn't as tall as Mike.
　　3 The TV isn't as expensive as the computer.
　　4 The cat isn't as thin as the dog.
　　5 Arsenal isn't as good as Liverpool.
　　6 Today is as cold as yesterday.

4 **(a)** 2 slowly 3 easily 4 happily 5 fast 6 badly
7 well 8 far

(b) 2 He had to run fast.
3 He drives very slowly.
4 He doesn't write clearly.
5 My secretary types quickly.
6 I did the test easily.

(c) Paul 1.7m, £50, F, 4th
David 1.5m, £200, B, 1st
Fred 1.6m, £100, A, 2nd
Richard 1.8m, £500, C, 3rd

5 **(a)** TAPESCRIPT/ANSWERS
1 as good as gold
2 as black as night
3 as quick as a fox
4 as soon as I know
5 as fast as I can
6 as white as snow

6 Stop it   hold on   I'm off

7 **(b)** 1 a 2 c 3 d 4 f 5 e 6 b

8 2 b 3 a

TAPESCRIPT

James I guess you had a great time, eh, Phil?
Phil Well, yes – I mean, the World Cup Final!
My dad and I really enjoyed it!
James What did you enjoy most?
Phil Well, you know, it was a really good game, you know,
good football really, and Ronaldo's second goal was
fantastic, but the best thing for me was the fans, the
Brazilians, all the drums and music – it was great to be
there with them, dancing and singing.
James What did you do at the end of the match?
Phil Well, we decided to stay a bit – you know, we saw
the Brazilians getting the World Cup and everything,
we didn't leave the stadium until about an hour after
the game had finished!
James Wow!
Phil And by then we were pretty hungry, and my dad
wanted to go to a Japanese restaurant for some sushi,
but I don't really like sushi, so we just walked a bit and
then went back to our hotel on the Underground and
got some food there.
James That's a bit boring, isn't it?
Phil Not really – I mean, there were Brazilian fans
celebrating in the hotel too! Lots more music and
singing …

POSSIBLE ANSWER

It was 10pm and I was worried because I was late for the party.
I got in my car and drove as fast as I could to the party.
Suddenly, I saw a dog run into the road. I tried to stop, but
I lost control of the car and hit a tree.

Writing tip
Version 2 is more interesting because it contains more
description, such as adverbs and adjectives.
1 *It was a fantastic experience; … thousands of happy*
people; … couldn't wait to get to our seats.
2 adjectives: *fantastic, excited, huge, modern, happy.*
adverbs: *really, loudly.*
3 linking words: *so, and.*
4 *them; inside.*

9 POSSIBLE ANSWERS
1 She walked slowly into the room and sat down heavily
in the chair.
2 My alarm clock didn't ring so I was late for work.
3 The meal was delicious/fantastic.
4 My favourite restaurant is an Italian one. It's the best
in town.

Unit check

1 2 difficult 3 quiet 4 tidy 5 near 6 easy
7 boring 8 new 9 young

2 2 c 3 a 4 a 5 c 6 b 7 a 8 c 9 a

3 2 I think ice hockey is one of *the most* dangerous sports.
3 You are *taller than* me.
4 Her work is really *good.*
5 Carol is *the tidiest* girl in our class.
6 The film on Sunday was *more interesting than* this film.
7 Wait a minute! I can't run *as fast as* you!
8 My pronunciation is *terrible.*
9 That new laptop isn't *as expensive as* I thought.
10 I think this is *the worst* CD of all time!

4 Our world

1 **(a)** b 4 c 1 d 6 e 5 f 2

(b) 2 P 3 C 4 P 5 C 6 P 7 P

(c) 2 a 3 b 4 d 5 c 6 e 7 f

(d) 2 might go 3 might not do 4 'll be
5 might not take 6 might have 7 won't do
8 'll be

2 **(a)** 2 fumes 3 pollution 4 atmosphere
5 power station 6 recycling 7 rubbish 8 litter

(b) 2 f 3 b 4 a 5 g 6 d 7 e

(c) 2 forests 3 pollution 4 fumes 5 warming
6 litter 7 picking 8 clean 9 rubbish
10 recycle

3 **(a)** 2 cut down 3 will rise 4 goes up
5 will start 6 won't get 7 dies 8 will be

(b) 2 If I'm good, will you buy me a present?
3 If I see James, I'll give him your message.
4 If it rains, they will arrive late.

5 What will you do if he doesn't phone?
6 My sister will lend me her mobile if I ask her.
7 If you haven't got any money, I'll give you some.

(c) 2 unless   3 if   4 if   5 if   6 unless

4 TAPESCRIPT/ANSWERS
1 They won't come.
2 They want to go to bed.
3 I won't be here.
4 So you want to play squash?
5 I think you might be right.
6 You said you're my teacher.

5 2 pollute the atmosphere   3 will disappear
4 too dangerous   5 solar energy   6 from the sea
7 hydro-electric dams

6 (b) *Environment* is a noun and *environmental* is an adjective.

(c) Noun
pollution   increase   warming   recycling

Verb
pollute   waste   recycle

Adjective
energetic   powerful   wasteful   warm

7 2 ✓   3 ✓   4 ✗   5 ✗   6 ✓

TAPESCRIPT

Aunt June So, what's your school like, Mike? I mean, I know you like sports – has the school got good facilities?
Mike Oh, yeah. There's a really good gym, and really big sports fields. The sports facilities are great!
Aunt June Do you have lunch at school?
Mike Yes, I do – and actually, the food is pretty good. It's the usual things, you know: hamburgers, pizzas, chips, that kind of thing, but I like it!
Aunt June OK, good. But tell me about the teachers!
Mike Ah, the teachers! Well, you know, you can't have a school without teachers! And the teachers at our school, they're OK. I mean, some are better than others, of course, but most of the teachers are nice.
Aunt June Good!
Mike But the problem is, I think the lessons are too short. All the lessons are 45 minutes. Well, sometimes we get double lessons, an hour and a half, but 45 minutes really is too short, I think.
Aunt June That's interesting! Not many students at school complain about the lessons being too short! What else don't you like?
Mike Hmmm. Well, I think the uniform's awful! Green and black! It's horrible. And I hate wearing ties – and of course we have to wear a green and black tie.
Aunt June And I'm sure you hate the school rules too!
Mike Actually, no. The rules are OK. You know, the usual things: no running in corridors, no mobile phones in the classroom, things like that. But I think the rules are OK.
Aunt June Wow! So it seems like it's not a bad school.

8 (a) 1 lessons, facilities, meals
2 Write to school website, say what's wrong and suggest a solution.
3 100 Euros

Writing tip
2 Secondly ...   3 Perhaps ...   4 Some people ...
5 Finally ...

Jennifer starts her second idea with 'secondly'.

She starts her last main idea with 'finally'.

She gives examples of other activities by using 'perhaps' and 'some people ...'.

She introduces her closing sentence with 'to sum up'.

Unit check
1 2 fumes   3 pollute   4 will   5 may not   6 renewable energy   7 atmosphere   8 litter   9 waste   10 recycle

2 2 b   3 c   4 c   5 c   6 b   7 b   8 a   9 b

3 2 I won't have time unless Kate *helps* me.
3 Do you think people in the future *will have* cars?
4 If pollution increases, more animals *might die* out.
5 If you don't say you're sorry, Jane *may be* angry.
6 If we *do not* use more renewable energy, we'll soon run out of oil.
7 I think that in the future, we *won't* drive cars.
8 I *might* go to Spain on holiday this year, but I'm not sure.
9 Scientists think there *will be* more climate changes in the future.

(5) Canada and the USA

1 (a) 2 aren't we?   3 can't she?   4 didn't they?
5 doesn't he?   6 can she?   7 did they?
8 haven't they?

(b) 3 ✓   4 ✗ doesn't he?   5 ✗ didn't you?
6 ✓   7 ✓   8 ✗ hasn't she?   9 ✓

(c) 2 didn't you?   3 aren't you?   4 won't you?
5 isn't he?   6 can't he?   7 is it?   8 shouldn't you?

2 TAPESCRIPT/ANSWERS

(a) (b)
1 aren't you? D
2 aren't you? U
3 doesn't she? U
4 do they? U
5 can't I? D
6 won't you? U

3 (a) **British:** pavement   lift   trousers   underground   flat   rubbish
North American: sidewalk   elevator   pants   subway   apartment   garbage

(b) 2 lift 3 underground 4 vacation
5 pants 6 sidewalk

(c) 1 colour 2 theatre 3 kilometre 4 travelling

4 (a) Past simple
was/were began came drank ate went
knew saw wrote

Past participle
been begun come drunk eaten gone
known seen written

(b) 2 f 3 a 4 d 5 b 6 e

(c) 2 yet 3 already 4 yet 5 yet 6 already

(d) 1 B: I've already eaten the hamburger, but I
haven't finished the vegetables yet.

2 A: Has Maria already gone to Sally's house?
B: Yes, but she hasn't come back yet.

3 A: I've already bought the new Green Day CD.
B: Really? Have you listened to it yet?

4 A: Have you gone to sleep yet?
B: No! And you have already asked me
three times!

5 (a) 2 I've just phoned Jenny.
3 We've just arrived.
4 My parents have just gone out.
5 The film's just finished.

(b) 2 She's just bought an ice cream, but she hasn't
eaten it yet.
3 He's just written a letter but he hasn't posted it yet.
4 She's just bought a new CD, but she hasn't
listened to it yet.

6 2 Sure 3 Off we go! 4 hold on 5 Nice one

8 (a) 1 lift ✓ 3 taps ✓ 4 petrol ✓ 7 lorry ✓

TAPESCRIPT

Josh ... and American people are really friendly, very nice
– only we had a few problems understanding them
sometimes!
Sally Really? Why? Because they use different words?
Josh Well, sometimes – like, for example, we went to a
restaurant the first night in New York, and at the end
my dad asked for the bill and the waiter looked at him
and said, 'Oh, you mean the check. OK, sir'!
Sally Uh huh.
Josh And of course in the hotels you see signs for
elevators, not lifts, and in the bathrooms and toilets
there are signs that ask you to turn off the faucets.
Sally Faucets?
Josh Yeah, you know on basins, what the British
call 'taps'.
Sally Really? I didn't know that one.
Josh Yeah, and you know we rented a car for a few days?
Well, when we went to fill the car with petrol, my mum
asked for petrol and of course the guy didn't understand.

Sally They call it 'gas', don't they?
Josh That's right. And then of course there are things
like trucks.
Sally What we here in Britain call 'lorries', yeah?
Josh Yeah, but the American ones are huge: they're
about 20 metres long and have got twenty wheels or
something!
Sally And Americans certainly do pronounce things
differently, too, don't they ...

(b) bill – check
tap – faucet
petrol – gas
lorry – truck

Unit check

1 2 popular 3 Have you heard 4 yet 5 wicked
6 apartment 7 already 8 subway 9 garbage
10 nice one

2 2 b 3 c 4 c 5 a 6 a 7 a 8 a 9 c

3 2 She's just come home but she *hasn't eaten* yet.
3 Don't worry! *I've already cooked* your dinner.
4 It wasn't your Maths teacher, *was* it?
5 They love tennis, *don't they*?
6 I have just *done* my homework.
7 You have already *eaten* everything!
8 Paddy didn't phone, *did* he?
9 I don't want to see the film – *I've* already *seen* it.

(6) Growing up

1 (a) 2 is grown 3 is visited 4 's written 5 are made
6 are visited 7 are written 8 are grown

(b) 2 Portuguese is spoken in Brazil.
3 My watch is made of gold.
4 The World Cup is held every four years.
5 Many different things are sold here.
6 How many pizzas are eaten every day?

(c) 2 e 3 b 4 f 5 a 6 c

(d) 2 Foreign money is changed here.
3 Colour films are developed here.
4 Fresh food is served here.
5 Cameras are repaired here.
6 English lessons are given here.

(e) 2 A new computer is sold every day.
3 Computer programs are designed in that
company.
4 Mistakes are made in grammar exercises.
5 A lot of new houses are built every year.
6 Football is often played on Saturdays.

2 (a) 1 baby 2 toddler 3 child 4 teenager
5 adult 6 pensioner

(b) 2 baby 3 child 4 teenager 5 pensioner
6 toddler

3 (a) 1 We're not allowed to   2 I'm not allowed to
3 You're not allowed to   4 doesn't let   5 don't let
6 doesn't let

(b) 1 aren't allowed to
2 aren't allowed to
3 are allowed to
4 aren't allowed to
5 am allowed to
6 aren't allowed to

(c) 2 My parents don't let me stay in bed late
at the weekend.
3 My brother lets me ride his bike.
4 Our parents let us invite our friends to our house.
5 Our head teacher doesn't let us use
our mobile phones inside the school.
6 I don't let our dog come into my bedroom.

(d) 2 We are allowed to wear jeans to school.
3 We aren't allowed to run in the school corridor.
4 My sister lets our cat sleep on her bed.
5 My parents let me put posters on my wall.
6 Teenagers aren't allowed to go into that club.

4 (a) TAPESCRIPT/ANSWERS
know, show, low, throw, go /əʊ/
now, sound, loud, round, shout, town, house, down,
allowed /aʊ/

5 4 seventeen   5 sixteen   6 New York   7 vote
8 twenty   9 China

6 (c) /maʊs/ /ðəʊ/ /streɪt/ /kəʊm/

7 (a) He's inviting her to his birthday party.

(b) No, she can't.

(c) 2 F   3 T   4 T   5 F   6 T

Unit check

1 2 baby   3 given   4 toddler   5 child   6 let
7 adult   8 allowed to   9 get married   10 pensioner

2 2 a   3 a   4 b   5 b   6 a   7 c   8 a   9 b

3 2 My father *doesn't let* me stay up late during the week.
3 Last week *I didn't let* my little sister use my camera.
4 You *aren't allowed* to play football here.
5 Thousands of people *are killed* in car accidents
every year.
6 Ice cream *is made* with a lot of sugar.
7 At my school we are not allowed *to eat* in class.
8 My dad always lets me *use* his squash racket.
9 Are they *allowed* to wear jeans?

7 Have a laugh!

1 (a) 2 I've had my bike for two years. ✓
I have my bike for two years. ✗
3 A: How long are you here? ✗
B: Since eight o'clock.
A: How long have you been here? ✓
B: Since eight o'clock.
4 I haven't been to school since last week. ✓
I haven't been to school for last week. ✗
5 My mum has worked here for three months. ✓
My mum has worked here since three months. ✗
6 I've seen that film three times. ✓
I see that film three times. ✗

(b) 2 has been   3 has had   4 have told
5 have helped   6 has asked   7 have arranged

(c) 2 How long have you had it?
3 How long has she been there?
4 How long has he worked there?
5 How long have they been there?

(d) 2 loves / has taken
3 have had / don't play
4 has worked / enjoys
5 have bought / prefer

(e) 2 has lived   3 loves   4 is   5 plays
6 has not played   7 want   8 has got   9 hope

2 (a) 2 since Saturday / for two days
3 since yesterday / for 24 hours
4 for six months / since last July
5 since last weekend / for a week
6 since I was 11 / for a very long time

(b) 2 They have lived in this house since 1998.
They have lived in this house for … years.
3 I have been ill for three days.
I have been ill since Sunday.
4 My aunt has had her car since 2001.
My aunt has had her car for … years.
5 We have had this computer since 1999.
We have had this computer for … years.

(c) 2 They haven't played football for two weeks.
3 He hasn't cut it / had it cut for three months.
4 I haven't been out since yesterday.
5 My girlfriend hasn't phoned me since Saturday.
6 I haven't seen a good film for a long time.

3 (a) TAPESCRIPT/ANSWERS
1 <u>Where</u> have you <u>been</u>?
2 How <u>long</u> has he <u>been</u> <u>there</u>?
3 My <u>parents</u> have <u>bought</u> a new car.
4 <u>James</u> has gone <u>home</u>.

(b) TAPESCRIPT/ANSWERS
1 He's been here for <u>ages</u>.
2 We've <u>lived</u> here for <u>a</u> <u>long</u> <u>time</u>.

3 I've <u>had</u> this bike for <u>three</u> <u>months</u>.
4 We <u>haven't</u> <u>eaten</u> for <u>two</u> <u>hours</u>.

4 2 had   3 made   4 made   5 had   6 making
7 made   8 made

5 2 I reckon   3 to be honest   4 I see   5 get a move on

6 (**b**) has been interested in computing since he was 12
has already written
has been his teacher

7 1 b   2 a   3 b   4 a   5 c

Unit check

1 2 make me   3 for   4 makes fun   5 fun   6 time
7 made fools   8 funny faces   9 haven't   10 since

2 2 c   3 b   4 a   5 a   6 b   7 a   8 c   9 a

3 2 I *have lived* in this house for three years.
3 She's had her dog *since* last Christmas.
4 I haven't seen him *for* two years.
5 They love making fools *of themselves*.
6 Don't make fun *of her*. It isn't fair!
7 I think you *made* a mistake when you told your mother.
8 Sarah and Tricia *have been* my friends for many years.
9 You *have told* me that five times since last week!

(8) A great film!

1 (**a**) 2 My sister prefers going to the cinema.
3 He promised to come to my party.
4 I don't mind cooking.
5 My cousin is learning to drive.
6 We offered to do the washing-up.
7 Our teacher decided to give us a test.
8 My friend can't stand watching films on video.
9 My brother always refuses to do the washing-up.
10 I agreed to let him use my computer.

(**b**) 2 helping   3 to help   4 washing   5 playing
6 to wait   7 to wash   8 waiting   9 to play
10 to speak

(**c**) 2 enjoy studying   3 decided to buy   4 promise to
be   5 refuses to lend   6 offered to buy
7 want to live   8 doesn't mind doing   9 prefers
swimming / prefers to swim   10 can't stand
getting up

(**d**) 2 can't stand washing-up   3 offer to help
4 don't mind going   5 prefer watching
6 learning to drive   7 hope to   8 promise to come

2 (**a**) a 6   b 8   c 1   d 4   e 3   f 2   g 7   h 5

(**b**) 2 thriller   3 western   4 romance   5 comedy
6 science fiction   7 action   8 drama

(**c**) 2 about   3 storyline   4 soundtrack   5 actor
6 acting   7 special effects   8 set   9 director
10 ending

4 2 luxury hotels   3 private yachts   4 magazines
5 paparazzi   6 goldfish bowl   7 cosmetic surgery
8 marriages

5 (**b**) TAPESCRIPT/ANSWERS
1 <u>spec</u>ial   2 <u>eff</u>ects   3 pre<u>fer</u>   4 <u>prom</u>ise
5 <u>mag</u>azine   6 <u>act</u>ress   7 <u>sound</u>track   8 <u>thrill</u>er
9 de<u>sign</u>er

6 (**a**) The film, *Gangs of New York*, directed by Martin
Scorsese, is almost three hours long. It stars Leonardo
DiCaprio, Cameron Diaz, Daniel Day-Lewis and Liam
Neeson.
It's about gangs of men in the streets of New York, in
the middle of the nineteenth century.
Di Caprio plays the role of Amsterdam, a boy who saw
his father killed by Butcher Bill, played by Day-Lewis.
Amsterdam comes back to New York many years later,
looking for a way to kill Butcher Bill. When he is in
New York he falls in love with Jennie, played by
Cameron Diaz.

7 a 5, 8, 4   b 1, 7, 2   c 2, 6   d 5, 3, 4

TAPESCRIPT

A **Teenage boy 1** What do I like in a film? Well, I think
the most important thing for me is that a film has to
have a good plot! You know, a storyline that interests
me, that makes me want to know what's going to
happen in the end. Oh, and I like happy endings too!
Things that aren't important to me
are things like special effects, you know? I don't care
about that. And I don't care who the actors are – but
of course, good acting is very important for me, if
I'm going to really enjoy a film.

B **Teenage girl 1** What's important for me in a film?
Well, I like films with my favourite actors, of course
– famous actors and actresses like Nicole Kidman,
Brad Pitt, those people. So I really liked *Gangs of
New York*. Leonardo DiCaprio and Cameron Diaz –
wow! Erm, and I like lots of action in a film, and
special effects too – that's why I love the James
Bond films. Well, I like them because of Pierce
Brosnan too, of course! So that's it – famous actors,
lots of action, good special effects, and I'm happy!

C **Teenage boy 2** Well, actually, I'm not really into films
that much. I don't go to the cinema very often.
When I do go, you know, with some friends from
school, the things I really like are the special effects
and the photography. Some films have got great
special effects, and I love that – and I really like
seeing beautiful things that have been well
photographed, you know? I don't care much about
the acting or the story, to be honest, and I don't
know the names of many actors or actresses, but
I enjoy the photography and the effects!

D **Teenage girl 2** If I'm going to enjoy a film, well, then it's got to have a really good story. I love romantic films, you know? And, erm, I think it's important for a film to have a good soundtrack – I like good music while the film's going on. So those two things are important: good story and music. And I guess the other thing that's important for me is good acting. It doesn't matter if the actors and actresses are famous or if they're completely new – there has to be good acting.

Unit check

1 2 getting 3 like 4 watching 5 imagine 6 going
7 refuse 8 walking 9 to go 10 to get

2 2 c 3 a 4 c 5 a 6 b 7 a 8 b 9 c

3 2 Nick doesn't mind *talking* on the phone for hours.
3 Nick really hates *tidying* his room.
4 I wanted *to go* to the cinema, so I called my friends.
5 You can go if you promise *to be* back soon.
6 My parents can't stand *listening* to loud music.
7 Our cat refuses *to eat* meat.
8 You promised *to help* me, Jane.
9 I don't mind *doing* housework sometimes.

9 Disaster!

1 **a** 2 broken 3 heard 4 sent 5 spoken 6 lost
7 found 8 given

b 2 was killed 3 was stolen 4 was found
5 arrived 6 were interviewed 7 wasn't invented
8 were sold

c 2 The telephone was invented by Alexander Graham Bell.
3 The Harry Potter stories were written by J.K. Rowling.
4 The 2002 World Cup was won by Brazil.
5 The first aeroplane was flown by the Wright brothers.
6 The Titanic was sunk by an iceberg in 1912.
7 La Gioconda was painted by Leonardo da Vinci.
8 The Great Pyramids were built by the ancient Egyptians.

d 2 are broken 3 are damaged 4 was hit 5 were damaged 6 was destroyed 7 were killed 8 were introduced 9 are built

e 2 100,000 soldiers were killed in the war.
3 The door was left open last night.
4 All the books were printed on time.
5 The main railway station was closed yesterday.
6 All my money was stolen.
7 My suitcase was taken to my room.

f 2 lived 3 appeared 4 was pushed 5 was given
6 were killed 7 produced 8 travelled 9 made
10 was heard 11 were thrown 12 produced

2 TAPESCRIPT/ANSWERS
1 k<u>n</u>ows, an<u>sw</u>er 2 <u>w</u>rote, <u>wr</u>ong 3 Li<u>st</u>en, an<u>sw</u>ers
4 cli<u>mb</u>ing, bu<u>i</u>lding 5 bu<u>i</u>lt, ca<u>st</u>le

3 2 avalanche 3 killed 4 damage 5 wave 6 volcano
7 fire 8 injured 9 sea 10 bomb 11 destroyed

4 **a** 2 an 3 an 4 an 5 a 6 an, a

b 2 a 3 the 4 a 5 a 6 the 7 the 8 a
9 The 10 a 11 the 12 the 13 the

c 2 the 3 a 4 an 5 a 6 the 7 the 8 the
9 an 10 an 11 a 12 the

5 2 sort of 3 I reckon 4 got a point 5 get rid of

7 2 Edo (Japan), 1710, 200,000
3 Lisbon (Portugal), 1755, 80,000
4 Quito (Ecuador), 1797, 40,000
5 Shaanxi (China), 1556, 800,000

TAPESCRIPT

Dr Harris ... but that's dollars in 1906, not dollars today. So, you can see, the San Francisco earthquake was a really terrible event – one of the worst in history.
Interviewer But not the worst? What do we know about other terrible earthquakes?
Dr Harris Well, we know that there were earthquakes before now – I mean, before our times – but of course we don't know exactly how big they were and how many people died.
Interviewer But do we know about some of them?
Dr Harris Well, we have a good idea. For example, there was an earthquake in Sicily, in southern Italy, in 1693. We think 60,000 people died. Then in about 1710 – er, we don't know for sure – in Japan, there was a city called Edo, where Tokyo now is, and ... erm ... we believe that 200,000 people or so were killed.
Interviewer That's incredible. 200,000?
Dr Harris Yes, that's right. Erm ... other great earthquakes ... erm ... well, the city of Lisbon, in Portugal, erm, in 1755, it was hit very badly, erm, about 80,000 people died. And in 1797, in Quito, in Ecuador, over 40,000 people were killed.
Interviewer So the one in Japan was the most terrible ever?
Dr Harris Well, no. There was an earthquake in 1556, in China, in an area called Shaanxi ... erm ... There are records, you know. China's a very advanced civilisation, and ... erm ... we think that the number of people who were killed was about 800,000.
Interviewer Good heavens! 800,000!!
Dr Harris Yes indeed. It was probably the worst ever natural disaster to ...

8 **a** 1 Harry Truman
2 Mount St Helens, Washington
3 He was killed by the volcanic lava.
4 84

(b) 1 Students' own answers.

2 No, probably because sending a helicopter would have been too dangerous for the rescue team.

Unit check

1 2 killed 3 avalanche 4 earthquakes 5 wave
6 injure 7 floods 8 lose 9 volcano 10 destroy

2 2 c 3 c 4 a 5 b 6 c 7 a 8 b 9 c

3 2 When was the Golden Gate Bridge *built*?
3 A house in the city centre was *destroyed* by fire.
4 *Romeo and Juliet* was *written* by Shakespeare.
5 A lot of money was *lost* in the big earthquake.
6 This song *was* written by the Beatles in 1968.
7 These houses *were* built many years ago.
8 *Was* the fire started by a cigarette?
9 No, I haven't got *a* Walkman.

(10) A place to stay

1 **(a)** 2 Be quiet, please! There's too much noise in here.
3 I think we get too many tests at school.
4 Jack was sick because he ate too much ice cream yesterday.
5 I put too much sugar in my coffee.
6 You always ask me too many questions!

(b) 2 isn't enough 3 isn't enough
4 aren't enough 5 aren't enough
6 aren't enough

(c) 2 too many, not enough 3 too much, not enough
4 too many, not enough 5 not enough, too many

2 **(a)** TAPESCRIPT/ANSWERS
/ɔf/ cough
/ʌf/ tough, enough
/uː/ through

3 **(a)** 2 chimney 3 TV aerial 4 garden 5 door
6 roof 7 garage

(b) 2 housing 3 chimney 4 garden 5 stairs
6 floor 7 cottage 8 window
The mystery word is 'bungalow'.

4 **(a)** 2 Qinghai 3 tents 4 month 5 jumpers
6 walking boots 7 three weeks 8 send his gran a postcard

(b) 3 B 4 A 5 A 6 B 7 B 8 A

(c) 2 f 3 b 4 d 5 e 6 a

(d) 2 I'll watch 3 my dad's going to buy
4 We're going to visit 5 I'll phone
6 I'll take 7 I'll do

5 **(a)** 2 *Crocodile Dundee* 3 18 4 Adelaide
5 barbecues 6 has got 7 cousins 8 the insects

(b) 2 sport 3 different 4 outside 5 relaxed
6 talk 7 British 8 warm 9 way

6 **(b)** 3 N 4 V 5 V 6 N 7 N 8 V 9 N 10 V

7 **(a)** There are seven rooms.

(b) 1 F 2 F 3 T 4 T 5 F 6 F 7 T

Unit check

1 2 semi-detached 3 garage 4 garden 5 too much
6 floor 7 chimney 8 housing 9 detached 10 enough

2 2 b 3 a 4 b 5 b 6 a 7 c 8 b 9 a

3 2 He can't come with us. He hasn't *got much/enough* time.
3 I'm really happy because *we're going* to the zoo tomorrow.
4 I'm tired. I think *I'll* go to bed.
5 That bag's heavy. *I'll* carry it for you.
6 I can't buy that shirt – I haven't got *enough money*.
7 We couldn't get on the bus – there were too *many* people.
8 Next year, *we're* going to visit my uncle in France.
9 There *aren't* enough houses in our city.

(11) Your mind

1 **(a)** 1 everything 2 nothing 3 someone 4 no one
5 nowhere 6 somewhere 7 all of them

(b) 2 Some of them 3 somewhere 4 nowhere
5 everything 6 nothing 7 no one 8 none of them

(c) 2 no one 3 all of them 4 everywhere
5 someone 6 something 7 none of them
8 nowhere

(d) 2 is 3 are 4 is 5 was 6 have 7 knows
8 was

2 **(a)** 2 forget 3 memory 4 memorise 5 brain
6 mind
The mystery word is 'remind'.

(b) 2 memorable 3 memorise 4 memory 5 mind
6 remind

(c) 2 visual 3 musical 4 mathematical 5 verbal
6 interpersonal

3 **(a)** 2 must 3 mustn't 4 mustn't 5 mustn't
6 must 7 must

(b) 1 b i 2 a ii b i 3 a ii b i 4 a i b ii

(c) 2 mustn't 3 mustn't 4 doesn't have to 5 mustn't
6 don't have to

(d) 2 doesn't have to 3 don't have to 4 mustn't
5 mustn't 6 doesn't have to 7 mustn't

5 2 mates 3 wonder 4 never mind 5 sort of 6 come on

Writing tip

The boy forgot the date of his father's birthday and also the CD his father wanted.

2 then   3 after that   4 in the end   5 finally   6 then

7 **(a)** 1 d 2 b 3 e 4 a 5 c

(b) Jane uses *suddenly*, *then*, *after that*, and *in the end* in her story.

TAPESCRIPT

Mack Hi Jane, what's the matter? You look like you've had an awful day!

Jane I have! It's been terrible!

Mack Why? What happened?

Jane Well, this morning I was walking to school and I was almost there, and suddenly I remembered that today's Friday.

Mack So?

Jane Well, Friday's the day we have swimming practice at school – and I'd forgotten my swimming costume, so I had to run back home to get it. Then, when I got home, I couldn't remember where my costume was. It took me about fifteen minutes to find it.

Mack So you were late for school?

Jane Yes. The teacher had a real go at me when I got there! And you know, after that, things got even worse!

Mack Worse?

Jane Yes – in the afternoon there was an English test, and I hadn't done any revision for it.

Mack Why not?

Jane Well, to be honest, I didn't remember that we had a test! Well, in the end it was OK – I think – I mean, I think I didn't do too badly.

Mack Well, never mind. Anyway, I'll see you at Tony's birthday party tonight, OK?

Jane What? Oh, no! Tony's birthday! And I haven't bought him a present!

Mack Oh, dear – you have got a bad memory!

Unit check

1 2 remember 3 some of them 4 someone 5 imagine 6 forget 7 memorise 8 bad memory 9 remembers 10 remind

2 2 a 3 a 4 a 5 c 6 a 7 c 8 a 9 b

3 2 Maria *doesn't* have to study – she remembers everything.
3 You *don't have to* cook. There are lots of sandwiches left.
4 My room's very messy – there are clothes and books *everywhere*!
5 I invited lots of friends, but *no one* came. I was all alone!
6 Please can you remind me *to* phone John this evening?
7 It's really warm outside. You *don't have to* put three pullovers on!
8 My visual memory is excellent, so I *remember* pictures easily.
9 Please *remind* me to give you back the money.

12 Music makers

1 **(a)** b 5 c 1 d 6 e 4 f 2

(b) 2 Have you been trying to phone me?
3 It has / It's been raining for ten days.
4 I've been tidying up since eight thirty.
5 I've been using a digital camera since 1998.
6 What has / What's she been doing? I think she's been running.

(c) 2 I have / I've been working really hard.
3 The sun has /The sun's been shining all day.
4 She has not / She hasn't been studying hard enough.
5 You have / You've been eating all morning.
6 Have you been waiting long?
7 Has he cleaned his car?

2 **(a)** TAPESCRIPT/ANSWERS
1 A: How <u>long</u> have you been <u>waiting</u>?
   B: I've been <u>waiting</u> for <u>three hours</u>.
2 A: <u>Where's</u> she been <u>living</u>?
   B: She's been <u>living</u> in <u>London</u>.
3 A: What's he been <u>doing</u>?
   B: He's been <u>looking</u> for a new <u>flat</u>.

3 **(a)** 2 a 3 f 4 b 5 e 6 c

(b) 2 a ✓ b ✗ 3 a ✓ b ✗ 4 a ✓ b ✗
5 a ✓ b ✗ 6 a ✗ b ✓

(c) 2 My brother has always wanted to meet your sister.
3 I hope my teacher won't be angry. I've forgotten my homework.
4 Great! I've done all my homework. Now I can watch TV.
5 She's awful. She has / She's been talking about herself all evening.
6 He's written four emails this morning.
7 My father has / My father's been using the computer since eight o'clock this morning!

(d) 2 twenty 3 has he lived 4 thirty-five
5 has he made? 6 thirty 7 has he been married?
8 has he been working

(e) 3 I've won the lottery!
4 He's crashed/dented his parents' car.
5 He's been playing computer games.
6 He's been running.

4 **(a)** 2 folk 3 heavy metal 4 classical 5 jazz, reggae

(b) 2 clarinet 3 violin 4 saxophone 5 trumpet
6 flute 7 drums 8 guitar 9 keyboards

(c) 2 personal stereo 3 live 4 hi-fi 5 singles

5 2 F 3 F 4 F 5 F 6 F 7 T

6 2 b 3 e 4 a 5 d

7 a 6 b 3 c 2 d 5

Unit check

1 2 has been collecting   3 has collected   4 singer
5 listen   6 have been playing   7 plays   8 drums
9 rock   10 saxophone

2 2 c   3 c   4 b   5 b   6 b   7 c   8 c   9 b

3 2 Maria *has* been learning the flute for a month.
3 Claire's *been* at home for a month.
4 How long *have you* been waiting here?
5 He's *been* talking on the phone for an hour.
6 Sue and Cath *have been* riding their bikes for two hours.
7 Hi Mum. Has Peter *phoned* this morning?
8 How many CDs have U2 *made*?
9 You look tired. What have you *been doing*?

(13) Doctor's orders

1 (**a**) b 1   c 4   d 6   e 3   f 2

(**b**) 2 hospital   3 painful   4 health   5 patients
6 tablet   7 treat   8 hurts

(**c**) 2 hurt   3 temperature   4 stomach ache
5 sore   6 pain

2 (**a**) 2 who   3 which   4 where   5 who   6 who
7 where

(**b**) 2 where   3 that/which   4 that/which
5 who   6 that/which   7 where   8 who

(**c**) 2 d   Robert Ballard is the man who found the
Titanic.
3 a   N'gol is a ceremony that/which boys on
Pentecost Island take part in.
4 g   A leech is a creature that/which sucks blood.
5 b   San Francisco was the city that/which had a
terrible earthquake in 1906.
6 c   Budapest was the city where Laszlo Biro
invented the ballpoint pen.
7 e   Longhouses are buildings that/which the Iban
people live in.

3 (**a**) 2 We often used to go to the park.
3 That shop used to be very cheap.
4 My father used to play the guitar in a band.
5 My brother didn't use to enjoy Maths.
6 Did you use to have bad dreams?

(**b**) 2 used to like, eat
3 used to play, don't play
4 used to be, is
5 didn't use to go, go
6 loves, used to hate
7 didn't use to read, read
8 Did you use to go, stay

(**c**) 2 She used to go to bed at 9pm but now she goes
at 11pm.
3 She used to watch TV but now she reads a lot.

4 She used to play tennis but now she plays
football.
5 She didn't use to like dancing but now she loves it.
6 She didn't use to like Maths but now she does.

4 (**a**) TAPESCRIPT/ANSWERS
1 We used the Internet to find the information.
2 I used to go to bed early when I was young.
3 Who used my personal stereo?
4 My dad used to work in an office.
5 Did he use to play tennis?
6 Did she use my bike?

5 2 ended up with   3 you're kidding   4 never mind
5 hang on to

7 1 b   2 c   3 a   4 a   5 c   6 b

TAPESCRIPT

1 **Woman 1** I'm really sorry I'm late. I missed the
bus to the airport and I had to take a taxi.
Man 1 Oh, don't worry. The plane's delayed
anyway. Look, why don't we go and have a drink
before we check in for our flight?
Woman 1 Good idea.

2 **Teenage boy 1** Got a pen you can lend me?
Teenage girl 1 You know, it's strange – you've
never got a pen! Can't you afford them?
Teenage boy 1 Ha, ha. Come on, just lend me a
pen, OK?

3 **Woman 2** Hello. Can I help you with anything?
Teenage boy 2 Erm … yes, I saw in an article that
I was reading that it's possible to buy trainers
for children – with little lights in them.
Woman 2 Yes, that's right, but I'm afraid we
haven't got any at the moment. We should have
more next week.

4 **Man 2** Excuse me. I'm looking for a shop called
'Fun Reading'.
Woman 3 Oh, yes. Is that the place where you
can get children's books?
Man 2 That's the one. I want to get something
for my daughter to take to school.
Woman 3 Well, I think it's in Baker Street – that's
just over there …

5 **Man 3** Well, not long now and we'll be at the
airport. Are you OK in the back there, Jenny?
Teenage girl 2 Not really, Dad, no. Do you think
we can stop for a minute?
Man 3 OK – we've got plenty of time. Let's stop
and get something to eat.

6 **Woman 4** Annie, are you daydreaming again?
Teenage girl 3 You sound just like my teacher!
Woman 4 Well, I'm sure your friends don't sit
around all day looking out of the window.
Haven't you got homework to do?

8 **(a)** Dr Christiaan Barnard. He performed the first human heart transplant operation.

(b) 1 South African
2 South Africa and USA
3 1967
4 Louis Washkansky
5 Just over 18 months
6 He spent a lot of time in nightclubs and knew famous people. He also did free operations for hundreds of sick people.

Unit check

1 2 ended up with 3 who 4 temperature 5 sore throat
6 tablet 7 that 8 hurts 9 ambulance 10 treat

2 2 c 3 a 4 c 5 c 6 a 7 b 8 b 9 b

3 2 He used to *be* a Manchester United fan.
3 The people *that/who* did that were stupid.
4 When I was five I used *to* swim in the river behind our house.
5 The police found the person *who* robbed the bank.
6 That's the town *where* I was born.
7 I didn't *use* to like Art very much.
8 *Did you use to* like eggs?
9 Did your parents *use* to read you stories?

14 If I had …

1 **(a)** b 6 c 5 d 2 e 4 f 1

(b) 1 'd have 2 had, 'd go 3 didn't have, would smell
4 'd like, were 5 'd buy, weren't 6 'd go, have

(c) 2 left, 'd have 3 knew, 'd tell 4 will be, know
5 didn't have, would you read 6 didn't eat, wouldn't be

(d) 2 If we had a computer, we could send emails.
3 If I didn't love music, I wouldn't spend all my money on CDs.
4 If I were a good player, I'd be in the school team.
5 I wouldn't be fit if I didn't do a lot of exercise.
6 If my uncle didn't speak such good English, he wouldn't watch American TV programmes.

(f) 2 e 3 a 4 b 5 f 6 c

(g) POSSIBLE ANSWERS
2 I'd go to bed if I were you.
3 I'd eat something if I were you.
4 If I were you, I'd talk to the teacher/your parents/the head teacher.
5 If I were you, I'd count sheep.
6 If I were you, I'd listen in class / do my homework!

2 **(a)** 2 screen 4 keyboard 5 drive
6 printer 7 mouse
The mystery word is internet.

(b) 2 search engine 3 download 4 start up
5 log on 6 save 7 provider 8 burn

3 **(a)** TAPESCRIPT/ANSWERS
1 I'd open the window.
2 They eat it.
3 I'd ask her out.
4 We'd love ham sandwiches.
5 They listen to some music.
6 We'd have a really good time.

4 1 mouse 2 eyesight 3 lonely 4 creative
5 responsible 6 movement 7 life 8 overweight
9 arm 11 addicted

6 2 a 3 b 4 b 5 a 6 c 7 c 8 d 9 a 10 d

Unit check

1 2 printer 3 screen 4 logs on 5 net 6 search
7 downloads 8 crashes 9 had 10 didn't

2 2 c 3 b 4 c 5 a 6 b 7 a 8 b 9 a

3 2 If you helped me, *I'd be* happy.
3 She'll be really happy if you *invite* her. / *She'd* be really happy if you invited her.
4 If they *had* the money, they could buy the house.
5 If you could buy anything, what *would* you buy?
6 If you *could* live anywhere, where would you want to live?
7 If I were you, *I'd* talk to the teacher.
8 If you could go on a holiday, where *would* you like to go?
9 We *would buy* a new house if we won the lottery.

15 Lost worlds

1 **(a)** a 2 b 3 c 1 d 6 e 8 f 5 g 7 h 4

(b) 2 f 3 d 4 a 5 h 6 g 7 e 8 b

(c) 2 had left 3 had not studied 4 had visited
5 had eaten 6 had lost 7 had shut
8 had you seen

(d) 2 was, had broken
3 didn't buy, had spent
4 wasn't, had not invited
5 had forgotten, went
6 looked, had put

(e) 2 did not give 3 was 4 became 5 allowed
6 had been 7 continued 8 won 9 had worked
10 became 11 had not been

2　**a** TAPESCRIPT/ANSWERS

2　It was the best pizza I had ~~ever~~ eaten.
3　My mum <u>had</u> a great idea.
4　It was the best idea my mum had ever <u>had</u>.
5　We <u>had</u> a holiday in Italy.
6　My family ~~had~~ always wanted to go there.

3　**a**　2 tourist　3 decorator　4 explorer　5 professor
6 cyclist　7 farmer　8 footballer　9 owner
10 journalist

　b　2 explorer　3 driver　4 tourist　5 scientists
6 manager　7 journalist　8 receptionist
9 decorator　10 archaeologist

4　2 give it a go　3 though　4 stuff　5 good luck

5　**b**　2 hope<u>ful</u> – adjective
3 program<u>mer</u> – noun
4 relax<u>ation</u> – noun
5 comfort<u>able</u> – adjective
6 hope<u>less</u> – adjective
7 lov<u>able</u> – adjective
8 imagin<u>ation</u> – noun

　c　-ation – explanation, information, installation,
relaxation, transformation
-ist – scientist, archaeologist, artist, tourist, violinist
-er/-or – actor, climber, decorator, painter, swimmer

6　2 b　3 a　4 c

TAPESCRIPT

Greg　It was brilliant, we flew from London to Lima
in Peru, my dad and I, and then we flew to another
city called Cuzco, a really old place up in the Andes
mountains. We stayed in a small hotel overnight –
it was cold, too! And the next morning, really
early, you know, about half past six, we went to the
train station and took the train.
Friend　Were there many people on the train?
Greg　Oh, yeah. All tourists like us – lots of
Americans. A lot of them were quite old as well. It
was really full, though. Every seat was taken. But it
was a really exciting journey!
Friend　Why? What happened?
Greg　Well, we'd been about three hours on the train,
I think – yeah, it was about half past nine – and
the train was going really slowly round a bend, and
suddenly there was like a thump noise, and the
train stopped, and I could see that the first part of
the train was leaning over!
Friend　Wow!
Greg　Yeah, you see, it had rained a lot the night
before, and some mud had come down from the
mountains and was on the tracks, where the train
goes … and the wheels of the first part of the train
slipped on the mud and came off!
Friend　Wow! Was anybody hurt?
Greg　No – I mean, two or three people fell over and I
think one elderly lady hurt her arm, but that was
all … luckily!

Friend　So what did you all do?
Greg　Well, we heard someone say that it was only
five kilometres to Machu Picchu, so my dad and I,
and some other people too, we just started walking
in a group along the tracks. It was a really hot day,
but it was a beautiful walk beside a river, and it
took us about two hours, but then we got to
another place and took a bus up to Machu Picchu!
Friend　And what was it like?
Greg　Wow, it's a fantastic place! …

Unit check

1　2 footballer　3 receptionist　4 owner　5 decorator
6 driver　7 photographer　8 explorer　9 artist
10 cyclist

2　2 c　3 c　4 a　5 b　6 c　7 b　8 c　9 c

3　2　When we *had visited* the museum, we went to
the cinema.
3　He had lived in London for ten years before he
moved to the USA.
4　She came home late because she had *met* some friends.
5　We couldn't have dinner because all the restaurants
had closed.
6　There wasn't any food left because my sister *had eaten*
it all.
7　When I got there, my friends *had* already left.
8　I was going to pay the bill but my friend had already
paid it.
9　The room was cold because someone *had* left the
window open.

16　Good or bad luck?

1　**a**　Present perfect
Past perfect – They said they had never been
to London.
Past perfect – They said they had seen a great film
the week before.
Was/were going to – He said his uncle was going to
live in Paris.
Could/couldn't – She said she couldn't come
on Saturday.
Would/wouldn't – He said he would give it back the
following week.

　b　2 would be　3 had never been　4 had stolen
5 was　6 didn't have　7 didn't want　8 was trying
9 was going　10 could take

　c　TAPESCRIPT
Sandra　Hi. My name's Sandra. This is Claudia.
Claudia　Hi.
Sandra　We arrived here at two o'clock.
Claudia　Yeah, that's right. Some of the rides
here are very good!
Sandra　Yeah, very good! But you know, the
queues are <u>very</u> long!

Claudia Yeah – and we think it's very expensive here, too. Bye!

Josh Hello. My name's Josh, and ... erm ... I think this is a great place! Erm ... all the rides are cool, but my favourite is The Elevator. I've been on it three times already, and I'm going again!

Mitsuko Hi. I'm Mitsuko. Erm ... I don't like the park very much! Erm ... you know, some of the rides are very scary, and I can't go on them! So ... erm ... I won't come here again.

d Sandra and Claudia

Sandra and Claudia said they had arrived there at 2 o'clock. They said that some of the rides were very good, but they also said the queues were very long and they thought it was very expensive there.

Josh

Josh told me he thought it was a great place. He said all the rides were cool, but his favourite was The Elevator. He said he had been on it three times already and that he was going again.

Mitsuko

Mitsuko said that she didn't like the park very much. She said that some of the rides were very scary, and she said she couldn't go on them. She also told me that she wouldn't go there again.

2 **a**

b 2 improvements   3 management   4 information
5 calculation

3 **a** 2 She asked me if we were having pizza for supper.
3 She asked me if she could paint some pictures.
4 She asked me if I would clean the carpet. / She asked me to clean the carpet.
5 She asked if I was angry with her.
6 She asked if I still loved her.
7 She asked if you were coming home late.
8 She asked if she could stay up until midnight.

b 2 Which one do you want? How much are they?
3 What street are we in? Where do you want to go?
4 What's the time? Why haven't you got a watch?
5 What does 'savoir' mean? Where's your dictionary?

c 2 Alan asked Jane if she could help him.
3 Marco asked his dad what time it was.
4 Mike asked Steve if Maria was going to the party.
5 Belinda asked Alicia how old she was.
6 Andy asked Mr Jones if he had marked the tests.

4 **a** 2 a   3 f   4 b   5 g   6 d   7 c

b 2 If Alex had listened to the questions, he wouldn't have got the answers wrong.
3 If he hadn't got all the answers wrong, the other kids wouldn't have laughed at him.
4 He wouldn't have felt really miserable if the other kids hadn't laughed at him.
5 If he hadn't felt really miserable, he wouldn't have eaten a huge lunch.
6 If he hadn't eaten a huge lunch, he wouldn't have been sick later on.
7 If he hadn't been sick later on, his mother wouldn't have called the doctor.

7 **a** Yes, the writer enjoyed the film.

b 2 T   3 N   4 F   5 F   6 T   7 N   8 N

Writing tip

b 1 Dear   2 First of all,   3 but   4 Secondly,
5 because   6 I think   7 Finally,   8 In my opinion

Unit check

1 2 management   3 equipment   4 entertainment
5 improvement   6 communication   7 calculation
8 education

2 2 a   3 a   4 c   5 c   6 a   7 a   8 c   9 a   10 a

3 2 If you'd told me before, I *wouldn't have* made this mistake.
3 If I *had had* more money, I would have bought you a present.
4 I wouldn't *have* helped her if I'd known that!
5 He told me he *had* been away the week before.
6 If she hadn't told me, I *wouldn't have known* about the problem.
7 Mum told me that she *had lived* in Paris when she was 18.
8 Claire asked us where we *had gone* last year.
9 He asked me *if I was* hungry.
10 They wouldn't *have* been late if they'd left earlier.

Acknowledgements

The publishers are grateful to the following contributors:

Pentacor Book Design: text design and layouts